"*THE WOMANLY ART OF BREASTFEEDING is not a textbook. It is by itself a work of art. Every pregnant woman, every young mother should share the atmosphere this book spreads.*"

—Michel Odent, MD
Obstetrics, France

"*Now that many self-help groups flourish, it is notable that La Leche League started in 1956, long before it was widely recognized how much people with similar problems and loving hearts could help each other by organizing. Surely it is notable that this organization of breastfeeding mothers now offers authoritative courses for physicians and other health-care professionals.*"

—Niles Newton, PhD
Professor of Behavioral Sciences
Northwestern University Medical School

"*The newborn baby has only three demands. They are warmth in the arms of its mother, food from her breasts, and security in the knowledge of her presence. Breastfeeding satisfies all three.*"

—Dr. Grantly Dick-Read

# The Womanly Art
## of
# Breastfeeding

*"As your Surgeon General, as a pediatrician, and as a woman, I wholeheartedly endorse breastfeeding.*

*"La Leche League's history of support to mothers is commendable and most valuable.*

*"I am pleased to extend congratulations to La Leche League International in celebration of your 35 years as a supporter and promoter of breastfeeding."*

—Antonia C. Novello, MD, MPH
Surgeon General of the United States

# The Womanly Art
## of
# Breastfeeding

Thirty-Fifth Anniversary Edition

Revised and Updated

A PLUME BOOK

PLUME
Published by the Penguin Group
Penguin Books USA Inc., 375 Hudson Street, New York, New York 10014, U.S.A.
Penguin Books Ltd, 27 Wrights Lane, London W8 5TZ, England
Penguin Books Australia Ltd, Ringwood, Victoria, Australia
Penguin Books Canada Ltd, 2801 John Street, Markham, Ontario, Canada L3R 1B4
Penguin Books (N.Z.) Ltd, 182-190 Wairau Road, Auckland 10, New Zealand

Penguin Books Ltd, Registered Offices: Harmondsworth, Middlesex, England

First published by Plume, an imprint of New American Library, a division of
Penguin Books USA Inc.

First Printing (Fifth Edition), June 1991
10 9 8 7 6 5 4 3

Published by arrangement with La Leche League International.

Book design by Kim Stuffelbeam
Fifth edition revised and edited by Judy Torgus
Photo credits are listed in the Appendix.

 REGISTERED TRADEMARK—MARCA REGISTRADA

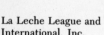

LIBRARY OF CONGRESS CATALOGING-IN-PUBLICATION DATA
The Womanly art of breastfeeding—5th ed., 35th anniversary ed.
      p.  cm.
    ISBN 0-452-26623-8
    1. Breastfeeding.    I. La Leche League International.
RJ216.W72    1991
649′.33—dc20                                         91-15005
                                                       CIP

Printed in the United States of America

BOOKS ARE AVAILABLE AT QUANTITY DISCOUNTS WHEN USED TO PROMOTE
PRODUCTS OR SERVICES. FOR INFORMATION PLEASE WRITE TO PREMIUM
MARKETING DIVISION, PENGUIN BOOKS USA INC., 375 HUDSON STREET, NEW
YORK, NEW YORK 10014.

$W$e dedicate this book with much love to the many caring parents who have helped make La Leche League what it is today, and to our patient, loving husbands and children, all of whom helped the seven of us learn the womanly art of breastfeeding

This book could not have been written and the basic principles underlying the work of La Leche League would not have withstood the test of time, had it not been for the unfailing counsel of Doctors Herbert Ratner and Gregory White, who have wholeheartedly supported us from the earliest days of the League. For this, we are most grateful.

# CONTENTS

# CONTENTS

# *Foreword*

The seven Founders of La Leche League joined together to begin the special family called La Leche League 35 years ago.

Family is the cornerstone of La Leche League. The family helps, protects, and supports the breastfeeding couple.

Family is what happens the moment a couple becomes three—or more. Family is a single parent and a child or children. Family is multi-generations under one roof. Family is an important unit in the eyes of La Leche League.

Family is the feeling we get from La Leche League in one form or another. When we read THE WOMANLY ART OF BREAST-FEEDING, we feel a renewed commitment to family life and to our children.

Family is what those of us who volunteer for La Leche League feel, as we form instant friendships with our co-workers. We know we are accepted and appreciated. We have an instant bond—our commitment to family. That's what La Leche League is all about! The 40,000 members and La Leche League Leaders all over the globe symbolically join hands and hearts as we endeavor to help mothers and babies everywhere with breastfeeding.

The Board of Directors of La Leche League International congratulates the Founders and the entire organization on our 35th Anniversary. If you are a breastfeeding mother, or plan to become one, we invite you to join with us and become a part of this multi-cultural, vibrant, healthy, and happy family of La Leche League.

Together we will help make more and more good things happen for mothers and babies worldwide, preserving the spirit and
intention of that first small "family" of seven in 1956, who brought
us together.


*Gail A. Berke, Chairman*
**LLLI Board of Directors**
*Massachusetts*
*1991*

# *Foreword*

**Reprinted from the Fourth Edition**

In the summer of 1960 I was working on my book, *Nursing Your Baby,* and I went to Chicago to interview some women who'd started an organization to help nursing mothers: La Leche League. Edwina Froehlich answered the phone at the number I had been given to call, so I went to her house first. Edwina remembers looking out the window and seeing me and my children trailing up the path "like a mother duck with her ducklings." I remember Edwina's kind eyes, and a house drowning in stacks of paper; as Executive Secretary, Edwina was handling all of the incoming phone calls and correspondence singlehandedly, and the new organization was already receiving some 800 letters a month from nursing mothers. Marian Tompson's house was similarly awash: she and her family and whoever else had time to help were writing, collating, stapling, addressing, and mailing out 4000 newsletters a month. The need was great; the job they were doing was monumental.

The seven founders of La Leche League, all busy mothers, never thought about the organization growing, but it did. By my next visit, La Leche League had an office. Of a special sort. Everyone came and went through the back door. The central room was not a reception room, as you would find in most offices, but a kitchen; you had to go through the kitchen to get anywhere else, so it was used as a handy gathering place. I interviewed the founders while we all prepared and ate a big salad at the kitchen table, and my children played with the toys in the next room—the Conference Room. It's the only Conference Room I've ever seen in which there are piles of pillows on the floor and baskets of toys for visiting children to play with during meetings.

From the beginning, La Leche League was putting something back into the culture that had accidentally been left out: a recognition of the value of children, the importance of family, and most especially, the naturalness of learning mothering skills from another woman. Breastfeeding is learned behavior; and biologically we are designed to learn it from other nursing mothers, not from male doctors, or textbooks, or authorities who never nursed a baby. La Leche League made that possible; first through a series of meetings, phone calls, and letters, then through an ever-growing cadre of group leaders, all nursing mothers themselves, and eventually through written materials published by the League. They reviewed the medical research, and learned to sort out factual medical information from prejudiced opinion. And they kept the focus of the organization very clear: mothers helping mothers to breastfeed.

La Leche League helps mothers to stand up for their rights, and their babies' rights, without confrontation and clamor, but effectively. Once while attending a La Leche League conference I was asked to appear on a TV show with a distinguished pediatrician along with some local League Leaders (and their nursing babies, of course). The pediatrician had me in a sputtering rage in no time, as he spouted misinformation and harmful cliches—"Today's mothers are too nervous to breastfeed...." "A baby that doesn't stay on a four-hour schedule isn't getting enough milk...." and so on. During the cab ride back to the conference hotel, I was surprised when one of the League mothers said, "I think I'll start taking my child to that pediatrician." "Why?" I asked. "Well, he's a very knowledgeable pediatrician, so I know he can handle medical situations, which is all I need. Of course, he doesn't know anything about breastfeeding, but I don't need him for that anyway and that's probably because he doesn't see any successful nursing mothers in his practice. So when he sees me and my kids, he'll learn." I said I thought that was more than generous of her. "Oh, it's fun," she said. "I've already converted four doctors that way."

That's La Leche League. And that's why they are so successful. As I write this in 1987, they have 9,000 active Leaders, all over the United States and Canada and in 43 other countries. They help more than 300,000 breastfeeding women a year, through meetings, hospital reference services, 24-hour telephone hot lines, and publications, including most especially THE WOMANLY ART OF BREASTFEEDING. And they still confine themselves with great discipline to their one task: women helping women learn about mothering, through breastfeeding.

La Leche League and the women in it are almost certainly the most powerful single force behind the rennaissance of breastfeeding in the United States. When I met the founders in 1960 only a small percentage of US mothers left the hospital breastfeeding, and fewer still kept it up for six months or more. Now across the country 60% of new mothers are breastfeeding. Hospital schedules accommodate nursing mothers now, instead of thwarting them. Formula companies have to admit that breast milk is best. Doctors hand out good advice instead of malarky. A lot has changed.

But new nursing mothers still need one thing most: other nursing mothers to encourage, inform, and befriend them. La Leche League International provides that. When the doctor says "Wean," or the husband says "Don't nurse," or a relative says "You don't have enough milk," La Leche League is there, with the facts and the friendship. That kind of help, the spirit of La Leche League, is an integral part of THE WOMANLY ART OF BREASTFEEDING, a product of many, many League mothers' experiences. This fourth revised edition will continue to help many thousands of new mothers to know the joy of successfully breastfeeding their babies.

*Karen Pryor*
**Behavioral Biologist**
**Author of** *Nursing Your Baby* **and** *Don't Shoot the Dog*
**1987**

# *Foreword*

**Reprinted from the Third Edition**

$\mathbf{F}$ew pioneers are graced with seeing their efforts recognized by society at large. The founders of La Leche League International, however, are such pioneers. They have seen their work flower and bear fruit. They have seen the impact of their work upon their culture.

From their own personal experiences, the founders recognized the benefits of breastfeeding to both mother and child. They also recognized the widespread antipathy toward breastfeeding in the culture at large, and in the hospital environment in particular. They saw clearly the oppressive effect this antipathy had upon women who wanted to breastfeed their babies, and the deprivation it imposed upon mothers and their infants. To offset the detrimental effect of these negative attitudes, they banded together to share the joys of breastfeeding with other young mothers and, in 1956, organized La Leche League.

In La Leche League's early years, breastfeeding was a lost art, and bottle feeding was in its heyday. It was a time when doctors (but not infants) paid lip service to breastfeeding. "Breastfeeding is best," they proclaimed, "but bottle feeding is just as good." It was their success with artificial feeding of hospitalized sick infants, and other infants in unusual circumstances, that led doctors to this belief that bottle feeding was, in fact, just as good. Then, as indications for bottle feeding insidiously broadened, it was only a matter of time until the unusual—bottle feeding—became the usual, and the customary—breastfeeding—became the rarity. Such conversion is seen frequently in medical practice: in the shift of the place of birth from home to hospital; in the increase of circumcision, episiotomy, obstetrical analgesia and anesthesia; and the forceps and stirrup delivery. Unbelievably, the operative delivery—cesarean section—is, today, becoming the usual and the nonoperative delivery, the unusual.

Physicians, comfortable with modern science and technology, were, in the case of bottle feeding, misled by gross nutritional standards such as weight gain and apparent freedom from nutritional diseases. Unfortunately, they did not reflect on the boasting of the formula industry that each new discovery was **the** discovery that would make the artificial product equal to human milk. The very fact that there were "new discoveries" annually proved the futility of their claims. This should have suggested to physicians that the natural was a standard unattainable by the artificial; that the thousands of laboratories, the countless scientists, and the annual expenditure of millions and millions of dollars devoted to research were a measure of our extensive ignorance of the workings of nature. Although raised on the theory of evolution, which taught that survival meant fitness, the doctors of the day disregarded the tailor-made, eminent fitness of breast milk for the young of each species and ignored the fact that the species-specific breast milk had had the longest clinical trial of any food ever made for the young. Physicians were, in effect, pitting their knowledge and experience against nature's knowledge and experience. They were bound to lose.

The founders of La Leche League, and their legion of followers, opted not for science and technology, but for nature as the repository of wisdom. They did not entrust the development of the mother-infant relationship to the vagaries of scientific advance, but rather, they placed their faith in nature and the promptings of the heart, a mode by which nature communicates many teachings. It was in the seventeenth century that Blaise Pascal, in his famous *Pensées*, wrote. "The heart has its own reasons, which reason does not know." How wise LLL mothers were. Their faith, which led them to accept nature's obvious norms, kept them ahead of the scientists. As one LLL Leader wittily stated, "A fanatic is a breastfeeding mother who for twenty years and against great odds has been doing and believing what physicians have only now discovered is a scientific truth."

When THE WOMANLY ART OF BREASTFEEDING first appeared, it was the only book on breastfeeding published in the United States which was written for breastfeeding mothers. In those days, in most parts of the country, the incidence of breastfeeding at the time of hospital discharge was less than ten percent, and the duration was short, a matter of weeks. Only a few hardy souls managed to nurse as long as nine months. The breastfeeding climate was oppressive. Mothers desiring to breastfeed were looked at askance by hospital personnel because of their refusal to enter the world of emancipated womanhood. Physicians, for the most part, were indifferent, unenthusiastic, and unhelpful. In the hospital and at home, when the slightest nursing problem arose, medical personnel, relatives, and friends were prompt to urge bottle feeding as the foolproof solution.

With the inception of LLL, a remarkable reversal occurred. The new mother, full of the maternal promptings of nature, was no longer alone, unassured, insecure in the newness of her relationship to her child, wanting success, but fearing failure. She now had someone to turn to for practical help, a woman who had been there, who could provide the encouragement and support she needed. The value of this woman-to-woman help is paramount, especially during the period of transition when the mother-infant relationship shifts from the invisible to the visible, from the bodily womb to the spiritual womb (the womb with a view), and from an involuntary, effortless, passive system of nourishment to a voluntary, dynamically active mode of nourishment. This transitional period, with the uncertainties that accompany it, is not unlike the honeymoon or any other period of interpersonal adjustment. In addition, LLL gave the new mother (as well as the old) a bible, THE WOMANLY ART, an invaluable resource for the breastfeeding woman.

Dramatic changes have resulted from La Leche League's efforts. Today, instead of a small minority, the majority of women are opting for breastfeeding. Today, instead of one book on breastfeeding there are dozens, some better than others, but none matching THE WOMANLY ART—the distillation of the accumulated experiences of thousands of LLL Leaders and millions of mothers. Today, increasingly, hospital personnel, relatives, the mass media, and others are becoming friends of breastfeeding.

Finally, we must express our debt to medical scientists for their dramatic findings of the past decade and to the American Academy of Pediatrics and the Canadian Paediatric Society, which as a consequence of these findings, made an unreserved commitment to breastfeeding in a joint statement issued on the occasion of the International Year of the Child in 1979. The definitive establishment and acceptance of the unmatchable superiority of breastfeeding and breast milk were in a way, a coup de grâce to bottle feeding. Though the latter has its role, no longer can it be thought of as an equivalent substitute for the nurturing and nourishing qualities associated with breastfeeding. The scientific findings were twofold.

One was the discovery and the recognition of the remarkable protective properties of breast milk against infectious diseases. This discovery will go down in the annals of medicine as one of the most striking examples of nature accomplishing multiple goals through a single means. It extends the healing power of nature (*vis medicatrix naturae*) to the preventive as well. What mothers knew all along— that breasfed babies are freer from illness than bottle-fed babies— scientists have not only affirmed for modern times, but have confirmed by discovering the mechanisms that bring it about. Nursing mothers knew the **fact**; medical scientists know the **reasoned fact**— the reasons why. Breast milk prevents a multiplicity of infections that modern medicine not only cannot prevent, but sometimes cannot even cure. Even when modern medicine can cure what it doesn't prevent, there are always the attendant problems: the sickness itself, the parental anxieties, the emotional trauma of hospitalization, and the expense and complications of treatment. Since a major part of the protective properties of milk center about the human immunoglobulins and countless numbers of live human cells, it is no longer possible for formula manufacturers to mimic breast milk. Unlike the apparent matching of the nutritive properties of breast milk, matching a living tissue such as breast milk with its living cellular capacity to manufacture its own antibodies is an entirely different order of probability.

The other striking advance was the uncovering and elucidation of the maternal attachment phenomenon. What nursing mothers did by natural inclination and intuition, and learned experientially, scientists corroborated experimentally. The mother knew the fact, the scientist, subsequently, the substantiated fact. It was not a case of science replacing art, but of science illuminating a natural, maternal act which is part of the art of motherhood. Researchers simply delivered the scientific backup for what nursing mothers were accomplishing all along. Of tremendous importance is that maternal attachment adds the affective to the cognitive; i.e., the emotional to the intellectual, the outreach of love to rational comprehension. Only now are we beginning to grasp the extent to which the undermining of the maternal attachment process with its reciprocal bonding of infant to mother has contributed to the maternal and adult delinquency of a sick society.

This brings me to the publication of this third edition of THE WOMANLY ART OF BREASTFEEDING. It marks a milestone, namely a sign and a symbol of the universal acceptance of the unique benefits and superiority of breastfeeding. THE WOMANLY ART, with its womanly know-how, is bound to play a critical role (as in the past it has played a major role in the renascence of breastfeeding) in converting today's universal assent into actuality. The reward? Mothers and infants will become bosom friends, and society will reap the benefits. In the words of mid-eighteenth-century philosopher, Jean-Jacques Rousseau, "Would you restore all to their primal duties, begin with the mothers; the results will surprise you."

*Herbert Ratner, MD*
*Editor,* Child & Family Quarterly
*Visiting Professor of Community and Preventive Medicine*
*New York Medical College*
*1981*

### Excerpted from the Third Edition

The genuine call to help other human beings is a powerful message that attracts outstanding people. La Leche League has been blessed by attracting to its ranks extremely able, ethically sensitive women who give their abilities and energy, first to their own families and then to helping other families through La Leche League. They have had the courage to do this in a society that downgrades motherhood and in which most women are raised to ignore the importance of their biological heritage, making them feel they should act like men, even to muting their unique ability to totally nourish their infants themselves.

Example is the best teacher, and it is La Leche League mothers breastfeeding in their homes — and discreetly outside their homes — who have helped to awaken the industrial world to a value almost lost: the closeness of the breastfeeding mother-baby couple. Anyone attending a League meeting sees tangible evidence of the health and well-being of breastfed babies. How beautiful and alert and agreeable those babies usually are!

Now that many self-help groups flourish, it is notable that La Leche League started in 1956, long before it was widely recognized how much people with similar problems and loving hearts could help each other by organizing. Not only is La Leche League now an outstanding model of a self-help organization, but surely it is notable that this organization of breastfeeding mothers now offers authoritative courses for physicians and other professionals which give them continuing education credits.

This book can do much to help yet another generation of babies get a good start in life. The warmth and maturity of the authors shine out on every page — a remarkable document illustrating their philosophy in life and their broad and exceptional wisdom about babies and breastfeeding. This revised edition is probably the most authoritative text for mothers on breastfeeding that has ever been developed, since it is based not only on research, but on vast practical experience.

*Niles Newton, PhD*
**Mother of four breastfed babies, and**
**Professor of Behavioral Sciences**
*Northwestern University Medical School*
*1981*

# Foreword

*Excerpted from the Anglicized Edition*

If I had a very large, shiny, gold medal. I would like to present it to La Leche League on behalf of the hundreds of thousands of women who—like me—have learned so much about the art of breastfeeding and mothering from the combined wisdom of the League mothers.

Breastfeeding isn't always easy—it never has been—but it is particularly difficult in an age in which technology is revered and nature is often prevented from taking its course. Because of society's enthusiasm for the bottle earlier in this century, the traditional female helpers largely lost their age-old knowledge of how to help women breastfeed and look after their babies.

La Leche League has been at the forefront of the return to breastfeeding and to the particular sort of mothering that tends to accompany successful breastfeeding. Internationally it is by far the largest self-help group and it continues not only to support individual women but to educate those—whether lay or professional—who wish to help others. One of its prime roles now is to help women in developing countries whose babies are endangered by the far-reaching effects that a swing to bottle-feeding can have.

In a society in which the feminine tends to be repressed in both women and men, La Leche League's values are very welcome. The masculine, goal-oriented, achievement-centered aims presented to young people are not the only ones worth having. There is a time and a place for them, yes, but there is also a much needed place for the feminine, process-centered way of thinking that allows us to enjoy moments in time without always thinking to the future. Nurturing a baby or a young child as he or she grows is much more rewarding if mothers, fathers, and anyone else involved allow their feminine side the freedom to respond, love, care, share, and lead. Looking after others well is only possible if you look after yourself and the League helps women to do that, too.

Breastfeeding is a womanly art that is a true celebration of feminine values and its far-reaching effects enrich not only the individuals involved but also society as a whole.

*Dr. Penny A. Stanway, MRCS, LRCP, MBBS*
**General Practice**
*Surrey, England*
*1988*

T his is the manual for the worldwide organization called La Leche League, the foremost authority on breastfeeding. Its principles are simple, its truth obvious.

Today's woman wants fulfillment in every stage of her life — and for the totally feminine stage of mothering, this is *the* resource book.

Women are deluged by how-to books, written by "experts" with university qualifications and no personal experience. This is different — it is written by the true experts in the field, *mothers.* It has been derived from the accumulated wisdom and experience of many thousands of women over a thirty-year span.

These experts know their subject so well that they are able to write it down in such a way that the reader feels, "Of course, that's only sensible and reasonable." This is how this book reads, but don't be misled — this is the most valuable book I know for today's mother. Its wisdom is deep, its scope wide; it gives not only the feet-on-the-ground, "how to" advice from before baby, through breastfeeding, to nutrition for the older child but also a whole philosophy for mothering that applies from the babe in arms to the toddler and preschooler and forever.

During my nineteen years of parenting, I have had contact with many organizations, books, and people. They have helped me at various stages and then I have grown past them. La Leche League and THE WOMANLY ART OF BREASTFEEDING have continued to be a source of both information and inspiration.

*Dr. Ruth Schell, MB, ChB, Dip Obs, MRNZCGP*
**Family General Practitioner**
*New Zealand*
*1988*

Our century has been called "the age of professionals." In "the age of professionals" every person is first a consumer or a client. For every human need, for any "problem," you can find the right expert, who belongs to an established profession.

In the middle of this century, at the time when "the age of professionals" had reached its climax, some breastfeeding mothers felt the limits and even the inadequacy of services given by experts. Where breastfeeding is concerned, experts can only give information, or advice, or care. But breastfeeding mothers need more than that. They need first a shared self-confidence. Thus was broken the illusion that any kind of need can be satisfied by professional services. Thus was born La Leche League, a mother-to-mother help group, a model for any kind of help group.

The role of La Leche League is of paramount importance in our special society, where the family is commonly reduced to the small nuclear family. This role is still more important after a hospital birth. Even in the best hospitals, you cannot help disturbing the beginning of the mother-infant relationship, that is to say, the beginning of breastfeeding.

An art cannot be learned in a textbook, like a medical discipline. But THE WOMANLY ART OF BREASTFEEDING is not a textbook. It is by itself a work of art. Only breastfeeding mothers have the capacity to transmit beliefs, convictions, confidence, attitudes toward life. . .and authentic knowledge, which is different from information. Every pregnant woman, every young mother should share the atmosphere this book spreads.

*Michel Odent, MD*
**Obstetrics**
*France*
*1988*

# Foreword

*Excerpted from the German Edition —*
*Handbuch fur die stillende Mutter*

The publication of a German version of THE WOMANLY ART OF BREASTFEEDING is a welcome and important tool for safeguarding and reinforcing a natural asset for infants and an essential part of mothering for women. From its 40 years of experience in working with mothers and children, UNICEF is convinced that breastfeeding is a vital element of child protection — not only does it offer nutritional and immunological protection, but it also bonds mother and child together in a mutually satisfying relationship.

A breastfed child is offered the best possible start in life whether born into an affluent or a disadvantaged home. Breastfeeding provides a solid base of good health and love upon which to build.

This alone is argument enough to make breastfeeding worth fighting for. But there is even more. Asserting that nature has in fact provided the best possible nutrients for babies — perfectly adapted to their growth needs, their digestion, and their immunological needs — to a degree that science cannot imitate, is reasserting that mothers are in fact the most important in assuring their infants' health. And providing mothers with the information they need to meet the various problems that might arise, is empowering them to withstand the different pressures to place their infants' life and health in someone else's hands.

For all these reasons, UNICEF has made breastfeeding a central plank in its strategy to reduce the rates of infant morbidity and mortality around the world, and to support women in their function as nurturer of the world's children.

Much has been done, much has been won, in this effort to reaffirm the importance of breastfeeding, and La Leche League has been at the vanguard of this movement.

UNICEF applauds this effort to reach out to new audiences, to bring to new groups of women the support and the knowledge they need to give their children what they need and deserve—the best possible start in life.

*Uffe W. Konig*
**Director, UNICEF**
*Geneva*
*1986*

The importance of breastfeeding for infant and young child health continues to be reinforced as new scientific evidence about its unique nutritional and immunological qualities becomes available. More recently attention has been focused on the way in which breastfeeding helps establish a sound caring relationship between mother and baby, and also on the role breastfeeding can play in helping delay a too early subsequent conception. While all these qualities are of primary importance to babies and their mothers in developing countries, there can be no doubt that breastfeeding must be promoted and protected in developed countries, too.

Breastfeeding, however, has, over the last four decades, proved to be a highly labile behaviour and one that requires constant support if it is to be performed successfully. Regrettably, in many situations this support to the mother has remained limited. It is for this reason that the work of La Leche League has become so singularly important. As a source of guidance, encouragement, and information to mothers, as well as providing a context in which they can come together to share ideas and discuss breastfeeding and everyday child care issues, La Leche League and its book THE WOMANLY ART OF BREASTFEEDING have proved to be a vital resource to mothers and health workers alike. We welcome the publication of the German version of this book.

*World Health Organization*
**Maternal and Child Health Unit**
*Geneva*
*1986*

# *Foreword*

*Excerpted from the Italian Edition —*
*L'Arte Dell'Allattamento Materno*

$M$ilk is an irreplaceable nutriment for the early period of life in mammals: it is a species-specific food, and most probably it is actually individual-specific. In fact, its characteristics differ not only from species to species, but also from baby to baby. The milk of a mother with a premature baby has, for example, a greater protein content than that of a mother who has given birth at term and, moreover, there are more than reliable studies which show that infants who have truly been undisturbed in their relationship with the mother and not misled by intolerable intrusions (pacifiers, bottles of water, or solids) cause the breast to produce each time the quantity and quality of milk which is needed at that particular moment. The feeding of babies with an atypical milk which has been perfected and improved compared to its parent, cow's milk, should only be used as a prosthesis, i.e., it should be used exclusively where there is not and cannot be any mother's milk.

The monster of formula feeding is thought to be more suitable because it is more "scientific" than antiquated breastfeeding, although this is never confessed in words. Formula feeding has found a valid ally in another monster, a son of the same ignoble union: the nursery, i.e., the "hospital creche" for healthy neonates: that ignoble Prussian-style barracks which still infects the maternal-infant structures with its presence in all too many Italian hospitals, even those of modern construction and finishings.

This is the translation of a book written by more than one person: they are parents who have been able to successfully raise their children through breastfeeding, in a social, medical and pseudoscientific situation which is basically against feeding babies with mother's milk.

"To write a book is less than nothing if the book written does not change people" said Giuseppe Giusti, a poet from the first half of the last century.

I hope, in fact I am sure, that the Italian translation will make this book much more than nothing, because it will change not so much the parents themselves, but the health workers, if they are able to see and hear.

*Dr. Lorenzo Brailanti*
*Italy*
*1990*

# Foreword

*Excerpted from the Dutch Edition—*
*Borstvoeding Geven-een Vrouwelijke Kunst*

Nursing a baby is unique, providing an indelible and intimate experience for mother and child. But also in other aspects breastfeeding is something irreplaceable. Even now new aspects are being discovered: the structure of the proteins in human milk, the protective properties against several infections, reducing the rate of food allergy, the presence of specific growth factors, the natural spreading of pregnancies, the prevention of certain illnesses at a later age, and the automatic adaptation of milk supply to the demands of the child. In all it is impressive how perfectly human milk is adjusted for the short and long term needs of the growing human infant.

Unfortunately in the period between 1945 and 1975 breastfeeding was not highly regarded. At the end only half of the number of newborns started with breastfeeding and only one out of nine babies was still nursing fully or partly at the age of three months.

Later the time came in the Netherlands when mothers began getting together, exchanging ideas concerning the art of breastfeeding, and discovering mothers' need to support each other, sometimes correcting and stimulating each other. Breastfeeding is an art which we nearly had forgotten, the experience had nearly vanished when left in the hands of the professionals. The organization of self-help mother's groups started, their expertise increased, and international studies and publications proved their worth.

Through the activities of these mothers' groups much was achieved. By proper advice and support it proved that many problems were avoidable or could be solved. The percentage of babies who started out nursing increased within ten years from 50% to 70%; the percentage continuing until three months increased from 11% to 30%; the percentage of babies nursing for six months or over increased from 2% to 20%. Also the pleasure of nursing a baby increased greatly.

In conclusion: it is safe to say that for 99% of the babies to be born in the Netherlands, breastfeeding will be preferable in all aspects. It will be their mothers' duty to fight for this right. It is hoped they will be supported by their partners, by maternity personnel, nurses, doctors, and midwives, for whom this book is also intended.

*Guus de Jonge*
**Professor of Pediatrics**
*Vrÿe Universiteit of Amsterdam*
*1990*

*Translated for LLLI by Henk and Margreet Brethouwer.*

# Introduction

Breastfeeding a baby—what could be more natural? Just cradle that precious newborn in your arms and offer him your breast. It sounds easy enough.

Breastfeeding a baby is simple and natural—if you know how to do it and what to expect. But it takes information and encouragement and some motherly know-how to nurse a baby, as the seven of us who founded La Leche League quickly discovered with our first breastfeeding attempts. How often should you nurse? How long on each side? How do you know if baby is getting enough to eat? What other foods does he need? And what if he seems hungry again only an hour after he has been fed?

When the seven of us found each other in 1956 and formed La Leche League, answers to such questions were as scarce as mother's milk itself. But we had breastfed a combined total of twenty-four babies, and by then had a good idea of what did and didn't work, what was and wasn't helpful. The secret of success in nursing a baby, we had discovered, was having the right information and having another breastfeeding mother to turn to for advice and reassurance.

In THE WOMANLY ART OF BREASTFEEDING we have attempted to put a philosophy about being a mother and nurturing an infant between covers. This book is our way of sharing the sense of satisfaction and fulfillment countless mothers have found through breastfeeding their babies, and the special joys that are awaiting as you embark on the great adventure of motherhood.

Our first two editions, published in 1958 and 1963, were based largely on our own personal experiences. The third edition, published in 1981, was enlarged and expanded to include the combined wisdom accumulated from thousands of breastfeeding mothers who had shared their stories and experiences with us. The fourth edition included new information, reflected current medical research, and continued the tradition of providing practical suggestions based on the experiences of breastfeeding mothers from all over the world.

This current edition commemorates the organization's thirty-fifth anniversary. While it is not a major revision, specific information has been updated where necessary throughout the book and current research is reflected in the chapters on the benefits of breastfeeding.

You will notice that we write from the perspective of a household consisting of husband, wife, and child or children. Some have pointed out to us that this is not a realistic approach nowadays. But we are convinced that breastfeeding and mothering progress more easily in such an environment. From personal experience, we also know that this situation does not always hold true in real life. Sometimes the father is missing from the family, and mothering then becomes a solitary endeavor. It is not an easy situation for a woman to be in. But no matter what else happens in her life, a mother can take great satisfaction in breastfeeding her baby and staying close to him. Her efforts in this regard bring a feeling of accomplishment that will increase in value as time goes by.

Our wish is that every mother anywhere in the world who wants to breastfeed her baby will have the information and support she needs to do so. Yes, breastfeeding is simple and natural — and an exquisitely beautiful way to nourish and nurture a new life.

*We appreciate and applaud
the fact that babies
come in two genders, but
in this book, we refer to baby
as "he," not
with sexist intent,
but simply for clarity's sake,
since mother is unquestionably "she."*

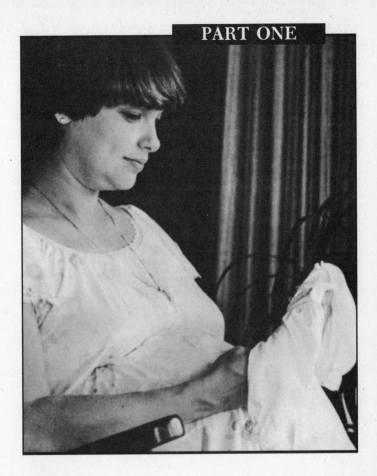

# PART ONE

# Planning to Breastfeed

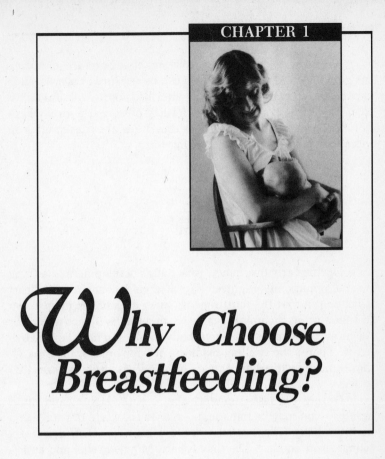

**CHAPTER 1**

# *W*hy *Choose* Breastfeeding?

Breastfeeding is the most natural source of nourishment and security for your baby. For many mothers, breastfeeding is a fulfillment of what it means to be a woman. Pregnancy, childbirth, and breastfeeding comprise a special phase in your life—one that is bound up with an extraordinary array of emotions.

Expecting a baby brings with it a sudden realization that your life will never be the same. You recognize a need to learn more about being a mother, but you may feel doubt and uncertainty about being able to cope.

You may even share the feelings of this mother: "When I was expecting my first baby, my husband and I didn't feel comfortable about becoming parents. We had no friends or relatives living near us who had babies. We were confused by what we read, what we were told, and what we felt....After four years and two breastfed babies, we now feel better about being parents and we also know what to listen to—our hearts."

As you watch your body grow and change to accommodate the growing child within you, you can be reassured that your own capabilities to care for your baby after he is born will also adjust to meet your baby's needs. Breastfeeding offers a beautiful transition for mother and baby alike as they learn about each other in those first hours and days following birth.

# A Special Journey

During early pregnancy, your baby's development is nothing short of remarkable. Eighteen days after he is conceived, his heart is beating. About the fourth month or so of your pregnancy, you feel the flutter, the unmistakable stirring that is like no other. It's the revelation of a new life. Your body changes to meet your baby's needs. There's the swelling readiness of your breasts, the expanding cradle of your womb. You are beautiful, as lovely as a tree that is heavy with fruit.

During the last trimester—the seventh, eighth, and ninth months—you may be impatient, eager to complete this stage and have the baby. Then, often when you least expect it, you feel a twinge. And another. The time is here. Mingled relief and anticipation can bring a catch in your throat. Today, sometime soon, your baby will be born!

The doctor or midwife is contacted, and the preliminary details are taken care of. You settle down to the work of giving birth. This day is like no other, and your mind, your whole body, centers on the process that is taking over inside of you.

The birth force rises, swells as a great wave, peaks, and recedes. You try to concentrate on relaxing, on willing your muscles to cooperate. In the welcome interim between contractions, there's time to rest.

The tempo quickens. Contractions are strong, they come quickly. You've probably never worked harder in your life. Labor is a fitting term! Just when you're most likely to feel exhausted and discouraged, you hear the reassurance of those who are with you—"Don't give up! We'll soon have a baby!"

And, at last, there is the moment you've been waiting for all those months, the bursting forth, the moment of blessed birth! As you catch your breath, you hear his cry. Was a sound ever before so priceless?

The umbilical cord is cut, marking the first separation. Who is to bridge this change of worlds for your newborn, who will soothe him and let him know he is again secure? Who better than his mother?

Again your body cradles him. You touch him, kiss his cheek, stroke his damp little head. Will he nurse? Perhaps. At some time within the first hour or so he will take the breast. You hold him close and he nuzzles your breast. His tiny mouth grasps your nipple. It seems no less than amazing! You and your baby can relax. After the enormous effort of giving birth, this is sweet reward.

Without thought or conscious effort on your part, your milk will come. You can look beyond to the many days together as a nursing couple. The security and warmth of your arms, the ready comfort of your milk, the familiar smell and pulse of your body are all precious food to fill out your baby's body and quicken his mind and spirit. Such accomplishments take time. But is there a more awe-inspiring task? This is the ageless beauty of mother and child—a time of grace and peace.

You'll hug him to you, intensely aware of his dependence upon you. Of course he will grow, will reach out, and eventually leave you. But not for a while. Give yourself time together; let there be no regrets. Together you'll begin to weave a new cord to replace the one so recently severed. This one will be plaited simply and naturally by your continuing closeness through many unhurried days. Not to be cut, it will form the first link to all human love and understanding.

But perhaps, instead of the natural birth you prepared for, you have a cesarean delivery. Or the months of waiting are not long enough, and the baby arrives prematurely, to be whisked away for specialized care. For the moment there is little sense of rapport with the baby.

These things happen. They may slow down a mother's and baby's start as a nursing couple, but they need not end it. Given the right support, mothers and babies have untold levels of strength and adaptability. Mothers through the ages have happily breastfed their babies, and you can do it, too.

The groundwork is laid before your baby is born. Nothing is more important in your advance planning than your preparation for breastfeeding. There is no better time to start than now.

# Best For Baby—Best For You

When you breastfeed your baby, you're providing him with the best possible infant food. No product has ever been as time-tested as mother's milk. Breast milk contains all the nutrients your newborn needs and is more easily digested and assimilated than any other infant food. As reassuring as this is, superior nutrition is only one of the many advantages you and your baby gain from breastfeeding.

Putting your newborn to the breast within minutes after delivery causes the uterus to contract and reduces the flow of blood. It also results in the uterus getting back in shape more quickly than it would if you were not breastfeeding

With his small head pillowed against your breast and your milk warming his insides, your baby knows a special closeness to you. He is gaining a firm foundation in an important area of life—he is learning about love.

As his tiny mouth eagerly milks your breast, your baby is performing an exercise that promotes the proper development of his jaw and facial structure. Breastfeeding also encourages a normal weight gain for your particular baby, which is good insurance against a future tendency toward obesity.

There is no better safeguard for your baby against the onset of allergies than breastfeeding. A diet of your milk alone for about the first six months of his life readies his body for other foods. It protects him against infection as well as allergies. Living substances that are unique to your milk inhibit the growth of harmful bacteria and viruses in his still maturing system. With fewer health problems, you can look forward to having a happier baby.

Breastfeeding—lactation—was meant to follow pregnancy and childbirth. The milk-producing breast represents a healthy progression in the natural sequence of reproduction that includes pregnancy, birth, and lactation. Nursing mothers find that breastfeeding is a naturally pleasurable experience.

The mother who is totally breastfeeding—not giving bottle supplements or solid foods—seldom becomes pregnant before her baby starts receiving other foods. Her first menstrual period may be delayed for six months or more following her baby's birth, especially if baby nurses often. Breastfeeding uses up extra calories, so it will help you lose weight faster in the coming months.

Breastfeeding results in an appreciable saving of time, effort, and money when compared to formula feeding. Minutes and hours of a mother's time are not diverted to the preparation of baby's milk.

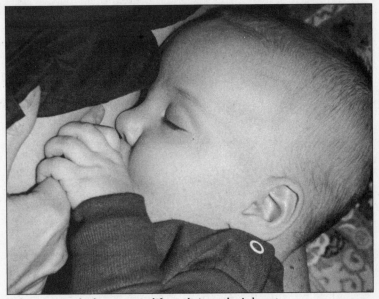

*Babies receive the best start in life at their mother's breast.*

Feeding the baby is a time to relax. Day and night, automatically and accurately, milk is made and stored in the breasts. The temperature is always ideal; the supply is pure and practically unlimited.

Breastfeeding helps us appreciate the different yet complementary ways that men and women can participate in raising a child. If you have older children, breastfeeding the baby contributes toward their sex education. For a parent, it is an educational process itself, of a rank and value equal to a course of study at any prestigious institution of learning.

Breastfeeding is the best start in life for a baby. Unlike so much that is considered "best" and is often beyond even one's wildest dreams, in this instance the best is yours to give.

## SOLID BACKING

If you had been a new mother living in Rome in the year 180 A.D., there is a good possibility that you would have heard the following advice from the physician Galen, who gave public lectures on anatomy and physiology. "For if one places the nipple in the mouth of the newborn, they suck the milk and swallow it eagerly. And if they chance to be distressed or to cry, the best appeasement of their unhappiness is the mother's nipple put in their mouth."

Closer to our own time, the man who is usually referred to as the father of the modern natural-birth movement, Dr. Grantly Dick-Read, said, "The newborn baby has only three demands. They are warmth in the arms of its mother, food from her breasts, and security in the knowledge of her presence. Breastfeeding satisfies all three."

Dr. Ashley Montagu, noted anthropologist and social biologist, wrote the following in 1971 in his book, *Touching:*

*What is established in the breastfeeding relationship constitutes the foundation for the development of all human social relationships, and the communications the infant receives through the warmth of the mother's skin constitute the first of the socializing experiences of his life.*

More recently, the American Academy of Pediatrics and the Canadian Paediatric Society have stated that they "strongly recommend breastfeeding." Their joint statement, issued in 1979, is widely recognized as a sweeping endorsement of breastfeeding.

The pediatricians state, "We believe human milk is nutritionally superior to formula," and conclude that "the overall nutritional superiority of human milk remains unchallenged." As you might expect, their report stressed the importance of breastfeeding in those parts of the world where housing and sanitary conditions are inadequate. "For much of the population in developing countries," it reads, "both economic and health considerations speak conclusively for breastfeeding." A more surprising finding concerns areas that enjoy a high standard of living. Even in these areas less illness is reported among breastfed babies than among bottle-fed infants. The latest technological and medical advances notwithstanding, "new information suggests that significant advantages still exist for the breastfed infant." The report notes that breast milk is the only source of important elements that help to protect the newborn baby during the time his own immune system is maturing.

The pediatric groups also spoke of the emotional bond that develops between a breastfeeding mother and her baby. "Early and prolonged contact between a mother and her newborn infant can be an important factor in mother-infant bonding and in the development of a mother's subsequent behavior to her infant."

The Paediatric Society in New Zealand states, "Evidence continues to accumulate that an important contribution to child and possibly adult health can be made by an increased prevalence of breastfeeding."

The Kinderzentrum, the Institute for Social Pediatrics and Youth Medicine of the University of Munich, West Germany, considers breastfeeding "a primary measure in preventive pediatry."

The banner slogan at the World Health Organization reads, "Breastfeeding, a basic part of life." The World Health Organization has also gone on record as urging, in strong terms, that steps be taken to counteract the spread of artificial infant feeding in high-risk populations.

UNICEF, an agency of the United Nations concerned about the welfare of children, has made breastfeeding a central plank in its strategy to reduce the rates of infant morbidity and mortality around the world.

In 1985, James P. Grant, Executive Director of UNICEF, wrote about the life-or-death consequences of the decision to breastfeed:

*Almost unnoticed, many nations are now moving to preserve a vital element of child protection—breastfeeding.*

*Breastfeeding is a natural "safety net" against the worst effects of poverty. If the child survives the first month of life (the most dangerous period of childhood), then for the next four months or so, exclusive breastfeeding goes a long way towards canceling out the health difference between being born into poverty and being born into affluence. Unless the mother is in extremely poor nutritional health, the breast milk of a mother in an African village is as good as the breast milk of a mother in a Manhattan apartment. . . . It is almost as if breastfeeding takes the infant out of poverty for those first few vital months in order to give the child a fairer start in life and compensate for the injustice of the world into which it was born. . . .*

*In many cities of the developing world, the incidence and duration of breastfeeding has begun to fall precipitously [in recent years]. . . . The result can be a doubling or trebling of malnutrition, infection, and infant deaths.*

An increase in the incidence and duration of breastfeeding is also one of the goals of the United States Department of Health and Human Services. C. Everett Koop, then Surgeon General of the United States, gave the following testimony before a Congressional subcommittee on nutrition in 1989:

*Breastfeeding should be actively promoted in all maternal and child health programs. Health experts worldwide agree that breastfeeding is the optimal way to nurture infants and should be practiced whenever possible. I use the term "nurture" deliberately since it means "to feed and care for during growth". . . .*

*There is abundant evidence that human milk is designed to enhance optimally the growth, development, and well-being of the infant. A mother's milk provides the best protection for her infant against specific infections. This cannot be duplicated in infant formula. . . .*

*A decisive way to promote child health in the US in the next decade will be to implement effective breastfeeding promotion programs so that the unique and important benefits of breastfeeding can be made available to protect health, nourish, and optimally develop infants in all segments of our society.*

# The Key to Good Mothering

Even though your milk is important to your baby as a food and as a source of elements that protect him against infection, breastfeeding is more than a method of feeding your baby. Breastfeeding is the most natural and effective way of understanding and satisfying the needs of the baby. An experienced mother made the observation, "Nursing the baby is the do-it-yourself kit for learning good mothering."

One explanation of breastfeeding's effect on mothering lies in the fact that a nursing mother is physically different than a non-nursing mother. She is in a different hormonal state. Because she is breastfeeding, she has a high level of prolactin—the "mothering" hormone.

*Getting to know your baby helps you learn how to meet his needs.*

We all know that motherhood can be very demanding, and breastfeeding helps balance the give-and-take of caring for a young child. It serves as a bridge from mother to child, child to mother. Lucy Waletzky, MD, a psychiatrist who breastfed her children, explains:

*The more intimate bodily communication inherent in the breastfeeding situation leads to a feeling of psychological oneness with the child, which allows the mother to satisfy her own dependency needs (needs to be cared for and loved) at the same time she meets the baby's dependency needs. A mother's dependency needs may be accentuated postpartum by pain, fatigue, and the psychological stress of adjusting to new motherhood. When her dependency needs are thus met, her resentment of the child's dependency (often a very difficult problem) is alleviated, and the positive maternal feelings can flourish unencumbered.*

## WHAT IS MOTHERING?

Mothering is caring for your baby, communicating with him and encouraging him to communicate back. It encompasses all of the many things that you will do to keep your baby healthy and comfortable, to help him grow in body and spirit. Breastfeeding is an unequaled form of communication between mother and baby. All of the senses can be brought into play. Your baby tastes your milk. He knows you through the smell of your skin and your milk. He experiences a sense of closeness to you by feeling your skin next to his. In the nursing position, he can easily look into your eyes. He hears your voice. The many times that you nurse your baby tell him, "Yes, you are safe. You are doing all right!" and he, of course, communicates back to you that he feels loved and is reassured. It is a learning and comforting experience for both of you.

From time immemorial, mothers have comforted their babies at the breast. They know that a few minutes of nursing can soothe an upset child's feelings of fear or anger. Nothing is more reassuring to a small one than being close to mother and tasting her warm milk.

In explaining how breastfeeding improves the interaction between a mother and her baby, Dr. William Sears, pediatrician and father of six, writes:

*Breastfeeding mothers respond to their babies more intuitively and with less restraint. The baby's signals of hunger or distress trigger a biological response within the mother (a milk let-down), and she feels the urge to pick up the baby and nurse him. This responsiveness rewards both mother and baby with good feelings. If a mother is bottle-feeding her response to her baby's hunger or distress cues is quite different. She must initially divert her attention away from the baby to an object, the bottle, and take time to find and prepare it. Research has shown that a baby's memory span in the first six months is from four to ten seconds. The time it takes to produce a non-biological response, such as bottle-feeding, is usually longer than the baby's memory span. The bottle-feeding baby does not receive the same immediate reinforcement of his cues that a breastfeeding baby does. In my practice, I have noticed that breastfeeding mothers tend to show a high degree of sensitivity to their babies, and I believe this is a result of the biological changes that occur in a mother in response to the signals of her baby.*

Good mothering means babying the baby, accepting that his wants and his needs are the same. It includes holding him when he is too full to nurse, but he is not yet ready to sleep. Mothering is changing a diaper or playing peek-a-boo. It means recognizing that each child has an inexhaustible need to be loved for what he is—a person with his own individuality. As he grows, his needs will change. A toddler needs freedom and guidance, with an ever-watchful eye. The manner in which these early needs are met, or not met, has a great deal to do with a child's response to people and situations in later life. The way the child is mothered is important not only to mother and child, but to society as well. Marian Tompson, one of La Leche League's founders, observes, "No matter how far our world advances technologically, the decisions of how to use that technology still have to be made by people. And so the kind of people we produce is crucial to the direction our world takes. You know that raising a loving, caring child is the most important contribution any of us can make to the progress of the world."

## GETTING TO KNOW YOUR BABY

Mothering is not something you can learn from a book. We can tell you, for instance, that most young babies like the secure feeling of being snugly wrapped up and cuddled. We can tell you that at about three months, most babies like company. They like to be propped up in the midst of the family. Instead of wanting to be fed or cuddled, what they often want is just to be sociable. These may be perfectly true observations for many babies—but *your* newborn may prefer to have his arms and legs free, or *your* three-month-old may be overstimulated by too much activity and end up feeling miserable. You have to be sensitive to the individual needs of your own baby.

The sensitivity that helps you do the right thing at the right time comes from knowing your baby. It develops as you spend time with him, but it develops more quickly, and to a greater degree, if you are nursing your baby. The very closeness and intimacy of breastfeeding give you a quicker and surer perception of the feelings and needs of this tiny person, and help you to know how to meet them.

Ann Van Norman, a mother from Ontario, Canada, tells how breastfeeding helped her learn about her baby's needs:

---

*I thought I had prepared myself for motherhood before Sarah's birth. I learned about diapering, bathing, and breastfeeding, but there was no way to prepare for "mothering." I found out that mothering is only learned by doing. Learning to respond flexibly to baby's needs for love, care, and stimulation, putting our own desires on temporary hold, and accepting the constancy and intensity of baby's needs are lessons only learned by living them.*

*I believe nursing has helped make my learning relatively painless, mainly through the positive reinforcement I have received from Sarah. She showed me how much I was needed and loved. Nursing her meant that I had to take time to respond, relax, and reflect. I am a different person now. Sarah has changed me from a compulsive time-and-task-oriented tiger to a go-with-the-flow housecat.*

---

Your joy in mothering grows as you experience the quick, strong feeling of affection so natural between a nursing mother and her baby; as you develop an understanding of your baby's needs and gain confidence in your own ability to satisfy them; and as you see the happy dividends from this good relationship as the baby grows. As one nursing mother, Shirl Butts, from Louisiana, expressed her feelings:

---

*Those who have never nursed a child might find it hard to understand just how special a nursing relationship can be. Now as I nurse my second child, I can appreciate what I missed with my toddler, whom I did not nurse.*

*My favorite moments are spent just before bedtime, nursing my four-month-old daughter. We snuggle together in our rocking chair, her tiny mouth eagerly searching for the warmth of my milk, until at last she latches on and drifts into peaceful sleep. Her chubby little hand is outstretched on my arm, her cheek nestled against my*

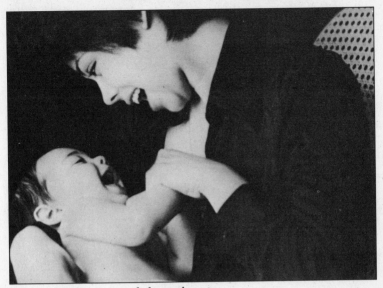

*Breastfeeding brings rewards for mothers, too.*

*breast. I continue to rock, lovingly studying every crease and fold of her soft body. Times like this make me look forward to the next night and the next. Sometimes she stops nursing to look up at me and give a big smile as if to say, "Thanks, Mom!" and then resumes nursing again. Those moments make me wish time would stand still.*

Breastfeeding is not a *guarantee* of good mothering, and bottle feeding does not rule it out. The most important thing is the love you give your baby and the fact that you are doing your best to be a good mother. Mary White, another of LLL's founders, reminds us:

*We're all learning, all the time. We're all still reaching up to the top of the ladder, and we've all got a long way to go. But for each and every one of us, the person from whom we can learn the most is our own baby; listen to him. Give to him; in the giving we are growing, as mothers and as women. As we watch him grow and thrive, we are watching an achievement we can really be proud of.*

# CHAPTER 2

# *P*lans Are Underway

$P$lanning for a new baby is one of the most exciting adventures in the life of a couple. You will dream the dreams that belong exclusively to parents. Your family's future is full of hope.

Planning usually begins with making practical arrangements. You'll select a doctor, look into childbirth education classes, and attend La Leche League meetings. Then your attention will turn to the need for rearranging the priorities in your life. Babies take time, and adjustments will have to be made. How can you change a routine here or eliminate an activity there in order to fit the new family member into your already busy life?

From long experience, we have learned that whenever a routine comes into conflict with the needs of one of the family members, it's the routine that has to give. "People before things" is a handy slogan to remember.

It should be said, too, that this change of emphasis is not a temporary interlude, with life reverting to its former style once the baby is older. Having a baby, loving a child, is forever. New experiences, endless opportunities, and depths of feelings that you can know in no other way lie ahead of you.

True, the investment in a new baby is enormous. As you are probably well aware, the financial output is a definite concern for many couples. But money is seldom the most critical or the rarest commodity that parents must provide. The coin that has greater value and is more difficult to part with is that which represents the continuous giving of one's self, emotionally and physically. Babies have no way of knowing how much it costs their parents to tend to them, worry about them, and love them day and night. They can't know, of course, until they themselves become parents someday. Then the gift is recognized and passed on as lovingly as it was given.

# Plans for the Baby's Birth

We learned early in the League's existence that a woman's experience in giving birth affects the beginning of breastfeeding and many of her attitudes about being a mother. Alert and active participation by the mother in childbirth is a help in getting breastfeeding off to a good start.

Childbirth can be a rich, joyful, and maturing experience. Those of us who have given birth without drugs or medical intervention know that helping a baby to be born and hearing his first cry can be a crowning moment of achievement in the life of a woman. Doctor William Hazlett expressed it well when he wrote, "The more a woman accomplishes in her feminine, natural functions, knowingly and willfully, particularly in labor, in the birth of her infant, and in its nourishment, the more she learns, both intuitively and consciously. The more she appreciates herself and in so doing, the more her self-appreciation radiates toward her infant and others—her husband, her other children, and society."

Having a baby is a natural, normal function for which a woman's body is superbly designed. The healthiest birth situation for both mother and baby is one that is completely drug-free. Almost all mothers are physically able to deliver their babies without medical intervention. You do need a doctor or trained midwife attending the birth of your baby but this is similar to having a lifeguard on duty in case there are complications. In the natural, normal birth, it is not the doctor who delivers the baby; it is the mother.

Advance preparation can pay off for you and your baby by resulting in a safer, happier birth experience. You and your husband can begin to prepare for this event by learning as much as you can beforehand. Many of the fears, doubts, and misconceptions you may have about childbirth will disappear as you become better informed and more confident. Attending childbirth classes will help you learn about the process of giving birth as well as how to participate and cooperate in the event. In addition, childbirth options are explained in many books that are listed in the Appendix.

With concentration and practice, you can learn relaxation techniques that are invaluable in the first stage of labor. Then in the second stage of labor, by pushing with contractions, you move your baby out of the womb and into the world, perhaps even into his father's hands. The experience of seeing and holding his newborn bonds a father to his child and to the mother of his child in a special way. When you are all together—mother, father, and baby—you "claim" each other for your own.

If all goes well, you'll be able to hold your baby immediately after birth and put him to your breast. The outflow of love and warmth to your child at this time is a spontaneous continuation of the comfort and security he has known for so long before his birth. This early contact can be very soothing and satisfying for both of you. Nursing the baby soon after birth encourages your milk to come in and starts you on your way as a breastfeeding mother.

## TIMES HAVE CHANGED

Fortunately for today's mother-to-be, attitudes and procedures related to childbirth and breastfeeding have changed dramatically in recent years. Anne Carducci from Maryland tells of her experiences.

*In 1971 it was difficult to find childbirth classes for anyone who wanted a prepared, natural delivery. Our hospital offered expectant parent classes that explained labor and delivery, but there was not very much in the way of options. Rooming-in was offered in some hospitals, but it was considered just as strange as having fathers present in the labor or delivery room.*

*Our hospital had three-hour schedules during the day for breastfed babies. They said they brought babies at night on demand, but it was always every four hours. I got very little rest in the hospital, because I was concerned about my baby.*

*My, how we've learned and grown in fifteen years! My last baby was born a little over a year ago in the birthing room of our local hospital. It was a natural delivery with my husband present. We stayed at the hospital twelve hours, and our daughter never went to the nursery at all. It was a wonderful experience. After twelve hours of almost constant nursing, our baby actually gained two ounces over her birth weight. So many of the things we had to fight for fifteen years ago have now become part of the routine for new mothers. And I, for one couldn't be happier.*

## CHILDBIRTH OPTIONS

Nowadays, mothers are approaching the birth of their baby as the natural, normal event it really is, instead of a medical situation. They are looking into options to the traditional hospital birth. Home birth and free-standing birth centers are becoming popular choices in some areas. Hospitals have responded to this by offering birthing rooms and family-centered care to replace the traditional labor and delivery rooms. Many of these changes have been in response to the patients' demands.

Judy Unruh, from California, gave birth to her two daughters in the hospital. When she was expecting her third child she planned to return to the same hospital. But at her doctor's suggestion she visited the new Birthing Center. The positive atmosphere and the enthusiasm of the staff made her decide she wanted to have her baby there.

*When we arrived at the Birthing Center to have the baby, we were told to go right to the room we had chosen ahead of time. There weren't any strong hospital odors, no*

*people rushing around, no papers for Gary to fill out
while I was wheeled off down a long hall without him.
We just walked together to our room.*

*There is always some amount of anxiety in starting
labor, but the atmosphere at the Birthing Center was so
relaxing that it had a calming effect on me. The thing
that meant the most to my husband was his feeling that
he belonged there. No one made him feel that he was in
the way. (The comfortable recliner in our room helped,
too.)*

*I can remember how great it felt to be able to get
up and shower to relieve my back labor and to take a
walk out in the hall when I felt the need to walk. I
wasn't confined to bed; I was in control.*

*Several hours later, our third daughter was born. She
never left us to go to the nursery with harsh lights and
lots of other crying babies. She remained in our quiet
room with us. We could hold her when she wanted to be
held and feed her when she wanted to be fed. Gary and I
both were there when the pediatrician checked her.*

*Even though it was my most difficult labor and
delivery, it was our happiest. My husband and I look back
on our daughter's birth with good memories and love for
all the wonderful people who have worked so hard to
make having a baby an enriching experience for the entire
family.*

You'll want to find out as much as possible about the choices
available as you plan for your baby's birth. Books listed in the Appendix will be helpful or you may want to contact an organization called
NAPSAC (National Association of Parents and Professionals for Safe
Alternatives in Childbirth), which is also listed.

## THE CESAREAN QUESTION

The cesarean birth rate in the USA was 5.5% in 1970 and
increased to 24.4% of all births in 1987, according to the National
Center for Health Statistics. This means one-fourth of all births are
done by cesarean, an alarming fact that many health professionals
consider to be an epidemic.

The decision to perform a cesarean is a serious one, often made at a critical point in labor when parents are not likely to question their doctor's decision. Parents will want to thoroughly discuss their doctor's views on the need for a cesarean birth early in the pregnancy. A few doctors have come to believe that cesareans are always necessary for twins, babies who are breech, and so-called "prolonged" labor. Other doctors view cesarean deliveries as only a last resort and find that in many such cases all that is needed is a little more time and patience. With proper medical support and care, most babies, even the big ones, can be successfully delivered vaginally with greater safety for both mother and baby.

The incidence of prematurity, respiratory distress syndrome, and other complications is far higher with cesarean deliveries, and the likelihood that the baby and mother will be separated from each other, often for some time, is much greater. Morbidity and mortality rates are higher for mothers who have cesarean births. The mother is more likely to experience infection, pain, and discomfort, as well as psychological effects such as depression after a cesarean delivery.

If your doctor thinks it may be necessary to plan on a cesarean birth for your baby, don't hesitate to consult another doctor before making this decision.

If you have already had a previous cesarean birth you should know, too, that many mothers have had subsequent vaginal deliveries. It is not always necessary to have another cesarean. Frequently the reason for the first cesarean delivery does not apply to subsequent births. Organizations such as C-SEC or VBAC can offer further information about this. (See Appendix.)

A growing number of doctors and hospitals permit fathers to be there for a cesarean birth. Mothers appreciate the comfort and support, and fathers are glad to be able to participate in the birth of their babies. Discuss these options with your doctor.

One mother, Debbie Pollock from Wisconsin, tells of some things a mother can discuss ahead of time in order to achieve a positive cesarean birth experience:

*Communication with your doctor during pregnancy is as important for a cesarean birth as it is for a vaginal delivery. If a problem occurs during or after the birth, a cesarean mother is at a disadvantage and may have a difficult time handling conflict, as she is already dealing with surgery and medication.*

*One key factor in a positive cesarean birth and speedy recovery is to use a minimal amount of drugs, and if possible, experience some hours of healthy labor. Spinal or epidural anesthesia will allow you to be awake for your baby's birth, and your baby will be more alert than if you receive general anesthesia.*

*To get breastfeeding off to a good start, mother can see to it that her baby receives no supplements. Moments after birth, my husband carried our son from the operating room to the nursery, remained there for a few minutes with him, and then carried him to me in recovery. The baby nursed for the first time within an hour after birth.*

*If a private room is available, father, mother, and baby may be given permission to room together. In this case, baby need never be separated from mother, as dad can be there to help. Some hospitals have a form to sign, releasing them of certain responsibilities once baby and mother are rooming-in.*

*Mothers can experience many different emotions after a cesarean birth. It was important to me not to dwell on what happened and burden myself with guilt and regrets, but rather to absorb and cherish every moment of the present with my newborn.*

# Health Professionals Who Care

There's no doubt about it—your choice of health care providers makes a difference. The doctor or trained midwife who attends you in childbirth will greatly influence how your infant is delivered, and the physician caring for your baby afterward can affect the course of breastfeeding. Even the doctor who prescribes medication should you become ill must take both you and your nursing baby into consideration. A doctor who has had little opportunity to learn about breastfeeding may be readily inclined to take the baby off the breast when treating either you or your baby. Such a move is rarely necessary.

Many young couples are devoting a considerable amount of time and care to finding health care professionals whose priorities are similar to their own.

Attendance at La Leche League meetings and childbirth education classes is a good way to learn about other parents' experiences. As you become better informed, through reading and talking to others, you'll know the questions to ask in order to learn more about a doctor's or a hospital's practices.

Your first step will probably be to select the doctor or trained midwife who will attend the birth of your baby. Seek out a doctor who does *not* routinely use medications or IVs during labor, who does *not* routinely induce labor or use fetal monitors, who does *not* routinely give anesthesia or do episiotomies. Ask about the percentage of cesarean births in his or her practice and at the hospital where your baby will be born.

You may want to meet and talk with several health care professionals before selecting one. Before the interview, write out a list of the points you want to discuss. When you make this appointment, ask what the fee will be for a consultation visit. Tell the receptionist you do not want a complete examination.

Find out, too, if the doctor is in a group practice with other doctors. You'll be interested in knowing if an associate physician, rather than your doctor, might attend the birth of your baby. Be sure to find out if the associates are also willing to respect your wishes.

After discussing your concerns with your doctor, it's a good idea to put in writing what is acceptable to all of you and ask the doctor to indicate his or her agreement by signing your list. (Of course, a doctor must reserve the right to change procedures in any emergency.) Take this with you to the hospital. Mothers say that producing their signed list was often all the authority needed to stop someone who was ready to administer a routine procedure or medication in childbirth or give the baby the usual supplemental bottle in the nursery.

## THE BABY'S DOCTOR

When you are choosing the doctor who will care for your baby, you'll want to find someone who is knowledgeable about breastfeeding and has a positive attitude toward it. A family doctor may be caring for both you and your baby and you can discuss breastfeeding at your prenatal visits. Otherwise you will be selecting a pediatrician to care for the baby after birth. Make an appointment to talk to the doctor before the baby is born and let him or her know that you plan to breastfeed your baby. Ask questions. Are most of the doctor's patients breastfed? How does he or she deal with situ-

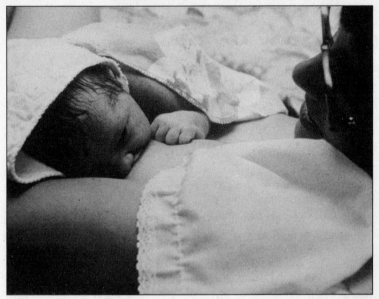

*Talk to your doctor ahead of time to be sure that you and your baby can enjoy breastfeeding soon after birth.*

ations such as slow weight gain? A doctor who has not dealt with many breastfed babies may want you to give supplementary bottles or recommend that you start solid foods too early. If you are not satisfied with the answers you receive, shop around for another doctor. If this is not possible for you, discuss your concerns with the doctor and explain why breastfeeding is so important to you.

## A NEED TO DIALOGUE

When dealing with health professionals, you may have to take the initiative in letting them know what you want. A simple, direct statement can begin a dialogue between the two of you. "Doctor, I need to discuss this with you. It's important to me." When there's a need for medication or hospitalization for the baby, you need a doctor who will treat him yet not interrupt breastfeeding—or do so as little as possible. Staying close to your baby at a time of illness, nursing him when possible, is always best.

If the doctor who is treating you or caring for your baby is not willing to discuss the options you prefer, you may want to seek another medical opinion. The American Medical Association calls this right of the patient the Fifth Freedom.

# Preparing Your Nipples

As you talk to other mothers about your plans to breastfeed your baby, you will probably hear stories about sore nipples. At one time, nipple soreness was a common reason for mothers to give up breastfeeding so a great deal of emphasis was put on the need to "prepare your nipples" before your baby was born. In recent years, it has been found that the major cause of nipple soreness is incorrect positioning of the baby at the breast and/or improper sucking techniques. While there are still some types of nipple preparation a mother can do during the last few weeks of pregnancy, nipple preparation is no longer considered a major prerequisite to successful breastfeeding.

Kittie Frantz, RN, CPNP, who is a La Leche League Leader and also the Director of the Breastfeeding Infant Clinic at the University of Southern California Medical Center, was one of the people who first emphasized the importance of correct positioning. In evaluating 300 breastfeeding mothers, she found that 57% reported nipple soreness and 43% said they were not sore. Kittie reports on her findings:

*We observed a difference in the two groups — in the way mother held the baby and the way the baby accepted the breast into his mouth. When we taught the mothers with sore nipples the technique we observed the mothers without sore nipples to be using, they almost all exclaimed that the pain significantly lessened or, in most cases, vanished.*

More information on correct positioning of baby at the breast can be found in the chapter called "Your Baby Arrives."

## WHAT YOU CAN DO

Some women apply a lubricant to their nipples and breasts to moisturize their skin during pregnancy. Any skin cream you normally use will do fine. There is a pure, medical grade of anhydrous lanolin called Lansinoh® that has been developed especially for nursing mothers. It can be used during pregnancy to moisturize the nipples. (See the Appendix for more information.)

Soap can be very drying so it should be avoided entirely in the nipple area. Rinsing with plain water when you bathe will keep the nipple area clean. When your baby is nursing, the Montgomery glands that surround the nipple secrete a substance that kills bacteria. There is no need to use alcohol or other antiseptics on your nipples. If you can go without a bra for part of each day, your nipples may benefit from the air and the light friction of your outer clothing. Some women are uncomfortable going braless and wear a nursing bra with flaps down.

For some couples, a normal part of their love-making includes caressing the breasts and sucking the nipples. This can also serve as a form of nipple preparation. It can be a natural way of preparing the wife's breasts for the coming work of nourishing their child.

## BREAST MASSAGE

Gentle breast massage will help you feel more comfortable handling your breasts and can be useful later on if you need to express your milk. Support one breast with both hands, your thumbs above and fingers underneath. Press your fingers and thumb together gently as you slide your fingers forward from the chest wall out toward your nipple; circle the breast with this gentle massaging motion. Then switch to the other breast.

Another type of breast massage involves using your fingers to press gently on one area of your breast and moving your fingers in a circular motion on one spot. After a few seconds, move your fingers to another spot. Start at the top of your breast and spiral around the breast toward the areola using this massage.

## CHECK FOR FLAT NIPPLES

In order for the baby to suck effectively, he will need to draw your nipple far back into his mouth. If you have flat nipples, the baby may have a problem latching on correctly. If you do nothing else in the way of nipple preparation, at least check for flat or inverted nipples.

To bring the nipple out, place a thumb and forefinger near the base of the nipple and gently press together. You'll be able to feel where the larger mass of the breast tissue ends and the nipple begins. Then, holding the nipple, slowly pull it out, and gently turn it up and then down. Some authorities believe doing this exercise

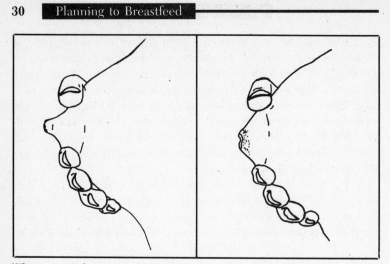

*When you gently squeeze the areola, a normal nipple protrudes, as shown on
the left. A flat or inverted nipple retracts.*

several times a day with each nipple will increase the elasticity of
your nipples and help baby grasp them more easily.

If you try these nipple pulls and find that your nipples do not
come out far enough for you to grasp them easily, you may have
flat or inverted nipples. Squeezing or pinching gently about an inch
behind the base of the nipple should cause the nipple to project
away from the breast.

One method for encouraging the flat nipple to be more outgoing was developed by Dr. J. Brooks Hoffman of Connecticut. Place
a thumb on each side of the nipple. Your thumbs should be directly
at the base of the nipple, not at the edge of the areola. Press in
firmly against the breast tissue and at the same time pull the thumbs
away from each other. You'll be stretching out the nipple and loosen-
ing the tightness at the base, which will make the nipple move up
and outward. Dr. Hoffman recommends that you repeat this stretch
five times first thing in the morning moving your thumbs around
the base of the nipple.

## INVERTED NIPPLES

If you find your nipples do not come out at all when you do
these exercises, then you may have what is called inverted nipples.
An inverted nipple shrinks back into the breast when the areola
is squeezed. Some inverted nipples appear as though they're pushed
in all the time. One mother who had this type called it "the folding
model of the nipple world." A full-size nipple is there, ready and
able to do the job for which it was intended, but left on its own,
it folds back into the breast instead of coming out when the baby
tries to nurse.

Inverted nipples respond to care. The best treatment for a flat or inverted nipple is the use of breast shields or shells that are designed specifically to draw the nipple out. Breast shields are comfortable to wear, lightweight, and inconspicuous under your bra. You can begin wearing them during pregnancy for a few hours a day and gradually increase the time. There are two sections to each shell, the bottom part, which has an opening for the nipple and fits directly over the breast, and the top part, which holds the bra away from the emerging nipple.

The breast shells are available from La Leche League International's Catalogue and many La Leche League Groups; complete instructions come with them.

Occasionally, when flat or inverted nipples are discovered after the baby is born and there's a problem getting started, these breast shells can be worn between feedings to correct the condition.

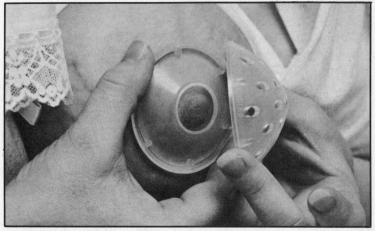

*Use of the breast shell for inverted nipples.*

## EXPRESSING COLOSTRUM

During pregnancy, your breasts begin producing colostrum to prepare for the task of feeding your baby. You may notice a few drops leaking from your nipples during the last few weeks of pregnancy, or some may leak out if you massage your breasts.

At one time, experts recommended squeezing a few drops of colostrum from your breasts every day, but this has not been proven to be helpful in preventing engorgement or sore nipples. Follow your own doctor's recommendations.

At most, you only want to express a few drops of colostrum from each breast. Gently massage it into your skin. Don't worry if you don't get any at all—it will be there when your baby nurses.

# What to Wear—
# Nursing Fashions

You'll probably be glad to shed your maternity garb after your baby is born and your figure changes to the smaller tummy and the temporarily fuller bust of a breastfeeding mother. Actually, you can make almost any clothes do for nursing, but a few special items can make life easier.

During pregnancy, and when the milk first comes in, the breasts often enlarge, and the support of a well-fitted bra can be most welcome. Let comfort be your guide. If you usually go bra-less, you may not need to wear one while breastfeeding.

You may find that you are more comfortable with a bra designed for nursing mothers. The traditional nursing bra has a flap on the cup that is opened for feedings. We suggest that you start with two or three bras and try them for fit and ease of use before purchasing more. Bras purchased during the last weeks of pregnancy should have extra room both in the cup and around the rib cage. The breasts will enlarge after the baby is born and the milk comes in, and nursing bras must be fitted with this in mind. A bra that is too tight, either around the ribs or in the cup, can cause a plugged milk duct or breast infection, and you don't want that to happen!

When trying on nursing bras in the store, be sure to note how the flap is attached in front. You'll want a fastener that you can manage with one hand so that you don't have to put the baby down every time you open or close the cup. You can also purchase washable or disposable nursing pads which fit inside your bra and absorb the milk that may leak from the nipples between feedings. A folded cotton or linen handkerchief works well, too, but avoid using the no-iron variety—the finish often retards absorbency.

Half-slips are probably the handiest while nursing, but you can adapt full slips to your needs by replacing the adjustment clip with a small piece of a Velcro-type fastener. For outer apparel, two-piece outfits—skirts, jeans, slacks, or shorts with a loose top or sweater are ideal. With your top, blouse, or sweater lifted from the waist for nursing, the baby covers any bare midriff. When wearing a blouse that buttons down the front, you can unbutton from the bottom up. If you wear a three-piece outfit, with a jacket or shawl, you will be able to nurse so unobtrusively that the person sitting next to you won't know that your baby is having lunch.

*Clothing designed for breastfeeding allows baby to nurse discreetly.*

La Leche League publications often carry ads for nursing bras and clothing designed especially for nursing mothers. Today's breast-feeding mother has her choice of many fashionable and comfortable styles of clothing designed with special openings for discreet breastfeeding. Recently, a trade organization has been formed by companies who specialize in designing clothing for breastfeeding mothers. Their aim is to make nursing fashions as widely available as maternity wear. The Association for Breastfeeding Fashions is listed in the Appendix. They can send you a listing of their member companies.

## NURSING DISCREETLY

This brings us to a concern you may have about breastfeeding. You may worry about feeding the baby while you're away from home or when other people are around. As the American Academy of Pediatrics noted, "It is a curious commentary on our society that we tolerate all degrees of explicitness in our literature and mass media as regards sex and violence, but the normal act of breastfeeding is taboo."

Embarrassment is a reason mothers sometimes give for not breastfeeding or for weaning within the early weeks. Interestingly, studies of breastfeeding mothers show that the mothers who stop early seldom know another nursing mother and have no one to help them in their new undertaking. Experienced breastfeeding mothers know how to nurse a baby so discreetly that only the mother and the baby are the wiser. Breastfeeding can be as private as a mother wishes it to be, yet it need not unduly confine her and her baby.

There may be occasions when someone is extremely sensitive to the prospect of the baby being put to mother's breast when others are present. Breastfeeding mothers note that, at such times, discretion can be the better part of valor. Some mothers find it easiest to leave the room for a few moments just to get the baby started on the breast. Then, with baby nursing contentedly, a shawl or lightweight blanket can be draped over your shoulder to cover the baby and you can return comfortably to your group of friends.

A mother from California, Sue Ellen Jennings Austin, tells how attending La Leche League meetings helped her learn how to nurse discreetly:

*I have managed to feed my baby in just about every place imaginable, from teenage brother's basketball games to our church Christmas party. This came about gradually of course—after practicing in front of the mirror and becoming brave in desperate situations, but most importantly after observing other mothers nursing discreetly at LLL functions and being able to share my concerns with them.*

Don't let a concern about feeding your baby in public keep you from enjoying the advantages and convenience of breastfeeding. In Chapter 5, we offer more tips on trips and outings with your breastfed baby.

**CHAPTER 3**

# *Your Network of Support*

How can we adequately convey to you the tremendous value of being in touch with other nursing mothers? No book about breast-feeding can equal talking to an experienced nursing mother and seeing her happy baby. When you know a woman who enjoys being a nursing mother, you have access to a continuing source of information and inspiration. It is our hope that you can join with other mothers and together find the same reinforcement and satisfaction that we have known.

The best place we know of to receive this mother-to-mother support is your local La Leche League Group. Attending LLL meetings during your pregnancy is the ideal preparation for breastfeeding and a good way to learn what being a mother is all about. Betty McLellan, a League member from Ontario, puts it this way:

*I have a background in psychology, but it was attendance at LLL meetings and the example of a wonderful Leader that showed me alternatives to many of the typical ways of handling children in our culture. The "psychology of mothering" is learned best from other mothers and comes through loud and clear at La Leche League meetings.*

# La Leche League Meetings

"Doesn't breastfeeding just come naturally? My great-grandmother never went to a La Leche League meeting, and she nursed all her babies." "Why should breastfeeding women need a worldwide organization for support?" Many who are unfamiliar with La Leche League ask these questions. More and more mothers today are choosing to breastfeed their babies, but they may not understand just how much a support group like La Leche League can help them enjoy the experience.

When La Leche League was formed more than thirty years ago, breastfeeding had become a lost art. Mothers had begun seeking advice from medical professionals about caring for their babies instead of learning from the wisdom of other mothers.

Today, La Leche League gatherings are held monthly in all parts of the world. The information is divided into topics for a four-meeting series. As no two series of meetings are ever exactly alike, many mothers continue to attend for many months beyond the first series and even for many years. A membership fee allows a mother to attend Group meetings for a full year.

LLL meetings are often held in the home of a La Leche League member. All mothers are encouraged to bring along their nursing babies. The meetings are conducted by an experienced breastfeeding mother who has been qualified to represent La Leche League. She presents a somewhat structured outline of information at each meeting, but these meetings are not classes; they are open, informative discussions. At the LLL Group meetings in your area, you will learn about much more than the basics of breastfeeding.

The first meeting of the series is usually about the advantages of breastfeeding. You will discover benefits of breastfeeding that may have never occurred to you—results of research on the value of human milk and mothers' own stories of breastfeeding advantages. Many mothers have remarked after this meeting, "I knew that breastfeeding was good for my baby and good for me, but I didn't know how good it was. This information makes me feel more confident than ever in my decision to nurse, and it makes me feel proud to know that I am doing something so wonderful for my baby."

At the next meeting, the discussion usually centers on the family and the breastfed baby. Mothers share tips on how to get off to a good start in the hospital and at home with the new baby. Knowing what to expect in the way of procedures and routines at local area hospitals can be helpful to a new mother. Easing the emotional adjustment of all family members, lightening the work load, establishing a good milk supply, and preventing problems from ever beginning are all topics of discussion.

Another meeting covers basic breastfeeding techniques and problem-solving. You can receive specific advice from the best breastfeeding experts in the world: experienced nursing mothers. The overall message is that no matter what problem may arise, there is almost always a solution that does not require weaning the baby.

At another meeting, the proper diet for the lactating and pregnant woman is discussed, as well as starting the baby on solid foods and when and how to wean the baby. Often discipline of toddlers is also explored at this meeting.

Almost all La Leche League Groups have an extensive lending library available to their members. Current titles on breastfeeding, childbirth, parenting, and nutrition that may not be widely available can be found at LLL meetings. Most groups also have books, booklets, and breastfeeding-aid products for sale to LLL members.

## ALL MOTHERS ARE WELCOME

All women who have an interest in breastfeeding are invited to attend La Leche League meetings. All mothers are accepted with open arms at La Leche League: mothers of all races and religions, single mothers, working mothers, and mothers whose philosophy on various aspects of infant care and childrearing may differ from La Leche League's. Each mother is encouraged to take from the League's philosophy what seems sensible and helpful to her. The ideal time to begin attending is during pregnancy, because the information received in advance may prove to be vital to a mother when her baby arrives.

After her first League meeting one pregnant mother commented, "I have read all the books, and didn't think there was anything else I needed to know. I learned so much more tonight than I expected to." Another mother, Heather Karlheim from Ohio, had a similar response after attending La Leche League meetings:

*As a pharmacist and avid reader, I spent the months of my first pregnancy reading everything I could find on topics related to birth, breastfeeding, and childrearing. I anticipated my child's birth with confidence.*

*Since I have a close friend who is a League Leader, I knew a little about LLL through her, but I was not convinced that I "needed" such an organization.*

*In my fifth month of pregnancy, I was persuaded by a co-worker, who was also expecting a baby, to accompany her to a La Leche League meeting. This meeting was a real turning point for me. La Leche League aided me by providing specific suggestions and lots of reassurance from other mothers.*

*As the months passed and my daughter and I became a happy nursing couple, I continued to benefit from League meetings and friendships made there.*

*As I look back now I can't believe how naive I was, thinking that I could "learn it all" from books. La Leche League has been, for me, a safe island in the tumultuous sea of first-time motherhood, and you can bet I'm not about to jump back into the water alone!*

## WHY IS IT NEEDED?

Though the majority of mothers today are breastfeeding when they leave the hospital, within a few months, weeks, or even days, most of them switch to the bottle. Why? Insufficient milk supply, breast infections, embarrassment, fear of criticism from relatives, and general confusion are some of the reasons. These problems are not the inevitable lot of the nursing mother. They can be avoided for the most part, or resolved with the correct information and support. Should a problem arise, a mother can call her La Leche League

*La Leche League meetings offer information and support in a friendly, informal atmosphere.*

Leader for help at any time. Sometimes just being able to dial the phone number of a sympathetic, informed mother who has had breastfeeding experience is the key to the resumption of a successful breastfeeding relationship.

Ruth A. Lawrence, MD, a physician who breastfed her own children and the author of *Breastfeeding: A Guide for the Medical Profession*, agrees that mothers need information and support as they learn about breastfeeding:

*Breastfeeding is not a reflex; it is a learned process. In our present culture, many women have never witnessed an infant at the breast. When a woman is called upon to nurse her own infant, much of her success depends on a learning process. Successful lactation depends on proper information.*

Mothers who attend LLL meetings soon find there is more involved than basic breastfeeding information. There is something very special about the sharing and companionship of other mothers. Cynthia Webb, from Montana, found this out:

*When I was seven months pregnant and wondering if I could survive pregnancy and parenthood, I found a place that celebrates motherhood in a quiet, sustaining fashion: my first La Leche League meeting.*

*I believe motherhood touches the soul of a woman in a way that nothing else can....After being infertile for ten years, motherhood came as quite a surprise to me. Without LLL, I'd probably still be in shock. League members have helped me cope with many situations. Problem-solving and support are important, but so is having a place to share the special joys of each days' experience. An LLL meeting is a haven for all of these things.*

And another LLL member, who wrote to us anonymously, told how La Leche League helped her to overcome memories of her own unhappy childhood.

*The reason I am so grateful to La Leche League is that it has helped me understand what "mothering" means and has given me confidence with my own children. My own upbringing was scary and chaotic. I was terribly afraid of becoming a mother. By having a stable nursing relationship I was able to tune in physically and emotionally to the needs of my baby.*

*At meetings I saw other mothers at peace with their infants and toddlers, learning like me and still available to be learned from. I became friends with several of these mothers and that, too, has enriched my life and my children's lives. And of course, those things that enrich us are of benefit to my husband as well.*

*I read your bimonthly magazine, NEW BEGINNINGS, including all the back copies in the Group's library. I am grateful I received adequate doses of support in favor of nursing to counterbalance the negative input I had received.*

Sally Olson, from Nebraska, already breastfed two babies when she attended her first La Leche League meeting. Her third son was just a month old. She explains:

*I really went to the meeting to meet some other mothers, as we had just moved to a new town and I did not know a soul. I found what I went for—fellowship with other nursing mothers—but I also found much more. The mothers in my Group and the LLL information sheets and the books found in the LLL Group library helped me to put into words and actions what I felt in my heart.*

## HOW DO I FIND LA LECHE LEAGUE?

There are several ways for you to find out the name of your local La Leche League Leader. In large cities, you may find La Leche League listed in the white pages of your telephone directory. In smaller communities, the Group may not be able to afford such a listing. You might check at your local library to see if they have information about a nearby LLL Group. If you are attending childbirth classes, your instructor may know of an LLL Group in the area. A local newspaper may have LLL meeting notices from time to time so they may know the local Leader's phone number.

You can also write or call LLLI Headquarters for the name and number of your local Leader. Our business hours are from 8 AM to 3 PM, Central Time; the phone number is 708-455-7730. In the USA, you can use our toll-free number to find the name of a local Leader. Call 1-800-LA LECHE. The address is: P.O. Box 1209, Franklin Park IL 60131-8209 USA.

When you join LLL, you participate in an international mother-to-mother helping network, a valuable resource for parenting help and support. Your annual dues bring you six bimonthly issues of NEW BEGINNINGS, a magazine filled with stories, hints, and inspiration from other breastfeeding families. Members receive our LLLI Catalogues by mail and they are entitled to a 10% discount on purchases from LLLI's wide variety of outstanding books and publications on breastfeeding, childbirth, nutrition, and parenting. Your membership dues also support La Leche League activities. Additional benefits of LLL membership may also be available; they will be explained by your local Leader or in current LLL publications.

Even mothers who cannot attend LLL Group meetings find the support they need through LLL membership. Elizabeth Hunsaker was living in Belgium, far from her family and friends, when her first baby was born. She writes:

*I had always wanted to breastfeed because I had read it was best for the baby and that it helped to create a special bond between mother and child. I bought many books on caring for a baby, and I joined La Leche League. Our baby boy is now ten months old and is still nursing. It has been an experience I will always treasure. But it hasn't always been easy, and at times I felt very frustrated and discouraged.*

*Receiving NEW BEGINNINGS helped me through a lot of trying times and made my nursing experience a happier one. Reading letters from other mothers who had the same experiences and the same attitudes about nursing made me feel as if I weren't alone and that it was worth the effort.*

And another mother, Elena Hannah from Newfoundland, found a friend's collection of back issues helped her get through some difficult times.

*When I was almost overwhelmed with problems I was having with my first baby, a friend sent me her two-year collection of back issues. As soon as I started reading them I felt I had found what I needed. Reading others' stories, many of them with problems more serious than mine, put everything back in perspective for me, and the main message seemed to be: "You can do it! You can overcome the difficulties!" By the time I finished devouring the collection I felt calmer and more confident. So today I want to say: Thank you to all the moms that shared their stories with me, and thank you, La Leche League for having such a wonderful publication.*

Soon thereafter, Elena paid her membership dues and started receiving NEW BEGINNINGS on a regular basis.

Is La Leche League just for brand new mothers? The answer is "no." Experienced mothers provide the backbone of LLL Groups because they can offer the advice and encouragement that helps a new breastfeeding mother cope. But mothers of older babies and toddlers find advantages, too, from their continued association with La Leche League. Elizabeth Hormann, who is an experienced mother and La Leche League Leader, writes:

*Why would anyone want to continue with LLL once their children are weaned? It is not always easy to explain, but support is a large part of the reason. LLL addresses more than breastfeeding; there is a philosophy of mothering that grows from our experience as nursing mothers and that philosophy is not widely shared outside League circles. We need each other, especially as our children get beyond infancy and develop more facets to their personalities.*

    *Mothers of toddlers are particularly likely to need the kind of support LLL provides. Shifting gears to care for toddlers is not easy.*

Above and beyond information, La Leche League offers a special advantage to mothers summed up this way by one La Leche League Leader: "LLL gives me an opportunity to surround myself with the kind of people that I want in my life: caring, intelligent, family-oriented women who look on their children as assets, and who enjoy being mothers."

## BEYOND THE BASICS

In addition to the basic meetings offered by LLL Groups all over the world, special meetings are often scheduled in response to the interest of the mothers in the Group. Toddlers' Meetings are held routinely for mothers who want to discuss meeting the needs of their older babies and toddlers. Employed Mothers' Meetings may be scheduled when several mothers in the Group want to discuss routines that are specifically directed to combining working and breastfeeding. Couples' Nights or Fathers' Meetings give men the opportunity to share their experiences with one another.

In addition, La Leche League periodically sponsors International and Area Conferences. These are one, two, or three day events providing information on breastfeeding and parenting that goes beyond the topics of regular LLL meetings. Doctors, health professionals, and experienced parents lend their expertise to a variety of sessions throughout the day. Often luncheons are scheduled featuring a special guest speaker or allowing time for open discussion. Mothers, fathers, and babies enjoy the opportunity to spend the day together at an LLL Conference.

At International Conferences which are held every other year, thousands of parents and professionals from all over the world meet to share their experiences and expertise. La Leche League International also sponsors annual Physicians' Seminars on Breastfeeding. These seminars are officially recognized and accredited by major medical associations.

La Leche League has been a source of inspiration and encouragement for breastfeeding mothers for more than thirty years. If there is an LLL Group in your community, we urge you to become a part of this mother-to-mother network.

# PART TWO

# The Early Months

**CHAPTER 4**

# Your Baby Arrives

$\mathrm{T}$he newborn child is a rare and incredible sight. He seems so tiny and helpless, yet he does have certain survival skills that were not generally recognized until recently. Held up close, a newborn baby can see his mother's face clearly, and in fact has a preference for the human face. He can also hear quite well. For a period during the first hour of life, most newborns are quietly alert and receptive. A lively and intricate exchange of messages passes between the mother and the baby who are together at this time. The hours and days immediately after birth also seem to be an especially sensitive period for a mother to form an attachment to her newly arrived baby.

In their book, *The Amazing Newborn*, Marshall Klaus, MD, and his wife, Phyllis, tell about research that has changed attitudes about a newborn's capability:

*When our own children were born, we were not aware of all their amazing talents and abilities. At that time, most everyone—including doctors—believed not only that infants could not see or focus their eyes, but also that they certainly would not respond to or recognize their mother's voice. No one talked about the possibility that an infant could imitate facial expressions, respond to rhythms of language, reach for objects, and start to learn at such an early age....*

*Right after birth, within the first hour of life, normal infants have a prolonged period of quiet alertness, averaging forty minutes, during which they look directly at their mother's and father's face and eyes and can respond to voices. It is as though newborns had rehearsed the perfect approach to the first meeting with their parents.*

# Baby's First Feeding

**The sooner you put your baby to the breast, the better.** Most babies are ready and even eager to nurse at some time within the first hour. The sucking reflex of a full-term healthy newborn is usually at a peak about twenty to thirty minutes after he is born, provided he is not drowsy from drugs or anesthesia used during labor and delivery. If this prime time to begin nursing is missed, the baby's sucking reflex may be less acute for about a day and a half.

Early nursing is mutually beneficial to mother and baby. Aside from getting breastfeeding off to a good start, your newborn's immediate nursing hastens the delivery of the placenta. You will have less blood loss because the baby's sucking causes the uterus to contract. For the baby, being so close to his mother is comforting, and the first milk, the colostrum, is priceless as a source of protective immunities against disease.

When mothers are able to greet their newborns by cuddling and nursing, and infants remain with their mothers to nurse at will, breastfeeding usually progresses with few problems. Mother and baby need to be together early and often to establish a satisfying relationship and an adequate milk supply.

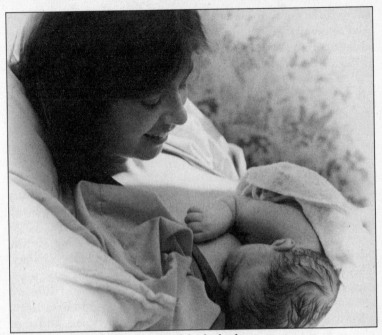

*Baby's first feeding is a sweet reward for both of you.*

Your first attempt to breastfeed your baby is a learning experience, a get-acquainted effort for both of you. There are many variations in babies' responses. He may only nuzzle at your nipple or lick it a few times. You will be very emotional from the excitement of giving birth and you may feel awkward trying to position your baby at the breast. It will be hard for you to relax if there is a lot of activity going on around you.

The important thing is to hold your baby close, talk to him and comfort him. Cup your breast in your hand (as described in the sections that follow) and tickle your baby's lips with your nipple. If he opens his mouth wide, pull him in close to you so he can easily grasp the nipple and all or most of the areola, the darker skin area that surrounds your nipple. He may take a few sucks and fall asleep. Or he may let go and prefer to look around at his new surroundings. This first opportunity to nurse sets the stage for the hours and days ahead when you and your baby will be getting to know each other.

If medical complications prevent you from breastfeeding immediately after your baby is born, all is not lost. You and your baby can make up for lost time once you are able to be together and begin breastfeeding. In a later chapter of this book, we discuss breast-feeding in certain medical situations or unusual circumstances. You'll also want to be in touch with your local La Leche League Leader if difficulties or special problems arise.

# Getting Started

Getting your baby started at the breast smoothly and easily will soon be second nature to you. Nursing a baby is actually much less involved than any description of the process.

One benefit of attending La Leche League meetings during your pregnancy is seeing other mothers breastfeeding their babies. This can help you more than photos or written explanations because you can observe a variety of mothers with babies of different ages and sizes who have adopted comfortable ways to breastfeed. They will probably be using pillows, cushions, footstools, and armrests to help them position their babies for nursing. Of course, no two mothers and babies are alike and as a baby gets older and nurses well, correct positioning becomes less of a concern.

## BREASTFEEDING IN SLOW MOTION

The following steps explain the correct way to position your baby at the breast in order to ensure that baby sucks well and gets plenty of milk and also to prevent nipple soreness and pain.

**1. Position yourself properly.** It's easiest to get started breastfeeding the first few times if you are sitting up. Sit up in bed, in a comfortable armchair, or rocking chair. Pillows are a must. Use them behind your back, under your elbow, and on your lap to support the baby. Use a footstool to bring your knees up. You should be relaxed with none of your muscles straining.

**2. Position your baby properly.** Baby should be lying on his side with his whole body facing you. His head should rest in the crook of your elbow. His back should be supported by your forearm and you can hold his bottom or upper thigh with your hand. Baby's ear, shoulder, and hips should be in a straight line. His head should be straight, in line with his body, not arched back or turned sideways.

Baby should be held up at the level of your breast so you are not leaning forward to reach him and he is not straining to reach your nipple. Using a pillow on your lap will help.

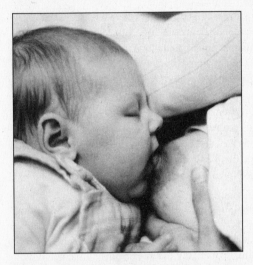

**3. Offer your breast to the baby.** Cup your breast with your free hand, supporting it with your fingers underneath and your thumb on the top. Your thumb and index finger should form a "C." Be sure your fingers are well behind the areola.

**4. Encourage baby to latch on properly.** Tickle baby's lips with your nipple. If baby turns his head away, gently stroke his cheek on the side nearest you. The rooting reflex will make him turn his head toward you. Then try again to tickle his lips, talking to him and encouraging him to open his mouth. When baby opens his mouth **wide**, quickly center your nipple in his mouth and **pull** baby toward you with the arm that is holding him. It's important to pull baby in very close to you, not move forward toward baby. It may

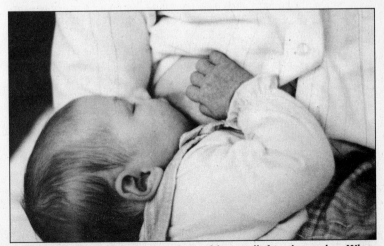

*Baby's whole body is facing his mother and he is pulled in close to her. When sucking correctly, his mouth covers most of the areola.*

take a few tries to coordinate your actions with baby's reactions so that all goes smoothly. If baby gets frustrated, you may have to stop and soothe him a bit before starting again.

**5. Effective sucking techniques.** In order to suck effectively, the baby must get a large portion of your areola into his mouth along with the nipple. The milk sinuses that must be compressed in order to release the milk are located under the areola. Baby's gums should completely bypass the nipple and cover about one inch of the areola behind the nipple. Be sure your nipple is centered in his mouth; it should be above his tongue. Baby should be pulled in so close that the tip of his nose touches your breast. He will still be able to breathe quite well. If baby's nose does seem blocked by your breast, try lifting up your breast or pulling baby's body in closer to you rather than pressing down on the top of your breast.

**6. Nipple soreness or pain.** If your baby is latching on and sucking correctly you should not feel any painful pressure on your nipple. If baby seems to be sucking incorrectly or you feel pain as he nurses, you may have to make him stop and start over again. Break the suction by putting your finger in the side of baby's mouth and either pressing on your breast or gently pulling on baby's cheek. Don't let your baby continue to suck incorrectly because it leads to nipple soreness and poor sucking patterns can be hard to correct later on.

If soreness or nipple pain continues check for these possible causes:

- *Do not let baby slide onto the nipple, stopping short of the correct sucking position. Be sure he opens wide to take the nipple far back into his mouth.*
- *If baby persistently clamps down too hard as he starts to suck, depress his lower jaw with your finger by pulling down on his chin as you tell him to "open" in a clear, commanding tone of voice.*
- *If nipple pain continues, pull baby's lower lip down while he is nursing and check to see if his tongue is visible between his lower lip and the breast. If you cannot see his tongue, baby may be sucking it along with your nipple. Take baby off the breast and restart him, being sure his mouth is open very wide and his tongue is below the nipple when he latches on.*

**7. Effective sucking patterns.** Many babies know exactly how to suck correctly from the moment they are born. Others take a few days to learn and need specific guidance as outlined above with lots of comfort and patience. But once baby is sucking properly you will take great satisfaction in watching him. As baby sucks vigorously, the muscles in his face work so hard that even his ears wiggle. You can see the strong action of his jaw muscles and hear him swallowing. Then once his initial hunger is satisfied, he becomes relaxed, sucking less vigorously, with fewer swallows, as he enjoys the closeness and comfort of being at his mother's breast.

# Other Breastfeeding Positions

It's a good idea to vary the positions you use to breastfeed your baby. When you are holding the baby at a different angle, he is putting pressure on different areas of your nipple, breast, and areola and this will help to prevent soreness. Also, it can be useful for you to know how to breastfeed your baby in different positions.

## LYING DOWN TO NURSE

You may be more comfortable breastfeeding your baby lying down in the early weeks. You will need to use pillows to support yourself and the baby. At first, you may need some help getting the baby positioned properly so he can latch on correctly. Lie on your side with a pillow under your head. Have baby lying on his side facing you with his mouth in line with your nipple. Place your arm under him with his head on the crook of your elbow. Lean back into the pillows that are behind your back and offer your breast to the baby by supporting it with your fingers underneath and your thumb above, well behind the areola. Encourage the baby to latch on properly by tickling his lips until he opens his mouth **wide**. Then quickly center your nipple in his mouth and **pull** him in close so he can suck effectively.

After you get baby started, you may want to place a pillow behind his back to hold him close and tuck your arm under the pillow supporting your head if that's more comfortable for you. Some mothers also place a pillow between their knees. To change sides, sit baby up and pat his back to see if he needs to bring up a burp, then hold him flat against your chest and roll over on your back. Lie on your other side and position baby at your other breast. This is especially good for mothers who have had a cesarean birth; while

*With baby in the football hold, mother can see how baby is sucking. Notice that baby's legs are bent upward and his toes are peeking out behind mother's shoulder.*

still in the hospital you can use the side rails on the bed to help you roll over.

## THE FOOTBALL HOLD

Another useful position for a mother to learn is the football or "clutch" hold. Position baby with his legs under your arm and his head resting in your hand. Again, you'll need to use pillows to bring baby up to the level of your breast. When you pull baby in close to latch on, be sure his legs are not pushing up against the back of the chair. If this seems to be happening, bend his legs upward, behind you, so his bottom is pressed against the back of the chair. This position is helpful for babies who are having trouble latching on as it gives the mother good visibility of what's going on and good control of baby's position as he latches on.

## FOLLOW THESE PROCEDURES AT FIRST

Since it is important that the young baby learn to suck effectively, we recommend that you use these techniques step-by-step when you and your baby are learning. After a while, when both of you are breastfeeding experts, you can use whatever positions and procedures are comfortable for you. You will sometimes see photos of mothers using just two fingers to position their breast for the baby to latch on. At one time, this technique was recommended and some mothers do find it effective. But more recently it has been found that positioning the thumb and forefinger to form a "C" allows the mother to support her breast and avoid pressing on the areola or squeezing too hard.

## THE MILK-EJECTION REFLEX (THE LET-DOWN)

After the baby has been sucking vigorously for several minutes, many mothers feel a tingling sensation and notice a strong surge of milk. This is known as the milk-ejection reflex or the let-down. It occurs several times during a feeding, and mothers sometimes notice that milk drips from the other breast when a let-down occurs. Baby usually responds to the let-down by more frequent swallowing. Even if you don't feel a tingling in your breast, you'll know a let-down has occurred by watching baby's pattern of sucking and swallowing. Sometimes, hearing your baby cry will initiate a let-down even before he starts to nurse.

Occasionally a baby will be caught off guard by mother's strong let-down and responds by choking and sputtering a bit. It's a good idea to keep a towel or clean diaper handy to mop up the drips as you sit baby up and let him catch his breath.

Some mothers do not feel the milk-ejection reflex at all, but it is still occurring if their babies are nursing well. For other mothers, the tingling sensation may be very strong, especially in the early weeks. One mother, Jo Ellen Carson from Georgia, had the following thoughts about the let-down:

*One quiet evening as I nursed my daughter to sleep, I reflected on the term "let-down" and I began to wonder how this term came to be used in regard to breastfeeding. It usually means disappointment and hurt. The total opposite is what occurs when I nurse my infant daughter.*

*The breastfeeding let-down was by then a very familiar feeling to me, yet it can't really be described. My daughter sucked and wriggled and sucked some more to coax the milk out. After a few brief moments, I felt the fullness—almost an ache—my breasts seemed hard and ready to overflow. And then the change in her breathing as she began drinking in with long, slow gulps, eyes closed, in utter peace and abandonment.*

*I looked down at this small being who was cradled against my body. As I stroked her soft, sweet skin, I felt the overwhelming release of love which, to me, is what the let-down truly is.*

# Engorgement— When the Milk "Comes In"

Your milk will become more plentiful, or "come in," at some time between the second to the sixth day after delivery. Before that time, your baby will get colostrum, which will provide him with all of the nourishment he needs, plus important elements to protect him against infections. It takes about two weeks before the colostrum totally disappears from your milk.

A combination of factors influences when a mother's milk becomes more plentiful. Nursing the baby soon and often after birth encourages milk production. An unmedicated delivery and having your baby with you make an important difference. It also helps if you are reasonably at ease. For most mothers, being in the familiar surroundings of home, with the freedom this gives you to cuddle and nurse your baby frequently, is all that is needed to bring in the milk.

When the milk becomes more plentiful, your breasts may seem fairly bursting. You feel as though you could satisfy twins—or triplets! This fullness is due to a condition called engorgement. It comes about because additional blood has rushed to the breasts in order to assure that there will be adequate nourishment for the new baby. It is like the marshaling of the grand army—all the forces come to the fore to get things in good working order. The extra blood, along with some swelling of tissues, produces the engorgement. It occurs most often in first-time mothers, although this also varies among individuals. Some mothers notice only moderate or little fullness with their first babies, while other mothers become equally engorged with later babies.

In the usual course of events, engorgement subsides in a matter of days. But while the breasts are engorged, it is especially important to continue to nurse the baby frequently, since emptying the breasts relieves the congestion. A comfortably warm shower, followed by a nursing, often reduces engorgement. Some mothers find applying heat helps to relieve engorgement; others use ice packs. In some hospitals, they suggest alternating the two.

A gentle breast massage may also help to relieve engorgement. Sometimes the engorged area is mainly in one part of the breast, perhaps high up toward the arm. With the palm of your hand, gently stroke the breast downward toward the nipple. This is most effective when done under the shower or while leaning over a bowl of warm water and sloshing the water over the breasts.

Cynthia Webb, from Montana, tells how her La Leche League Leader helped her to overcome the problem of engorgement and get off to a good start breastfeeding her daughter:

*The day after we got home from the hospital was the day my breasts became engorged. With the baby crying in the background and the sample bottle of formula from the hospital looking temptingly easy, my LLL Leader gave me advice and solutions that had us back on the right track in half an hour.*

*It took Kelli and me a little longer to really get the hang of nursing. Then one day everything seemed to fall into place. The reward for perseverance has been tremendous. Kelli has shown me the gentle joys and subtle pleasures of motherhood. More than the baby at the breast, it's the first smile of recognition, little arms around my neck, a sleepy head on my shoulder, or snuggling under the covers during an early morning feeding.*

Engorgement can present a problem if the fullness causes the nipples to flatten making it difficult for the baby to latch on properly. It may be helpful to pump or hand-express some milk first to relieve the fullness. Sometimes holding a cold washcloth or ice pack on your nipple will help to bring it out. Breast shells, made of hard plastic, can also be used between feedings to draw out flat nipples. (Do not confuse these with nipple shields which are worn over a mother's nipples during feedings. These are sometimes recommended for flat nipples but they are seldom helpful and often contribute to nipple confusion and sucking problems. They should be avoided.)

# How Long to Nurse?

At one time new mothers were often told to limit nursings in the first few days to three or five minutes on each side at each feeding, and to work up to about ten minutes on the third or fourth day. Such advice does not take into account the fact that it may take two or three minutes for the milk to let down in any quantity, especially in the early days. Nursing for less than five minutes could mean that the feeding would end almost before it started. And once the milk is flowing, the slight soreness that may be felt when the baby starts to nurse subsides. Keep in mind that, in the beginning, nursing frequently—every two hours or so—is easier on the nipples and at the same time stimulates the production of milk. Frequent nursing can also help to prevent jaundice in your newborn.

We also know now that correct positioning of the baby at the breast and proper sucking techniques are the best protection against nipple soreness, so limiting baby's time at the breast is not necessary to prevent sore nipples.

The length of a breastfeeding session should be determined by the baby's interest and response. He will usually suck eagerly, swallowing often, for the first ten minutes or so. Then the flow of milk may decrease and he begins to doze or lose interest. That's the time to switch him over to the other breast. You may want to stop at this point to burp him or change his diaper, and then get him started on the other side. As long as he is sucking correctly, you can let him nurse as long as he wants on the second side.

## TAKING BABY OFF THE BREAST

If you must end a nursing session while baby still has a firm grip on your nipple, you can comfortably remove your baby either by gently pressing the breast away from the corner of his mouth or by pulling back on his cheek near the corner of his mouth. Pulling your baby off the breast may be painful, and it can also be damaging to your nipples.

## ONE SIDE OR BOTH?

Most mothers find it best to offer both breasts to the baby at each feeding. The added stimulation of suckling baby on both breasts is a way of keeping pace with his increasing interest in nursing and his need for more milk. In addition, the breasts will not become overfull.

At each feeding, alternate starting sides. For instance, if at one feeding you start nursing on the right and then switch to the left, reverse the order for the next feeding. You'll be using the last used side first and the first, last. To help remember the starting order, mothers have come up with all kinds of ideas from fastening a small safety pin on the bra on the side used last to transferring a small ring from hand to hand. There's even a Nursing Reminder that can be attached to your bra to remind you which side was used last. See the Appendix for details.

If you do forget, your baby and your own full breast will probably soon let you know you've offered the "wrong" side. No harm is done if this happens from time to time; there's no need for you to worry about it.

### "EMPTYING THE BREAST"

Sometimes mothers are told to empty their breasts completely after each feeding by pumping out whatever milk the baby may leave. This is not really practical because, first of all, the lactating breast is never empty; there will always be another drop of milk, and yet another. Secondly, we have yet to find a mother of a normal, healthy baby who found such emptying to be necessary in order to build up a good milk supply.

If you should have a baby who does not suck well at first, as might be the case with most premies or an occasional full-term baby, you will have to pump after each feeding in order to provide sufficient stimulation to keep up your supply and to provide your own milk for your baby.

### KEEPING YOUR NIPPLES CLEAN

There is no need for special cleansing techniques for your nipples either before or after nursing. The Montgomery glands that surround the nipple secrete a substance that kills bacteria. When you bathe or shower, use only plain water on the breasts and nipples as soap can be drying. It is important to wash your hands before a nursing session, especially while you are in the hospital.

## BURPING THE BABY

During a feeding a baby sometimes swallows air that needs to be expelled or burped if the little one is to be comfortable. Your experience with your own baby will be your best guide as to when and if he needs burping. Some breastfed babies never seem to need burping, while others will swallow air when mother's breast is very full and the milk comes quickly. The baby who by nature is a "gulper" is always a likely candidate for burping. Burping is one of the things to try whenever the baby is fussy.

There are any number of ways to burp a baby. You can try placing your baby on your shoulder and gently patting his back. A clean diaper or receiving blanket tossed over the shoulder will absorb any milk that comes up. Just holding your baby in a more or less upright position will bring up most air bubbles in an easy and relaxed way. Another tried and true method is to raise baby, slowly, to a sitting position. When he is very small, take care to support his head and back, and hold him in this position for only a few moments. Some mothers rest the baby, tummy down, across their knees and rub or pat his back. Try burping the baby when you switch from one breast to the other during a feeding and again when your baby is through nursing. If there is no burp after a few moments, you can forget the idea—unless, of course, he is fussy.

Anytime your baby burps especially heartily, see if he wants a little more milk. The big bubble may have made him feel full when he really wasn't. But if baby falls asleep at the breast while nursing, you don't need to disturb him with the burping routine. Lay him down carefully, either on his side or stomach, not on his back. When he is lying on his side, any milk he might spit up will run out of his mouth and not upset him.

## HICCUPS

We'd also like to mention hiccups here. Little babies seem to be prone to them, often hiccupping after every feeding. Don't worry about them; they're perfectly normal and more upsetting to the parents than the baby. If you like, you can let the baby nurse for a few more minutes. This may stop the hiccups.

# Hospital Routines

Hospitals want what is best for the patients, but often their size and bureaucracy come between their good intentions and the kind of care you need. Be prepared to speak up for what you want. Often, getting what you want is simply a matter of persistence. One mother said that whenever she was told "I'm sorry, we can't do that" in answer to a request, she would say that she did not want anyone to go against hospital policy, but that she would like to talk to someone who had the authority to alter the policy. Carrying her appeal up the line did at times result in a happy resolution of the problem.

## YOU MAY NEED HELP

Assertiveness takes energy, of course, and may be an effort that you aren't up to at the time. Your husband can be your partner in helping to bend or bypass routines that hamper your breastfeeding efforts. You concentrate on caring for the baby, and he can take the position of running interference against red tape and regulations that get in your way. After all, this is *your* baby, a fact that is sometimes obscured in the delicate balance between institutional and parental authority.

Susan and Larry Kaseman of Virginia tell of their experience when their son Peter was born.

*As my husband, Larry, and I planned for the birth of our second child, our major concern was that our family be together as much as possible. When a cesarean became necessary, we quickly changed plans, but not priorities. With a combination of diplomacy and determination, Larry communicated our wishes and began a dialogue with the hospital staff. They would state hospital policy, we would offer an alternative, and they would consider and sometimes cooperate.*

*"May I please have my baby?" became my theme throughout my hospital stay. I had been reluctant to refer to our first child as "my baby" for fear of being thought an over-possessive mother. I have since decided it is an effective way of emphasizing to myself and the staff exactly who has the primary responsibility.*

*Again and again I found that exceptions could be made to many of the rules. Peter was brought to us in the recovery room, two hours old and sleepy, but eager and able to nurse. What a tremendous help that contact was! When a nurse said an injection of painkiller would make me too woozy to be trusted with Peter, I declined the injection and she found a milder, oral drug that worked well enough.*

*Throughout my hospital stay, I had to keep asking for Peter. If one person refused to bring him, I'd ask someone else. Staff members were generally cooperative in responding, but seldom offered to bring him. I felt like a minority of one because of my "unusual" ideas, and was grateful for the reassurance of those who agreed with me.*

*My initial concern had been that Peter be with me so I could meet his needs, but I was continually amazed at the strength of my need for him—how much better I felt, physically and emotionally, when he was in my arms, and how difficult it was when he was in the nursery.*

## NO SUPPLEMENTS—FREQUENT NURSING

In the hospital your constant refrain should be that you *do not* want your baby to be given bottles of water or formula in the nursery, and you *do* want to be able to nurse him often. This is very important, because supplementary formula is one of the greatest deterrents to establishing a good milk supply. Frequent nursing is not only important in establishing a good milk supply, but it will also help to prevent jaundice in your newborn. **Your milk is regulated by what your baby takes, and the more he nurses, the more milk your breasts produce.** If your baby is given a bottle, he will take less from the breast. Also, your baby will be confused by the change from mother's soft nipple to the harder rubber nipple.

A baby is particularly vulnerable to nipple confusion in the first few days because he is learning how to suck properly. If he is given bottles at this point, it may be a long hard struggle before he learns to breastfeed effectively.

If you do not have rooming-in, be sure to let everyone know that you want your baby brought to you as often as he wants to be fed. This should be at least every two hours during the day and whenever he wakes at night. Babies need to be fed at night and if your newborn is not brought to you, he may be receiving a bottle of water or formula in the nursery.

## ROOMING-IN

Problems caused by hospital routines can often be avoided if it is possible for you to room-in with your baby. Rooming-in allows you to have your baby in your room for all or most of the time. You care for the baby, and others care for you. Connie Horenkamp of Illinois tells of her experience:

*My first two children were totally breastfed, but they were forced to live those first precious days behind the glass wall of the hospital nursery. I spent many hours standing at the window making sure everything was all right. When Marissa was born, hospital policy was more relaxed and I was more determined; we roomed-in together. We nursed frequently, napped together, and just cuddled. The first day she slept very little as she adjusted to her new life, but I was able to phone a Leader for the reassurance I needed. Now I keep remembering (three months later) how Marissa slept in my arms and in the arms of my husband. Those first days were ours in which to grow together. I went home confidently knowing my baby.*

Laurel Cohen of New Jersey planned on having rooming-in when her daughter, Debbie Sue, was born, but she was informed that the required private room was not available. The baby would have to be in the nursery, and feedings could be only every four hours. Laurel was in a double room with another patient, but when the woman left soon afterward, Laurel went immediately to the supervisor's desk. Could she pay the private room charge and have her baby with her? A call to the business office procured the needed permission, and a delighted Laurel reported, "I had my dear little baby with me all day."

## SLEEPING OR SCREAMING?

If you are able to have rooming-in or at least nurse your baby on demand, you won't be bothered with problems that can be caused by hospital feeding schedules. Still, there may be times when baby is not waking up to be fed as often as he should. A newborn needs to nurse at least 8-12 times in twenty-four hours.

If your baby has been sleeping for more than two or three hours, try gently to awaken him. Rough handling is very disturbing to a newborn, but you can jiggle him a bit, rub his head, talk to him, stroke his cheek with your nipple; try rubbing his feet or blowing on them.

One suggestion is to sit baby on your lap with his chin in your hand and bend him forward at the hips. Usually he awakens in just a few seconds. If not, try walking your fingers up and down his spine. Or gently bring him from a horizontal to a vertical position, one hand supporting his head, the other holding his bottom.

You can also try undressing him or changing his diaper. If nothing works to awaken him, you may have to give it another half hour or so and then try again. If the nurse comes to take him back to the nursery, be sure to let her know the baby did not wake up to nurse and should be brought back for a feeding as soon as he wakes up. Make it clear that you do not want your baby to be given a bottle in the nursery.

If for some reason your baby is crying very hard before you get a chance to start feeding him, a little patience may be needed to calm him down before he's ready to nurse. Try rocking him or putting him over your shoulder and patting his back. Sing a soothing melody—baby will be calmed by hearing your familiar voice. Then try offering him your breast and see if he calms down and starts to suck. If he's not ready yet, try a few more minutes of calm mothering to help him relax.

With either the sleeping or screaming baby, squeeze a few drops of your milk into his mouth to give him a taste of what he's missing. We do not advise putting anything else, such as honey, on the nipple to entice the baby to take it. Anything other than your milk can cause a reaction in a sensitive baby. Also, these products may have impurities in them which could cause problems for baby— a certain type of botulism spores, for example, can be found in honey. It should not be given to babies under one year old.

# Breastfeeding-Aid Products

Experience has taught us that breastfeeding proceeds most smoothly when kept as simple and natural as possible. But there are some circumstances when a product designed to aid breastfeeding can be helpful. Breast pumps and other breastfeeding-aid products may be available from your local LLL Leader. Some are also sold through the La Leche League International Catalogue. See the Appendix for details.

## BREAST PUMPS

Not every breastfeeding mother will need a breast pump. If a mother needs to remove milk from her breasts on a short-term basis, she can usually learn to use the techniques explained for hand-expression in Chapter 7. But there are situations when a breast pump is useful, for example, when a mother is saving her milk for a premature or sick baby, when a mother plans to return to work, or when a mother and baby must be separated for other reasons. More information on breast pumps can also be found in Chapter 7.

In the hospital, you may be advised to use a breast pump to relieve engorgement. If used for this purpose, be sure to pump only enough to soften the breast for baby to grasp the nipple. You will probably not need to do this for more than one or two feedings.

## BREAST SHELLS OR BREAST SHIELDS

These two-piece hard plastic shells are the same ones recommended for use during pregnancy to correct flat or inverted nipples. They can be used between feedings to draw out flat or inverted nipples that were not treated during pregnancy. One type of breast shell has large holes that allow air to circulate around the nipples. These are also recommended when air is needed to treat sore nipples.

Milk often collects in these breast shields but it should not be saved or fed to the baby. It should be discarded.

## NASAL SPRAY

You may be told about a nasal spray that is used to bring on the milk ejection or let-down reflex. Such artificial intervention is sometimes suggested for a tense and nervous mother or one who is very doubtful of her ability to breastfeed. A seriously delayed let-down in the first week of breastfeeding can sometimes be helped by short-term use of this oxytocin nasal spray, but long-term use is seldom necessary or recommended.

## NIPPLE SHIELDS

A nipple shield looks like a regular rubber nipple and is worn over the mother's own nipple during a feeding. From our years of experience, we know without a doubt that nipple shields are an invitation to trouble. Their use is almost never justified, and they create many more problems than they solve. The impulses to the brain that normally come from a baby sucking directly on his mother's nipple are fewer, and the secretion and let-down of the milk is slowed.

A baby who has become accustomed to sucking on a nipple shield is usually upset when his mother tries to take it away. With patience and understanding, a baby can be weaned from the rubber nipple but it is no easy task. You may be able to start baby nursing on the shield, and after one or two minutes when the milk is flowing well, whisk it away and put baby directly on mother's nipple. Once the baby is accustomed to the real thing, the shield can be thrown away.

If you are given a nipple shield to use in the hospital, we suggest that you refuse it. If your baby has already become accustomed to nursing with a nipple shield, your LLL Leader may be able to offer specific suggestions that will help him learn to suck effectively.

# Leaving the Hospital

Nowadays, mothers don't usually stay in the hospital more than two or three days after their baby is born. Some mothers have found it wise to leave for home even sooner than that. Even the most progressive hospital cannot duplicate the relaxed atmosphere and the freedom you have at home to mother your baby as you choose.

Karen Stange of Nebraska asked the doctor if she could go home from the hospital soon after birth if there were no problems. Karen explains how it worked out:

*T*he *doctor said the baby should be observed for twelve hours, but after that we were allowed to go home. Thus began three of the best days in eleven years of marriage. All of us got to know each other better than ever, and Clay seemed to thrive on the added love of five-year-old Sean and three-year-old Eric. The evening of Clay's true birthday all five of us sat in our home and, I'm sure, glowed with the love we felt.*

*Larry took three days off and we did nothing but be a family. We had few visitors as no one realized we were home. I was free to rest as I chose, and needless to add, breastfeeding went very well. For us it was a time that will be remembered fondly all our lives.*

You can do yourself and your baby a favor by not taking any formula home from the hospital. You won't need it, and if it isn't in the house, you won't be tempted to use it at one of those moments of doubt that most mothers have. The take-home packs of formula are simply advertising, a promotion for artificial infant feeding. Research has shown that these formula gift-packs interfere with a mother's determination to breastfeed.

Hospitals have become much more consumer-conscious in recent years and want to know what patients like or dislike about their hospital stay. By taking a few minutes to write a personal letter or fill out a patient questionnaire stating your preferences, you can support the practices you found helpful and point out the ones you'd like to see changed. Your suggestions could make it easier for the next breastfeeding mother giving birth in that hospital and, who knows?—you may find a delightfully improved atmosphere during *your* next visit.

If for some reason your breastfeeding experience in the hospital has not been the best or if you could not relax, don't fret. The hospital stay is now in the past. When you are at home with your baby, you will be able to breastfeed him. Thousands of mothers have done so and you can, too.

# CHAPTER 5

# At Home with Your Baby

There is a sense of joy and satisfaction on everyone's part when your newborn is settled at home, in the heart of the family. Things are as they should be—you are all together. You'll find your mothering skills improving every day. But don't be surprised if you feel unsure of yourself and even a bit panicky at times. The care of this tiny baby is yours day and night, and the realization can seem overwhelming at times.

Most of us can say that we've been there; we know the feeling. One of La Leche League's founders thinks back with amazement at her own ineptness when she and her husband brought their firstborn home:

*The picture is vivid in my mind. Baby was lying in her basket, which was beautifully done up with a frilly, ruffled liner that I had made before she was born. She was crying*

*her heart out, oblivious to this finery. She had been fed
and changed and was supposed to sleep. I remember
thinking, "If only she were old enough to talk. She could
tell me what is bothering her." Unfortunately, I was not
yet aware of a far more basic form of communication
with a little baby—a caring touch. How much more
effective than speech! How simple if only I had picked
her up! Instead I was feeling somewhat put out at the
turn of events, disappointed in myself and my baby.*

Think of the baby's first four to six weeks as an adjustment
period for both of you, a time of getting to know each other. Your
baby is mastering the skill of nursing to bring in milk, and your
body is fine-tuning the system for producing it. It's not unusual for
a new mother to feel as though her breasts are "bursting" with milk
one day, and then be frantic a few days later because she thinks
"there's nothing there."

Is the baby getting enough? Why is he crying? Haven't we all
asked ourselves these questions and more? A good many of us announced firmly at some point in those early weeks that breastfeeding was "impossible." But at the urging of a supportive husband or
with the help of another nursing mother, we decided to keep going
for just a few more days.

Nowadays, new mothers have the advantage of being able to
call an LLL Leader when questions or problems arise. She can give
you reassuring answers and mother-to-mother encouragement. Diane McAleer, a mother from Florida, is still enjoying her breastfeeding relationship with her one-year-old daughter. But she recalls
the early weeks:

*The first six weeks were rough but well worth it. It took
a while for me to recover from my daughter's long,
difficult birth. We made it through together—Tiffany
receiving the best through my milk and her nursing
helping me to get back into shape. Six weeks, I had been
told, was the magic number. I was told not to give up the
idea of nursing until after that period, as both mother and
child need time to adjust to one another. We had problems
in the beginning, but nothing that a phone call to one of
my LLL Leaders could not resolve.*

# Babies Are to Love

Through doubts and anxious moments, remember—babies are to love. The task of caring for your new baby will not seem nearly so awesome if you keep this thought in mind. "Tender loving care" is what the very best authorities recognize as the prime need of babies. Look to your own baby. Is he happiest when snuggled close to you, nursing very often, perhaps even every hour? Or does he respond best when laid down after a nursing and patted to sleep? Your baby's well-being, comfort, and security are your guides.

James Kenny, a clinical psychologist, who together with his wife, Mary, has authored many books and articles about childrearing, writes about baby's needs:

*The needs of the infant are urgent. They are necessary for survival. When adults meet these needs day after day and week after week with reasonable consistency and promptness, the infant gradually develops a sense of trust.*

There is a beautiful simplicity about the care of the young baby that does not apply at any other stage of childrearing. With sureness we can say that **a baby's wants are a baby's needs.** The wants of a two- or three-year-old, however, may not always be what he needs. Parents will not respond any less lovingly then, but their approach will adjust to the changing world of the mobile child.

In THE HEART HAS ITS OWN REASONS, author Mary Ann Cahill, one of La Leche League's founders, talks about the needs of a newborn:

*From living in the womb with the umbilical cord supplying all his needs, he has progressed to a position outside of, but near, mother's body. He is meant to be within close proximity of her warm breast and the sound of her voice. It is nature's careful way of providing a transition from the infant's old world to his new one. The little newcomer has the freedom needed to grow, yet is assured of continuous, loving support. The all-important mother-child bond replaces the umbilical cord.*

With your newborn, "giving in" to him is good parenting. Feed him according to his own time schedule. Comfort him when he is upset. But, you may ask, won't such permissiveness spoil the baby? This question is asked by many parents who are sincerely concerned about their children and want to do what is best.

A mother, grandmother, and League Leader, Marion Blackshear, had this to say on the matter of spoiling and babies. "When you think of a piece of fruit as spoiled, you think of it as bruised, left on the shelf to rot, handled roughly, neglected. But meeting needs, giving lots of loving care, handling gently, is not spoiling. I could carry this a step further and say that a piece of fruit is at its best when left to ripen on the tree, its source of nourishment— and a baby is at his best when held close to his source of physical and emotional nourishment—his mother."

And others agree. Dr. William Sears, author of THE GROWING FAMILY SERIES, says, "Spoiling is a word that should be forever stricken from parenting books....Babies do not get spoiled by being held. Babies 'spoil' when they are not held."

And in his classic book, *How to Really Love Your Child,* Dr. Ross Campbell explains:

---

*W*e cannot start too early in giving a child continuous, warm, consistent affection. He simply must have this unconditional love to cope most effectively in today's world.

---

## HOW MANY TIMES DO I FEED THE BABY?

Throughout this book, we refer repeatedly to feedings "every two or three hours" since it is a common time span for babies' appetites. And it is a fact that when baby's tummy is filled often enough, and mother's breasts are emptied regularly enough, most breastfeeding problems are avoided. But no timetable can tell you how often you should nurse your baby. Some babies, some of the time, will nurse more often than every two hours. Others will nurse less often, or perhaps go for one longer stretch at night.

Some people are more comfortable with the explanation that a newborn usually breastfeeds 10-12 times in twenty-four hours. This way, a mother is not watching the clock to see if two hours have passed since baby's last feeding.

Mothers who live in a world that is not as mechanized and scheduled as ours would be aghast at the thought of regulating the comfort their babies receive at their breasts. In a study of New Guinea tribeswomen, it was found that infants nursed about once every twenty-four minutes. The babies were carried close to their mother's body all the time and an average feeding lasted about three minutes.

In the *Journal of Tropical Pediatrics and Environmental Child Health,* guest editor Babette Francis wrote:

---

*Successful lactation is an expression of a woman's femininity and she doesn't need to count how often she feeds the baby any more than she counts how often she kisses the baby.*

---

# Nursing Manners

As parents soon learn, babies have distinct personalities, and nowhere is this more apparent than in the way each little person approaches the important matter of eating. With our first babies some of us had preconceived ideas of how babies should nurse—beautifully mannered, of course, with no starts and stops or spitting up. With later babies, we found it much more revealing and entertaining to relax and observe each new stylist. You may find that your baby will fit one of the following descriptions. On the other hand, he may create a style that is strictly his own.

## THE LEISURELY DINER

This young miss or mister thoroughly enjoys mealtime, which may be just about all of the time, especially in the early weeks. Intervals between nursings will lengthen as he grows older, and while he will probably always enjoy unhurried dining, he'll become much more efficient about drinking his fill. Once you are sure that he is gaining well, you can on occasion end a nursing after twenty minutes or so, feeling confident that he will not go hungry. A bonus with this type of baby is the opportunity to take it easy and cuddle lots.

Sometimes the leisurely diner can be encouraged to suck more effectively with some "switch nursing." After he has been nursing on one breast for about ten minutes you'll probably notice his sucking and swallowing slows down. It's time, then, to switch him to the other side. A new supply of milk may encourage him to finish his meal a bit more efficiently. If he slows down again, but still wants to suck, switch him back again to the first side.

## THE NIP AND NAPPER

The nip and napper has much in common with the leisurely diner, although he tends to drop off to sleep (nap) after a few minutes of nursing (nip) and repeats this sequence rather often.

This is another instance when switch nursing can encourage more efficiency. As soon as baby starts to doze, switch him to the other breast. If he's really sleeping soundly, but you know he hasn't nursed enough to be full, try burping him or changing his diaper before switching to the other breast.

A baby who spends too much time sleeping at the breast instead of sucking well could be headed for a problem with slow weight gain. You'll want to work at encouraging him to suck well and watch for wet and soiled diapers to be sure he's getting enough to eat. (See the information in the next section under "Is Baby Getting Enough?")

## THE NO-NONSENSE NURSER

Feedings are a down-to-business operation with this youngster. Once beyond the early stages of learning about breastfeeding, nursing time may be over in ten or fifteen minutes or less. He may be a baby who is only willing to nurse from one breast at each feeding. There is little opportunity for a dinner time tete-a-tete with the no-nonsense nurser. But look for a big smile, sometimes with milk trickling from the side of his mouth, at the end of a nursing before he moves on to the next challenge.

You may want to be sure that a baby who only nurses for short periods of time is given the opportunity to breastfeed often enough.

There may be a question about whether he is getting enough to eat at these short, quick feedings, so again, you'll want to watch for wet and soiled diapers to be sure he's getting enough milk.

## THE WHAT-GOES-DOWN-TENDS-TO-COME-UP TYKE

Is this a personality or a physical trait? No matter, it is unmistakable. While almost all babies bring up a little milk occasionally after a feeding, this little one spits up regularly after feedings and in-between time. He is happy enough and gains weight, but you wonder whether he's keeping enough milk in his tummy to keep on gaining. The information in the next section will help you determine if he's getting enough to eat.

He may or may not speed through nursings. Some babies spit up because they're getting too much milk too quickly. If your baby gulps and gasps just after you have a let-down, try taking him off the breast for a moment or two as the milk rushes down. Have a diaper handy to catch the overflow. Let baby start nursing again as the milk flow slows to a rate he can handle. Some babies may even let the overflow trickle out of their mouths, which is a nice way of alleviating the problem. Your main response to this characteristic should be very gentle handling, with no sudden movements. Too vigorous burping can bring up milk that would otherwise stay in the baby's stomach. Gentle handling after a feeding will help your baby keep down his lunch. It may help to raise the pad or mattress in baby's bed or basket by an inch or two at the head end as laying baby flat is sometimes what triggers the spitting up.

Occasionally a baby will finish nursing as usual and promptly bring up what seems to be the entire feeding, perhaps even with jet-like force. If the baby does not show any signs of illness—no fever or unusual crying—it is probably just one of those things. After things calm down a bit and you've cleaned up the mess, go ahead and nurse the baby again. Of course, you'd want to check with your doctor if this happens often.

A handy supply of diapers or small towels is a help in protecting your clothing with a spitter in the family. And along with diapers, take extra changes of clothing for baby when going out. As Dr. Gregory White has observed, "in a healthy baby, spitting up is a laundry problem, not a medical problem."

Getting bigger is a sure cure for this tendency in a baby. While spitting up is a nuisance at the time, there is less odor and staining with breast milk than there would be if baby were formula-fed. And really, what's a little milk between a mother and her bosom buddy?

## ABOUT THE PACIFIER

Be forewarned that the pacifier can create more problems than it solves, often because it works too well. Pop it into a crying baby's mouth, and the room is suddenly blanketed with silence. What could be handier? But therein lies trouble. The use of a pacifier has a way of sneaking up on you by making it so simple to take the easy way out. While a pacifier can sometimes substitute for mother's breast, it is never a substitute for mother. A League Leader from Great Britain, Christine Blissett, explains that the English term for a pacifier is "dummy." "This is exactly what it is!" she adds.

Used judiciously, however, for a short period of time and in a limited number of circumstances, a pacifier can be a help to the breastfeeding mother. Sucking can be very soothing to a newborn, and a pacifier may be convenient when you find yourself in a situation where you absolutely can't nurse him. A pacifier may satisfy him briefly until you can.

The "pacifier habit" develops when it's used routinely, for instance, as a way to put the baby to sleep. Ordinarily, if your baby likes to fall asleep sucking, let it be at the breast. You have the best pacifier in the world from baby's point of view. And more nursing at the breast means more milk for the baby.

If your baby sucks on a pacifier regularly every day, your milk supply could be adversely affected and the baby may not gain well.

# Is Baby Getting Enough?

How will you know if your baby is getting enough milk? He is probably getting enough to eat if he nurses every two or three hours. Is he "filling out" and putting on weight? Growing in length? Active and alert? A "yes" to these questions is an indication that your baby is thriving.

A quick, easy way to reassure yourself that your infant is getting enough milk is to check the number of wet diapers. If he has six to eight really wet diapers a day, he is probably getting plenty of milk. Frequent bowel movements are also a sign that baby is getting enough to eat. For the first six weeks or so, a breastfed baby will usually have two to five bowel movements a day.

From time to time, your doctor will weigh the baby as a way of measuring his physical progress. Some babies never lose an ounce from the day they're born, and put on weight with the greatest of ease. Most babies lose some weight during the first week but get back to birth weight by two to three weeks of age. After that, a pound a month (453 grams), or four to seven ounces a week, is usually considered an acceptable gain, although some babies gain as much as a pound a week. Family characteristics and the baby's individual makeup need to be considered. Remember—healthy, happy babies come in all shapes and sizes. Both the quite fat and the very slim baby can be normal and healthy. Neither bigness nor smallness is a reason for concern as long as the baby's food is breast milk and nursings are according to his needs. If you feed your baby in the way that is naturally intended for the human infant, his weight gain will be what is natural for your particular child.

With regard to baby's size and appetite, Malinda Sawyer of Missouri noted, "Mothers who give birth to large babies and mothers who give birth to small babies have at least one thing in common: They can expect to have their ability to totally breastfeed the baby questioned."

Marian Tompson, one of La Leche League's founders, remembers when two of her nieces had identical weights of seventeen pounds—but one baby was six months old and the other was one and one-half years old. Yet the doctor for each was satisfied that the baby was healthy.

If you are having any problems with your milk supply, or if your baby is not gaining at least four ounces a week, see the sections later in this book on "Increasing Your Milk Supply" (in Chapter 7) and "Slow Weight Gain" (in Chapter 17).

## LEAKING

A common occurrence while you are breastfeeding is for milk to drip from one breast when baby starts to nurse on the other. If your breasts are very full or engorged, there is good reason to let the milk come out rather than hold it back. It's a great way to relieve that full feeling. To catch the overflow and keep yourself dry, hold a diaper or something equally absorbent under your breast.

Sometimes a breastfeeding mother will find her milk is leaking at inopportune moments. This is most likely to occur during the first weeks of nursing. Suddenly, to your dismay, you realize that milk is leaking from your breasts. Often, it is nearly time for a feeding and the sight, sound, or even the *thought* of your baby triggers the let-down reflex.

Nursing mothers have learned that pressure applied directly against the nipples will keep the milk from dripping out. If you notice the tingly, stinging sensation of the let-down—or if you feel milk starting to leak—fold your arms across your chest and apply pressure with the heels of your hands directly on your nipples. Another unobtrusive way to stop leaking is to rest your chin on your hands and press against your breasts with your forearms.

There are nursing pads available in drug stores and maternity shops that are designed to absorb leakage. Some are disposable; others can be washed and used over and over again. You'll want to avoid pads that have a plastic liner as they can keep air from getting at your nipples. Some mothers make their own pads by stitching together circular pieces cut from old diapers or other absorbent material. The pads can be washed along with baby's other things and reused. A folded cotton or linen handkerchief works well, too, but avoid the no-iron variety as they are less absorbent.

The possibility of your milk leaking when you least expect it can lead to a certain amount of embarrassment, as Sue Ellen Jennings Austin, from California, recalls:

---

*I* remember an early outing with our first nursing baby. I had carefully planned to be out between his every-two-hour nursings and was even armed with a water bottle in case (heaven forbid!) he should want to nurse in public. We were strolling down the aisle of a grocery store when a woman approached me and whispered, "Excuse me, Miss, your milk is leaking."

Glancing down at the floor, I was horrified to see a trail of milk all around me and my shopping cart. Panicked, I clasped both arms across my chest. It was only then I realized that the milk had not come from me but from a milk carton in my shopping cart that had overturned.

---

# BUT WHERE HAS ALL THE MILK GONE?

When the milk comes in and your breasts feel quite full, you are of course overjoyed and supremely confident that you will have plenty of milk for your baby. Then the engorgement goes away, and you may find yourself thinking that the milk must be gone, too. At this point you may feel discouraged. You begin to wonder, "Have I lost my milk?"

You haven't, we can assure you. The absence of that full feeling and dripping is no indication that the amount of milk you have for your baby has diminished. The making of milk is an almost continuous process. As the baby takes some out, more comes in. Just keep nursing, and your eager eater will be rewarded with milk, even though you do not feel "full."

The more often your baby takes milk, the more milk you will have. When a mother has twins, there is twice the stimulation to the breasts to produce milk, and so she has enough for two babies. When your baby nurses less often or with less vigor, the amount of milk you produce decreases accordingly. If it drops too low to suit his needs, he will want to nurse more often. With added nursings, your breasts will respond by making more milk.

As you will see, breastfeeding is an excellent example of the law of supply and demand in operation. **Problems arise when rigid feeding schedules, bottles of water, or supplementary feedings hamper the natural balance.** It takes a little while to establish a good balance between baby's appetite and your milk supply, so be patient. The first six weeks are sometimes the most challenging. This is the time when you'll really want to be in touch with other breastfeeding mothers, especially your La Leche League Group.

Breastfeeding becomes easier as it continues. As your baby's personality emerges, the fun increases. There are smiles and love pats. The time you spend with baby at your breast helps you get to know each other in very special way. The concerns of the early weeks will soon give way to the enjoyment awaiting you in the months ahead.

## BABY'S BOWEL MOVEMENTS

For the first few days after birth, baby's stool will be very dark—greenish-black—and sticky. It may be a nuisance to wipe off his little bottom, but it's a reassuring sign that all is well with baby's digestive system. This first stool is called meconium. Nursing the baby soon after birth assures that your baby will get the colostrum he needs to help get rid of the meconium.

Once the meconium is cleared out, the stool of the baby who is receiving only mother's milk differs a good deal from that of the formula-fed infant. The stool of the breastfed baby is usually quite loose and unformed, often of a pea-soup consistency, and may be yellow to yellow-green to tan in color. The odor, unlike that of the bottle-fed baby's stool, is mild and not unpleasant.

Frequency of bowel movements varies from baby to baby and even from week to week with the same baby. Some babies may have frequent bowel movements that are little more than a stain on the diaper. At first, your baby may have a bowel movement with every nursing. This is definitely not diarrhea in the breastfed baby. It is a sign that he is getting plenty of milk. As he gets older, he may have only two or three large bowel movements a week, or sometimes only one a week. As his bowel movements decrease in frequency, they will increase in volume. There is room for considerable variation among perfectly normal breastfed babies. Even an occasional green, watery stool is not a cause for worry in the otherwise healthy baby. Bowel movements can also change in color after exposure to the air.

Happily enough, because breast milk contains enough water for his needs, your breastfed baby does not get constipated. Constipation (hard, dry stools) has nothing to do with the time interval between bowel movements. Some older breastfed babies go five to seven or more days between bowel movements and have perfectly normal, though very profuse, stools.

Babies sometimes fuss just before or at the time they have a bowel movement, and a change of position may help them. Some can get down to business more easily when in a semi-reclining position, either in your lap or in an infant seat. Others want to brace their feet against something. If you hold the baby against your shoulder, hold one hand under his feet. If your baby is one who seems to have a difficult time with this, you might try helping him by sponging the rectal area gently with warm water. If that doesn't help, some doctors suggest inserting just the tip of a rectal thermometer. This is seldom necessary, and there's no need to bother unless your baby has a real struggle and seems very uncomfortable.

# Caring for Your Baby

As a very new little person, your baby continues to need many of the same conditions that helped him to grow in the womb. He needs to be close to you most of the time, whether awake or sleeping. Being close to you is very reassuring to your newborn. The rhythms of your breathing and heartbeat are familiar to him. In addition, he has been hearing your voice since about six months before he was born, so talking to him in soft, loving tones is especially soothing. For the time being, you are his world.

As Herbert Ratner, MD, philosopher and long time friend and advisor to La Leche League, states, "It is a wise and providential nature that gives each newborn his or her private caretaker and tutor—the mother."

Selma Fraiberg, professor of child psychoanalysis at the University of Michigan Medical School and author of many books and articles on child development, talks about baby's needs:

*In the biological program of mother and baby there are built-in guarantees for the satisfaction of the baby's needs that ensure the formation of human bonds in the first eighteen months of life. The mother is the primary "need satisfier," and that need satisfaction should lead the infant through a series of stages in the first year in which the mother is loved more than any other person in his small world.*

Viola Lennon, one of La Leche League's founders, tells a story of a young mother who had what seemed to her a hundred and one problems. Vi recalls: "I invited her over for a visit. As she sat down in the living room with me, she immediately began asking questions. Soon I noticed she was not listening to my answers but was watching me handle my baby, Marty, who was rather fussy that day. I nursed him, walked him, bounced him, rocked him, and carried him with me to the kitchen while I made a pot of tea. Finally, she blurted out, 'Does he often act this way?' When I said yes, she smiled and said, 'I don't think I have any real problems. I just didn't know that babies needed all that attention.'"

## KEEP YOUR BABY CLOSE

Along with whatever else you are doing during the day, you will want to have your baby close to you as a matter of course. You don't have to have him in your arms every minute, although you will be holding him often, both when you are nursing and between times (as he needs this contact). But you will just want to be there because what your baby needs most of all is you. No one else can take your place. To him, there is nobody quite like his mother.

In many cultures it is the custom for mothers to be practically inseparable from their babies during their first years, with the baby either strapped to his mother's body or sleeping cuddled next to her. In these cultures, it is unusual to hear a baby cry.

So it is not surprising that a recent study found that more human contact makes for a happier baby. Those babies who spent more time being held or carried either in mother's arms or in a baby carrier—even while contented or asleep—cried less. The younger the baby, the more dramatic were the results: Three extra hours of carrying a day reduced the amount of crying in a four-week-old infant by forty-five percent.

These findings confirm what our motherly instincts tell us— that plenty of loving contact does not "spoil" a baby or make him more demanding, but instead helps him feel more comfortable and happy in his new world.

For many mothers, owning some type of baby carrier is essential. Helen Nichols of Massachusetts can't say enough "in praise of the baby carrier." She writes: "As with breastfeeding itself, the benefits of the baby carrier are not entirely for the baby. In fact, as I discovered, mother receives a generous portion of them. I could cook, clean house, wash dishes, care for the older children, even sew while Benjamin slept blissfully in his cozy nest. It was, purely and simply, the very easiest thing to do."

When you are considering what kinds of equipment you'll need for your new baby, remember that very little specialized baby equipment is really necessary; more important to the baby are mother's sweet milk and loving arms. Lee Stewart of Missouri sums up the subject well: "Children's natural values are very human and simple. They want to be held and loved. They want to be with those who care for them. They want to be comfortable. Given a choice between the warmth of human values and material values, babies will almost always choose the human."

A mother from New York, Michele Acerra, gives credit to La Leche League for helping her learn about her baby's needs:

*I* want to thank La Leche League, not only for the breastfeeding information, but for their outlook on babies and mothering. There are many baby gadgets and gimmicks around these days to substitute for mother's time and closeness. I don't think our society is really comfortable with babies and their simple needs: security in mother's presence and the best possible food, mother's milk.

# Taking Care of Mother

As a brand-new mother, you may find yourself concentrating so completely on your baby that you forget about taking care of yourself, so a quick review of the basics of "mother care" is worthwhile here. Mother care isn't elaborate or demanding; it involves mostly commonsense things that are important to any new mother, breastfeeding or not.

Good food, plenty of fluids, and adequate rest come quickly to mind. We also include in our list the need for plenty of loving exchanges—if only a hug or a quick squeeze of a hand—between the new baby's parents. Such shared moments will help keep you going during this demanding time in your life.

Choose between-meal snacks carefully. A nursing mother gets hungry almost as often as her baby, and there's the temptation to nibble on sweets. Choose instead nutritious snacks such as fresh fruit, raw vegetables, or cheese. Getting enough to drink can be taken care of by keeping unsweetened juice or water handy at all times.

Sufficient rest is right up there with the most important recommendations for a new mother. In the days immediately following your baby's birth you will want to spend a good part of your day relaxing. A certain amount of being up and about provides needed exercise, but this is the time to enjoy being pampered. "Mothering the mother" is an integral part of the care of a new mother and baby in many cultures.

A handy rule of thumb for a new mother is to sleep, or at least rest, whenever baby dozes. Even the baby who "never sleeps" catnaps more often than parents may realize. True, the times when the baby sleeps are probably not when you are accustomed to sleeping, and it will take some discipline on your part to set aside what interests you at the moment, close your eyes, and think "sleep." When baby's eyes close at the breast, settle back in your chair with your feet up, your little bundle still in your arms, and try to drop off to sleep. And even if you can't sleep, just closing your eyes, forgetting work that needs to be done, and relaxing can be refreshing.

Other times, mothers find that lying down, closing their eyes, and listening to soft music for ten minutes or so is refreshing. Try it! Think of tension draining away as water drains from a basin. Or snuggle with baby and a book. The important part is to forget about those things which "must be done." Remember, "people before things," and that includes you!

Every so often, take a moment to think through the ways to make the most of this time in your life. Use your own good judgment as to what is or is not important. Your baby and the rest of the family, too, need and appreciate a mother who is relaxed and feels good about herself.

## A NURSING CORNER

Many breastfeeding mothers find it convenient to set up a comfortable spot for their nursing sessions. Since you'll be spending a lot of time there in the early weeks you'll want everything as handy as possible to save time and effort.

You'll probably start with a comfortable armchair or rocker. We'd go so far as to say that a rocking chair is one of the most essential items you'll need for your new baby. A footstool is another handy item as it helps to lift your knees when positioning your baby for breastfeeding. There's nothing like putting up your feet to help you relax!

Lots of cushions or pillows are another essential aspect of your nursing corner. You need these to properly support yourself and your baby for comfortable feedings.

*Taking good care of yourself helps you to meet baby's needs in a calm, loving way.*

A good reading lamp should be nearby, as there will be occasions when you'll want to lean back and enjoy reading a book or magazine as baby nurses the time away. A small table allows you to keep a large glass of water or juice within easy reach—something you should bring along every time you sit down to nurse the baby.

You might want to keep a stack of diapers, a wastebasket or diaper container, and other baby items (wipes, undershirts, and a few small blankets) close at hand. With these essential supplies always nearby, you can feed and change baby with a minimum of effort.

## VISITORS—A HELP OR HINDRANCE?

Friends or relatives may offer to help out when you have a new baby. While an extra pair of hands is always welcome, some well-wishers may bring advice and comments that are not at all helpful. Be specific about the kind of help you would appreciate—a nice hearty casserole or a nutritious dessert perhaps. Don't be afraid to ask your mother or mother-in-law to stop at the grocery store if you need supplies—or to throw a load of laundry in the washer when they stop by to see the baby.

It may seem unusual for you to sit back and be waited on by your guests—but that's very much the way it should be for a new mother. If you enjoy visiting with friends, then welcome them but let them know you won't be up to the role of "perfect hostess" for a few weeks. One way to reinforce this message is what one mother calls "robe play." Slip into your robe when the company knocks on the door, even if you have been wearing daytime clothes. Without saying a word, the message is conveyed that you are not yet up to entertaining as usual.

In general, a new mother can be as active as she wants to be, provided that she stops whatever she is doing the instant she begins to feel tired. You will find that this little reminder covers a multitude of new-mother indiscretions. By taking care of yourself in the early weeks, you will feel better in the months ahead.

## WHEN RELAXING ISN'T ENOUGH

If your baby happens to be one of those fussy, active babies who is always looking for mother's attention and who thrives on change, you may find it hard to follow our advice to relax and take it easy. If this is the case, you have our sympathy, because we've had this kind of baby too, and we know how trying it can be. The very busy, alert baby is almost always more content as he gets older and can do more for himself. He can't wait to conquer the world on his own!

If you find that you just can't relax, ask yourself if you are trying to pack too much into your day? We hope you have taken to heart our remarks about the baby being more important than housework or other commitments. But if you do find yourself tense and jittery and you know the baby will want to nurse again soon, take a breather for a minute or two. An exercise break can do wonders. The activity will loosen tight muscles and perk up the blood circulation. There are new books and videotapes available that explain exercise routines that include your baby. (See Appendix.)

Weather permitting, look forward to a walk outdoors each day. Take baby with you, of course, in his carriage or baby carrier. The fresh air, sunshine, and change of scenery will do both of you a world of good.

It may be that, when you begin to feel on edge, you could be hungry. How long has it been since your last meal? Why not eat a piece of fresh fruit or nibble on a tasty piece of cheese? A hard-cooked egg, ready in the refrigerator, will furnish you with the staying power of protein. A slice of whole-grain bread with peanut butter is also quick and good. Or brew a fragrant cup of hot tea to drink as baby nurses.

The end of the day is often a troublesome time for mothers and babies. Clare Vetter of Kentucky tells of one particularly trying evening that worked out well in the end:

*After a very busy day, my son, Isaac, was too "wired-up" to nurse. Of course, I was worn out also and perhaps a bit low on milk supply. Each time Isaac would start to nurse, he would stop suddenly, sit up, and fuss loudly.*

*My husband Tom came in and put on his new record, a lovely relaxed piece, Pachelbel's Kanon. The music seemed to be just what our family needed. I stood up with Isaac in one arm and the three of us began a lively yet soothing waltz. Our dance was spontaneous and improvised, and our aching muscles seemed to work out their pains. Gazing into Tom's eyes I remembered our first dance at a college waltz party ten years ago. There is so much more to our lives now than then!*

*The canon ended too soon. Bathtime, storytime, then bed and lights out. Isaac and I lay nursing and the melody played itself again inside me; and there was milk. Sometimes a little romance helps.*

## NEW BABY BLUES

Occasionally, a woman feels down or depressed for no particular reason following the birth of her baby. "There I was, holding my beautiful new daughter in my arms, knowing that I had everything to be thankful for, yet I was dissolved in tears," one mother remembers. Another mother described the feeling as "combat fatigue following delivery." Dr. James Good, a wise family doctor, once pointed out the similarities between the depression a mother may feel following the delivery of her baby and that which often sets in the day after a special occasion. The anticipation and planning that filled the months before have come to an end. A high point of participation is over, and a period of adjustment follows.

This emotional seesaw may also arise as a result of the change of hormones in your body from a pregnant to a nonpregnant state. It is usually short-lived, but if the feeling persists, you may want to check with your doctor. Breastfeeding and having your baby close to you will help you to deal with this transition. The hormonal changes are more gradual when you breastfeed. The old standbys, eating well and getting enough rest, are important in helping you feel well, both physiologically and emotionally.

Marlene Edelman of New Jersey stresses the benefits of being in touch with La Leche League:

*At our last La Leche League meeting our Leader asked all of the mothers to share what they liked most about breastfeeding. One mother said that she considered the League meetings to be one of the advantages of breastfeeding. Her answer caused me to look back on the influence La Leche League has had in my life.*

*I became pregnant shortly after we moved to a new state. During my pregnancy I had no friends in our new home town and I was very lonely.*

*I attended my first League meeting because after three months of breastfeeding I was still having considerable difficulty with sore nipples and breast*

*infections. I was looking for information and consolation
that things would get better. I went home from that first
meeting with some helpful information and returned for
the next three meetings.*

*It hadn't occurred to me to continue past those first
meetings, but the Leader called to invite me, so I went.
Now, sixteen months later, I am still attending LLL
meetings. I have found they are more than just a place to
learn about breastfeeding. I've learned about the
nutritional, emotional, and physical needs of growing
babies and ways of coping with people who ask, "Are you
still nursing?" I've found a place where people understand
why my career is my family. And, I've finally found
friends. Friends who have joined together with their
children to form a playgroup. Friends who understand
how frustrating it is to be housebound on a long winter
day.*

*LLL has meant so very much to me. I hope
someday to be able to give other mothers what I have
found there—a warm, accepting environment where I'm
encouraged to love and nurture my child in the way I feel
is best, beginning with breastfeeding.*

# Going Out? Take Baby Along

You don't have to be a stay-at-home with a breastfed baby.
Baby can go right along with you almost everywhere you want to
go. In the early weeks, it's a good idea to pace yourself—take things
easy—for your own sake. A brief shopping trip or a visit to see the
proud grandparents are good starters and can be a refreshing break
in the everyday routine. When you're ready to go, baby and a diaper bag are easy bundles to take along.

Feeding your baby or comforting him at the breast is no problem, since it is possible to nurse inconspicuously almost anywhere.
In most parts of the world no one gives a second thought to the
sight of a nursing mother. But if you feel more comfortable nursing your baby without drawing attention to the fact, this can be
easily accomplished.

Two-piece outfits are probably the most convenient for nursing away from home. A loose-fitting sweater or overblouse can be lifted from the waist for easy nursing. You remain covered on top, and a diaper or small blanket can be a casual cover-up. The never-out-of-fashion shawl also lends itself to discreet nursing. Maternity shops and specialty catalogues now feature special tops for nursing mothers with concealed openings for nursing. Many La Leche League publications carry advertising from companies who specialize in fashionable clothing designed for discreet nursing.

It's a simple matter to conceal the whole operation. You will need only a minute or so of privacy to get baby started at the breast. Once he's nursing, your baby could be sleeping in your arms for all anyone knows. Many large stores, airports, train stations, and shopping malls have rooms set aside for mothers and small babies. Another possibility when shopping in a large store or shopping center is a visit to the women's clothing department. If it isn't too crowded, you can relax in a fitting room while you nurse the baby. If you sew or just enjoy looking at fashions, take a nursing break in the pattern department—one with comfortable stools at the pattern-book counter.

You will soon be able to devise a way to nurse inconspicuously to suit any occasion. At the beach, a large beach towel thrown casually over your shoulders and arms can serve as a kind of private tent for your nursing baby.

As a new breastfeeding mother, you may feel more at ease about nursing in different situations if you practice inconspicuous nursing at home first, with your husband or a good friend as critic. Mothers find that it doesn't take long to smooth out their performance. A Nevada mother, Charlene Brown, recalls:

*After the birth of our daughter, Dawn Michelle, Fred and I were invited to speak about our experience at a childbirth class. Toward the end, Dawn decided that she wanted to nurse. I continued answering questions as I put her blanket over her head and my shoulder, and she took the breast. One of the expectant mothers commented that I certainly had a unique way of quieting my baby— throwing a blanket over her head! I explained that the baby was nursing. Fred later said that I was getting to be such a pro, I didn't even pause in mid-sentence.*

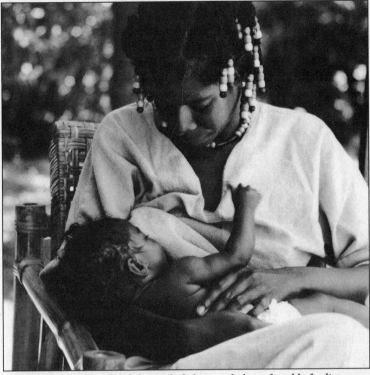

*Learning how to breastfeed discreetly helps you feel comfortable feeding your baby anywhere.*

## BREASTFED BABIES GO EVERYWHERE

A little advance planning or innovative thinking will often keep a young one and his mother together and happy. When Mary White was the matron of honor at her sister's wedding, she brought a babysitter along for the specific purpose of holding her three-month-old baby during the ceremony. Between the ceremony and the reception, Mary slipped off, nursed the baby, and was back in the receiving line in time to shake a few hundred hands.

The women in the League Group of Hull, England, drew up a list of the places they had gone with their nursing babies. In many of the situations, they felt it would be difficult to feed or comfort a bottle-fed baby. Lynne Emerson wrote the following account:

*Bridget said that she's nursed in restaurants, doctors' and dentists' offices, and in church. Christina took the*

*minimum of equipment on a canalling holiday compared
with another bottle-feeding mum on another boat. She has
also nursed baby Sarah in the changing room at the local
sports centre. Lynne said she had nursed at a wedding
reception, in a snow blizzard, while stuck in her car when
her ten-minute car trip turned to all day after the car
broke down, while football spectating, and on the beach.*

*I nursed Lucy, when only three months old, at a one-
day yoga seminar. The yoga teacher was skeptical at first,
but I assured her Lucy wouldn't distract the class. Our last
excursion (to see the local pantomime) was really exciting.
The whole family went, and there were a few raised eye-
brows when we walked in, but afterward people remarked
how good the baby had been. We hope this will help dispel
the myth that breastfeeding the baby is confining.*

## TRAVEL PLANS

On longer excursions, babies make good travelers if some
thought is given ahead of time to their special needs. Breastfed babies
have logged a phenomenal number of hours in the air. Judy Sanders
of Washington flew halfway around the world to New Zealand with
her daughter, Maria. Judy reports that it was easy to travel with
Maria because she was breastfed. Wearing a caftan-type dress with
hidden zippers was comfortable and convenient for discreet nursing.

You'll want to check with your specific air carrier for their
regulations before planning a trip by plane. They may provide special infant safety seats or suggest you bring your own. Reserving
a bulkhead seat will give you some extra room. Pack your tote bag
with baby's diapers, soft toys, and a change of outfits—just in case
your luggage does not land at the same time or place that you do.
Nursing your baby at takeoff and landing will lessen the pressure
on his ears, but this may not be possible if baby is restrained in
a seat belt. This may be a time when a pacifier would be useful.

Kay McFerrin of Texas tells of her family's vacation:

*Last summer we traveled to Acapulco, Mexico, with our
infant daughter, Monica. Thanks to breastfeeding, our little
girl was a delightful travel companion. Monica was six
months old then, and still on just mother's milk. All she*

*needed for the trip was her mother, some diapers, and a bathing suit. We all had such a marvelous time. I had no worries such as what to do if the room doesn't have a refrigerator, or what if I don't take enough formula, or how will I warm the bottles, or how to take formula and feed baby away from the hotel, or any other problems a bottle-fed baby and mother might face. No matter where we were—beach, sightseeing, poolside, or plane—wherever Monica got hungry, she just did what came naturally.*

*At night we never had to bother with baby beds, we just tucked our baby in with us as we do at home. She didn't care where she was—no insecurity for her! She was happy just being with her mother and daddy. It never even occurred to us to leave her out of this adventure.*

Lisa Gehring from Ohio tells about bicycling with her daughter. She and her husband ride a tandem bike, and they fastened the baby's car seat to a special trailer that attached behind their bike. She writes:

*My husband and I, being avid bicyclists, decided that we didn't want to give up our favorite hobby just because we had a baby....we would take her along!*

*Since Heidi is totally breastfed, going bicycling with her couldn't be any easier. We just put her in the trailer with her diaper bag, and off we go. It's great not having to pack bottles and formula.*

*When Heidi was four months old, we participated in a two-day tour along the south shore of Lake Erie. Whenever Heidi would get hungry, we would take a break. She had her lunch at a park on the shore of Lake Erie. We did attract quite a lot of attention, and at rest stops Rich would answer questions regarding our tandem and trailer. Meanwhile Heidi would nurse inconspicuously, oblivious to the crowd gathered around our bike.*

*We believe that a happy family is one that enjoys going places and doing things together. Taking Heidi with us is so easy that we would never dream of leaving her with a sitter. We're planning a cross-country ski vacation this winter, and guess who's going with us? That's right, have baby—will travel!*

## IF YOU MUST LEAVE YOUR BABY

If you must leave your tiny baby for a short time—and the shorter the time the better—leave him with someone he is happy with when you are around. Be sure to leave the baby well fed and contented. Don't rush—babies can sense when mother is in a hurry to get away. When he is happy and settled, then go off. For some time you won't leave him for longer than an hour or two, and then only occasionally. Since you don't want your little one to miss you or go hungry, you'll want to be back soon.

Some mothers like to have the added security of leaving a bottle of expressed breast milk stored in the freezer in case it's needed while they're gone. (Information on expressing and storing breast milk is found in Chapter 7.)

Mothers often ask about leaving a bottle of formula when they're gone. We cannot recommend that you do that. Leaving your own milk assures that your baby will continue to receive his favorite food. Does one bottle of formula make that much difference? We wish we could say that it doesn't, but we can't. Even one bottle of formula can be a problem for some babies because of the risk of allergy. Animal studies have also shown that introducing formula may upset the balance of enzymes and nutrients in the digestive system and interfere with the protective qualities your milk provides.

## ALONE IS LONELY

You won't want to leave your baby any more than you have to because babies need their mothers. It's a need that is as basic and intense as his need for food. "That's all well and good," you may be thinking, "but what about me? I have needs, too."

Of course a mother has needs, and sometimes other responsibilities and obligations cause a mother to be away from her baby more than she wants to be. But you may be surprised to find how strong the bond is that develops between you and your baby. A mother often finds that when she does leave her baby for that long-awaited "night out," she worries so much about how the baby is getting along that she doesn't really enjoy the occasion!

Dr. William Sears, pediatrician and father of six, explains how this can happen:

*When mother and baby are separated, both of them miss out on the full benefits of a continuous mother-infant attachment. When mother and baby spend most of their*

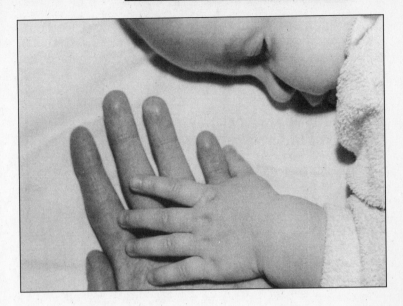

*time with each other, responding positively to each other's
cues, they get in harmony with each other....not only does
the mother help the baby develop, but the baby also helps
the mother develop.*

Mothers do grow along with their children. Judy Kahrl from
Ohio tells of her experience in gaining an understanding of her
baby's need for her:

*One thing that helped me when I wanted to leave the
baby was to remember that a baby has no sense of time.
When he is left, he thinks it is forever. He can't
understand that his mother will be back later tonight or
whenever. Also, what seems like a short time to parents,
for instance a weekend, is proportionately speaking, a long
time in the baby's life. It has helped me to try to look at
this from the baby's perspective, his sense of time, his
understanding of the world. Of course, we mothers have
needs, too, but because of our maturity, we are better
equipped to cope with ours, to postpone them for a bit. A
baby's needs are immediate.*

# CHAPTER 6

# *A* Time to Learn

The early weeks of caring for your new baby are a time of adjustment for both of you. Mothering is a learned skill and your baby is the best teacher you could have. As you learn to respond to your baby's needs, your baby learns to trust that his needs will be met. Marshall Klaus, MD, and his wife, Phyllis, talk about this in *The Amazing Newborn:*

*The mother appears to be especially open and unusually receptive in the first weeks of her child's life to learning about and perceiving her infant through all her senses. The infant's talents, abilities, and wide range of senses are each matched by parallel sensitivities and alertness on the part of the mother. There is a mutual interest in eye-to-eye contact. A mother's use of a high-pitched voice in talking to her infant coincides with the infant's attraction to*

97

*speech in the high-frequency range. The timing of speech
stimulates both the parent and infant to move to its
rhythm. An infant's cry will stimulate milk production.
During breastfeeding, the distance between the parent
and the infant's eyes is about eight to ten inches, an
optimum distance for a newborn to see his mother. . . A
feedback loop pervades the relationship between mother
and baby.*

This chapter talks about some of the things you'll need to learn
as your mothering skills develop.

# Why Is My Baby Crying?

The sound of a baby crying is not easy to ignore. It is not intended to be. Your baby's cry is *meant* to be disturbing, for it is
his most important means of communication. Only by crying can
he let you know that he needs you to help him—to come to his rescue. Something is bothering him or frightening him. It may be that
he is hungry, or he may be lonesome for you. He only knows the
security of your presence when his body is next to yours; as far as
your baby is concerned, you might as well be on Mars as on the
other side of the house. Vi Lennon, one of LLL's founders, recalls
that she once asked an older child to pick up the crying baby and
hold him while she finished frying chicken. Her helper responded,
"I already tried that, but it's no use. He's having an attack of loneliness for you."

In *Creative Parenting*, Dr. William Sears explains:

*Babies do not cry to annoy, to maliciously manipulate, or
to take advantage of their parents in an unfair way. They
cry because they have a need. To ignore the cry is to
ignore the need. A baby is not spoiled if he is picked up.
He is more apt to be spoiled if he is not picked up.*

# RESPONDING TO YOUR CRYING BABY

When a baby cries, a nursing mother's immediate instinctive response is to offer her breast. Whether it's been ten minutes or two hours since baby was fed, a few minutes of sucking may be all he needs to settle down. Baby's appetite can vary from day to day, so he may really be crying because he's hungry. Or perhaps he just wants the comfort of being close to you. Either way, nursing him may be the answer.

But what if that's not what he wants after all? Then you need to check into other solutions. Perhaps he's too warm, or maybe he's too cold. Perhaps something he is wearing is causing the problem. Try removing all of his clothes. Look for a pin or rough label, or something binding around his leg or arm—sometimes a hair from mother's head can wrap tightly around baby's toe. Look him over carefully from top to bottom, just to be sure that nothing is hurting him or irritating his tender skin.

If he seems too warm, try leaving him in just a shirt and diaper. If the room is chilly, try wrapping him in a soft blanket. Some babies feel more secure if they are wrapped up snugly, or swaddled.

Once he is snug and dry, offer him the breast again. This time, he just may drift off to sleep. But sometimes the baby doesn't want to nurse, or has downed so much milk he repeatedly spits it up, and still he cries. What then? Try holding him against your shoulder and with a background of soft music or your own lullaby, glide through the house doing the "baby waltz." Some mothers put the baby in a baby carrier and vacuum the rugs. The droning noise of the vacuum cleaner and the accompanying body movements often lull the baby to sleep. How about a drive in the car? Or a stroll outdoors? A warm bath may soothe and relax both of you—try taking baby into the tub with you.

A time-honored way of soothing a crying baby is time spent in the trusty rocking chair together. A steady rocking rhythm, some gentle patting on his back, and perhaps a soothing lullaby can work their magic on the fussiest of little ones. In fact, Becky Conley from Illinois swears by her "magic rocker":

*No matter how hectic the day or how frantic the world may seem, we can retreat to the arms of our rocker, and be suddenly oblivious to it all. Peace descends on us; tensions float away;, and love surrounds us like a cloud. We can go anywhere we please in our rocker. Over the year since Eli was born, we've been to desert islands, mountain ranges, endless beaches, and on a few, very special occasions, to what surely must have been heaven.*

Some babies cry because they are overtired, but they aren't happy being held as they fall asleep. Try laying your baby in his cradle or on a blanket on the floor and talk or sing to him softly as you pat him gently. He may continue to fuss for a few minutes, then close his eyes and drift off to sleep. You'll soon know if he is truly tired and ready to sleep or not. If he becomes increasingly more anxious (even five minutes is a long time for a baby to cry), pick him up again.

Babies are sometimes fretful for reasons that no one, not even a mother, can understand. If you can't calm your baby right away, try not to let it upset you. "Don't take it as a personal rejection of you," a mother who has gone through the experience advises. Your baby will always benefit from a calm, loving mother. In handling any tiny baby, you have to move slowly and gently. Fast, jerky motions and loud noises may startle him. If he is already upset for some reason, accept the fact and work from there—slow and easy.

## SHOULD BABY CRY IT OUT?

While holding and carrying the baby may comfort him, it may also elicit some stern advice from friends and relatives. The notion still persists that the baby who cries when put down, but is soothed when held, should be laid down gently but firmly to "cry it out."

Sometimes a mother wonders if it really makes a difference if the baby cries in her arms or in a crib. It makes a considerable difference. Jan Wojcik of Florida puts the matter in a different light by asking how any of us would feel if we were the ones who were upset. "If we were crying, wouldn't we feel better if someone were around to reassure us? To care that we were upset? Wouldn't we wives feel rejected if our husbands were to say, 'Go into the bedroom. I don't want to be around you until you regain control of yourself.' Don't we want to be loved in times of stress as well as in times of happiness?"

Our suggestion to the mother of a fussy baby is: Don't let your baby cry alone. The comfort and security extended by your loving arms is never wasted. Love begets love. Then, too, the next thing you try may be just the right thing to ease baby's discomfort and restore peace and serenity to the house.

## BABY THE BABY

You can't spoil a baby; his wants are his needs. **His need to be lovingly held when he is upset is as strong and important as his need to be fed and kept warm and dry.** So, if your infant stops his crying when you pick him up and hold him, just keep on holding him and be happy that you are there to satisfy this important emotional need. By all means, "baby" the baby.

Dr. Lee Salk, Pediatric Psychologist and Director of New York Hospital-Cornell Medical Center, has written, "The baby whose cries are answered now will later be the child confident enough to show his independence and curiosity. But the baby who is left to cry it out may develop a sense of isolation and distrust, and may turn inward by tuning out the world that will not answer its cry. And later on in life, this child may continue to cope with stress by trying to shut out reality." As for crying being good exercise for a baby's lungs, Dr. Salk says, "If crying is good for the lungs, then bleeding is good for the veins!"

## A FUSSY TIME OF DAY

Some babies have a regular fussy period, often late in the afternoon, that occurs predictably day after day. At other times, the baby is good-natured, and there doesn't seem to be any particular cause for these fussy spells. The baby is not uncomfortable, as with colic, but is not happy either. Folklore refers to this time as the "Granny Hour," meaning that a loving grandmother is needed who has nothing more urgent to do than rock and cuddle the baby.

Your husband may not always be home at baby's fussy time but it can be a great comfort if he can take over for a spell. The change of loving arms and voice often relaxes an upset child. While your husband and baby watch the fish swimming in the fish tank or the cars passing by, you may want to take a refreshing shower—it can really help wash the tension away.

# Babies Who Are Colicky

When a tiny baby has long periods of hard crying, and seems to be in some sort of physical discomfort for which there is no apparent reason that you or your doctor can discover, he is often said to be colicky.

"Colic" is a catchall word meaning essentially "loud, persistent screaming for undetermined reasons." As many causes of colic are put forth as there are doctors who have studied it. As far back as the turn of the century, colic was referred to in one widely used pediatric text as "a scientifically inaccurate and unsatisfactory term which serves such a useful purpose in practice and covers so well a multitude of abdominal pains that it maintains its place in our medical books." The same loose definition could apply today; doctors still seem to know little or nothing about the true cause of this kind of crying.

In his book, THE FUSSY BABY, Dr. William Sears has this to say about colic:

*I* suspect that colic is the result of many causes, temperamental, physiological, and environmental, that overwhelm a baby's immature coping skills....In light of present knowledge about colic, the best anyone can do is to comfort the baby and minimize the factors that may contribute to the baby's fussiness.

So what can a mother do about colic? Calm, gentle handling is essential. Many doctors feel that frequent, shorter feedings are easier for baby to handle than long feedings. But a colicky baby may be soothed by lots of sucking, plus the extra cuddling that comes with nursing, so what do you do then? Try feeding him from one breast only during a two- to three-hour period. He may want to nurse a number of times during that time span; just keep to the "empty" breast. After two hours or so, switch to the other breast and again limit nursings to one side.

If your baby shows signs of colic, you'll want to be sure he gets nothing else but your milk. Avoid giving formula, juice, or water. Some babies also react to vitamins, especially those with added fluoride.

Occasionally, something the mother eats might be a possible cause of colicky symptoms in her baby. Some possibilities include certain vitamins, food supplements such as brewer's yeast, large amounts of caffeine or foods or drinks with artificial sweeteners. In some instances, a food such as milk (or foods containing milk) in the mother's diet can make her baby uncomfortable. (This is more

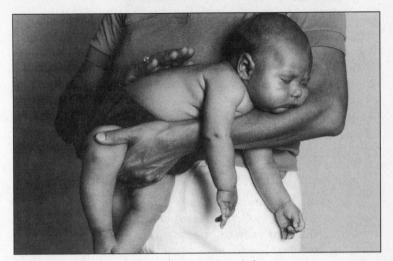

*The "colic hold" often provides relief for a fussy baby.*

likely to occur if there is a history of allergy in the family. It is explained later under Allergies.)

Mothers of colicky babies have come up with a variety of ways to comfort and soothe them. Sue Nobriga Buckley of California talks about a "colic hold" that helped her daughter feel better.

*Although Lara gained weight quickly and proved to be alert and healthy, every evening found us rocking or walking her back and forth for hours before her crying and wailing gave way to sleep. After five weeks of steady evening and occasional daytime crying sessions, we were hesitant to visit her grandparents. When we did visit, Lara typically acted pleasant during most of the day, only to start in loud and long in the early evening. As usual no one could comfort her until her grandfather picked her up, laid her astraddle his arm with her head slightly higher than her feet, and proceeded to immediately rock her to sleep. Amazed, we imitated his way of holding her whenever Lara began to act colicky, and almost every time the new way of holding her quieted and comforted her.*

A soothing, pleasant bath proved to be a refuge for Judy Wesockes and her baby daughter, who live in Florida:

*When Amy has an attack of colic, usually between eight and ten in the evening, we go into a warm, deep tub and stay there for the duration of her attack. The moist heat, holding her, and relaxing all help. She gets almost immediate relief, but if we get out of the tub, the symptoms return. So we stay in, and I add more hot water as needed.*

Knowing that your breast milk is the best possible food for your baby will help you to be relaxed and calm. It's one less thing to worry about, and baby will be spared the risks that come with changing formulas. The warm closeness of the nursing relationship and your gentle, loving ministrations will help ease your baby through this trying time.

## HIGH NEED BABIES

As you read through this section you may be saying to yourself, "But I've tried all those things and my baby is still fussy." It may be that you have the kind of baby that Dr. William Sears talks about in his book, THE FUSSY BABY. He explains it this way:

*In the first few days or weeks, parents begin to pick up on clues as to the temperament of their baby. Some parents are blessed with so-called easy babies. Others are blessed with babies who are not so easy....the term "fussy baby" is a bit unfair....I prefer to call this special type of baby the high need baby. This is not only a kinder term, but it more accurately describes why these babies act the way they do and what level of parenting they need.*

Dr. Sears assures parents that having a high need baby can be a blessing. He points out that high need babies bring out the best in their parents. He says, "Those same qualities which at first seemed to be such an exhausting liability have a good chance of turning out to be an asset for the child and the family."

If you want to find out more, you can buy a copy of THE FUSSY BABY from your local bookstore or your La Leche League Group. For details, see the Appendix.

# Growth Spurts

Some time after the first week or two the baby who has been peacefully nursing every three hours may suddenly want to dramatically increase the number of times a day he is fed. No sooner does he drift off to sleep than he is up again, nuzzling the bedding or his fist, looking for something to eat. You may hear comments to the effect that it was a nice try, but breastfeeding just isn't working.

Tune out such remarks. This increase in the number of nursings is normal. Medical writers in old textbooks referred to such periods as "frequency days." They recognized that more frequent nursing builds up the milk supply to meet the growing baby's increasing need. So settle in with baby for a few "frequency days." Even the skeptics would be hard-pressed to think of anything else you could be doing that is more important than giving your baby the best possible nourishment.

Twenty minutes of fairly vigorous nursing every hour or so is more effective in building up your milk supply than less frequent, longer sessions at the breast. Most babies eventually settle into a fairly consistent pattern of nursing, one that is right for each particular child. These increases in frequency usually show up in relation to growth spurts. Like the rest of us, babies are hungrier at some times than others. Rather than check out the refrigeraton, baby looks to mom. Baby's appetite temporarily gets ahead of his mother's milk supply.

Mothers commonly report such a fussy period coinciding with a growth spurt between the third and sixth weeks. If this happens, put baby to the breast as often as he wants to nurse. With extra nursings, it isn't long before your milk production steps up to meet his need. The interval between nursings will soon lengthen, and baby will be his old self again. The extra rest that comes to you with more frequent nursing may be exactly what the doctor would order. It may be that the tempo of all you are doing has picked up a little faster than is good for a new mother. Nature and your baby combine forces to help you get much needed rest.

When your baby is three months old, more or less, there is often another fussy period. It is probably due partly to a jump in appetite, and again, increased nursings will generally take care of this part of the difficulty. It is still too early for solids for most healthy babies, so don't risk an allergy to new foods by introducing solids too early.

Another factor in the three-month fussy period, which you may or may not experience with your baby, is that he stays awake longer and is taking a greater interest in the world around him. Fussing may also indicate a need for company and action. Keep him in the center of activity. Settle him near you in a safe spot on a blanket on the floor where he can really stretch out. He will enjoy music, movement, and people going by. As he gets older, he thrives on change and variety. As he becomes more aware of the world around him, the sights and sounds of the family group are wonderful stimulation for his senses. People often notice and comment on the early alertness and responsiveness of the baby who is part of the family group, who is talked to and sung to and smiled at often.

# Nighttime Needs

During the early months, it is especially desirable for the baby to nurse at least once during the night. Your young baby is growing at a phenomenal rate and has a physical need to be fed during the night. Also, your breasts can become engorged and uncomfortable if you go for five, six, or more hours without a feeding, and in the morning baby might have trouble getting started at the breast because of the fullness.

A study of nursing mothers in West Nigeria by Jelliffe and Jelliffe revealed that babies as old as ten months received not less than twenty-five percent of their breast milk at night. So it is not at all unusual for your baby to want to nurse at night.

In his book, NIGHTTIME PARENTING, Dr. William Sears points out that babies sleep differently than adults and he says that babies aren't designed to sleep through the night.

Dr. Sears goes on to say, "Sleep problems occur when your child's night-waking exceeds your ability to cope." One secret of coping with your baby's need for night feedings is to develop your skill at nursing the baby lying down. If you feel awkward when you first try to nurse in bed, continue to experiment with different positions and lots of pillows. Once you can feed the baby while comfortably stretched out, you've eliminated much of the work of mothering for about eight of the twenty-four hours in a day. In order to see what you are doing in the early weeks without turning on a bright light, consider keeping a small flashlight on the nightstand or under your pillow. Or leave the light on in the closet with the door ajar. To change sides with a minimum of strain when nursing while lying down, simply hold baby close to you with both arms and roll over.

When your baby wakes at night, just tuck him into bed with you, start nursing him, and the two of you can drop off to sleep again together. It is quite safe—we have all done it, and so have mothers all over the world for centuries. The babies love the warm closeness, which usually helps them drop off to sleep sooner than they might otherwise.

Nighttime nursings in bed allow for greater skin contact and touching. Mother and baby are not encumbered by layers of clothing. In his book on the importance of touching to the development of the person, anthropologist Ashley Montagu states, "The infant's need for body contact is compelling."

You may have heard stories of a parent rolling over on the baby in bed. Don't worry; your healthy, normal baby, even when very small, can move his head and in some way let you know if a blanket is over his face or if he is feeling closed in. Mothers say that they quickly develop a sixth sense about allowing room for the baby.

If you're worried that the baby may fall off the bed there are a number of ways to avoid this. Pull his cradle or bassinet next to your bed. When close by, it's convenient to scoop him into your bed when he cries, and if it is high enough it serves as a guardrail to keep baby from falling when he's in your bed. Or you can purchase a guardrail that fits along the side of your bed to keep baby safe.

A resourceful mother in Pennsylvania, Pat Muschamp, uses a blanket to keep her baby from moving away from her after she has drifted back to sleep. Place baby's blanket diagonally on the bed, like a kite. You lie down with the inner corner under you and baby next to you on the blanket. Pull the outer corner of the blanket across baby's body and tuck it under your body. Your baby is wrapped snugly against you, and there is no worry about falling.

Some mothers wear a bra to bed at night. This is not necessary, but if you find you're more comfortable with some kind of support, choose a bra that is big enough or stretchy enough to allow for expansion if your breasts fill during the night hours.

# WHEN WILL HE SLEEP THROUGH THE NIGHT?

Probably the reason this question ever assumed the proportions it has is because of the inconvenience of nighttime bottle feeding—getting up with the baby into what may be a chilly house, waiting while the bottle warms, fighting sleep, and being fearful that baby or bottle may be dropped. As a nursing mother, you are spared such inconvenience, so when you hear that a neighbor's baby sleeps through the night and yours doesn't, ask yourself, "Is it really that important?" Isn't the important thing that your baby is content and happy and you can satisfy his needs at night as well as during the day? To a baby, it makes no difference whether the sun is up or the world is hushed in darkness. His need for mothering remains. It is no less important at night than during the day.

As to when he will sleep through the night, it's impossible to say. Babies are human beings, and each and every human being in the world is different from every other. Some babies will sleep through the night at an early age, and some will not. This is as true of bottle-fed babies, by the way, as it is of breastfed babies. And not infrequently, the little one who sleeps through the night one week is waking the next.

In NIGHTTIME PARENTING, Dr. Sears discusses ways of encouraging sleep and also causes of sleep disturbance in older children. He tells how mother and baby can develop harmonious sleep cycles which make it less disturbing for a mother to be awakened when her baby cries.

Getting up in the night is never a favorite part of parenting. But there are ways to cope, to come to terms with the situation. How you react can make a considerable difference in how it affects you. We know the truth of this because many of us learned it the hard way. Pat Yearian of Washington says she gradually came to the realization that she could change the up-at-night syndrome by changing her attitude. After all, a mother's reactions to interrupted sleep are up to her. Pat writes:

*If you resent the interruptions to your sleep—and haven't we all come to believe we need a full night's rest?—you will face each day more frustrated and trying harder and harder to fit the baby into your sleep pattern. On the other hand, if you can adjust your mental attitude to one of greater acceptance, you will find yourself able to enjoy those quiet moments in the night with your infant who needs to be held and nursed, or with your toddler who just needs to be with someone. Acceptance of interrupted sleep doesn't come right away. In fact, for many of us it has taken a baby or two to fully appreciate their needs. When you begin to notice that your sleep can be interrupted many times a night, and yet you are able to face the next day with a smile, your attitudes are changing.*

Dr. Gregory White, an experienced family practice physician, once commented on the subject of sleep in a talk he gave to parents:

*A lot of people think they are entitled to a night's sleep. Nobody's entitled to a full night's sleep and very few mothers get one. Many people do at one time or another during their lives, and I'm all for it. But no one's entitled to it, whether she's a new mother or not, if someone needs her. If a lazy, self-indulgent, old man like me can get out in the middle of the night to help people he hardly knows, certainly a mother can do this for her own child.*

## NIGHT WAKING GOES ON

Even if your baby begins sleeping almost all night when he's a few months old, that may not be the end of your nighttime parenting role. Toddlers often wake up at night for a variety of reasons. Many one-year-olds have erratic eating habits and may wake up really hungry during the night. If you think that this could be the reason your toddler is waking at night, be sure there are nutritious foods available to him frequently during the day and offer him a good bedtime snack. Perhaps he is thirsty. Offer your toddler water often, especially in warm weather.

The older baby or toddler who wakes a number of times at night may be bothered by teething. Even though there doesn't seem to be much of a problem during the day, his gums may hurt more at night when he isn't distracted by a busy daytime world. Have you ever had a mild toothache that started throbbing madly just as you were dropping off to sleep? A toddler cannot express what he is feeling in words, but since frequent waking during the night is so common in children during their second year, teething might have something to do with it.

Fatigue or aching muscles might cause a busy toddler to be wakeful. There are other possibilities. Is he getting enough fresh air and exercise? Was there tension during the day caused by such things as long shopping trips or visiting? A frightening experience? Were there enough hugs and kisses? Too many restrictions? If your answers to these questions satisfy you, and your toddler is still waking at night, blame it on whatever you like and remember that it will pass. Whatever the reason, nursing seems to offer special comfort in satisfying nighttime needs.

# The Family Bed

Rather than try to change their children's need for parenting at night, many families have decided to change sleeping arrangements. After all, what babies and young children are seeking is not all that strange—they just want to be closer to those who love them.

The custom of mother, father, and young child sleeping together at night is "an age old concept in childrearing which has been practiced throughout the ages, throughout the world," Tine Thevenin writes in her book, *The Family Bed.* She addresses the fears and questions that parents in our part of the world commonly have on the subject, and she probably touches the heart of the matter when she comments, "I have been asked numerous times if it is not bothersome to have our children sleep with us. To this I reply that it is no more bothersome than their presence in our family."

Dr. Herbert Ratner, editor of *Child and Family* and longtime Professional Advisor for La Leche League, has encouraged the use of the family bed for a long time. And Dr. Hugh Jolly of London says, "Psychoanalysts may be firm in their advice that parents must never allow their children into their beds, but those who have practiced it know better and have not had any dire consequences to face—just the opposite."

Dr. William Sears uses the term, "sharing sleep," because he emphasizes the fact that physical closeness causes mother and baby to share sleep cycles. But he doesn't leave out fathers. He points out that fathers report they feel closer to their babies when they sleep together.

Dr. Penny Stanway, a noted British doctor, had this to say about sleeping with her children. Penny and her husband, Andrew, also a physician, have two daughters and a son:

*Ben and Amy slept in our bed. Amy stayed in our bed till she was about one and then she moved in with Susie in a double bed. It was similar with Ben. He stayed in with us until he was about sixteen months and then went into a double bed with his sisters. I think nighttime is very hard with our built-in belief that we should be able to have our own beds and sleep with our husbands. It is fairly rooted in our culture, and any departure is met with quite a lot of criticism from friends and relatives. But I wouldn't give up that first year or so with a baby in bed. It is so much easier.*

The beauty of bedding down as a family is that it can be customized to suit each individual family's needs. Some mothers choose to return the baby to his own bed once he is fed and settled. In other households, the crib and separate room for the baby are abandoned, and an all-night family bed is adopted. Sleeping arrangements are as varied as families, and we share only a few of the many experiences of couples who have tried this innovation.

Ann Parker's story is rather typical. This Indiana mother explains that for the first six months after birth, baby Bryan slept in his parents' room, but in his own bed. Ann writes:

*I kept going back and forth every few hours to nurse him, and one time I caught myself asleep, sitting on the side of the bed, with baby in arms. I could have dropped him, and that really scared me! From then on I nursed him in bed lying down, but as soon as he stopped nursing, I would take him back to his bed. That plan didn't work all the time, since I kept falling asleep while he was nursing. But in the morning, I felt better. I had slept longer and without as many interruptions. My husband's sleep wasn't disturbed either, and so Bryan began sleeping with us.*

Quite often one parent is enthusiastic about bringing the new baby into bed, but the other has reservations. In the Zavari household in Michigan, husband Hassan was born in the Middle East, where a baby sleeping with his parents is a natural part of life. Joan Zavari tells of her reaction to some of her husband's ideas.

*When Hassan suggested breastfeeding, I didn't hesitate. However, being of a conservative nature, I put my foot down when he suggested putting two beds together and sleeping family style. How would I make the beds? I found lots of excuses, When Stevie was born, I soon found out that some babies wake up five or six times at night. Hassan didn't even say, "I told you so," when I suggested putting two beds together so he could sleep with us.*

By age two or so, many youngsters will proudly take to a conventional bed of their own, although it will be easier for short legs to reach if the spring and mattress are placed directly on the floor. With a full-size mattress you can lie down next to your little one if he wakes up. It's less disturbing for you to then move back to your bed than it would be to move him. For the child who is ready for his own bed, but still wants to be near you once in a while, a sleeping bag or air mattress and blanket can be stowed under your bed and pulled out to make a cozy spot.

An Ohio mother of seven, Martha Pugacz sagely commented a number of years ago: "It's not wall-to-wall carpeting that families need—it's wall-to-wall beds!"

Are there other children in the family? If your little one has outgrown sleeping with you but he has an older brother or sister, consider some night pairing—two sharing one bed. Young children have probably slept together throughout time, and the arrangement has been beneficial. Before establishing the little one in the older one's bed, discuss the prospect with each, stressing the positive aspects of having a night buddy. Then make the move with great fanfare. On more than one night, you'll probably find your two youngsters soundly sleeping, like little puppies, a tangle of arms and legs. They don't mind in the least. Is there reason to worry about how you'll eventually discontinue the arrangement when the children grow older? Not really. They manage this on their own when they no longer need—or want—the companionship. Usually one unceremoniously moves the other out of the bed, but by that time,

*Mother and baby may both sleep better when they sleep together.*

they are older and quite ready to be on their own. It just means you'll have to get another bed.

## PRACTICAL ARRANGEMENTS

Many couples find that they can accommodate a baby and, perhaps, other little night visitors in the ready-made spaciousness of a king-size or queen-size bed. Those who do not have such a large bed can create one by fastening two twin-size beds or a double and a twin together with heavy-duty cord or wire. The space between the two mattresses is filled in with a blanket.

Once the baby is moving well on his own, there is the fear that he may fall off. There are guardrails you can buy that slide into place between the mattress and box spring. Taking the spring and mattress off of the frame and placing them directly on the floor reduces the danger of a fall.

An Indiana couple went a step further and, without pounding a nail, constructed a guardrail to keep their active baby from going overboard. Letitia Hoffman and her husband, Rick, had moved a spare bed into their room to make their family bed the width of two full-size beds. Parts of the baby's bed were used to baby-proof it. Letitia tells us:

*Rick and I dismantled the crib. We put the two crib ends and one railing at the foot of the family bed. They are held upright between the mattress and the end boards. The other railing goes up the side of the bed and is secured with heavy string to the bed frame and end rail. The opposite side of the bed is against the wall. This leaves about a two-foot opening to get in and out of bed, which is easily blocked by pillows or a body.*

If you have a standard double bed and a crib, you may want to try the solution used by a Wisconsin family. Judy Haugen describes their sleeping arrangement:

*At the point of investing in a king-size bed or building a trundle, we came upon what we feel is a better method of enlarging our sleeping area. We have an adjustable crib. By raising its mattress to dressing-table height, flipping the side rail down, and lowering the legs to playpen level, we can make it the same height as our bed. When the crack between the beds is covered with an extra blanket, we have the perfect bed for our one-year-old who needs early morning snacks and pats.*

*Since the beds are separate, we do not disturb him, and most of the time he does not disturb us. If he whimpers during the night I only need to reach out and rock his crib (the casters have been replaced by springs) without even opening my eyes. If he is hungry I can pull him to me and, after nursing him, push him back to his bed without sitting up.*

When the big bed seems crowded (even though it may be almost the size of the room) because everyone is huddled over in one spot (yours), you may wonder if this time of intense togetherness will ever come to an end. It does, and your reaction at the time may not be what you thought it would be. Ann Backhurst of Michigan tells of her experience:

*Amy, age four, sleeps alone willingly all night. When Emily was about eighteen months old, she indicated an interest in sleeping in the crib. She now sleeps all night in it. Ken and I have our queen-size bed to ourselves again; to my surprise, I find that I really miss having the little girls sleep with us. While living through a difficult time with sleeping arrangements, I thought we would never see the end of this "family bed"—I couldn't wait. Now that it's over, we have cherished memories of a little person snuggling up on a cold winter night, or reaching out and putting an arm around one of us and knowing that all was secure.*

Parents will find many practical suggestions on meeting their children's nighttime needs in the book we have referred to several times in this chapter—NIGHTTIME PARENTING by William Sears, MD. Copies are available from your local LLL Group, La Leche League International, or a bookstore. See the Appendix for details.

# Babies, Beds, and Sex

You may be wondering—if baby's going to be sleeping in your bed, what happens to your marriage? Is there a survival plan for new parents?

We can offer some suggestions, but in the final analysis you and your husband are your own best authorities on what is the most loving, satisfying sexual relationship for you. Sex, like breastfeeding, is ninety percent mental attitude and ten percent technique. Both sex and breastfeeding flourish on the power of positive thinking. Needless worries can be counterproductive. The joy that you experience with the arrival of your baby will spill over into other areas of your life.

## COMMON MYTHS AND QUESTIONS

**With the baby nursing so often and possibly sleeping in our bed, will there by any time for my husband and me to be alone together?** Absolutely. We have all found opportunities: You will have to outwit the baby, but there are two of you. Consider a change of time and place. Where there is a will, there is a way.

Babies usually have one fairly long period of deep sleep. Take advantage of it. If your baby is easily disturbed, leave your bed (carefully) for the spare bedroom or the floor in the living room.

If baby is awake, you might try combining romance and distraction by lining up an array of lighted candles. Little babies are fascinated by the flickering lights. Some soft music is another possibility.

Few married couples can expect complete freedom all of the time, without interruptions, to make love. There are the everyday outside demands from a job and from others who have needs. Restrictions do not go away as the children grow older and leave the parental bed. Ask any couple with teenagers. But you have a lifetime together to share your love. Tomorrow can be even better than today.

**My breasts are tender, and it's uncomfortable when my husband touches them. Also, I'm concerned. Can sexual foreplay affect the milk?** No. Your milk will be fine. Don't worry about passing germs from your husband to the baby on the nipples. Your baby is already exposed to family germs and there are special glands that keep your nipples free of germs when baby nurses. Nursing does not make your breasts off limits to your husband. The feeling of fullness and tenderness comes mostly in the early days of nursing and is temporary. You will notice it less if you nurse the baby just prior to making love. Your breasts will not be as full, and the baby will be more apt to sleep. But as one husband says, "Engorgement is gorgeous!"

At the time of a sexual climax, some women also have a milk let-down. The husband is often as surprised as his wife the first time it occurs, since the milk literally sprays out. Not all women experience this at a climax, and it lessens as the let-down reflex is better established. The hormones that produce the let-down are also present at the time of an orgasm. Keep a towel nearby for drying off.

When breastfeeding, a woman has a greater interest in sex; OR: When breastfeeding, a woman feels less desire for sexual relations. The response to both of the above is "yes" some of the time and "no" at other times. There are no pat answers.

After childbirth one woman may enjoy a feeling of great responsiveness. Giving milk and making love are very natural and exciting parts of her life. Another woman may notice the opposite. Her desire for sexual relations could better be described as understated, although she loves her husband as much as ever and wants to be close to him; in fact, she needs the reassurance of his affection. Such different reactions are not unusual or abnormal. All men and women have highs and lows in sexual desire at different times in life.

As a breastfeeding mother, it can probably be said that you feel good about being a woman and are at ease with the way your body functions. Breastfeeding is the completion of a woman's sexual cycle. There are marked similarities in the way a woman's body responds during breastfeeding and intercourse. It is a fulfilling time in a woman's life.

Fatigue, it must be said, is probably the greatest deterrent to sex for any new mother. Fit in a nap after dinner, if you can. Sometimes, even when you're feeling more tired than sexy, an extra output of loving effort on your part at the right moment could produce results that are a delight to both you and your husband.

**What about feeling "touched out"?** A mother once wrote to us, "After having my baby or toddler in my arms most of the day, I feel as though I don't want one more person touching me. I'm annoyed when my husband approaches me. Is this unusual? Can you help me?" We replied to this mother by telling her she was not alone. Many a mother, after spending a good part of the day holding the baby and having little hands cling and pat, finds herself thinking that the last thing she needs is more body contact. She's "touched out."

Our cultural heritage probably shapes this response at least to some extent. The person who grows up in a society where people maintain a certain physical distance from each other, and even family members seldom hug, may find the almost constant contact with a baby a new experience, one that takes some getting used to. Add to this the fatigue that comes at the end of the day for most mothers and young children, and there may not be the energy or inclination to feel romantic.

**The low estrogen level present during breastfeeding is often the cause of vaginal dryness.** There is some truth to this as estrogen is low when breastfeeding, but the solution to dryness is simple enough—a little more lovemaking ahead of time, supplemented, if need be, by a little lubrication such as KY jelly. An episiotomy can also cause painful intercourse, sometimes for many months.

**You were a wife before you were a mother, so your husband should come before the children.** This is very misleading. It isn't fair to put your husband and children in competition with each other for your time and affection. Whoever has the greatest need for love and attention at the time receives it. With maturity, gratification of want can be postponed for a time. Adults who are hungry can wait a while or find something to eat on their own. Babies cannot. With a little understanding, there needn't be a conflict. There is more than enough love to go around.

Dr. William Sears, pediatrician and father of six, reminds parents of the importance of their commitment to one another:

---

*F*or mother-baby attachment to work in the way it was designed to work, it must be practiced within the structure of a stable and fulfilled marriage....the whole family works together—mother-baby, father-baby, and husband-wife....You should not make an either-or choice among these relationships. You need to work at all of them because they complement each other.

---

This brings us back to the basic relationship. Loving husbands and wives want to please each other. They each try to respond to cues from the other. On one occasion, the wife puts forth an extra effort to respond to her husband's embrace, and on another, he puts her feelings and needs ahead of his own.

There's a time to give, and a time to take. With mutual good will and good humor, it all works out. One word of caution: don't keep score. Once you do, you're sure to lose.

# CHAPTER 7

# *C*ommon Concerns

The early weeks of breastfeeding are a time of learning for both you and your baby. Most of the time the process goes smoothly, but once in awhile, problems develop that threaten to interfere with or interrupt breastfeeding. Some of those problems are covered here, along with information to help you overcome any difficulties and continue to enjoy breastfeeding.

Additional information on special circumstances will be found in later chapters. If you still have questions or concerns, we encourage you to contact your La Leche League Leader. More than likely she can offer suggestions and encouragement based on your specific situation that will help solve your problem and allow you and your baby to continue enjoying the benefits of breastfeeding. We can assure you that it is rarely necessary for a baby to be weaned because of a breastfeeding problem.

# Avoiding and Treating Sore Nipples

Even though sore nipples can be very uncomfortable, they are certainly no reason for you or your baby to miss out on the advantages and pleasures of breastfeeding. Sore nipples often improve in a few days, even if you do nothing at all about them. Still, it's a good idea to give even slightly sore nipples some special attention to ease the discomfort and prevent complications.

## POSITIONING BABY

While studying breastfeeding difficulties encountered by mothers in the early postpartum period, Kittie Frantz, RN, CPNP, Director of the Breastfeeding Infant Clinic at the University of Southern California Medical Center, concluded that the most significant cause of sore nipples was the incorrect positioning of the baby at the breast.

There are two aspects to proper positioning: the position of the nipple in your baby's mouth and the position of your baby's body in relation to yours. When using the cradle hold, baby's head should be in the crook of your arm with your hand holding his buttocks. Baby's body should be turned on his side, facing you, with your nipple directly in front of his mouth so that he doesn't have to turn his head to reach it. Your other hand should support the breast with your thumb on top, behind the outer edge of the areola (the dark area around the nipple) and your index and second fingers below the breast, behind the outer edge of the areola. Tickle your baby's lips gently with your nipple so that he opens his mouth wide. Center the nipple quickly in his mouth and pull baby in very close. His mouth should be positioned as far back on the areola as possible before he begins to suck. His jaws must compress the milk sinuses which are located beneath the areola.

You can check once he is latched on to be sure he hasn't pulled in his lower lip along with the nipple. If he has, it should be gently pulled out.

Many mothers experience immediate relief from nipple discomfort when they begin positioning the baby properly. It is worth taking the time to reposition yourself and your baby until he is able to latch on correctly. If your nipples are very sore, it may also help

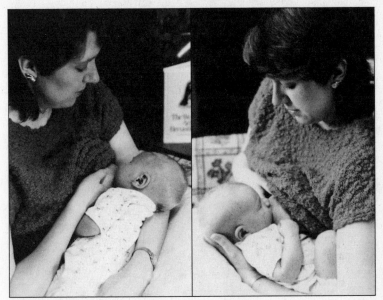

*Positioning baby correctly helps to avoid sore nipples.*

to change positions each time you nurse the baby. Sit up for one feeding, lie down for the next. You can try holding the baby in a "football hold" for some feedings. Hold his head in the palm of your hand and tuck his legs under your arm, close to your body. Changing positions puts the pressure on a different part of the nipple.

The way your baby grasps and releases the nipple is also very important in avoiding sore nipples. The nipple should not be sucked in, but rather put in when baby's mouth is open very wide. When removing him from the breast, always break the suction first using a finger to press down on your breast.

A mother who learned the importance of positioning her baby correctly to avoid sore nipples tells about her experience. Karen Price of British Columbia writes:

*My daughter Katie nurses beautifully. We are truly a happy nursing couple now. But the first four months I suffered terribly from sore and cracked nipples. I hope I can offer some encouragement to other women who may be experiencing a similar situation.*

*First of all, in my genetic makeup, no provision was made for protruding nipples. Before the baby came, I didn't even realize that this was unusual; I thought they would magically pop out when the baby was born. My*

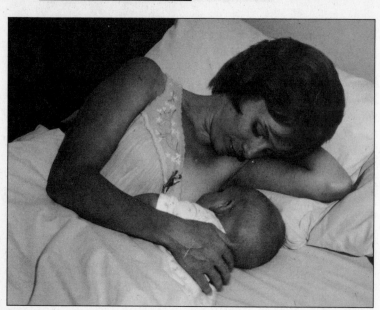

*Breastfeeding while lying down helps you get extra rest.*

next mistake was not attending La Leche League meetings ahead of time to see other mothers care for their babies.

We had several problems following Katie's birth. She had a hard time grasping my nipple in her mouth; this combined with a weak sucking reflex caused much frustration for us both. A week later, extremely sore nipples became the main issue. I now know that I was not positioning her properly at the breast. Because of the way I was holding her, she was stretching the areola around the nipple causing me pain and reducing the amount of milk she was getting. I dreaded each moment of nursing and cried through most of them because of the pain.

During that difficult time, I'd look down at the little being so helpless in my arms, whom I had wanted so badly, and somehow I was able to cope. This was one of the greatest sacrifices I have ever made, but the benefits are worth every moment of pain I experienced.

After learning to position her correctly at an LLL meeting, the pain totally disappeared. Now I can't wait for each nursing moment. Love does conquer all, but sometimes the right information is needed, too.

## LIMITING FEEDINGS

If your baby is positioned properly at the breast, there is no need to drastically limit the length of his feedings. It can take several minutes before the "let-down" occurs and the milk begins to flow, so by taking him off after three or five minutes, as some recommend, the feeding could end even before it starts.

Allowing your baby to nurse frequently, as often as he seems to be hungry, will actually minimize soreness; he will tend to suck with more vigor if he is ravenously hungry. Babies should nurse at least every two to three hours during the day in the early months.

## FLAT NIPPLES

Positioning the baby properly can be very important if your nipples are flat and difficult for the baby to grasp. If the problem is caused by engorgement, the swelling that may occur when the milk comes in, it may help to hand-express a little milk ahead of time to bring the nipples out.

Another remedy which many mothers have found helpful is the application of ice to the nipple. This eases nipple pain immediately and helps to bring out soft, small nipples or the nipple of an overly full breast. Ice applied immediately before nursing will usually make the first few minutes easier for both you and the baby. Crush the ice, wrap it in a wet cloth, and apply it to the sore area; or dampen gauze squares, put these into the freezer, and use as needed.

## AIR AND SUN

Often the tenderness you experience in the early days is chapping caused by the nipple being constantly moist. Studies by Niles Newton reported in the *Journal of Pediatrics* have shown that skin heals more quickly when left unmedicated, dry, and exposed to air.

Take advantage of the healing effects of breast milk by expressing a drop or two after baby is finished nursing, and rub gently into the skin. Allow your nipples to air dry afterwards. You may find it helpful to expose your nipples to sunlight for a few minutes or dry them very briefly with a hand-held hair dryer on a low setting.

If your nipples are tender, you can expose them to air between nursings by wearing hard plastic breast shells that are designed for that purpose with large air holes. (See the Appendix for information.) Or you can leave the flaps down on your nursing bra. If you are comfortable without a bra, discontinue wearing one while your nipples are sore. A soft, white cotton blouse or T-shirt will let air reach the nipples.

Avoid any kind of plastic lining in your bra or nursing pads. It can cause trouble by keeping in moisture and keeping out the air needed to heal your nipples. Wearing a bra that is too tight can also put pressure on your nipples and cause soreness. Avoid using nipple shields which are worn during feedings as they will not prevent soreness and their use almost always leads to further difficulties.

If soreness persists, you may want to try using an ultraviolet sunlamp to aid in healing. Sitting three feet from the lamp, cover your eyes with a very heavy towel and expose your breasts no more than one-half minute the first day, one minute the second and third days, two minutes the fourth and fifth days. If you notice a redness at two minutes, cut down to one minute and continue at that level for several days. **Be extremely careful always to protect your eyes while you are using the lamp; it is imperative that you time yourself with a clock or watch. Be careful about handling the bulb after use — it gets very hot; be careful not to get a sunburn from the lamp.**

## OINTMENTS

Most ointments sold for the treatment of sore nipples are not useful and some may even be harmful. Avoid any product that needs to be wiped off before the baby nurses. Ointments containing antibiotics, steroids, astringents, or anesthetic agents are **NOT** recommended because they are potentially harmful to both mother and baby. In addition, numbing the nipples may inhibit the let-down reflex. Antiseptic nipple sprays should also be avoided.

Ointment can worsen soreness if it prevents the baby from grasping the nipple and areola properly. Ointments can also keep out air and sunlight which are important to healing. Any ointment you use should be applied very sparingly.

Expressing a few drops of your milk after baby is finished nursing and rubbing it gently into your nipples will take advantage of the healing effects of breast milk.

Some mothers use anhydrous lanolin or pure vitamin E oil to soothe and moisturize sore nipples. Some caution is necessary regarding the frequent use of vitamin E oil.

A new type of hypoallergenic medical grade lanolin called Lansinoh® has been developed especially for nursing mothers. It does not have to be wiped off before baby nurses and has been found safe to use even by those who are allergic to wool. One study shows this type of lanolin is especially effective if the skin is cracked. For more information, see the Appendix.

## NIPPLE CLEANSING

Bathing with plain water is all that is necessary for your nipples. Avoid using soap on the nipples as it can remove the natural protective oils and predispose the nipples to cracking. Be careful, too, not to apply cologne, deodorant, hair spray, or powder near the nipples to avoid irritating the tender skin.

## SORE NIPPLES DO HEAL

Frequent opportunities to nurse and cuddle your little one, keeping him close day and night, will help to prevent and lessen nipple soreness. Lack of sleep and an inadequate diet may contribute to the problem. Try napping during the day, eating nourishing foods, and drinking plenty of liquids. Limit visitors, especially those who may discourage or upset you, and accept offers of help with the household while you and the baby rest.

There may be a relationship between apprehension on the part of the mother and sore nipples. Tender nipples may cause enough tension to hold back the let-down reflex. The delay in the milk may make the baby pull and tug on the nipple, making it even more sore—and creating greater concern on your part. What can you do about this? You can hand-express a little milk to start the flow, and you can make a deliberate effort to relax before nursing. You may want to ask your doctor to prescribe an analgesic to relieve the pain while your nipples are very sore.

Fortunately, sore nipples rarely last more than a few days, especially if you are following the suggestions given here. Pay particular attention to baby's position at the breast and continue to nurse every two hours. If soreness persists, your baby may be sucking incorrectly and you may need the advice of someone who has been trained to help babies learn to suck effectively. Check with your La Leche League Leader for recommendations or suggestions.

Some mothers have given up breastfeeding because of sore nipples. This is unfortunate because it isn't necessary. In a few very rare cases of extremely sore nipples, which might occur if baby has been sucking incorrectly for some time, it may be necessary to discontinue breastfeeding temporarily. During this time the mother may have to hand-express or pump her milk and give it to the baby from a dropper or a spoon. As soon as the nipples respond to treatment, the baby can be put back on the breast.

## THRUSH

If you suddenly get sore nipples after several weeks or months of comfortable nursing, you and/or your baby may have contracted thrush. (Thrush can also occur in the newborn period.) If the nipple area gets itchy and feels very tender, or if the skin becomes pink and flaky, you may have thrush. Thrush is a fungus infection that thrives on milk. It's not really serious, although it is a nuisance for you. It rarely bothers the baby at all. It may appear as white spots on the inside of your baby's cheeks, or on his gums. Your baby may also have a persistent diaper rash in connection with thrush, and you may have a vaginal yeast infection. Thrush can be related to taking oral contraceptive pills or an antibiotic. It is more common in warm, humid climates. You may have it on your nipples even when there is no sign of it in the baby's mouth.

Thrush may take several weeks to cure, but there is no reason to discontinue nursing. Your doctor may prescribe medication or other forms of treatment. Be sure to treat both the baby's mouth and your nipples. Others in the family may also require treatment.

Wash your hands thoroughly after using the bathroom, as this will help keep thrush from spreading. You must be persistent about treating thrush but it is no reason to discontinue breastfeeding.

## SORE NIPPLES IN LATER MONTHS

Another possible cause of sore nipples in later months is teething. Some babies' sucking pattern changes when their gums are sore, and this can temporarily cause nipple soreness. Try being more careful of baby's position at the breast and the way he is grasping your nipple. A change of nursing positions may help.

On occasion, mothers have developed sore nipples due to eczema. This most often happens when a baby who has started solids nurses while there are still particles of food in his mouth. When food particles come in contact with the sensitive skin of your nipples, eczema can result. This can be avoided by being sure that your baby's or toddler's mouth is empty when he begins to nurse.

Sometimes a mother will notice a small painful blister on the tip of her nipple. This is called a "milk blister" and could be caused by a plugged milk duct. Soak the nipple area in warm water several times a day and keep the area very clean. Try varying nursing positions so baby's mouth puts the least pressure on the blister. It may take a few days to heal completely, but resist the temptation to pop the blister yourself as this can lead to infection.

If you are nursing an older baby or toddler and suddenly notice that your nipples are sore, but none of the above reasons seem to be the cause, then there are some other questions that you can ask yourself. Has your little one been nursing more often, perhaps due to illness or a major change such as moving? Has he been experimenting with unusual nursing positions which might cause nipple strain and abrasion? When he grasps or releases the breast, has he been sucking the nipple in or pulling off without first breaking the suction? It is possible that you might be pregnant? One or more of these situations might cause sore nipples in even a veteran nursing mother.

When you are experiencing sore nipples or any kind of problem, it can be helpful to share your experience with another nursing mother, especially an LLL Leader. She may have additional insight into the situation. Sometimes, all you really need is support and encouragement to help you work through your problem or difficulty and see the brighter side of nursing your baby.

# Pumping and Storing Your Milk

When situations or circumstances occur that cause a mother to be separated from her breastfed baby, she'll need to know how to remove milk from her breasts by hand or by using a breast pump. She may also need information on how to safely store the milk she pumps so it can later be fed to her baby.

Some of the situations in which pumping will be needed include having a premature or sick baby who is unable to nurse, a mother planning to return to work, a need to relieve engorged or overfull breasts, or a situation where added stimulation is needed to increase a mother's milk supply.

*Hand-expressing your milk is easy and convenient.*

## HAND OR MANUAL EXPRESSION

One of the best techniques to learn is hand or manual expression. This is the least expensive and most portable method you can use. It may require some practice in order to make it work for you. In some cases, watching another mother hand-express her milk is the best way to learn how to do it.

With practice, many mothers are able to express several ounces of milk very quickly. Wash your hands before you begin. The basic technique is to place your fingers on your breast with your thumb above and fingers below so they form a "C." Push back toward the chest wall while squeezing your thumb and fingers together rhythmically just behind the areola (dark area of skin that surrounds the nipple). In the case of a very large areola, fingers should be positioned about 1" to 1½" behind the nipple.

Do not slide your fingers along the skin. Rotate your hand around the breast in order to reach all the milk ducts. Do this for three to five minutes on one breast; then switch to the other breast. Switching back and forth at least twice helps to increase the flow of milk.

You may find it more comfortable to use your right hand, but it's better to alternate, using both hands on each breast in order to reach more of the milk ducts.

Have a clean sterilized container ready to collect the milk. A Hand-Expression Funnel that fits on top of a baby bottle can be used to collect milk without spills or splashes. See the Appendix for details.

# THE MARMET TECHNIQUE OF MANUAL EXPRESSION†

Another hand-expression technique has been developed by Chele Marmet, a La Leche League Leader and lactation consultant who is the Director of the Lactation Institute in West Los Angeles, California. Many mothers who have been previously unsuccessful at hand-expression have found this method effective.

The key to the success of this technique is the combination of the method of manual expression and the use of massage to stimulate the milk ejection reflex. This technique can be learned by following this step-by-step guide. As with any manual skill, practice is important.

## DRAINING THE MILK RESERVOIRS

1. **Position** the thumb and first two fingers about 1″ to 1½″ behind the nipple.

   • Use this measurement, which is not necessarily the outer edge of the areola, as a guide. The areola varies in size from one woman to another.

   • Place the thumb pad above the nipple and the finger pads below to form a "C."

   • Note that the fingers are positioned so that the milk reservoirs lie beneath them.

   • Avoid cupping the breast.

2. **Push** straight into the chest wall.

   • Avoid spreading the fingers apart.

   • For large breasts, first lift and then push into the chest wall.

3. **Roll** thumb and fingers forward as if making thumb and fingerprints at the same time.

   • The rolling motion of the thumb and fingers compresses and empties the milk reservoirs without hurting sensitive breast tissue.

4. **Repeat Rhythmically** to drain the reservoirs.

   • Position, push, roll; position, push, roll.

5. **Rotate** the thumb and finger position to milk the other reservoirs. Use both hands on each breast.

†©1978, 1979, 1981, 1988, Chele Marmet. Used with permission.

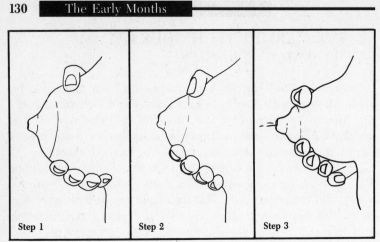

Step 1 | Step 2 | Step 3

*Notice how the thumb and fingers rotate to press in on the milk reservoirs.*

## AVOID THESE MOTIONS

• Avoid squeezing the breast. This can cause bruising.

• Avoid pulling on the nipple and breast. This can cause nipple damage.

• Avoid sliding fingers on the breast. This can cause skin burns.

## STIMULATING THE FLOW OF MILK

1. **Massage** the milk producing cells and ducts.

• Start at the top of the breast. Press firmly into the chest wall. Move fingers in a circular motion on one spot on the skin.

• After a few seconds move the fingers to the next area of the breast.

• Spiral around the breast toward the areola using this massage.

• The motion is similar to that used in a breast examination.

2. Next, **Stroke** the breast area from the top of the breast to the nipple with a light tickle-like stroke.

• Continue this stroking motion from the chest wall to the nipple around the whole breast.

• This will help with relaxation and will help stimulate the milk ejection reflex.

3. **Shake** the breast while leaning forward so that gravity will help the milk eject.

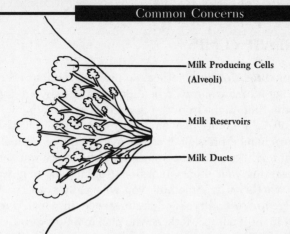

Milk Producing Cells
(Alveoli)

Milk Reservoirs

Milk Ducts

*How the Breast Works: The milk is produced in milk producing cells (alveoli). A portion of the milk continuously comes down the ducts and collects in the milk reservoirs. When the milk-producing cells are stimulated, they expel additional milk into the duct system (milk ejection reflex).*

## FOLLOW THIS PROCEDURE

This procedure should be followed by mothers who are expressing in place of a full feeding and those who need to establish, increase, or maintain their milk supply when the baby cannot breastfeed.

• Express each breast until the flow of milk slows down.

• Assist the milk ejection reflex (massage, stroke, shake) on both breasts. This can be done simultaneously.

• Repeat the whole process of expressing each breast and assisting the milk ejection reflex once or twice more. The flow of milk usually slows down sooner the second and third time as the reservoirs are drained.

The **Entire Procedure** should take about **20-30 Minutes.**

• Express each breast 5-7 minutes.

• Massage, stroke, shake.

• Express each breast 3-5 minutes.

• Massage, stroke, shake.

• Express each breast 2-3 minutes.

Note: If the milk supply is established, use the times given only as a guide. Watch the flow of milk and change breasts when the flow gets small. If little or no milk is present yet, follow these suggested times closely.

## BREAST PUMPS

Many breastfeeding mothers do just fine without ever owning or using a breast pump. When mother and baby are together most of the time, right from the beginning, and the baby is able to nurse often, a mother may have no reason to pump her breasts. If you learn hand expression, it can be used for the occasional times when you might need to save your milk or to empty your breasts. Before investing your money in a breast pump, you may want to consider whether it is something you will really need.

There are several types of circumstances in which a mother will want to use a pump. Mothers who plan to return to work when their babies are still very young can continue breastfeeding by pumping their breasts during their lunch hour and/or at mid-morning and mid-afternoon breaks while at work. They can refrigerate or freeze their milk for feeding to the baby later on.

A working mother will be looking for a breast pump that offers both ease and convenience. She probably needs to carry the pump back and forth to work with her and she needs to be able to use it quickly and efficiently. She also wants a pump that is easy to clean, perhaps even dishwasher-safe, to save time in her already busy day.

The mother who is pumping milk for a premature baby is in a situation where she needs both to establish her milk supply for the future and possibly to provide a specific number of ounces per day to meet her baby's present needs. However, she may not have the opportunity to actually nurse her baby for many weeks. She needs a pump that will closely simulate a baby's sucking action and initiate a good let-down reflex.

Some nursing mothers may decide they want to have a breast pump on hand just in case of a family emergency or other situation where they'll need to be temporarily separated from their baby. These mothers want to buy an inexpensive pump that just gives them the security of knowing it will be available even though it may never be needed. Breast pumps and other breastfeeding-aid products are available from most La Leche League Groups and from La Leche League International. See the Appendix for details.

## CHOOSING A BREAST PUMP

"Bicycle horn" pumps. At one time, this was the only type of breast pump available and it is still the least expensive. Suction is created by squeezing a rubber bulb, but care must be taken to avoid damage to breast tissue as the suction cannot be regulated. In addition, most of these pumps cannot be adequately sterilized. They are not recommended.

**Rubber-bulb pumps.** This type of hand-held pump is an improved version of the bicycle-horn pump. It uses the same principle of providing suction by squeezing a rubber bulb, but has two advantages: the milk goes directly into a storage container which can be sterilized, and the suction can be adjusted.

**Cylinder Pumps.** Several different manufacturers offer piston-type cylinder pumps with a wide variety of adaptations. All consist of basically two glass or plastic cylinders. The outer cylinder usually doubles as a storage container and baby bottle. Suction in these pumps is created by pulling the outer cylinder away from the breast. Many women report that this pump is quite comfortable to use and very effective at extracting milk from the breasts. Most of these pumps are small and lightweight, making them easy to fit into a purse, so they are convenient for the working mother. Most are also dishwasher-safe.

**The Loyd-B Pump.** This pump is an old standby, and for many years it was the only truly effective manual breast pump on the market. It is bulkier than most rubber bulb and cylinder pumps, but it comes apart easily and is still small enough to be carried to and from work in a large purse or tote bag. The pump works with a trigger-like mechanism (similar to the triggers on many household cleaner bottles), and most women report that it is both comfortable and effective.

**The Ora'Lac Pump.** This pump is unique in the method used to extract milk. Two tubes extend from the top of the collection bottle. One attaches to the breast shield, the other goes into the mother's mouth. The mother provides the suction which draws the milk from her breast directly into the collection bottle. The pump is small enough to fit into a purse and can be used while the mother is lying down.

**Battery-operated Pumps.** Battery-operated pumps provide a combination of convenience and portability. They are small, lightweight, and relatively inexpensive. Suction is provided by a small pump that operates on AA batteries saving mother the effort involved in using a hand pump. A battery-operated pump can be operated with one hand which is important in some situations.

**Semi-automatic Electric Pumps.** These small electric pumps require manual adjustment of the vacuum but offer the advantage of an electric motor to provide the suction. The new models are small enough to be very portable and moderately priced. A working mother who plans to pump her milk for several months could decide that buying one of these pumps would be a good investment.

**Full-size Electric Pumps.** An electric pump usually provides the most effective pumping action. Electric breast pumps are designed to provide an alternating pull and release suction which most closely resembles the sucking action of a nursing baby. Most mothers find these pumps to be gentle and efficient. These are the pumps of choice for the mother who is pumping her milk for a premature or sick baby who is unable to nurse at the breast. Because electric pumps are the fastest and easiest way to pump your milk, they provide the best stimulation for building and maintaining a good milk supply. This can be particularly important in a stressful situation.

Full-size electric pumps are expensive, but they are widely available on a rental basis. In the case of a sick or hospitalized baby (or mother), health insurance will often cover the rental fees when the use of the pump is prescribed by a doctor.

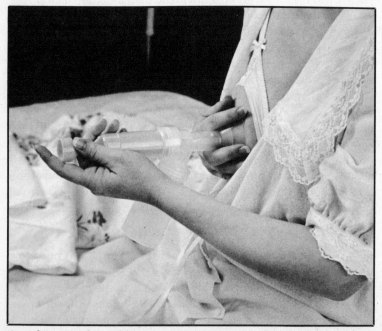

*A mother using the Medela manual breast pump.*

## BABY IS BEST

No breast pump can match the effectiveness of a baby in stimulating a mother's milk supply and extracting milk. This is partly because mechanical suction cannot duplicate the synchronized action of the baby's tongue, jaw, and palate, but it is mainly because the mother's emotional response to her baby is an important factor.

Learning the techniques of effective pumping requires patience and practice. But the rewards can be well worth your while if you are in a situation where you must be separated from your baby. Here are some tips that will help in any situation that requires you to pump your milk.

1. Follow the manufacturer's direction for any pump you use.

2. When using any kind of pump it's a good idea to moisten your breast before applying the breast shield. This improves the suction.

3. Be sure to go easy at first and use the lowest setting or the least amount of suction to get started. It is possible to damage sensitive breast tissue, so heed the first signs of discomfort. Pumping should not be uncomfortable and never painful. Reduce the strength of the suction, or the amount of time spent pumping. If discomfort occurs, check to be sure you are using the pump correctly. If necessary, switch to a different brand or type of pump.

4. Pumping in a quiet, relaxed setting will usually help the milk to flow more easily. Although this is not always possible in an office setting or a hospital nursery, it is worth the effort to try to find a secluded spot where you can pump undisturbed. Thinking about the baby or looking at a picture of him can do wonders in encouraging the milk to flow.

5. If you are planning to save the expressed milk to be given to the baby later on, be sure that your hands and the container you use to collect the milk are clean. Follow pump manufacturer's directions for cleaning the pump. Bacteria can accumulate if dried particles of milk are left in the breast shield, tubing, or collection bottle. If you are pumping for a hospitalized baby, there may be more specific precautions you need to take. Check with the nurses who are caring for the baby.

6. Research has shown that human milk can safely be kept at room temperature for 6 to 10 hours because of its ability to retard bacterial growth. You may need to be more cautious if you are expressing milk for a hospitalized baby.

7. Milk can be refrigerated for 3 to 5 days with no increase in harmful bacteria.

8. For longer storage, milk can be frozen and kept in a refrigerator-freezer for up to two weeks. In a separate door freezer it can be kept for up to four months. In a separate deep freeze that stays at a constant 0° F it can be kept six months or longer. Be sure to label and date frozen milk and use the oldest milk first.

9. It's a good idea to freeze your milk in small amounts varying from two to four ounces. You can always thaw more milk if your baby needs it. Once thawed, breast milk can be refrigerated for up to nine hours but should never be refrozen. Do not let milk stand at room temperature to thaw. Instead, thaw it quickly by putting the container under running water, first cold, then gradually getting warmer until the milk is warm. Do not heat the milk on the stove or in a microwave oven. More information on storing your milk and feeding it to your baby can be found in Chapter 8.

## TO EXPRESS MILK FOR A MILK BANK

Because breast milk has been found to be so important for sick or premature babies, nursing mothers are sometimes asked to donate their extra milk for these babies. In many hospitals, special milk banks have been established for this purpose. If you are asked to donate your milk, you will naturally consider your own baby's needs first, and you will probably pump or hand-express milk to donate only after feedings. If your baby is a little older, you might be able to express milk from one breast while the baby nurses at the other. This is less time-consuming, but can usually be done only if you are using a battery-operated or electric breast pump. Other methods usually require two hands.

The milk bank will probably have its own set of instructions and may even provide you with an electric breast pump to use. If you are donating your milk for a sick or premature baby, you must be scrupulously clean in your techniques for expressing and storing your milk. If you, your baby, or any other member of your household has been ill, you should not donate milk until everyone has been well for twenty-four hours.

When the time comes that you are no longer donating milk, cut down gradually on the pumping. If you have built up a milk supply much greater than your own baby needs, the sudden drop in demand might cause engorgement, just as sudden weaning would. Taper off gradually by pumping out some of the milk whenever your breasts feel overly full and uncomfortable. Or, see if your baby will help out with an extra nursing. He'll probably be happy to oblige.

# Breast Problems: Sore Breasts, Plugged Ducts, and Breast Infections

It sometimes happens that a nursing mother notices a very tender spot or a sore lump in her breast. This can be a plugged duct or a breast infection. Knowing what to do about it can clear things up quickly and avoid further difficulty.

Whatever the cause of a sore breast, there are three basic steps involved in treatment:

**Apply Heat; Get Plenty of Rest;** and keep the breast comfortably empty by **Frequent Nursing.** These procedures may sound deceptively simple, but immediate action can mean the difference between a few hours of discomfort and several days in bed.

**Plugged Ducts.** If a breastfeeding mother notices a very tender spot, redness, or a sore lump in her breast, this may very likely be caused by a plugged milk duct. What this means is that a milk duct has become inflamed because the milk is unable to flow through it freely.

Plugged ducts may be caused by any of the following—improper positioning of the baby at the breast, prolonged periods of time between nursings, giving supplementary bottles or overusing a pacifier, wearing a too-tight nursing bra or other clothing that constricts the breasts. If an older baby suddenly starts sleeping through the night, or nurses often one day and cuts way back the next day, a plugged milk duct may occur. Occasionally a plugged duct is caused by dried milk secretions covering one of the nipple openings.

Rest is essential at the first sign of a problem. If at all possible, you should climb into bed with the baby tucked in beside you for the remainder of the day. At the very least you should eliminate all extra activities and spend an hour or two relaxing with baby at your breast and feet off the floor. A plugged duct or a sore spot on your breast may be the first sign that you are trying to do too much. You would be well-advised to heed this warning and get lots of extra rest for a few days after you've experienced a plugged duct.

In addition to rest, there are some other things you can do to treat a plugged duct:

**Apply wet or dry heat to the affected area, and remove any dried milk secretions on the nipple by soaking with plain warm water.** Lean over a basin of warm water and soak your breasts for ten minutes or so three times a day, take warm showers, use hot wet packs, a heating pad, or a hot water bottle. Massage the affected area gently while it is warm, and nurse the baby or hand-express some milk immediately after treating the area with warmth. Getting the milk to flow while the breast is warm will help unplug the affected duct.

**Nurse the baby on the affected side frequently.** Nurse at least every two hours including during the night, as long as the breast is tender or warm to the touch. Nurse first on the affected side at each feeding. Frequent nursings will keep the breast fairly empty so the milk flows more freely.

**Loosen constrictive clothing, especially your bra.** If possible, you may even want to discontinue wearing a bra for a few days. If you are more comfortable with a bra, try wearing one that is a size larger or at least change to one that has a different cut or style. This should relieve any pressure that the bra you usually wear may have been putting on the milk ducts. Some mothers try to get by without a regular nursing bra by wearing a stretchy type of bra and pulling the cup up or down for feedings. This could be causing pressure on the milk ducts with the result that they are not emptied properly.

**Check the baby's position at the breast.** He should be on his side with his whole body facing you, and he should be able to grasp your nipple without having to turn his head. Most or all of the areola should be in his mouth. It is important for the baby to be positioned properly so that all the milk ducts are emptied at every feeding.

**Try changing nursing positions from time to time.** Lie down, sit up, switch from the rocking chair to the sofa to a lounge chair. Try nursing with baby in the football hold. A variety of nursing positions will give the baby a better chance to reach all of the milk ducts and keep them emptied. (See Chapter 4 for details on various nursing positions.) One position that may be particularly helpful in clearing up a plugged duct is to place the baby in the middle of a bed or a quilt or in your lap while you sit Indian-style (or get up on your hands and knees) and lean over him to nurse, with the breast hanging freely from the rib cage. This position may not be the most comfortable for you, but it can allow a plugged milk duct to be opened more easily.

## BREAST INFECTIONS

Prompt and proper treatment of a plugged duct will usually keep a breast infection from developing. However, if you notice the type of soreness or lump that is usually associated with a plugged duct, and it is accompanied by a fever or flu-like symptoms (feeling tired, achy, or run-down), you probably have a breast infection. A breastfeeding mother will sometimes find herself developing a breast infection when other family members suffer from colds or other types of flu.

It is important that you begin treating a breast infection immediately. The treatment for a breast infection is the same as for a plugged duct: **Apply Heat, Get Plenty of Rest,** and **Nurse Often.** If this course of action is begun quickly, you may not need further treatment for a breast infection. However, if you still have a fever after 24 hours, and other symptoms persist, you'll want to get in touch with your doctor. In this case, your doctor may prescribe medication. You'll want to continue getting lots of rest and nursing often while you take the medication.

It will not harm your baby to continue nursing when you have a breast infection. At one time it was standard procedure to recommend weaning if the mother had a breast infection. However, studies have shown that the infection clears up more quickly when the breast is kept empty. Also, the mother is much more comfortable than she would be after a sudden weaning. Antibodies in mother's milk protect the baby from the bacteria that may be causing the infection. Even temporary weaning is an unnecessary hardship at a time when you aren't feeling well in the first place.

If your doctor prescribes an antibiotic, be sure to take all of the medication that is prescribed. People sometimes stop taking a medication as soon as they start to feel better, only to have the infection or whatever reoccur in a few days. In the case of a breast infection, this would be hard on both you and the baby, so it's important to take the medication that is prescribed for you until it is gone. Antibiotics in general do not usually cause a problem for a nursing baby. If a doctor is wary about certain antibiotics, he can usually prescribe one that has been found to be safe to take while a mother is nursing.

If you find yourself with a second breast infection within a few days or weeks of the first one, chances are good that the original infection didn't clear up completely. Repeated breast infections do occasionally happen, but they are almost always a recurrence of the first infection rather than a brand new infection.

If you do find that plugged ducts or breast infections seem to occur frequently, you may want to look into your general health, being sure you are eating a balanced diet and limiting extra activities so you have enough time to relax and enjoy nursing your baby.

Donna Sutton, a mother from Iowa, found that the advice she received from her La Leche League Leader helped her recover when she had a breast infection:

*After being home from the hospital one week, I found myself with a sore breast and other symptoms of a breast infection. A consultation with a local physician produced the advice to stop nursing on the infected breast for at least four to five days, and express the milk by hand or breast pump. I knew that this was the wrong course to take, so after much deliberation I continued to nurse on both sides. My infection did not abate, and I could still feel a lump in my breast.*

*I finally called my local League Leader. Her advice soon made all the difference in the world. After applying warm packs, nursing often (especially on the affected side), and resting, the lump in my breast began to disappear. I still remember my Leader telling me that nothing should be more important at this time than nursing my baby. I realize now that if I had consulted her initially, the infection would have cleared up more quickly and been*

*less frustrating for Sarah and me. How many mothers
have received the wrong advice and been forced to quit
nursing?*

*I am grateful to my LLL Leader for her advice, and
I'm a firm believer that breast is best!*

## BREAST ABSCESS

In very rare cases, a breast infection may develop into an abscess. This usually does not occur if prompt treatment is initiated at the first sign of a problem. An abscess is a localized infection that may need to be surgically opened and drained. Usually your doctor can do this in his office or perhaps he'll want to do it at the hospital on an outpatient basis. If this procedure should be necessary, you can continue to nurse on the unaffected breast with no problem, but you may need to pump or hand-express your milk from the abscessed breast for a day or so. Keeping that breast empty will promote healing, but the incision may be too close to the areola for the baby to nurse without causing discomfort.

Remember that any of these breast problems can be an indication that you should carefully evaluate other things that are going on in your life. These symptoms are often a nursing mother's first clue that she should be taking better care of herself. Conserve your energy by keeping extra activities to a minimum and spend as much time as possible just relaxing and enjoying your baby without regard to schedules and deadlines.

## BREAST LUMPS

Most lumps in a nursing mother's breast are inflammatory, due to plugged ducts or a breast infection. Some are due to benign tumors (fibromas), a milk retention cyst (galactocele), and only in the very rarest of cases are they due to cancer.

If you have a lump that does not go away in a week with careful treatment for a plugged duct, we suggest that you consult a physician. Weaning is not necessary either for diagnosis or treatment of breast lumps. Mothers have had cysts removed, biopsied, and aspirated, without finding it necessary to wean. If your doctor is not familiar with the lactating breast, you may need to call his attention to this fact. It may be advisable to empty the breast by nursing the baby immediately prior to examination and/or whatever procedure the doctor may want to undertake. Nursing may be resumed again right afterwards, except after a radioactive Gallium breast scan.

One mother, Barbara Ann Paster of New Hampshire, worked closely with her surgeon to be sure she would be able to continue breastfeeding following surgery:

*Shortly after our second child, Sara, was born I noticed a lump in my breast just to the left of my nipple. I arranged to go in for the removal of the breast lump soon thereafter. Before the scheduled date of surgery, I sat down with my surgeon to discuss the nursing breast and how he could help me make my return to nursing go smoothly as soon as possible after the operation. While the surgeon had known I was nursing, he had never considered the problem of operating on a nursing breast. After our discussion he agreed to be especially careful during the surgery to cut as few milk ducts as possible.*

*Because my lump was deep within the breast, my surgeon ruled out anything less than general anesthesia, claiming that it was too tender an area to manage otherwise. To minimize engorgement, we worked out a plan for me to nurse Sara immediately prior to surgery. We also decided on dissolvable stitches, which would absorb after healing.*

*Sara was put to breast on my unaffected side as soon as I regained consciousness. The incisional area was dressed with as small a dressing as possible so as not to alarm her. Within twelve hours of the surgery I was able to nurse on the affected side.*

*I won't say it was comfortable. I found that putting some pressure on the dressing helped allay the feeling that she would pull the incision or my breast apart. By the second or third day it was quite tolerable. Putting my baby to the breast was more comfortable than trying to hand-express or use a pump. My surgeon was amazed at how well the breast healed.*

*My incision line follows the curve of the outer edge of the areola. The surgeon went in from there and excised the lump from almost directly under the nipple. Luckily it was fibrocystic in nature which meant it was not life-threatening.*

Another mother, Beverly Scott from Washington, found that surgery was not needed for her breast lump. She learned that the lump that formed in her breast when her son was ten days old was a galactocele, a milk-retention cyst. Fortunately, her doctor was familiar with this uncommon phenomenon and advised her to continue nursing and ignore the lump. However, by the time her son was twenty-one months old, the lump had enlarged to twice its original size and the doctor became concerned and suggested weaning. Beverly goes on to explain what happened:

*I was determined to continue with baby-led weaning. I decided to learn all I could about available options and then ask my doctor to proceed with treatment without waiting for Jesse to wean.*

*I talked to LLLI and received some helpful information regarding surgery during lactation. I contacted my obstetrician, summarizing my conclusions in a letter and then calling him. We agreed that he would go ahead and remove the fluid from the cyst immediately for diagnostic purposes. If surgical removal of the cyst was indicated, I would arrange with a general surgeon to have the procedure done on an outpatient basis under local anesthetic with minimal interruption of breastfeeding. However, that did not become necessary, as a laboratory analysis of the fluid confirmed the original diagnosis: The cyst contained only milk.*

*A woman who suddenly finds a large breast lump soon after giving birth should ask her doctor about the possibility of a galactocele before submitting to invasive treatment such as surgery. Ultrasound and/or aspiration could confirm the diagnosis if there was any uncertainty.*

Breastfeeding has been shown to reduce the incidence of breast cancer, nevertheless, there have been rare instances of a mother developing breast cancer while she is still nursing a baby. It is a good idea to learn how to do a monthly breast self-exam, and do it regularly. Any mother who discovers a lump in her breast that does not go away should have it checked by her doctor.

## OTHER BREAST SURGERY

Previous breast surgery usually need not stop a mother from nursing her baby even if she has had a breast removed because of cancer. Breastfeeding will not expose the mother to any greater risk of malignancy, nor will it harm the baby. And since milk production works on the basis of supply and demand, one breast will supply plenty of milk for the baby.

Mothers who have undergone breast augmentation surgery are usually able to breastfeed their babies. In some cases of breast reduction surgery (depending on the type of surgery that was done and on how extensive it was), breastfeeding may not be possible.

# Is Your Baby Getting Enough Milk?

There is nothing quite like the delight that comes from seeing your baby thrive and grow on your milk. As his arms and legs fill out and his cheeks turn plump and rosy, you can't help but glow with pride....and marvel at how perfectly your body is continuing to provide for all of his nutritional needs.

A baby's need for milk and his mother's ability to produce it in just the right quantity have been said to be one of nature's most perfect examples of the law of supply and demand. Until the advent of mass produced artificial formula, the very survival of the human race depended largely on a mother's ability to produce a sufficient quantity of milk to adequately nourish her baby.

There is nothing mystical or magical about producing enough milk to satisfy your baby's needs. Establishing and maintaining an ample milk supply is easy when you understand how the milk supply is regulated and what kinds of things are likely to upset the balance between the amount of milk the baby needs and the amount of milk that is produced.

**The more the baby nurses, the more milk there will be.** Understanding this "golden rule" of breastfeeding is the key to an abundant milk supply and a contented baby. Years ago, mothers were often told to wait four hours between feedings so that their breasts would "fill up." Many a mother and baby had a short-lived nursing experience due to this well-intentioned but erroneous advice.

It is now well understood that milk is produced almost continuously, and that the more often the baby nurses, the more milk

*Baby's round cheeks and happy smiles are good indications that he's getting enough to eat.*

there will be. Thus, the mother of a baby who is nursing every two hours will have a bountiful milk supply, while the mother who is trying to "hold off" the baby and nurse only every four hours will have considerably less milk. Frequent nursing at the breast signals the mother's body to produce a correspondingly increased amount of milk.

*You can be confident that your baby is getting enough milk if:*
   • He has six to eight really **wet diapers** and two to five **bowel movements** per day and is receiving nothing but breast milk—no supplemental water or formula. (A baby older than six weeks or so may have fewer bowel movements and still be getting enough to eat.)
   • He is **gaining weight** at an average of four to seven ounces a week or about one pound (453 grams) per month.
   At your baby's first checkup, weight gain should be determined from the **lowest** weight the baby reached rather than his birth weight. Most babies lose weight after birth and some babies take two to three weeks to regain their birth weight.
   • He is **nursing frequently** on both breasts at each feeding. Most newborns nurse every two to three hours or eight to twelve times in a twenty-four hour period. This is an average, and some babies may nurse less frequently while others nurse more often.
   • He **appears healthy**—has good color and resilient skin, is "filling out" and growing in length, and is alert and active with good muscle tone.

## "FALSE ALARMS"

Some mothers think they do not have enough milk when actually there is no problem with their milk supply. They worry about symptoms which have other causes or they're unfamiliar with the variety of patterns which are normal in breastfed babies. If your baby is gaining well and has plenty of wet and soiled diapers, there is no need to worry if:

*Your baby nurses very often.* Wanting to nurse frequently does not mean baby is hungry. Many babies have a strong need to suck or a need for continuous contact with their mothers. Frequent nursing assures that your baby *is* getting enough milk.

Breast milk digests more quickly than formula and places less strain on a baby's immature digestive system, so that the breastfed baby needs to be fed more frequently.

*Your baby's nursing habits, weight gain, or sleep patterns don't compare with other babies you know.* Each baby is an individual, and there are wide variations within the normal range.

*Your baby suddenly increases the frequency and/or length of his nursings.* Babies who are very sleepy as newborns often suddenly "wake up" and begin nursing more frequently. Babies also go through occasional growth spurts (frequently around two weeks, six weeks, and three months). During these times they nurse more often than usual to bring in more milk for their expanding needs.

*Your baby suddenly decreases his nursing time, perhaps down to five to ten minutes per breast.* He may simply be able to extract the milk more quickly now that he is more experienced at nursing.

*Your baby is fussy.* Many babies have a fussy period each day, often at about the same time of the day. Some babies are fussy much of the time. Fussiness can be caused by many things other than hunger, but often there is no discernible reason.

*Your breasts leak only a little or not at all.* Leaking has no relationship to the amount of milk you produce and often stops after your supply becomes established and regulated to your baby's needs.

*Your breasts suddenly seem softer.* This happens as your milk production adjusts to your baby's demand and the initial engorgement subsides.

*You never feel the let-down sensation or it does not seem as strong as it did before.* This may occur as time goes on. (Some mothers do not feel it at all; it does not mean that they do not have a let-down.)

# IF YOUR MILK SUPPLY IS LOW

If it seems that your supply is not meeting your baby's needs, then it is important to determine what is interfering with your production of milk. The following factors can cause or contribute to a lessened milk supply:

*Supplementing. Supplementing with even an occasional bottle of formula, juice, or water can interfere with a mother's milk supply. Supplements fill up the baby and cause him to wait longer for the next feeding, thereby decreasing his sucking at the breast. The more formula he gets one day, the less milk the mother's body will make the following day. Supplementing causes a mother's breasts to produce less, *not* more.

*Nipple Confusion. A baby can become confused by the bottle nipple, as it requires a different type of sucking. If your baby is not sucking properly at the breast, he will not be able to stimulate your breasts to produce enough milk.

*Pacifiers. Some babies are willing to meet their sucking needs with a pacifier, which may significantly reduce their sucking time at the breast. Pacifiers can also lead to nipple confusion.

*Using Nipple Shields. Nipple shields worn during feedings interfere with the impulses to the brain that normally come from a baby sucking directly on his mother's nipples. The milk secretion and letdown of the milk is slowed down—directly affecting the amount of milk the baby receives.

*Scheduled Feedings. Delaying the baby's feedings until the clock dictates a certain amount of time has passed can interfere with the supply and demand system of milk production. Feeding on demand usually assures an adequate supply.

*Placid, Sleepy Baby. Some babies sleep most of the time and nurse only infrequently and for short periods. If this describes your baby, and if he is having few wet diapers and not gaining weight, it is important for you to awaken him regularly, stimulate him with gentle handling, and encourage him to nurse at least every two hours. You'll need to decide how often he should nurse, until he learns for himself how to get enough to eat.

*Cutting back on the Length of Feedings. Long nursings can help assure an adequate milk supply. Cutting them short can prevent your supply from increasing as your baby's needs increase. On the other hand, a baby who nurses almost continually and never seems satisfied may not be sucking correctly.

*Offering only **One Breast** per feeding. After the milk is established, some mothers prefer to nurse at only one breast per feeding if baby is gaining well. But if you are working to increase your supply, use both breasts. The baby who nurses at only one breast will take in less milk per feeding, and each breast will receive less sucking stimulation.

## MOTHER CARE

A breastfeeding mother needs to take good care of herself in order to provide a good milk supply for her baby. Fatigue and tension can interfere with your let-down and contribute to an inadequate milk supply. Take the time to *really* relax every so often during the course of the day.

A poor diet can contribute to tension and fatigue, detract from your general well-being, and result in an inadequate milk supply. Many mothers feel better when they eat six small meals every day rather than three big ones. Good nutritional intake, and eating more often, may be the answer for you. Eat fresh fruits and salads, meats, cheese, nuts, and fish. Avoid poor quality foods such as cookies, crackers, candy, and the like.

Breastfeeding increases your need for fluids, as your body needs more fluids to make milk. Take a glass of water or juice with you each time you sit down to nurse the baby. If your urine is dark yellow in color and small in amount, you are not drinking enough liquids. What you drink is equally important. Water and unsweetened fruit juice are your best choices.

Sometimes problems with a mother's health can affect her milk supply and her baby's weight gain. If you are having any health problems, check with your doctor about them. Most medications are safe for nursing mothers, but some can adversely affect your milk production. If a doctor prescribes any medication for you, be sure to mention that you're breastfeeding.

The use of combined oral contraceptives can reduce milk production and also alter the nutritional quality of your milk. There is concern, too, about the long-term effects of hormones that are passed on to the baby through the mother's milk. Remember that breastfeeding delays the return of fertility for several months.

Smoking can also have a detrimental effect on your milk supply and your baby's well-being. Mothers who smoke may find that their babies gain better and are healthier when they cut down or stop smoking.

# INCREASING YOUR MILK SUPPLY

If you do find that some or all of the above factors have caused your milk supply to decrease, there are some positive steps you can follow to increase your supply of milk. If you are in a situation where you are concerned about your milk supply, it will be very helpful to get in touch with an LLL Leader. While we can offer you basic information here, she can often supply additional insight based on your specific situation.

If your baby is not gaining weight, or is losing weight, you'll want to be sure to keep in close touch with your doctor. There is always a possibility that a health problem is causing baby's slow weight gain. In addition to going over the points listed here to improve your milk supply, be sure to read the section in Chapter 17 on "Slow Weight Gain."

**NURSE FREQUENTLY** for as long as your baby will nurse. Plan to spend twenty-four to forty-eight hours (or longer if your supply is quite low) doing little else but nursing and resting. A sleepy baby may need to be awakened and encouraged to nurse more frequently.

**OFFER BOTH BREASTS AT EACH FEEDING.** This will ensure that your baby gets all the milk available and that both breasts are stimulated frequently.

**TRY SWITCH NURSING.** Switching breasts two or three times throughout each feeding will help to keep your baby interested in nursing and ensure that your baby receives the richest part of your milk. Watch baby's sucking and swallowing as he nurses, and switch to the other breast as soon as the sucking slows down and he swallows less often. For some babies, this will be about ten minutes on each side, for others it could be as little as two or three minutes. Be sure to use both breasts at least twice at each feeding.

**ALL YOUR BABY'S SUCKING SHOULD BE AT THE BREAST.** Avoid bottles and pacifiers as they can confuse the baby. Drinking from a bottle nipple requires a different type of sucking than nursing at mother's breast. If some supplement is necessary temporarily, it can be given with a nursing supplementer while baby nurses or by spoon. (See the Appendix for information about the nursing supplementer.) Pacifiers can interfere with the extra nursing that is needed when you are trying to build up your milk.

**GIVE YOUR BABY ONLY BREAST MILK.** Avoid all solids, water, and juice. If your baby has been receiving formula supplements you will not want to cut these out abruptly. You can gradually cut back on the amount of supplement as your milk supply increases, but you need to watch baby's wet and soiled diapers to be sure he is getting enough to eat. You need to be in touch with your doctor to monitor your baby's weight gain as you are cutting back on formula supplements.

**DRINK PLENTY OF LIQUIDS** and **EAT A WELL-BALANCED DIET.** Eat a wide variety of foods in as close to their natural state as possible. Try to have a glass of water or juice with you each time you nurse. **GET PLENTY OF REST AND RELAXATION.** Your milk supply will increase faster if you are relaxed and rested. Plan to do as little as possible for a while. Cut out *all* non-essential tasks. Be sure to take naps with your baby as often as possible. For relaxation, try a warm bath, soft music, exercise, or whatever works best for *you*. Try to spend at least a few minutes each day doing something special to pamper yourself.

After reading through this section, if you have any further questions or concerns be sure to get in touch with your La Leche League Leader and read the section later in this book on "Slow Weight Gain." Being in touch with other breastfeeding mothers through your La Leche League Group will offer you the support and encouragement you need to increase your milk supply. Your happy, healthy breastfed baby will soon provide the reward for your efforts.

# The Baby Who Is Pleasingly Plump

If your breastfed baby is a round little fatty, some may say he's gaining too much. While he may weigh more than the average shown on the doctor's charts, the baby on breast milk alone will not be overweight. According to Dr. Derrick Jelliffe, a totally breastfed baby who is "overweight" is not necessarily overfat or obese. Still, in a weight-conscious world, even baby fat is suspect, and the mother of a plump, fully breastfed baby may be told that her child should be put on a diet.

Heredity plays a definite role in determining a child's growth pattern, as became obvious in the Nixon family in Florida. Baby Alena weighed almost eighteen pounds at three and a half months, and her mother, Janice, was told that the development of a large number of fat cells in infancy would cause Alena problems later in life. This was Janice's first child and she was understandably upset. "But I thought back over all I had read or heard at the LLL meetings I had been going to since my eighth month of pregnancy," Janice recounted. "Was Alena happy and alert most of the time? Yes. Was she developing well in all other aspects? Yes."

Janice also remembered her mother telling her that she herself had been a very large baby, and she and her mother searched the family album for baby pictures. "A picture of my mother when she was a baby also showed her to be extremely chubby, and she was completely breastfed." Their findings were meaningful because, as Janice points out, "Neither of us has had a weight problem as an adult."

At the four-month checkup, Alena weighed in at almost nineteen pounds and was twenty-five inches long—way above the norms. Janice showed the doctor the family pictures:

*When the doctor saw the pictures, he was so impressed that he called in another doctor to look at them. They talked about the loopholes in the "fat cell" theory, and the obvious fact that fat babies do not always become fat adults. They both agreed that there was no reason for me to alter Alena's present care in any way. Absolutely no diet!*

There are hazards in limiting growth by putting a baby on a diet. The young child is a dynamic body builder, producing cells of all kinds, brain and nerve cells as well as fat cells. Researchers have observed that the flesh of the breastfed baby is firmer than that of a bottle-fed infant. There are no "empty" calories in breast milk, as there are in highly processed foods.

It must be remembered here that fat accumulated in the relatively inactive pre-toddler stage is preparatory for the highly active time when the busy toddler hardly has time to eat. It is not unlike the extra weight that a woman puts on during pregnancy in preparation for the extra demands of motherhood. We have found that by age two or three, the heavyweights among the tiny tots usually slim down beautifully.

Betty Scholz from Ohio confirms this with the story of her daughter's weight gain:

*Becky was a large baby at birth—nine pounds four ounces—and she thrived on breast milk. Many of our friends and relatives were worried about her because she was gaining so much weight. One week she gained fifteen ounces! Although she was exclusively breastfed, by the time she was six months old she was over twenty-one pounds.*

*Nature took its course, and eventually the rate of weight gain slowed down. Becky did not really enjoy eating solids until she turned one year old, at which time she was only twenty-two pounds. She is now a happy, healthy, sixteen-month-old toddler who drinks from a cup (she never did have a bottle), but still loves her "milky" several times a day.*

Some babies who start out tiny and petite at birth surprise everyone with their rapid gain. Ann Tutor from Japan tells how she handled critics with the comment, "We grow them big at our house!" She writes:

*Although Melanie weighed in at six pounds ten ounces at birth, by the time we left the hospital she was six pounds even and seemed to me the tiniest, prettiest little baby girl I had ever seen.*

*We attended our first La Leche League meeting when Melanie was one month old. She weighed nine pounds at her two-month checkup, and by the second League meeting we attended I began to notice that while Melanie had started out smaller than some of the other babies, she had caught up and even passed a few of her little friends. When she was about three months old, people began to casually mention how big my "dainty little girl" was getting, and at her four-month checkup I was surprised to find out that she weighed eighteen pounds.*

*When at six months Melanie weighed twenty-four pounds, she became a real conversation piece. While I was proud to have a healthy, happy baby, I began to worry about and even resent some of the comments about my baby's weight. Thank goodness my League friends and my wonderful doctor kept assuring me that as long as Melanie was totally breastfed we were doing great! My doctor even*

*A mother doesn't need to worry that her breastfed baby is gaining "too much."*

paraded Melanie around to his colleagues at one visit to show them this lovably round, totally breastfed baby.

Melanie is seventeen months old now and weighs thirty-one pounds, and while she doesn't yet have to worry about being called skinny, she has slimmed down considerably. We still get comments and questions about her once in a while, some of which still aggravate me, but I don't worry about Melanie's weight anymore. We're in no hurry to end our nursing days. While I hope that Melanie doesn't keep that cute round tummy and those dimpled thighs forever, I know she has had a wonderful start in being breastfed.

## WEIGHT PROBLEMS IN LATER YEARS

While some people may be concerned that too much weight gained in infancy will lead to obesity later on, the truth is that many factors contribute to weight problems in adults. Some aspects that are related to eating habits in childhood are automatically avoided when you breastfeed your baby and follow the other guidelines included in this book.

As a breastfeeding mother, you are not going to fall into the anxiety trap of monitoring how many ounces of milk your baby takes. You will not get into the habit of coaxing him to finish the last few ounces in a bottle. When you start solids, your child will probably be at least six months old. You will have bypassed the unnatural situation that comes when solids are given to the younger child, who automatically pushes out whatever is spooned into his mouth, making it difficult for a mother to know if her baby is hungry or not.

Breastfeeding is the first preventive measure against obesity in adult life. In fact, a recent study showed that breastfeeding protects against later obesity. Children who were breastfed were found to be less likely to be overweight in adolescence.

Good eating habits do start early, and you can be assured that your baby is receiving the very best nutrition available if he is breastfed.

# Did You Ever Hear of a Nursing Strike?

Occasionally a young baby will suddenly refuse to nurse for no apparent reason. This can be a real puzzle, especially if the baby is under a year old and probably not at all ready to be weaned.

A situation like this is called a nursing strike. It's baby's way of communicating the fact that something's wrong. It usually lasts from two to four days and requires some motherly ingenuity to figure out exactly what the problem is.

How can you tell whether your baby has gone on a nursing strike or has just decided to wean himself? A baby who is really ready to wean will usually be well over a year old, will be eating lots of solid food and drinking liquids from a cup, and will gradually lose interest in one nursing at a time. A baby who is on a nursing strike may not be eating much or drinking from a cup at all. He nurses fine one day and abruptly refuses to nurse at all the next day. He also shows signs of being obviously unhappy about the whole situation. He wants you to figure out what's wrong and solve the problem for him.

Consider the following possibilities: Is your baby teething? Does he have a cold or stuffy nose that prevents him from nursing easily? Does he have an earache that makes it painful to nurse? Are you anxious or upset about something? Babies respond to their mothers' feelings.

Has nursing become a stressful time, with too many outside interruptions or distractions? Have you been deciding when the baby should nurse and when he should stop, instead of letting him lead the way? Has the baby become dependent on a pacifier or his thumb, so that he routinely sucks quite a bit on either?

Has some recent change in your nursing pattern confused the baby? Has he had too many bottles? Been left with a sitter? Been repeatedly put off when he cries to nurse? Have you gone back to work, or are you worrying about what will happen when and if you do have to leave the baby?

Sometimes a nursing strike occurs after baby bites mother a time or two, and your understandable reaction has upset him. He bites, you jump or let out a startled cry. Baby is frightened, cries, and won't resume nursing for fear of another jolt or yell.

Sometimes the unexpected can cause a baby to refuse to nurse. Mary Shumeyko of New Jersey writes:

*The other day our twenty-month-old, Jonathan, bumped his chin. His mouth seemed to be bleeding a bit, so we wiped it off, I nursed him, and he continued playing. I went back to what I was doing. Several hours later, after happily nursing to sleep, Jonathan awoke crying in obvious pain. I offered him my breast. He tried to nurse, then drew away, crying harder. This continued all night, with Jonathan waking every half hour or so, and my husband or I walking the floor with him since he wouldn't nurse.*

*The next morning he seemed to feel better and tentatively asked to nurse. When he opened his mouth I discovered the problem: he had cut his tongue when he bumped his chin, and (after the initial numbness wore off) nursing obviously had been quite painful. My heart went out to him. Not only had he injured himself, but his standard "cure-all" hurt even more. Fortunately the mouth heals quickly, and he's once again nursing regularly. The episode was a good reinforcement for me, though. After one night of not nursing, I'm more aware than ever of how precious this beautiful relationship is.*

Even if you are not sure why the baby has gone on a nursing strike, you will want to help him get back to regular nursing as soon and easily as possible. Try nursing him when he is very sleepy, or already asleep. Many babies who refuse to nurse while awake will nurse when they are drowsy or asleep. Some babies are more likely to nurse if mother is walking about rather than sitting still. In any case, plan to devote yourself almost entirely to the baby for a few days. Lots of cuddling and stroking and maybe some relaxing time spent just with mom away from the hubbub of the rest of the family may calm the baby and encourage him to start nursing again. Rethink your priorities. You will both be better off and happier when things get back to normal again.

A mother from Guam, Becki Hallowell, found that calling her La Leche League Leader helped get to the bottom of her problem:

*We were on our third day of six-month-old Todd's refusing to nurse when I decided that something had to change. We were at wits' end, and I was in pain from engorgement. My husband had been very supportive but was finding the situation increasingly difficult as I became more and more upset. He begged me to call Linda, our La Leche League Leader. "She'll be able to help you," he said.*

*Linda and I talked it over, and she suggested the possibility of a nursing strike. I had been too close to the situation to recognize the problem, but soon realized we had all the usual causes and then some.*

*1) We all had bad colds.*

*2) Solids had been introduced on a trial basis and seemed to upset him.*

*3) We were all very tired and in a new situation with extra stress. Todd's grandparents, whom we hadn't seen in a year, were visiting us for a month. During their visit, Grandpa ended up in the hospital. There had also been two recent deaths in our family.*

*4) Todd had been biting me due to teething, and I had reacted strongly.*

*Our solutions were to relax and try to nurse him as often as possible, especially while he was sleeping. We also kept in close physical touch by my carrying him around the house in his usual nursing position.*

*After we began to try these solutions, the strike continued one more day (a total of four) and then nursing became easier. But it did take time to get back to normal. We found during this transition time that the swimming pool was perfect for relaxed nursing. Todd is a swimmer and loves the water. It took another week, but thanks to La Leche League and Linda, we're a happy nursing family once again.*

Carol Strait, an Iowa mother, sheds some light on another reason why some babies may refuse to nurse:

*W*hen *my two-and-a-half-month-old baby girl began refusing the breast, a thousand thoughts ran through my mind—I must be eating the wrong foods, maybe she was teething, I was probably too nervous (what nursing mother wouldn't be nervous when her new baby suddenly refused to nurse?), perhaps she was weaning herself—and even the fearful thought that she didn't like me! Quite by accident I discovered the answer to our problem. My first clue was that Christie always seemed fussier and wouldn't nurse just after I had showered and applied spray deodorant. I'm not sure what ingredients in the spray were responsible, but my problem was easily solved by simply switching from a spray to a solid stick deodorant. Now my little girl and I are a happy nursing couple again.*

## HOLIDAY WEANING

Another disruption in the normal course of nursing that sometimes catches mothers by surprise is the "holiday weaning syndrome." It occurs when holidays or other especially hectic times, such as moving, result in our getting so busy that we overlook our baby's needs. It's easy to put off that nice quiet moment of nursing when there are so many other demands on our time. In the midst of cooking, entertaining, shopping, and such, the leisurely closeness of the nursing relationship is temporarily or even permanently lost. Solids or bottles may be tried to tide baby over, or perhaps he's "good" and consents to wait—and wait—for nursing time to come around. And then suddenly, no one knows quite how, baby is weaned. Toni Pepe from Connecticut describes holiday weaning:

*A unique season in the private life of the baby has been cut short, and later, in the long days at home, come the regrets. Guard against holiday weaning. In the seasons of the world, these days of celebration return again and again—but the special season of nursing comes only once in the life of a child.*

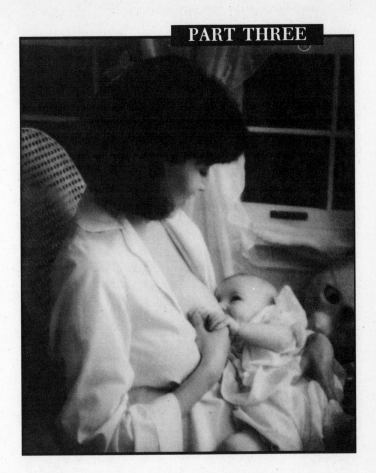

# PART THREE

# *Going Back to Work*

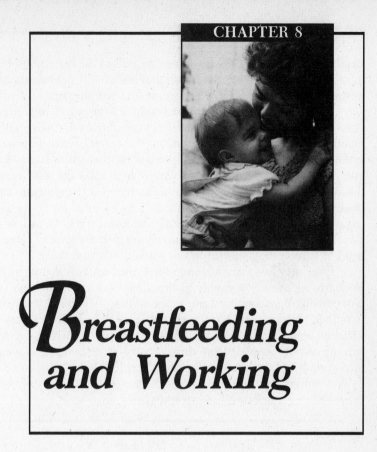

CHAPTER 8

# $\mathcal{B}$reastfeeding and Working

If you plan to return to your job after your baby is born, you may be wondering if you should even consider breastfeeding your baby. By all means, you can look forward to being a nursing mother. Not only is breastfeeding possible, many working mothers consider it easier than bottle feeding. Breastfeeding is a joy for both mother and baby. Usually, a quiet time with baby at the breast is the last thing on the agenda before mother goes off to work and the first thing she does when she returns home.

You may even be able to furnish your baby with all the milk he needs while you are gone. You may be thinking, "All right, but isn't breastfeeding difficult when a mother has to miss feedings?" It does take some extra effort, and it requires that you plan ahead, but isn't that true of most worthwhile things in life?

In many ways breastfeeding simplifies life with a baby. When at home there are no bottles to prepare, disruption of sleep can be minimized, and the one-on-one attention every baby needs is practically guaranteed despite the other demands of the household. In addition, the protection from illness that breast milk provides is an advantage that is especially important to a working mother.

In fact, the breastfeeding relationship may be particularly precious to the mother who is regularly separated from her baby. The emotional closeness can contribute to the special bond between mother and baby, helping to compensate for their time apart. As one working mother said, "I love being able to make the shift from the workaday world to the world of family with the closeness of breastfeeding." Another mother added, "I wish I could tell all working mothers how much easier, special, and joyful it is to breastfeed. I am surprised to find that some people seem sorry for me and others think it is so courageous to do the perfectly natural thing."

Charlotte Lee Carrihill from New York works full time as a stock broker but she was able to breastfeed her son Colin and is now nursing her daughter Laura. She writes: "The bond that we have built through these nursing experiences will be with us always. Through breastfeeding, I have learned more about mothering. I have learned to put 'people before things.' Nursing isn't only a way to feed your baby, it's a way to comfort and love your baby, too."

A mother from Indiana, Leslie Koczan, tells this story of her experience as a working breastfeeding mother:

---

*I knew that I had no choice but to return to work shortly after Laura's birth, although I would have dearly loved to stay home with her. I returned to work when Laura was only seven weeks old. She was so tiny and precious, and so very difficult to leave.*

*Our nursing relationship sustained us and strengthened our bond, despite the daily separation. For mothers who must work, I would strongly encourage breastfeeding. For me the major advantage was this: It was the one thing that I could do for my baby that the sitter could not do. It was a special bond between my baby and myself.*

*By seven weeks of age, Laura's need to nurse followed a fairly regular three-hour pattern. So, depending upon when she had last nursed in the morning, the sitter gave Laura a bottle of my milk about three hours later. I took my lunch hour to coincide with her next feeding and nursed her while eating my sack lunch. The sitter gave her another bottle three hours later, and I nursed her immediately after work. For each missed feeding, I pumped my breasts. I collected the milk in disposable bags, marked it with the amount and date, and stored it in a freezer at work. Each evening, I took that day's milk to the sitter's to be stored in her deep freeze until needed.*

*There were several important factors contributing to our success:*

• *I found a sitter close to my workplace, so I could be with Laura each noon. This also gave us an extra hour together driving to and from work. My sitter, coincidentally, had been very active in LLL and therefore was very supportive of my nursing.*

• *Laura was given a bottle only by the sitter. No bottles were ever given at home.*

• *My job was sufficiently flexible to allow me time to pump twice a day and to take my lunch hour beginning anywhere from 11:00 AM to 2:00 PM. Knowing that the need to pump would end as Laura got older made it more acceptable to my supervisor. It also helped keep up my morale when I became tired of pumping. After about three months, I was pumping only once a day and in another month, not at all.*

• *I became active in a local LLL Group who were very supportive and encouraging.*

• *Last, but definitely not least, I had lots of help from my older daughter and husband, who fixed sack lunches every morning, started dinner in the evening, changed diapers, and entertained the baby.*

# What Mothers Say

To find out more specific information about how employment affects breastfeeding, Kathleen Auerbach, PhD, a lactation consultant, La Leche League Leader, and editor of La Leche League's Lactation Consultant Series, surveyed 567 married and single employed nursing mothers.

When these women's responses were tabulated, certain patterns emerged. Of the factors Dr. Auerbach analyzed, how soon after their babies' birth the mothers returned to work seemed to have the most influence on the course of breastfeeding. This affected breastfeeding even more than the number of hours a week the mothers worked. Mothers who rejoined the work force when their babies were at least sixteen weeks old typically nursed longer than those who returned to work sooner. This may be because their milk supplies were solidly established and they had had more experience breastfeeding.

Whether the mothers worked full time or part time also affected how long breastfeeding continued. A greater percentage of the mothers working part time nursed their babies for at least a year. The longer a mother waited to return to work and the fewer hours per day she worked, the longer she was likely to nurse.

Another variable that influenced the course of breastfeeding was whether or not the mothers expressed their milk when they missed a feeding. Eighty-six percent of the mothers surveyed expressed milk by hand or pump while they were away from their babies and forty-nine percent fed their babies only breast milk until they were ready for solids at about six months. Mothers who chose to express their milk were more likely to nurse longer than those who did not.

Expressing milk offered five main advantages: 1) It helped keep up the mothers' milk supplies; 2) It provided breast milk for their babies, lessening the risk of sensitizing them to allergies through formula; 3) It prevented or relieved uncomfortable fullness; 4) It minimized leaking; and 5) It helped prevent plugged ducts or breast infections, which may develop if the breasts remain overly full.

Pumping or expressing seemed to accomplish its purpose best when it was done every three hours or so. For the mother who was away from her baby for six hours, two pumping sessions were usually sufficient. If mother and baby were apart for eight to ten hours, three pumping sessions seemed to be needed.

Breastfeeding problems (such as leaking, engorgement, and breast infections) were most commonly alleviated when the mothers began expressing milk at work or expressed their milk more often. Some mothers solved their problems by revising their priorities—making more time to be with their families and learning to leave work at the workplace.

When asked if they would combine breastfeeding and working with future babies, the responses were overwhelmingly in favor of breastfeeding. Eighty-two percent of the mothers said they would again choose to combine breastfeeding and working: eighteen percent said that with future children there was no doubt they would breastfeed, but they would make other choices regarding work, such as giving it up entirely, delaying their return until their children were older, or reducing their work hours.

*Working mothers usually find it best to nurse the baby just before they leave for work and as soon as they get home.*

One extremely important element was the mothers' motivation to continue breastfeeding. As one mother from New York put it:

*There were not problems—only situations to be dealt with. For me nursing was "the only game in town" and I didn't even consider weaning when I returned to work. Nobody and no situation could deter me. With this attitude, success was inevitable.*

## Proceed Slowly

The length of time a mother is able to spend at home with her baby before returning to work is an important factor in assuring success at breastfeeding. Also, a mother and baby have a great need to be together in the early months. Once you hold your baby in your arms you'll probably decide you want to delay returning to your job for as long as you can so you and your baby can enjoy this precious time together.

Bargain for as long a maternity leave as you can possibly manage. If at all possible, arrange to be home at least six to eight weeks after your baby is born. Three months at home with your baby is better yet. If you can stretch the time to six months, you will probably have seen him to the time when he begins to take other foods. The longer you can stay home with your baby, the longer both of you will enjoy the benefits of being together.

Stretching your maternity leave may mean using vacation time or accumulated sick or personal leave. Sometimes this leave will be paid, other times it will be an unpaid leave with an understanding that your job will only be held for a certain number of weeks or months. Some companies are willing to add an unpaid leave of six months or so onto a standard maternity leave. Policies are changing as more and more people, both men and women, request provisions for extended leaves for a variety of reasons. It is worth your while to look into the company's past treatment of employees who have received personal time off for whatever reasons.

Mothers and babies need time to be together in the early days and weeks. This is a special season in the life of a child, a time when mother and baby establish a relationship meant to last a lifetime. Whatever your plans for the future months, take time now to nurture this new human being.

In *Creative Parenting*, Dr. William Sears explains.

---

*Your commitment to parenting and your investment in the infancy period create a strong parent-infant attachment which helps prevent problems in later years. Infancy is the critical period for establishing bonds of love and security, and a trust in the environment.*

---

## TRY WORKING "MOTHER HOURS"

When the time comes that you can no longer postpone making a decision about returning to work, try to begin with a part-time schedule. Returning to work for three days a week will be easier on you and your baby than five days a week. Being separated for just six hours a day can make it easier to continue breastfeeding than being gone for eight or nine hours a day. Keep an open mind about such options. If you have specialized skills or years of training, your employer may be willing to make adjustments rather than losing you entirely.

# Some Practical Hints

If you plan to combine breastfeeding and working, you'll want to learn how to pump or express your milk. The milk you collect while separated from your baby can be given to him the next day. Expressing your milk will continue to stimulate your milk supply and avoid overly full breasts.

## SAVING YOUR MILK FOR YOUR BABY

No other milk or formula is as good for your baby as your own breast milk. Many mothers are able to provide enough milk to satisfy all their baby's needs while they are away. This involves knowing some techniques for storing breast milk properly and giving it to the baby. You'll want to be sure your sitter is aware of the need for certain precautions in handling the milk you leave for your baby.

New research has shown that human milk can safely be kept at room temperature for six to ten hours because of its remarkable ability to retard the growth of bacteria. Milk can be kept refrigerated for three to five days. For longer storage, it can be frozen after that. Frozen milk can be kept up to two weeks in the freezer compartment of your refrigerator, up to four months in a separate door freezer that is opened frequently. It can be kept six months or longer in a separate freezer that stays at a constant 0° F. Once the milk is thawed, it cannot be refrozen; if the freezer defrosts for any reason, the milk must be discarded.

After pumping or expressing your milk into a clean container, transfer it into a storage container, baby bottle, or plastic nurser bag. Use a separate container to refrigerate the milk each time you pump or express. These cooled batches can later be combined for a feeding or for freezing. You can add refrigerated milk to milk that is already frozen, just be sure the amount you are adding is smaller than the amount already frozen so it does not thaw the frozen milk. Allow room for expansion when filling containers for freezing. Do not tighten caps until milk is completely frozen.

Freeze the milk in small amounts varying from two to four ounces. There will be less waste this way as the sitter can choose the amount according to baby's hunger or usual feeding pattern. Always label each container with the month, date, and year. If your milk will be used in a situation where more than one baby is being fed, you'll want to add baby's name on each container.

When using plastic nurser bags, use them doubled to avoid tearing. Squeeze out the air at the top, roll down to one inch above the milk, fasten, and place into a container which will hold it upright until it is frozen solid. Plastic nurser bags are not recommended for long-term storage.

## COLLECTING YOUR MILK

There are a number of inexpensive manual breast pumps available today, but many mothers find that hand-expressing their milk is easy and convenient. (See Chapter 7 for more information on pumping or hand-expressing your milk.)

Don't be discouraged if the amount of milk obtained is small at first. With practice many mothers are able to pump several ounces in fifteen to twenty minutes. It is normal for the amount to vary from one pumping session to the next.

Follow the manufacturer's directions in caring for any type of pump. Usually it is necessary to clean the parts carefully after each use and sterilize the pump occasionally. Talk to other mothers about the types of pump they find effective. LLL does not recommend the type of pump which requires squeezing a rubber bulb to draw out the milk, as the mother has little control over the amount of suction and these are usually not very effective.

## WHEN AND WHERE TO PUMP

Some mothers start pumping and storing their milk ahead of the time they will be returning to work in order to have a reserve supply available. Others pump only while they are away and have enough for the baby's feedings on the following day. Some mothers pump once or twice a day in the morning or evening to be sure baby has enough to eat when they are gone. It is easy for some mothers to pump an ounce or two after baby has nursed.

The number of times you'll need to pump or express your milk while you are away from home will depend on the total length of time you are away from the baby as well as baby's age. It's usually best not to go more than three or four hours without removing milk from your breasts. If you are leaving a very young baby who has been nursing more often, you may need to pump or express your milk more frequently at first so your breasts do not get uncomfortably full or start to leak.

If your breasts start to leak at an inopportune time, apply firm pressure directly on the nipple for a minute or two. This can be done discreetly by folding your arms across your breasts. You don't want to do this too often, though, as it is better to relieve the fullness by removing some milk. You can purchase nursing pads to wear inside your bra to absorb this leakage. After a while, your breasts will adjust to your new schedule and you will have fewer problems with leaking.

Finding a suitable location for pumping or expressing your milk will depend on each individual situation. You may be able to use a private office, an isolated store room, or the women's lounge. You'll want someplace where you can relax and have some privacy. Some mothers find leaning over a sink helps avoid milk dripping on their clothes and makes use of gravity in removing the milk. Wearing two-piece outfits will make your pumping sessions less bothersome.

If you prefer to keep your milk cool and no refrigerator is available where you work, you can use an insulated thermos or small cooler. Put ice into the thermos in the morning to get it cold, then pour out the ice and add your milk. You can keep ice packs in the cooler and add the containers of your milk throughout the day. You can also use one of these methods to keep your milk cool on your way home.

## GIVING YOUR MILK TO THE BABY

Your milk can be given to the baby by bottle, spoon, cup, or eyedropper. You don't need to introduce the bottle in baby's first few weeks just because you'll be returning to work later on. Some babies refuse to take a bottle from mother when they know the breast is right nearby, but they soon become accustomed to taking a bottle from the sitter. Explain to the sitter that your baby may need some persuasion in learning to accept a bottle. Since you'll want the baby and the sitter to get to know each other before you actually return to work, these get-acquainted visits can be a good time for the sitter to get the baby used to taking a bottle.

The sitter needs to know that you plan to leave your own milk for the baby and what precautions will be necessary in handling it. Also be sure to emphasize that you do not want the baby given formula or other foods without your permission and that your baby should be held while he is being fed. Stress that you don't want your baby left to cry.

## OTHER SUPPLEMENTS

Mothers usually instruct the sitter to give the baby only breast milk if it is available. Any other supplement, if needed, should be prescribed by the baby's doctor. You'll be better off if your baby receives the fewest number of bottles possible. Liquids can be given by spoon or cup. As much as possible, you'll want to satisfy baby's sucking needs at the breast. If your baby is older than three or four months, consider asking your doctor if you could start some mashed banana as a supplement instead of introducing formula.

## FEEDING TIPS FOR THE SITTER

Refrigerated breast milk will separate as it is not homogenized. Shake gently to mix. If milk has been refrigerated in small batches, you can mix these together for a feeding. To warm the milk, hold it under warm running water for several minutes until it reaches room temperature or immerse the container of milk into a pan of water that has been heated on the stove. Do not heat the milk itself directly on the stove or in a microwave oven as valuable components of the milk can be destroyed.

To thaw frozen milk, hold the container under cool running water and gradually add warmer water until milk is thawed and warmed to room temperature. If hot running water is not available, heat a pan of water on the stove and immerse the container of frozen milk into the warm water. If necessary, remove the container of milk to reheat the water. If more than one container is being thawed, you can combine the milk for a feeding.

Breast milk that has been frozen and thawed can safely be kept refrigerated for up to nine hours and possibly longer. It was once thought that leftover milk had to be discarded, but recent studies have shown that breast milk actually retards the growth of bacteria so it is considered safe to refrigerate unused milk for later use. Thawed breast milk can be refrigerated for later use but should not be refrozen.

If baby seems hungry just before mother is due home, try to keep him satisfied with just a small amount of milk as mother will want to nurse the baby as soon as she arrives.

Be sure all bottles, nipples, or spoons used to feed the baby are kept clean. Washing your hands is important before feeding the baby and after changing his diaper.

# DELAY INTRODUCING THE BOTTLE

Many mothers who are planning to return to work may be tempted to begin using bottles early "to get the baby used to them." But there are several reasons why this can bring a quick end to breastfeeding. Giving formula in the early weeks is known to interfere with a new mother's milk supply. The amount of milk a mother produces is determined by how often her baby nurses and how much her baby takes from the breast. Giving formula during this adjustment period sometimes short-circuits this "demand-and-supply" process, reducing the amount of milk produced. The milk supply is usually well established by six weeks postpartum.

Another reason to delay giving bottles is to avoid confusing a newborn with an artificial nipple. Nursing at the breast requires more active participation from a baby than taking liquid from a bottle. If both breast and bottle are given during the impressionable early weeks, a baby may try to suck the breast as he sucks the rubber nipple. Babies who become nipple confused suck less efficiently at the breast and do not gain well or may refuse to nurse altogether. A pacifier sometimes produces this same effect. Once a baby is four to six weeks old and has had lots of practice nursing, nipple confusion is less of a problem.

Remember, too, that if baby does refuse the bottle, supplements can be given by spoon or cup until baby gets used to the change.

# ESTABLISH A ROUTINE

Time will be a most precious commodity in your life. When a woman combines mothering and working, she must be a miser with her time. Don't overlook the trusty baby carrier to help you catch up with household work and keep the baby close to you. It has proved a blessing to all of us at times. And don't be surprised if your baby becomes something of a "night owl," wide awake, bright-eyed, and busy in the center of family activities during the evening hours. Some working mothers tell us that they deliberately encourage an up-at-night, down-during-the-day sleeping pattern for the baby. If the baby sleeps for longer periods while mother is away, he will take fewer bottles during the day and be more eager to nurse in the evenings.

Try setting your alarm for at least twenty minutes before you have to get up. Nurse the baby during this time (even if he's still half asleep) so that he's more likely to be content while you dress and prepare for the day. Then nurse again just before you leave. It'll calm you both and make separation a bit smoother.

If you and your baby are separated for a considerable length of time, give special attention to your homecoming. Plan on sitting (or lying) down and nursing or playing with the baby for the first thirty minutes after you arrive home. Everyone will be more relaxed and dinner preparation won't be so chaotic. Keep nutritious snacks on hand for both you and the family.

Drink plenty of fluids and eat a nutritious diet of simple wholesome foods. Get most of your daily liquid in water, juice, or milk. The biggest problem mothers face is fatigue. This is especially true for employed breastfeeding mothers. Adequate rest will make life smoother and alleviate many problems.

Starting a new job, or even taking up where you left off in the old one, is very tiring for a new mother. One suggestion is to start back to work on a Thursday instead of a Monday so you'll have the weekend to recuperate before facing a full workweek.

Many working nursing mothers are able to nurse their babies full time on their days off or on weekends with no problem making the adjustment. If you have been pumping regularly while at work, your milk production will be about the same. (You can freeze the milk you pump on Friday for the sitter to give the baby on Monday.) Even if baby needs a supplement during your absence, frequent nursing on the weekend will supply him with plenty of milk, probably much more than you can remove by pumping. In this case, you may experience some fullness on Monday because of the increased stimulation over the weekend. It will make your pumping efforts easier.

## NIGHTTIME NURSING

Be prepared for more evening, nighttime, and early morning nursings. Bringing the baby to bed with you is a definite plus.

Lori Brewster, a mother of two from Michigan, found nighttime nursings very special. She and her husband work opposite shifts in the automotive industry so one of them is home while the other one is at work.

*T*he first time I was pregnant, I was sure that I wanted to nurse. I breastfed Matthew for eight weeks but weaned him when I had to return to work. I found out later that weaning was not necessary.

When I got pregnant for the second time, I knew that I wanted to breastfeed once again. This time instead of just turning to books, I contacted my local La Leche League Leader. That turned out to be the best phone call of my family's life.

Since the birth of Amy Rose five months ago, she and I have nursed happily. I returned to work after eight short weeks of leave, but brought to work my breast pump and cooler. While I am at work, I pump my breasts three times a day. On Friday I freeze bottles for Monday. While at home, I nurse on demand and love it.

The nights are very special for Amy and me. People think I am crazy when I tell them she nurses four or five times during the night. They wonder how in the world I can survive. They do not understand that she sleeps right next to me. Nighttime is my favorite time of the day.

After breastfeeding Matt and then going to bottles, I knew that I did not want to do that again. Bottles are such a hassle. Now when I get home, I just have to sterilize my pump and a few bottles and I am done and have the rest of the evening for my family. If you have never breastfed, you can't appreciate the convenience. Take it from one who has done both, "Breast is best."

I would encourage any mother to read all she can but also contact La Leche League for the support needed. If you are working full time, don't let that stop you from nursing your baby.

# Who Will Take Care of the Baby?

The most important task you will face before you go back to work is finding the best person possible to care for your baby while you are gone. Can you arrange for a family member to take over this responsibility? The baby's father is an obvious first choice, if he is available. The element of change for the baby will be minimized. A loving grandmother or an aunt who is already familiar to the baby are also high on the list of choices. A motherly neighbor may be interested in caring for your little one during the day.

Most people, though, are not fortunate enough to have a family member or friendly neighbor available as a sitter and must look further. They must then concern themselves with references and interviews. If the sitter is new to the baby, by all means have her come to your home a few times so the two of them can get acquainted before you begin working. Be sure to tell her that you are breastfeeding and explain in detail how you want the baby fed, what his likes and dislikes are, what his sleeping pattern is, and, most important, the fact that you do not want your baby to be left to cry. Let her observe your interaction with the baby so she can see how he is accustomed to being handled. And you can watch how the sitter and the baby relate to one another to be sure she is the right person to care for your baby.

Think about finding a sitter who lives close to your place of work rather than close to where you live. This would make it possible for you to visit the baby at lunch time or have the sitter bring the baby to you.

When choosing a sitter, look for someone who will give your baby as nearly as possible the same single-minded devotion and care that you give him yourself—someone who knows babies—who understands their needs. Will she sing to him? Talk to him? Rock him gently to sleep? Keep him dry and comfortable and always close by?

Constancy in nurturing is the means by which a child learns to trust others. A baby needs a loving, nurturing person, and this person should be the same someone, not an often changing parade of new faces and personalities. While a working mother naturally hopes to find such a reliable, loving substitute, she should also be aware that over a period of time, her baby will inevitably grow to love this "other mother."

You must also face the possibility that the patient, caring sitter you have this morning may announce at nightfall that she is moving away or taking another job. Such a disruption can be a serious loss for a young child.

Because of the unpredictability of finding and keeping a private sitter, working mothers may consider a day-care center as a solution. While there is a degree of permanence in a day-care center, here, too, workers come and go. And while the decorations may be charming, children under the age of three may not adjust well to a group situation. A young child was not meant to compete for attention with a large number of children of similar ages. Often a child will enjoy short play sessions in a preschool setting, but all-day care may become a threatening situation. Group care in a day-care center falls far short of meeting a baby's or toddler's need to relate to one person, to count on one person for loving attention at any time. The chances of illness and infection are also considerably greater when children are in a group setting.

In the New York Times Magazine, Sally E. Shaywitz, MD, had this to say about mother substitutes:

*We do not know enough about nurturing to be able to tell mothers that if they find a person or an institution that meets such-and-such standards that this will be an adequate mother substitute. We can list people's credentials, pinpoint the standards for a day care center, but just as breast milk cannot be duplicated, neither can a mother. We cannot put mothering into a formula and come up with a person who has the special feeling for your child that you do. . . . Just as everyone but a mother is excluded from nursing a baby, so they are also excluded from those immense feelings of satisfaction and inner unity with the child. . . .*

For many mothers, separation from the baby turns out to be the hardest part of returning to work. Lisa Bicknell Casey of Oklahoma tells what happened to her:

*I was allowed only two short months off after Jason was born. I spent most of those two months recovering from his cesarean birth. It seemed I was no sooner on my feet being the kind of mother I wanted to be, when it came time to return to work.*

*After contacting my LLL Leader, I purchased a breast pump, and the week before I went back to work, I dutifully pumped my breasts. It seemed so slow and awkward. I doubted I could ever pump enough to feed my beautiful boy. Thank goodness it got easier.*

*That first week of work I cried every day after leaving Jason at the sitter's, but I was blessed with an excellent sitter whom Jason took to immediately. This only upset me more. After all, every day I was replaced by a bottle and a sitter. Would my baby need ME?*

*Things proceeded well in spite of my fears. Then one day the sitter had to give Jason almost eighteen ounces of breast milk. I was ready to give up. How could I possibly keep up with his demand? Fortunately, this only happened once. Before long Jason had adjusted his nursing so he was taking only eight to ten ounces during the day and nursing frequently at night. I did not hesitate to take Jason in bed with us from the start, so I slept through many feedings and was never really sure just how frequently he nursed at night.*

*Jason refuses his bottle if he knows I am around, which reinforces my confidence as a mother. I know now that my baby does need me. Jason and I are able to share the kind of physical closeness that working might have denied us. For a mother who reluctantly returned to work, breastfeeding has been a godsend.*

A mother who plans to combine breastfeeding and working would do well to find the time to attend La Leche League meetings. Breastfeeding mothers who are separated from their babies regularly need the important support that comes from being with other nursing mothers. Your baby is welcome at LLL meetings.

Is it all worth it? Would it be better to give up breastfeeding if you plan to return to your job? One working mother who had bottle-fed a previous baby and is now breastfeeding puts it this way. "Breastfeeding simplifies many things for me, plus it helps to ensure that when I am home, I am spending time with my children." Another mother says: "My child benefited both physically and emotionally from the time we spent as a nursing couple!" And many others add: "I didn't want my baby to miss out on the benefits of breastfeeding just because I had to return to work."

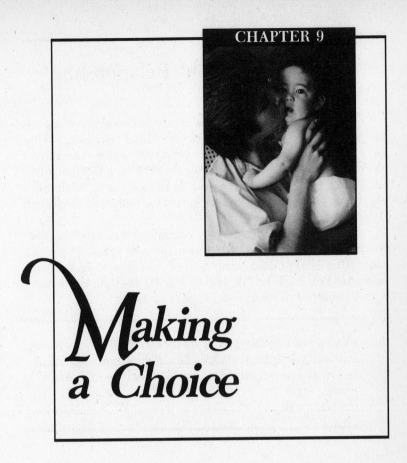

CHAPTER 9

# Making a Choice

Choosing whether or not to work outside your home after your baby is born is a complex decision. You'll want to take your time and evaluate your options before you reach a conclusion. Author Kaye Lowman talks about making this choice in her popular book, OF CRADLES AND CAREERS:

*A woman today is able to choose to be single or married, to pursue a career or to stay at home, to raise a family or to remain childless, to combine motherhood with a career or to make raising her children a full-time commitment. But make no mistake: the availability of so many options is a mixed blessing....Implicit in the freedom to choose is the obligation to choose wisely.*

# The Mother-Child Relationship

There are many important factors to be considered when you make the decision about returning to work after your baby is born. Let's take a look first at the mother-child relationship. This subject has fascinated the scientific community for a long time. A child's early years hold the clues to his future behavior as an adult. Society stands to gain or lose, depending on the soundness of mother-baby attachment.

La Leche League is strongly committed to a belief that babies and mothers need to be together in the early years. We are convinced that a baby's need for his mother's loving presence is as basic as his need for food. In THE HEART HAS ITS OWN REASONS, Mary Ann Cahill, one of La Leche League's founders, writes:

*No one can replace you as mother. From all the evidence, from all that is known about how babies grow and learn to live and to be competent adults, it can be said that a mother is the one most perfectly suited to be nurturer in the early years.*

Scientists hold that a child's initial one-to-one relationship with his mother is the foundation for emotional growth. From the security of the baby's ties to his mother he learns to relate to others. "The only true basis for the relationship of a child to mother and father, to other children, and eventually to society," Dr. W. Winnicott, a pediatrician from Great Britain, says, "is the first successful relationship between mother and baby."

In *Maternal Care and Mental Health,* John Bowlby, MD, a pioneer in the field of maternal-infant attachment, writes: "The mothering of a child is not something which can be arranged by roster; it is a live human relationship which alters the characters of both partners. . . .The provision of mothering cannot be considered in terms of hours per day but only in terms of the enjoyment of each other's company which mother and child obtain. Such enjoyment and close identification of feeling is only possible for either party if the relationship is continuous."

## SEPARATION BRINGS ANXIETY

In her book *Oneness and Separateness,* Dr. Louise Kaplan, psychologist and Director of the Mother-Infant Research Nursery of New York University, explains that an infant does not have an identity of his own at birth. Baby is in a state of oneness with his mother. Based on her work in mother-infant research, Dr. Kaplan states, "From the infant's point of view, there are no boundaries between himself and mother. They are one." The child must negotiate the move from oneness with his mother into separateness and a sense of individuality. It is a second birth that unfolds gradually in the first three years of life. Maintaining the early mother-baby relationship is extremely important to the successful completion of this journey.

And Selma Fraiberg, a professor of child psychoanalysis who wrote *Every Child's Birthright: In Defense of Mothering,* stated her views very emphatically:

*It has been determined that children who do not have the benefit of a single, sustained contact with a loving mother or mother-figure for at least the first three years of their lives, will—depending upon the degree of deprivation— manifest a diminished capacity to love others, impaired intellectual powers, and an inability to control their impulses, particularly in the area of aggression.*

A Canadian, Donna K. Kontos, PhD, consultant psychologist, comments, "There is at present no known substitute for a family environment for childrearing....Prolonged maternal separations cause distress to the child. All the research and all of the literature tell us that the best thing for an infant is to have a consistent good mother around most of the time."

Another psychologist, Dr. Joyce Brothers, recognizes the pressures on young mothers to work, yet notes, "I realize that the economic necessities of life often force us to do things differently than we would like. But when it comes to child raising, I am convinced that a woman should make every possible effort to spend the first three years with her child. It *does* make a tremendous difference."

The young child who is separated from his mother exhibits all of the classic symptoms of grief. He may cry unconsolably or withdraw into unnatural quietness. Regarding this separation anxiety, Humberto Nagera, Professor of Psychiatry at the University of Montana, points out:

> *When the child is confronted with the mother's absence his automatic response is an anxiety state that on many occasions reaches overwhelming proportions. Repeated traumas of this type in especially susceptible children will not fail to have serious consequences for their later development. . . . No other animal species will subject their infants to experiences that they are not endowed to cope with, except the human animal.*

## STAYING AT HOME—FOR NOW

How does a mother reconcile her own need for a healthy sense of self-esteem, achievement, and self-confidence with the needs of her baby? Many young women today are opting to put their careers "on hold" when the baby arrives. They see motherhood as a special season in their lives, one that they do not want to miss. The working world will still be there two or three, five or ten years from now. Stay-at-home mothers of young children often see themselves resuming their working careers once their children are older. They view the time at home as a short-period, "a sliver of time" when gauged against the many years that they can, and probably will, work outside the home.

Mary Ann Kerwin, one of LLL's founders, is a good example of this. After spending more than twenty years as a mother at home, deeply involved in caring for her large family, she found there was still "plenty of time for another career." Mary Ann began attending law school when her youngest child started high school. She adds:

> *Our children teach us much more than we realize. Being a mother taught me patience, perseverance, self-discipline, and hard work. After coping for twenty-four hours a day with children, no task seemed too hard.*

Judy Kahrl of Ohio appreciates the fact that it takes courage for a woman to stand in the face of society's pressure and say, "At this time in my life, and with this new person as my responsibility, I am going to use my resources of time and physical and emotional energy in the most effective way possible for the nurturing of that new life."

## DOES IT PAY TO WORK?

Perhaps you would like to stay home with your baby, but you can't see how you can manage without your paycheck. Home is where your heart is, but a job is where the money is—or is it?

Many of the women who are in touch with the League note that it is easy to think of one's take-home pay as "pure profit." Often the costs involved in working are overlooked, and some quick calculations of expenses versus income yield surprising results. There is the cost of a working wardrobe and transportation expenses getting to and from work each day. When you spend the day on the job, you probably prepare more expensive convenience foods or eat out more often. Figure out what child care for an infant would cost. Then sit down and approximate how much money these things add up to and subtract this amount from your income. You may very well find that there would be little net gain if you continued to work after the baby arrived.

When tallying up the funds that will be available to you if you stay home, consider the likelihood that you will drop into a lower tax bracket after you stop working. The tax savings alone may be substantial. Many mothers find that it doesn't "pay" for them to work outside the home.

## EARNING EXTRA MONEY

What if your financial situation is such that you feel you absolutely have to bring in some extra income? Happily more and more mothers have been able to combine working and keeping their babies with them. Many school buses make their runs with mothers behind the wheels and their babies securely in car seats behind them. Taking care of other mothers' children is another way to bring in extra income.

Many kinds of office work can be done just as well at home, so you might be able to interest your employer in having you do part-time work at home, coming into the office just long enough to pick up and deliver your work. It's this kind of flexibility in the working world that could be of great help to more families if it were more readily available to the trained woman who is also a mother.

If you are a good typist, get in touch with several different companies or secretarial services about free-lance typing at home, or run an ad in the newspaper. If you have a specialty like art, writing, photography, or public relations, you can develop a free-lance clientele and work out of your home. Giving music lessons is another good option. Or, if you are a teacher, contact local schools about tutoring in your home. Another possibility is to take baby along with you to your job. Given the right circumstances, an increasing number of women are finding that mothering the baby is compatible with their jobs.

A mother from Mississippi, Melissa McLain, tells about her situation: "When Megan was three months old, I returned to work. Luckily we have a family-owned business. My parents, brothers, and my husband, John, all work there, so it seemed only natural to take Megan along. We just work mornings. We don't always get a lot of work done, but everyone has fun." And Debi Drecksler from Florida adds, "I've been able to take my children along with me whenever I needed to work outside the home. My most recent job was as a Youth Director. I ran a day camp and, during the school year, an after-school enrichment program."

Jo Montgomery, from Washington, tells how she found a way to stay at home after her baby was born:

---

*Elizabeth was born on leap year day. I had planned on returning to work full time when she was three months old. By the time she was six weeks old, we had developed a solid nursing relationship. When I investigated day-care options, I became depressed. I felt cheated at the thought of leaving my precious baby.*

*I talked to my husband about my feelings. He was very supportive, and we both decided that I wouldn't return to work in June. I told my employer that I thought I might possibly return in September, but I couldn't make any promises.*

*Taking your baby to work with you, or working from home, are options worth considering.*

> *I had been working in the graphics field for six years, so I entertained the idea of putting my skills to work for myself at home. On July 1st I started my own business retailing wedding and baby announcements. Through referrals, my business has blossomed to include some commercial accounts, too.*
>
> *Taking your business home won't work for everyone, but it's worth thinking about. I am so glad I have gotten to know my daughter, Elizabeth, "full time."*

In the practical context of mothering a young child day after day, of changing and feeding him, returning his smiles, applauding his efforts to reach a toy, distracting him at times, or consoling him when tears appear, the mothers we have talked to make no distinction between the quantity and quality of time they spend with their babies. Mary Ann Kerwin, a founder of La Leche League, has observed, "Babies need quantities of quality time."

# Take One Step at a Time

If you are awaiting the arrival of your baby, you are probably thinking about what you should tell your employer regarding your future plans. From experience, many mothers insist: "Do not make any commitments before your baby is born. Be very firm on this."

You do not want the specter hanging over your head of having to return to a job by a certain date because of an agreement you made while still pregnant. Most businesses give a maternity leave, and will hold your job for you for a specified period of time after the baby is born. By all means take advantage of it, and give yourself that time to assess how much you and your baby need each other. For someone to expect you to promise away your future and that of your baby before you even have a chance to meet is tantamount to signing a blank check—no, it is worse.

Shirley Callanan, a mother from Utah, planned to work on a part-time basis. But after her baby was born, she wrote, "I really didn't know what to expect of motherhood or how I would feel, and it's hard to describe the feelings that flowed through me those first few days, weeks, and months of my daughter's life. I was needed by this tiny person; I knew I could not leave her with someone else, no matter how loving."

## EXPLORING OPTIONS

In OF CRADLES AND CAREERS, Kaye Lowman explores many aspects that are available to women who refuse to make an "all-or-nothing choice" between their careers and their families. Her book includes stories of women who have "reshaped the workplace in order to make it more responsive to their need to work and their desire to have a family." She goes on to explain:

*Whether a woman's need to work is financial, social, or emotional, the desire to be a parent may be equally strong....The career woman of the 80s understands her baby's need for her and the importance of being a meaningful part of her baby's life. And she realizes how much she herself will lose if she misses out on the opportunity to mother her own children....Careers can be put on hold; babies grow up and are gone. It was a wise*

*and thoughtful Mother Nature who brought babies into
the world needing to be breastfed and cared for, reminding us that mother and baby are very much a unit for
many months after birth and that they need to be together. To try to ignore or circumvent this physical and
psychological need is to tamper with one of the most fun-
damental and basic elements of human nature.*

Some women make one decision before their babies are born
and find their attitudes change once they become mothers. Such
was the case with Joy Cohen of New York.

*I have worked with children for eleven years: as an early
childhood teacher, as a teacher and therapist in a
therapeutic nursery, and as a psychotherapist caring for
seriously disturbed children and their families.*

*When I was pregnant, I believed that I would be
ready to resume my part-time psychotherapy practice after
three or four months. I couldn't have known then the
power and intensity of my baby's and my need for each
other. I wanted to give myself over totally to this new and
wonderful adventure called mothering. Slowly but surely I
did just that.*

*Those first few months passed quickly, and I began to
feel pressure to resume my practice. The children and
families with whom I had been working were anxious to
continue. My friends and family encouraged me not to give
up my career.*

*My own cultural stereotype of the woman who can
easily manage family and career during her children's early
years was being challenged. The only stimulation I felt I
needed was the stimulation of my baby nursing at my
breast. I wanted to savor every minute of my new life and
this delicately unfolding new relationship. I felt a crisis of
the heart upon me.*

*Fortunately, I did not have to work for economic
reasons, and my husband said that he had confidence in
me and that he would be supportive of any decision that I
made.*

*I had previously arranged to have my mother care for
Michael during my sessions. When I told her that I didn't
want to go back to work and felt the baby strongly needed*

*me, she told me that I was making a big mistake. I was
pained that my mother couldn't be as supportive as I
would have liked, but if I have learned anything from
helping people know their feelings, it was to acknowledge
and trust my own.*

*After much soul-searching, I decided to stop working
with my clients. The separations were difficult and sad
for everyone. I tried hard to stay connected to my own
heart and knew that what was best for me would ulti-
mately be best for all concerned. When I knew I would
no longer have to be away from Michael, I breathed a
long, deep sigh of relief. The internal and external work
had been difficult, but as I nestled in to nurse my baby
with the knowledge that I would not have to be away
from him until we were both ready, I knew that it had
been necessary work from which I had grown deeply as a
mother and as a person. I knew that I had made absolutely the right decision.*

For some mothers, even working part-time interferes with their
ability to mother their child. Elizabeth Golestaani, from Iran, is
one such mother:

*Until recently, I had always thought part-time work—say
two hours three times a week—was the ideal for the
mother of a small child. Add to this the great demand for
my English-teaching skills here in Iran, and I was under a
lot of pressure to return to work. So I did—and what a
mistake. It took me a long time to accept the fact that I'm
not Superwoman and that in my case working even part-
time is too much. I kept thinking that soon I would get
more organized or my toddler, Sa'id, would need me less,
and then all would be well.*

*The idea of "giving up my career" was so scary! I
kept wrestling with my thoughts and emotions. Then I
received the January-February issue of NEW BEGINNINGS.
In it, I read an article by a mother who had been in
exactly the same situation. She wrote about how important
it is for one to acknowledge and trust one's feelings, and
that helped me enormously.*

*I was finally able to decide to do what I believed was
right for me, which was to stop accepting teaching*

commitments while I have a small child. I still had to finish out the university semester, but just having made the
decision changed my attitude so much.

After just two days, I realized my feelings and
behavior towards Sa'id had changed. I was less irritable,
more loving, and the angry scoldings were replaced by
hugs and listening and eye contact. Life seemed so good
again.

I hadn't realized my teaching had such a bad effect
on my mothering until my decision to stop. It was hard
telling everybody "no more," but I kept reminding myself
"Sa'id first." For me, staying home allows me to be the kind
of mother I want to be.

# Choosing to Stay Home

"Becoming a mother is unlike almost any other experience,
and it is impossible for a woman to know beforehand how deeply
the experience will affect her. Until your baby is born and in your
arms, nursing at your breast, you cannot know what it means to
have a child, and then to leave a child." These words reflect the
thoughts and emotions of mothers who have decided to stay at home
full-time while their children are small.

One mother, Pat Smith from Pennsylvania, was faced with a
difficult choice during pregnancy:

*Of course I would return to work after having our baby!
This was a foregone conclusion during the several years my
husband Skip and I tried to conceive a child. We had rarely,
if ever, considered otherwise, because the reasons for my
continuing to work were so compelling: finances, lifestyles,
careers.*

*In many ways we followed the young suburban working
couple lifestyle. As happy consumers, we weren't quite ready
to relinquish some of our material well-being—like a
microwave oven. I still didn't have one. Among our peers, a
mother's right to work after childbirth wasn't questioned.*

Then there was the matter of careers. I had a promising future with a fine corporation owned by the major stock exchanges. In fact, I was due for a promotion into middle management that would mean relocation to New York at the company's expense.

Five months into my pregnancy, the New York promotion offer came, and it proved to be the undoing of my finances, career, and lifestyle. The offer was a fork in the road, because it brought into focus the commitment the new job demanded. Although the rewards were positively tantalizing, it didn't take me long to realize that I'd have little time or energy left for anything but part-time mothering if I were to pursue this career path.

Did I want to be a future vice-president of this corporation, or did I want to be a full-time mother? This was the question I had to answer once I accepted the premise that I couldn't be both. As I considered the question, images of the baby started invading my thoughts. They were fleeting, fragmented images at first, but when the images formed this scenario, I stopped cold: I saw myself wrapping the baby in blankets, taking him to the babysitter's house, holding him in my arms, then handing him over to someone else for the day. I knew right then and there that I would not go back to work after he was born.

For me, this was an irrational way to make a decision. I had a list of every rational reason to work, and at one single thought—separation from my little one—I tossed the list right out of the window. I resolved that I would do whatever was necessary to stay home with the baby.

Colin was born three years ago, and we have been almost inseparable ever since. In retrospect, my worries at the time seem trivial now. After all, we now own a home in a friendly, family-oriented town, a car, and all the comforts we really need. A real worry, as I see it now, is how I would ever have made it through a working day without my baby.

My ex-boss called me about a year ago and offered me my old job. I was delighted to decline. I told him I wouldn't even consider it.

And I don't need a microwave oven after all.

## A SENSE OF WORTH

The value of good parenting is never denied, but all too often it is unsung. Jobs in the marketplace have a highly visible rating system, usually, the higher the pay, the greater the prestige. The at-home mother has only one title, and there are no periodic raises telling her that she is doing a good job. But the rewards are there, right in the family, though they are much more subtle. A California mother, Emily Holt, discovered unexpected enjoyment in mothering. She reflects on the changes in her life that came with the birth of her baby. "I sit holding our five-month-old daughter, who is nursing so sweetly at my breast. I watch my husband's face light up with joy as she grabs his beard, laughing aloud. Oh yes, my job was wonderful as jobs go, but in these five short months, I have seen myself grow in a hundred ways, reaching for what is best in me to greet this beautiful new life. Sharing every delightful moment of our Sarah's discovery of our world, I realize how blessed I am to be a mother."

Carolyn Keiler Paul of New York doesn't think she's wasting her time by staying home with her children. She says "I think it's time we stop apologizing for being 'just a mother.' Childrearing is *not* a menial job. It calls for all our talents and resources. My college education isn't going to waste, because it has enriched me so that I may in turn enrich the lives of my children."

Harold M. Voth, senior psychiatrist from The Menninger Foundation, agrees that a mother's role is of the utmost importance to society.

*The* mothering function is one of the most important of all human events, but unfortunately, one of the least appreciated or regarded by society. Courage, trust, the capacity to experience intimacy, generosity, the ability to stand alone later in life, and much, much more, are a function of good mothering.

## A MAJOR INVESTMENT

Other mothers' stories can be inspiring and informative, but no one else can tell you what is the best course of action for you and your family. We can tell you about a baby's needs, we can tell you what works best to ensure successful breastfeeding, we can tell you how mothers have combined breastfeeding and working. And we can tell you about mothers who have discovered unexpected personal growth and fulfillment in staying home. But only you can make the decision that best reflects your own family's needs.

We encourage you to learn as much as you can, explore all the options that are available to you, and discuss these questions with others who have been faced with similar decisions and choices.

Attending La Leche League meetings can be a helpful source of information and encouragement. Talking with other mothers who are in situations similiar to your own can reinforce the choices you make. Whether you are an employed or at-home mother, you can look to La Leche League for support in breastfeeding your baby. We will not hesitate to answer your questions, delight in your progress, and stand by you in your decision to breastfeed.

Be as cautious in your decision-making as you would be with a major investment—the investment here is a critical period in your life and that of your baby. The early months and years set the course for the rest of your child's life, and they can never be recaptured. And as Dr. Marilyn Bonham, the psychiatrist who wrote *The Laughter and Tears of Children,* reminds us, "The outflow of (a mother's) love and affection for the very young child is pure gold in the bank."

# PART FOUR

# Life as a Family

# CHAPTER 10

# The Manly Art of Fathering

$A$ father's unique relationship with his baby is an important element in the child's development from early infancy. From our experience, we know without a doubt that breastfeeding is enhanced and the nursing couple sustained by the loving support, help, and companionship of the baby's father.

Nowadays, men no longer fit the stereotyped image of the father in the waiting room of the hospital, pacing the floor, while his wife delivers their baby surrounded by strangers. A father today is more often next to his wife during childbirth, supporting her and sharing the unforgettable emotions of this event. From the moment of birth, father and baby begin to get acquainted. The more a man can participate in the birth of his son or daughter, the more powerful and meaningful it will be. Just ask a new father who was at the birth of his child and be prepared to listen!

The metamorphosis that makes a man a father does not happen overnight. He usually acquires the title "father" much more quickly than he captures the spirit of fathering. In fact, men can't even count on the natural assistance of hormones that aid the mother. It has been said that when a baby is born, so is a mother. Fathers emerge more gradually, as Dr. William Sears, pediatrician and father of six, points out:

*Although mothers do indeed have a hormonal head start on developing their intuition, I believe that fathers also have natural nurturing abilities and, if given the opportunity to develop these abilities, fathers can indeed participate in the care and comforting of their babies.*

Sue LaLeike, from Florida, tells how father and daughter developed a special relationship:

*There is no way a father can take over a mother's role or vice versa—breastfeeding sees to that. But a nursing mother needs the baby's father to do his part by giving love to them both. The baby may not experience the closeness of nursing with Dad, but going for walks in the front-pack carrier, laughter and nuzzlings, the family bed, and even burping and diapering can all contribute to very intimate relationships at a very early age. Charlie's role has been important since our baby's conception. He has helped all along—he didn't wait. He caught and prepared fresh Rocky Mountain trout for me in the first weeks of pregnancy. He supported my views on birthing and nursing. He read and discussed and went with me to doctor's appointments and birthing classes. And then he held and cradled our beautiful daughter moments after her birth in a way that made me know that he was the only person in the world I trusted her with.*

*He made all the first moves, and it sure does show in the way our daughter cries, "Daddy—home—happy!" when she hears him opening the gate at the end of our driveway.*

# Fathers Get Involved

While more and more men are recognizing that breastfeeding is the natural and ideal way to feed the baby, some first-time fathers don't realize how much they can be involved during the breastfeeding period.

After birth, the intimate relationship between mother and baby continues. They are still a unit, and for some time mother will be the baby's sole source of nourishment. In language that is irrefutable, biology makes it clear that the mother-baby relationship is primary and should not be set aside. This relationship is unique and the prototype of all other relationships throughout life. A father's contribution is equally important, but it is different. Babies thrive on both.

Chris Phillips, from New Jersey, describes one way a father can spend time with his child:

*A lot of new nursing mothers seem to worry that Daddy will feel left out if he can't help feed the new baby. Not so! Actually, I think just the opposite is true. The lack of bottles seems to encourage a father to become more active in other areas of an infant's care and upbringing. My husband, Ronny, took on the job (or should I say joy?) of bathing our firstborn son, Nicholas, starting with his very first bath.*

*Everything went smoothly until Nicholas was about five months old and began to outgrow the kitchen sink. We discovered that bending over the tub was too much of a back strain for Ronny. He missed his special time with Nicholas. Thankfully, we came across a solution when someone told me about her husband taking their kids in the shower with him. What a terrific idea! It had never occurred to me that a baby would enjoy a shower, but why not? Nicholas had always loved the water; we would give it a try.*

*That was over a year ago and Nicholas still loves the shower. Of course, there are a few adjustments to make when showering with a baby, but all in all, bath time became a joy again and Ronny enjoys being an important part of his baby's life.*

In BECOMING A FATHER, a book written especially for dads, Dr. Sears encourages them to get involved with their children.

*Speaking as one father to another, let me share a secret with you: Babies are fun, kids are a joy, and fatherhood is the only profession where you're guaranteed that the more effort you put into it the more enjoyment you will get out of it.*

Some fathers take a while to grow into a nurturing relationship with their baby. Sally Thomas from Wisconsin writes about the changes as her husband developed more interest in their son:

*During my pregnancy, Eric, my husband, had surprised me with his interest and delight in my diet, exercise, and our growing baby. He was so supportive and interested in making our birth the kind of experience we wanted.*

*However, after we got home with our son, Eric didn't seem as involved. He'd hold Joseph only with my prompting and only for a very short time. He kept saying "He doesn't do anything."*

*When Joseph was a couple of weeks old I was talking to a friend about my concerns, and she told me that her husband had had a hard time relating to a tiny baby, too. She suggested I let Eric blossom as a father in whatever ways that he felt comfortable.*

*As the months went by and Joseph became more alert, Eric began to take more and more of an interest in his son. When Joseph became mobile and learned to like roughhousing, there was no holding Eric back. Soon Joseph seemed to prefer his daddy, and his face would light up at Eric's appearance.*

*I am thankful every day for our now fourteen-month-old toddler and his wonderful and supportive father. And I love to watch my two favorite fellows playing as Eric—the tough-guy father—leans over and whispers in Joseph's ears, "I love you so much. What would we ever do without you?"*

*Fathers are sometimes surprised at the intensity of their involvement in the breast-feeding relationship.*

## Fathers and Breastfeeding

Of all the sources of encouragement a woman may receive in breastfeeding, the support of her baby's father is the most meaningful to her. But for some women, support from the baby's father is not easy to come by. Perhaps a mother is a single parent and she is alone with her baby. She may need to look for support from friends or relatives. Or it may be that a married woman has a husband who is uncomfortable with the idea of his wife breast-feeding. A mother who faces these situations can still have a satisfy-ing breastfeeding experience.

Sometimes a father who had misgivings before the baby was born learns to accept breastfeeding as he sees his baby thrive on mother's milk. A mother's enthusiasm for breastfeeding often sparks a father's interest. A father who is hesitant can only begin to sup-port your decision to nurse the baby if he understands what it means to you.

Dr. Sears encourages fathers to support their wife's decision to breastfeed. He writes:

*I* am absolutely convinced of the superiority of human milk for human babies. I want to convey to new fathers a feeling from the bottom of my heart: **Do everything within your power to encourage and support the healthy breastfeeding relationship between your wife and your baby.** Breastfeeding is a lifestyle, not just a method of feeding. Providing understanding and support for the breastfeeding pair is one of the most valuable investments you can make in the future health and well-being of your family.

Men are sometimes surprised at the intensity of their reaction to seeing their wives breastfeed their babies. Archie Smith, a father from Texas, recalls his first impression:

*B*efore becoming an expectant father, I had never given much thought to breastfeeding. When my wife, Sheri, asked me what I thought about it, without hesitation I said I thought it was a great idea. It seemed to be the natural way. We talked more about it, and Sheri was eager to try breastfeeding.

After Angie was born the nurse handed her to Sheri and she began to nurse. Standing a few feet away I could feel the emotions flowing from one to another. Then seeing the smile of satisfaction on my wife's face, I knew we were a family. It was an experience I will long remember.

And another father, Dean Cook, also from Texas, adds his thoughts:

*B*efore our baby was born, my wife, Kathy, and I discussed breastfeeding, and we agreed our baby would be breastfed for at least six months, preferably as long as he needed it. I have long felt that there is no better way to *nurture a child. However, I soon discovered after reading the materials that Kathy brought home from her LLL meetings that I knew only a few of the benefits of breastfeeding. And after gaining some experience as an active father of a nursing baby, I became amazed at my own intense emotional involvement with nursing.*

# What Can Fathers Do?

Though mother is the only one who can nurse the baby, there are a number of things that no one else can do quite as well as a loving father. Have you ever watched a mother try to soothe a fussy baby by nursing and rocking and patting, and just about everything else she can think of, and then watched in amazement as the baby's father lifts the little one out of her arms, hoists him onto his shoulder, and promptly puts the baby to sleep! It is a trade secret known only to fathers; we don't know if it's the broad shoulders, the large, strong hands, or that deep baritone voice that does the trick. But no matter—we know that it works, and clever nursing mothers are the first to take advantage of it.

Babies are often their fussiest late in the day, mother is tired after a full day of baby care, and perhaps there is the added pressure of hungry children awaiting dinner. When dad arrives home, even though he may have had a hard day at work, he can often approach the baby in a more relaxed way than mother can at that point. Many fathers take advantage of this to establish their own special relationship with their babies.

In BECOMING A FATHER, Dr. Sears describes a special form of baby-soothing that only works for dads—he calls it "the Neck Nestle." Dad puts baby in a baby carrier on his chest and lifts him up a bit so baby's head nestles under dad's chin. Dr. Sears explains:

*In the neck nestle, father has a slight edge over mother. Babies hear not only through their ears, but also through the vibration of their skull bones. By placing baby's skull against your voice box in the front of your neck and humming or singing to your baby, the slower, more easily felt vibrations of the lower-pitched male voice will often*

The "neck nestle" is a unique way of comforting babies.

lull baby right to sleep. An added attraction of the neck nestle is that baby feels the warm air from your nose on his scalp. Experienced mothers have long known that sometimes just breathing onto their babies' faces or heads will calm them. They call this "magic breath." My children have enjoyed the neck nestle more than any of the other holding patterns.

What do fathers most enjoy doing with their babies? There are probably almost as many answers as there are fathers, but over the years we have observed that fathers seem to have a special gift for playing with even very young babies. While mother is often preoccupied with cuddling and feeding, father is likely to tickle baby under his chin, hoist him into the air, or bounce him on his knee. A caution may be needed about shaking a baby as this can be harmful, but movement and exercise are important to the baby's overall development. Babies thrive when provided with both gentle nurturing and lively activity. As Louise Kaplan, PhD, explains in her book *Oneness and Separateness*, "Fathers have a special excitement about them that babies find intriguing. . . .Fathers embody a delicious mixture of familiarity and novelty."

Fathers need to spend time with their babies in order to get to know them better and get "tuned in" to their needs. Watch for cues that baby is ready for some fatherly interaction. A hungry baby won't be at all interested in playing. But once baby has nursed his fill, dad can take over the burping, diaper-changing, singing, rocking, and cuddling. Some fathers enjoy bathing the baby—or bathing with the baby, soaking together in a warm tub. A gentle massage can be another form of interaction between father and infant.

Don't overlook the baby carrier. It's not just for mothers. Dr. Sears tells about taking early morning walks to the beach with his son, Matthew, in the baby carrier beginning when he was only a few weeks old.

Learning about the usual stages of a baby's development in the first year can help a father enjoy his baby more. It's important for him to know when his son or daughter is ready to play peek-a-boo, when to expect reaching and grasping, and when to encourage crawling and climbing. A father can play an important role in these stages of development and proudly watch his child's growth and advancement. GROWING TOGETHER: A PARENT'S GUIDE TO BABY'S FIRST YEAR, by Dr. William Sears, explains baby's stages of growth and development. See the Appendix for details.

# Husband and Wife— A Parenting Team

A husband and wife are a parenting team—each has an important and unique contribution to make to their child's development. They need to trust each other, respect each other's unique role, and help each other in times of stress. The most important thing you and your husband can do for your baby is to love one another.

The fact is that babies both expand horizons and rock boats. Your marriage will never again be the same. But it can be even more loving and it need never be dull. The silver and gold of future anniversaries are waiting. A prerequisite to attaining that treasure is putting your heads together now to chart your course.

There's a need to talk through the feelings that come with any important junction in life. We have referred to the emotions that a new mother often experiences, and it is just as reasonable to expect the father to react emotionally to his new responsibilities. A father and pediatrician, Jerald Davitz of California, tells fathers: "A very difficult feeling that most fathers have shortly after the new baby arrives home from the hospital is the unsettling sensation, 'Am I sure this is really what I want?' or 'Things were better before.' You need to understand you've got some reason to feel jealous and threatened at first, but these feelings will soon go away."

## COMMUNICATE YOUR FEELINGS

While talking with other young mothers, Martha Hartzell of Georgia found that communication between husband and wife about what is important to each can go a long way toward improving their relationship.

Mothers often find themselves totally immersed in nurturing and caring for their tiny baby. Some women have described their feelings about having a newborn as "like falling in love all over again." As one mother recalled, "I found myself head over heels in love with my baby. I found everything about her endlessly exciting and fascinating. I could hardly think about anything else. My feelings were so intense for several weeks that there seemed to be little room in my life for anything else."

Such a new and powerful emotion could well upset the equilibrium in a marriage. A husband may find himself feeling like a jilted lover and, to make matters worse, his wife is too preoccupied with the baby to even notice!

It helps to remember that today's intense involvement will become tomorrow's comfortable, easygoing relationship. A baby must be loved and cared for in order to survive, and this initial intensity between mother and baby is designed to assure that the baby's needs will be met. With plenty of time, and ongoing communication about their needs and feelings, mother, father, and baby will eventually settle into a new relationship that is comfortable and satisfying for all three of them.

First-time parents are often preoccupied with their new responsibilities. Both husband and wife are putting out a tremendous effort. They must be careful not to let their concentration on these new responsibilities isolate them from each other.

Psychiatrist Lucy Waletzky of Georgetown University, Washington, DC, found that husbands often experience some jealousy because of the closeness of the nursing mother and baby. She advises: "Effective communication between husband and wife should be encouraged before, during, and after the birth." Mother-

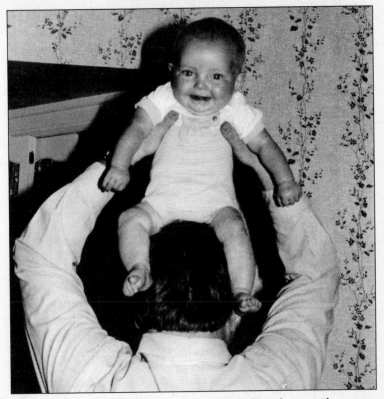

*Babies delight in the excitement of the activities fathers often provide.*

hood and fatherhood are new roles that need to be talked over and learned together. Time spent together during the first few weeks after the baby's birth can add a new dimension to a husband and wife's love for each other.

## THE REWARDS ARE GREAT

Being a parent is not easy, but it can be extremely rewarding. David Stewart, father of five from Missouri, has this to say:

*Parenting is not easy. It can try us to the point of frustration. But this frustration can be productive because it is the symptom of growth and expansion. I sometimes think that nature gives us children to force us to grow up ourselves....*

*Parenting is the greatest opportunity we normally re-
ceive to make good in this world. Your job may be important. Your volunteer activities may be important. But few
of us do anything so important as to make much difference in society a hundred years from now. But the way
you treat your children will matter a hundred years from
now. The attitudes you pass on to them will be passed on
to their children, who will pass them on to theirs....*

*Parenthood works in two directions: Good parenting
makes for happy children; but it also makes for happy,
fulfilled parents. It is not possible to give happiness without receiving it....*

Men seldom have the opportunity to discuss and share their
ideas about being fathers. This can be just as important for them
as it is for mothers. La Leche League Groups are not just for
mothers—activities are often scheduled where fathers can get together and compare notes about their role. Couples' Meetings and
Area Conferences provide these opportunities. In some local areas,
fathers are invited to attend regular LLL Group Meetings. Check
with your La Leche League Leader for details.

The book we've quoted throughout this chapter, BECOMING
A FATHER, by William Sears, is also a source of encouragement for
fathers. Copies are available from La Leche League Groups and
La Leche League International. See the Appendix.

To quote David Stewart, "Ever uncertain, ever unreliable, ever
unpredictable—most of life's offerings are fickle. Fatherhood is
forever."

# CHAPTER 11

# Meeting Family Needs

Throughout this book we talk about a mother meeting her baby's needs as though she and her baby were alone on a desert island. In reality, there are probably other family members whose needs must be met as well as household tasks that somehow must be accomplished. Faced with these responsibilities, you may be wondering just how you can keep things running smoothly while breastfeeding and caring for a newborn.

Over the years, League mothers have developed some techniques and tips that may help you. A basic recommendation is to always put people before things. Meeting the needs of family members should always come before immaculate housekeeping or caring for material possessions. Along with this, you'll want to remember that your family's priorities may not be the same as those of your next door neighbor or your favorite cousin (who doesn't have any children). Other people's standards or values may not be the ones that work out best for you and your family. Babies are small for such a short time. It would be a shame to waste those precious months trying to please others instead of enjoying your baby and meeting his needs.

# Housework and a New Baby

Top household efficiency and a new baby mix about as well as oil and water. Meeting baby's unscheduled needs makes a strict household schedule pretty much a thing of the past. This is not to say that a well-ordered life automatically becomes chaos at the moment of birth, but it is fair warning that you may want to reorganize your approach to household chores.

The key to survival is to simplify. Pick an afternoon to take a walking tour of your house, critically examining each room for items that should be removed, rearranged, or discarded. Do you hate to see the knickknacks on the bookshelf covered with dust? Then put them away and replace them with a fresh new plant that will brighten both the room and your spirits. How about that overstuffed closet where everything from ski gear to broken lamp shades seems to end up? If you take the time to clean it out while you are pregnant, it won't get on your nerves later. Discard the things that are beyond repair or that you no longer need—don't just move them somewhere else or they will soon be in your way again. Box up the things you want to keep and store in the attic or basement.

Whatever the season, do as much "spring cleaning" as you can before the baby is born. Light household chores are good exercise, and having them done will be a godsend later when you'll want to devote your time and energy to the baby. This sudden zeal for cleaning and readying the house so often felt by mothers during the last months of pregnancy is referred to as the "nesting instinct."

Give some thought to rearranging your cleaning supplies so that they are readily accessible (but stored in a high, child-proof cupboard). You'll want your supplies to be handy so you can quickly clean a bathroom mirror or scour a sink if you have a moment before stepping into your shower or while keeping an eye on a three-year-old in the tub. Your bathroom will be clean in minutes following bath time if you quickly wipe the mirror (already fogged), take a swipe over the sink and counter, and wipe up the water on the floor with a large towel, one that was already consigned to the laundry hamper.

In households where there is a baby, housework is nearly always done in quick snatches—a series of mini-cleaning sprints. Five to ten minutes at full speed in the kitchen, devoted to whatever is most bothersome to you—perhaps the breakfast dishes on the table or the grubby floor in front of the sink or refrigerator—will improve the looks of the house and give you a sense of accomplishment. Throughout the day, center your attention on what you have accomplished, beginning with the all-important work of nurturing your baby, rather than dwelling on the tasks that still need doing.

Make your bed or not, as it pleases you. Plumping up the pillows and tossing the covers back to air is a time-honored custom. Without a spread in place, you'll probably lie down to nurse the baby more often during the day. Keeping up with the dishes is about as easy as keeping up with the Joneses. If baby is not agreeable to having you do the whole job when the meal is over, fill the sink with hot soapy water and let everything soak until you can get back to it later on or the next morning. If you have a dishwasher, reload it during those times when baby is wakeful and wants to be held in your arms or snuggled in his baby carrier. Babies usually love the constant up-and-down and back-and-forth motions that accompany the loading and unloading process. Don't rush it. And many a fussy baby has fallen asleep in a baby carrier while his mother vacuums.

Little people and clutter seem to be inseparable. But clutter can be picked up and put out of sight quickly if you are equipped with a clutter-catcher—a cardboard box or other suitable container to carry with you as you whiz through each room depositing all the odds and ends that have been scattered about. This system enables you to de-clutter an entire house in fifteen minutes or so. The contents of the box can be sorted later when you have more time, but for now the house looks fairly straightened, and a visitor will be able to walk in the door without fear of skidding on a stray truck. Concentrate on immediately putting away the especially important items such as the car keys, which will drive you frantic when misplaced. Always putting your keys on a handy hook just inside the door could be one of the best habits you could get into. For safeguarding other small, valuable items picked up around the house during the day, the pockets in your jeans or an apron are indispensable.

Early in the morning, perhaps while you're relaxing with baby for an after-breakfast nursing, make a list of the "must do" chores for that day. Further refine your choices by selecting one, or possibly two, of the most important. Box off these top-priority items and plan on getting to them at the first opportunity, before you get caught up in another project or just the everyday chores. If it's something you can't do until later in the day, set your alarm clock or oven timer to ring at the appropriate time. Getting just one "top-priority" item crossed off your list every day will give you a feeling of accomplishment no matter how many things are left undone. Beware of going all out for cleaning, cooking, and scrubbing whenever the baby is taking a nap. Give some of that time to the other children, take a nap yourself, or relax with a project you enjoy.

## MEAL PLANNING

When there is a new baby in your life, mastering the art of advance meal preparation is as vital as knowing how to relax in a rocking chair. Many women prepare double recipes of stews, casseroles, spaghetti sauce, chili, and the like during the last weeks of pregnancy and put the extra portions in the freezer. We've heard of thoughtful friends giving the mother-to-be a "casserole shower," presenting her with meals which they have prepared and frozen in disposable pans, complete with instructions for cooking or reheating. And the lovely practice of bringing a meal to the new baby's family has certainly not lost its appeal.

After the baby arrives, let simplicity in menu-planning be your watchword. Make a list of your favorite one-step, no-fuss meals and be sure to keep the necessary ingredients on hand. A dessert or snack of fresh fruit is always quick and nutritious.

If you don't already have a slow cooker or crock pot, put it at the top of your list for the next gift-giving occasion. These marvelous cookers allow you to prepare your meat, potatoes, and vegetables at any convenient time during the day, and it's all ready to eat at suppertime with no fuss or bother when you're tired and the baby is most likely to need your undivided attention. If you are lucky enough to have a microwave oven, foods can be prepared quickly or cooked ahead of time and reheated when everyone is ready to eat. An inexpensive item that is helpful for a mother whose attention is often distracted from cooking is a metal plate that fits between a cooking pot and the stove burner and keeps the food from burning.

For help in meal planning, you will find many ideas in La Leche League's cookbooks, MOTHER'S IN THE KITCHEN, and WHOLE FOODS FOR THE WHOLE FAMILY. Both are collections of

*Keeping your toddler nearby while baby nurses helps keep you more relaxed.*

mother-tested recipes with an emphasis on good nutrition and easy preparation. For details, see the Appendix.

Nursing mothers should eat at regular intervals, and active children also need to eat often. To keep young temperaments soothed and tummies satisfied until mealtime, consider introducing salad snacks. Simply assemble an assortment of fresh, raw vegetables and fruits.(Note that raw carrots and nuts should not be given to toddlers.) Preschoolers can be happily occupied in the preparations by washing and tearing greens, pulling the strings from celery stalks, breaking the cauliflower or broccoli florets, shining the apples, and arranging them all on a platter. Prepare these early in the day and keep in the refrigerator for quick munching later on. The addition of cheese, slices of hard-cooked eggs, or strips of cooked meat will add protein and staying power.

Sitting down for a few minutes for a snack is a positive measure to divert youngsters when they're tired and hungry and perhaps getting irritable. You can create a happy atmosphere with music—a favorite recording or, better yet, a sing-along with mom. The songs from your childhood are fresh and dear to your children and can become a part of their heritage.

When it comes to getting your husband and older children off to work or school on time, advance planning can save the day. Betty Wagner, one of the LLL founders, managed by setting her alarm for about twenty minutes earlier than usual. Still resting in bed, she'd reset the clock for the regular time and nurse the baby. When she had to get breakfast and help the older children, she at least knew the baby would not be hungry in the midst of the morning rush.

One last thought on meal preparation: Now is the time to reinforce safety rules! When using the stove, turn in the handles of all pans so that children cannot grab them. Even babies still in their mothers' arms can reach surprisingly far. Keep knives and other sharp utensils where children cannot reach them.

## LAUNDRY

We are all amazed at how much laundry a new baby can generate and how quickly laundry stacks up once a baby joins the family. Before the baby arrives, try to be sure that all of you have the most ample supply of clothing that your budget will permit, particularly underwear and socks, so that you won't have to do laundry every day or two. Another item mothers like to stock up on is a dozen or more lightweight, inexpensive washcloths ("seconds") that often come packaged in bundles. They're handy for all kinds of mop-ups, and since they are thinner than regular washcloths, they are convenient to use when washing behind delicate, small ears and in the creases of chunky arms and legs.

Eventually the laundry has to be done, of course, and your own approach undoubtedly will depend on the kind of facilities available to you. Whether you depend on the neighborhood laundromat or have your own equipment, enlist your husband's help. If your husband isn't already familiar with the intricacies of a washer and dryer, the hour is at hand for him to learn! When you are doing the laundry, you can use a baby carrier to good advantage. Whether it involves trips to the laundromat or doing the laundry right at home, baby will be held and comforted, and you'll get clean clothes!

Consider using two or three inexpensive plastic buckets to soak clothing that might stain. Then you can run it through the washer at a time that is convenient. Some system of pre-sorting laundry is a great help, too. As a container fills, you can quickly see when you have a load of white or colored items, and you can drop them into the washer as time permits.

Your toddler will love to be in on the action of transferring laundry from the dryer to the basket and then helping sort the clothes. Long ago, many of us decided that a considerable amount of the laundry is just as serviceable when left unfolded. Undergarments, in particular, can be sorted—tops and bottoms—and put away in a drawer, in plastic bins, or on a shelf. Clean socks can be sorted into two baskets—one for white and the other for colors—and the older members of the family can each match their own pairs.

If you're in the habit of ironing some things, now would be the time to give it a second thought. Try the ten-minute test. Wear an ironed piece of clothing for ten minutes and notice how it takes on a more lived-in, rumpled look before too long. The same item, left as is straight from the dryer or line, often "shakes out" or folds smooth, and looks just as good after a ten-minute wearing. You'll wonder if it's worth the time and energy (your own and the electrical power) to take to the ironing board.

As you make plans for keeping up with the laundry, concentrate on ways to lessen it. To start, you may find that the large bath towels that are used for drying when jumping out of the tub can be recycled if they're spread out and hung to dry instead of bunched on a small towel rack. A towel can be fastened around a towel bar with a large safety pin or gripper snaps, so children can use it to dry their hands without having it end up on the floor and then inevitably in the hamper.

Popular speakers at one of La Leche League's Conferences were Peggy Jones and Pam Young, authors of the book, *Side-Tracked Home Executives.* They explained how they developed a system of organizing household tasks in order to accomplish necessary chores in the shortest amount of time. You might find their suggestions helpful.

## SAFETY TIPS

As you try to get some housework done or care for your other little ones, there will be times when you need a safe place to put the baby. The safest place for the baby is on a small rug or blanket on the floor. He can stretch and kick and look around to his heart's content.

Never leave your baby unattended in an infant seat on a table or counter. An active baby can easily scoot the seat across the smooth surface until, crash!, baby and seat are on the floor. A changing table can also be dangerous. Fasten your young baby securely or take him with you if you go for a forgotten item or to answer the phone or door. In just a few seconds, the baby who supposedly does not roll over can fall and be seriously injured.

A word of warning is in order, too, regarding walkers. Too many babies have fallen down the stairs in them. A walker also restricts the baby and denies him the opportunity to naturally develop his coordination of arms, legs, and eyes that comes with crawling. Safer and more comfortable for the baby is a type of infant seat that rests on the floor and has a cloth back and seat on a slightly springy, metal-tubing frame.

Most mothers do not find playpens useful or necessary. By the time baby can crawl, he wants and needs his freedom to explore. A high chair can be a convenience when the baby is older and ready to be eating solid foods, but a high chair can also be dangerous. Be sure the one you select has a wide base to prevent tipping over as well as a safety strap to insure that baby can't climb or fall out. Fasten the safety strap faithfully—it takes only a few seconds.

# Time for the Other Little Ones

You will find that generous portions of love and reassurance will go a long way toward helping your older child, the ex-baby, accept the demands that the new baby is making on your time. When the baby is fussy you can remind an older child, "Mary, when you were little and hungry, I always asked Elizabeth to be patient and wait because you needed to be fed (or rocked, or held, or whatever)." The child loves the idea of once having been the "star," and it's a happy thought that can always be reinforced with a hug. When feeding the baby, a nursing mother usually has an arm free for quick hugs or other important tasks.

There's a peace of mind in keeping your older child near you when you're nursing the baby, rather than having him off somewhere on his own. A popular suggestion is to arrange a nursing corner that accommodates at least three—mother, baby, and an older brother or sister. Have an extra chair or stool next to your rocker, with some interesting play items nearby. Change the assortment regularly; surprises are always fun. One creative mom, Marge Bazemore of Georgia, added a small table for a work surface, and she and son Russ enjoy a variety of activities while the baby nurses. Marge describes their favorite choices:

- *A cassette tape recorder. It's easy to operate and Russ enjoys hearing his voice as well as Phil's cooing.*
- *Simple puzzles.*
- *Playdough. I also keep a cookie cutter handy.*
- *Finger puppets.*
- *Crayons, paper, pencil, and coloring book.*
- *Pegboard. I made one out of a piece of ceiling board and used golf tees for the pegs.*
- *Viewmaster and slides.*
- *Books and family photo albums.*
- *Spools and a cord for stringing.*

From time to time, sit on the floor while nursing. You'll be at eye level with your toddler, and the whole floor is the play area. It's great for building with blocks or rolling a soft ball. This is especially helpful when the ex-baby is looking for extra attention. Jealousy toward the new baby often shows up when the baby is three or six months old, if it hasn't happened sooner.

The mother who is expecting her second child sometimes finds it hard to imagine that she will feel as close to the new baby as she does to the little one who is already here. Can there be the same

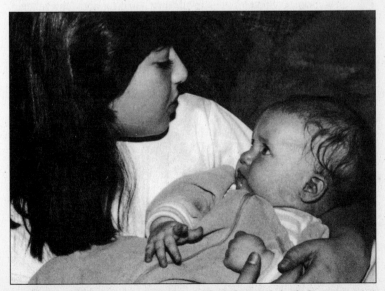

*School-age children are usually fascinated by babies and the feeling is mutual.*

strong love the second time around? The miracle of mother love is that it increases with each new birth. It is not diminished, not limited. It is not a pie that must be sliced into smaller pieces to accommodate extra plates at the table. With the new baby comes a resurgence of love for all of the family.

## LITTLE HELPERS

Toddlers love to help, and clever mothers find lots of things for little ones to help with. If you use nonbreakable dishes, your little one may enjoy setting the table, carrying one item at a time from the stack of dishes set out. Young ones never tire of the repetition of walking back and forth, especially when a smile and "thank you" accompany each dish that is delivered to the table. Shining the glass in a low window that has been sprayed with cleaner (or plain water) is another enjoyable pastime for budding artisans, (a task that is often signed by the young polisher pressing a small nose against the pane!).

Many toddlers seem to be fascinated with a hand brush or whisk broom and dust pan, so put yours to work under the kitchen table or some other open area. Old mittens and socks make great dusting mitts for little hands. If mother helps, too, even children who are barely walking will learn to put toys back in the toy box when it's time to clean up.

Preschoolers need lots of stimulating learning activities to keep them happy and out of mischief. A wonderful resource book is PLAYFUL LEARNING, by Anne Engelhardt and Cheryl Sullivan. Written for parents who want to organize an at-home preschool for their little ones, it can also be used on an individual basis. Craft projects, simple recipes, music and number activities, story-telling, and reading readiness are all included. The information about a preschooler's development can help you better understand your child's needs. For details, see the Appendix.

## DADS CAN HELP

An understanding husband is one of a nursing mother's most treasured assets. He can step in to provide you with a welcome respite when he is home, and your older one will thrive on the extra attention.

Dads are often masters at keeping toddler minds and hands busy when mother needs some time alone with the baby, or when she decides to take advantage of baby's nap time for a relaxing bath or some much needed rest. Father and toddler will both enjoy some toddler-size roughhousing, and who but daddy can add such excitement to stories by putting in all of those low, rumbling noises?

Fathers and their little ones often develop a new and very special relationship when a new baby joins the family. Let your husband know how much he is needed and appreciated, encourage him to spend some extra time with your toddler or preschooler, and be prepared to watch the two of them become the best of friends.

## OLDER CHILDREN

If you have older children, you're also probably wondering, "How can I possibly have enough time for them after the new baby arrives?" You ask if there won't be times when an older child will want your attention, and the baby will also need you. More than likely there will be, and this is when—and how—the mutual love and understanding that cement good human relationships are fostered. Learning to consider the needs of someone who is helpless before one's own needs is a valuable lesson for the older children. It is something that you will want to help them understand as much as you can.

In discussions about the arrival of the new member of the family, ask your older children to help you think of ways of managing and helping each other. Encourage them to remember that the new baby will be the only member of the family who is completely dependent on you—just as they were at that age. When thought of in this way, it's easier for a young person to recognize (if not always accept) that baby's needs must certainly come first.

The period before your new baby arrives is an excellent time to teach the older ones some new household skills. Select chores that match each one's ability and continue to work along with your child whenever possible. The children will learn from you, and humdrum chores, such as doing the dishes, can be transformed into special moments for sharing youthful hopes and problems. Children do not make appointments with their parents to talk over their deeply felt concerns. Such sharing takes place in the context of normal activities, during times when parent's and child's hands are busy, but their minds and hearts are in touch with each other.

Don't be surprised if your young helpers are less than enthusiastic at times. That's normal. Pour on the praise and be patient with your apprentice. We all need to feel needed, and children

*In the years ahead you'll be proud to watch your children grow in the warmth of a secure loving family.*

benefit from knowing that the family is depending on them to carry out their assigned jobs. We parents overlook a golden opportunity if we don't help our children learn to accept responsibility and to enjoy the self-esteem that comes with being expected to do a job and doing it well.

School-age youngsters in the family are generally very accepting of a new baby. They enjoy babies, and vice versa. Potential problems usually come from the variety of outside activities in which this age group is often involved and which demand a parent's participation. These often include driving to and from games or lessons, attending programs, or working together on special projects. Such a pace can be hectic for a mother who also has a new baby.

You will have to be realistic and firm in setting limits for the time being. Do only those extras that you and the baby can honestly manage. Your husband can be a big help here, spending extra time with the older children's activities whenever possible. If a particular program is very special to an older child, and neither you nor your husband can participate, be assertive in asking another parent to help you. For instance, a friend or neighbor could drive to and from functions for a few weeks; you can reciprocate later.

If you will be driving with the baby along, an infant auto safety seat is a must. If you use it faithfully, beginning with baby's first ride (possibly the trip home from the hospital), you and your baby will soon accept the procedure as a matter of course. Plan to nurse the baby before starting out in the car, so you and baby will be more relaxed.

You will be proud of your older children as they grow to understand the helplessness of the baby and accept the sacrifices they are asked to make. It has been gratifying to many of us to find that a crying baby is almost always disturbing to older children. They sense that something is not right, and they are happy again only when baby is happy. Looking ahead, you'll find that cheerfully putting the needs of the baby first, as a matter of course, is an example of caring for others that benefits everyone. It's a good way to educate your children for their future roles as loving parents.

# Developing a Parenting Style

Parents find themselves making many decisions as their children grow and family needs change. We all grow up with some idea of what it means to be a parent and raise children. Perhaps we were brought up in a loving, caring family and we choose our own parents as role models when we have children. Or possibly, our childhood was not a happy one and we want to offer a more secure environment to our own children.

Either way you'll want to make an effort to learn as much as you can about parenting, child care, meeting children's needs, and child development. You'll find books listed in the Appendix that offer practical information on these topics. Also, discussing these matters with other parents with values and concerns similar to your own can prove invaluable. La Leche League Groups offer this opportunity. Although the basic meeting topics are related to breastfeeding and young babies, additional topics are often discussed at Couples' Nights, Chapter Meetings, or informal get-togethers that are planned.

La Leche League Area and International Conferences offer further opportunities to expand your understanding of parenthood. Check with your local La Leche League Leader or LLLI for details of upcoming events you may be interested in attending.

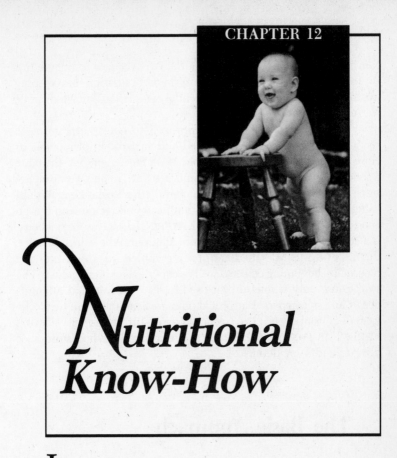

CHAPTER 12

# $N$utritional Know-How

If you already have good eating habits, there is no reason for you to make any major changes while you are breastfeeding. On the other hand, if you know that your eating habits need improvement, pregnancy and breastfeeding are good incentives to do this. Your baby's development during pregnancy depends to a great extent on good nutrition; your own health and well-being are also at stake. Your investment in your baby's welfare should provide strong motivation that will make it easier for you to change your eating habits.

Your baby will get off to a fine start on your milk. You will want him to build on this good start by giving him healthful foods when he is ready for them and by teaching him nutritionally sound eating habits that will become lifelong practices. The best way to accomplish this is by being a family in which everyone has good eating habits.

In this chapter, we include some general principles of food selection to help you learn how to choose the foods you and your family need to maintain good health. We urge you to pursue this topic further, reading other books on good nutrition and keeping up-to-date on dietary recommendations from knowledgeable sources.

La Leche League's basic approach to good nutrition is to recommend eating a well-balanced and varied diet of foods in as close to their natural state as possible. With few exceptions, the more a food is processed the more nutrients are lost. To help you prepare tasty and nutritious meals for your family, La Leche League publishes two cookbooks that include mother-tested recipes and tips on good nutrition. MOTHER'S IN THE KITCHEN, LLL's classic cookbook, is a collection of family favorites from all around the world. WHOLE FOODS FOR THE WHOLE FAMILY is a complete cookbook that can be used by beginning cooks as well as experienced family chefs. The recipes use only whole unprocessed foods with minimal amounts of salt and sweeteners. Both cookbooks are available from La Leche League Groups and La Leche League International. WHOLE FOODS FOR THE WHOLE FAMILY is also available in bookstores. See the Appendix for details.

# The Basic Approach

Some of the following suggestions have come from Dr. Herbert Ratner whose sensible approach to good nutrition is based on selecting foods in proper balance in order to meet all of our nutritional needs. He suggests the following:

- *Eat a variety of foods*
- *Eat a variety of animals and plants*
- *Eat a variety of the parts of animals and plants*

People instinctively seek a variety of styles and colors to decorate their homes and their bodies. The inner body also thrives on a diversity of foods with a wide range of flavors, colors, even textures—chewy, soft, firm, juicy, crisp. All the different textures, colors, and flavors of food reflect different food elements and values needed for the body.

In selecting foods, don't concentrate on four-legged animals, like the cow, to the exclusion of two-legged animals; or land animals to the exclusion of water animals. Don't limit yourself to muscle (for the most part the expensive cuts) such as steaks, chops, and roasts. Don't overlook liver, tongue, sweetbreads, hearts, kidneys, gizzards, soup bones, and the old-fashioned catchall: fresh sausage that you or your butcher make—free of chemicals, preservatives, dyes, and excessive amounts of fat. Remember also milk, cheese, and eggs.

In the plant kingdom, don't restrict yourself to a few vegetables to the exclusion of fruits, nuts, legumes, grains, and cereals; or green vegetables to the exclusion of orange and yellow vegetables. There are different parts of plants, too, that are edible. The parts don't have to belong to the same plant. There are leaves, including greens that go into a salad, as well as Swiss chard, collards, beet greens, kale, and cabbage. There are roots, like carrots, beets, yams, turnips, and onions. There are stems and tubers, including asparagus and potatoes, and the fruits of a plant, such as corn, string beans, and tomatoes, as well as apples, oranges, grapes, bananas, and melons.

Fats are needed in the cooking and preparation of some foods and they supply us with energy. There are animal fats and vegetable fats, solid fats and liquid fats. Animal fats include butter, cream, lard, and chicken fat. Fish oils, such as those used in cod-liver oil and vitamin A capsules, are also valuable. However, nutritionists today usually recommend moderate use of fats of any kind, particularly animal fats, because many people today consume excess amounts of fat.

## VARY YOUR MENUS

As you plan your family's meals, you'll want to provide variety in selecting foods. You can respect your own likes and dislikes as long as your dislikes aren't too numerous and as long as you do not impose your likes and dislikes on the rest of the family. After all, you don't want your children to grow up with restricted eating habits.

If there is a particular food you or other members of your family dislike, there is always a substitute. Cheese and yogurt are good substitutes for milk. Eggs are a good alternative to meat and fish, as are combinations of whole grains, nuts, dried peas, beans and lentils. This demonstrates one rule of nature. There is such a wide variety of foods that every culture in every age on every continent has had a varied selection of foodstuffs available to eat. This has resulted in a wondrous variety of national cuisines. Modern transportation and mechanization make possible a varied selection of foods throughout the year by sharing the productive seasons and rich bounty of other parts of the world with all of us.

## EAT NATURAL FOODS

Generally speaking, the farther one gets away from the natural state of a food, the less nutritional value the food is left with. Fresh foods are better than frozen or canned foods. Since cooking is one step removed from the natural state, some foods are better raw than cooked. This is especially true of fruits and vegetables, with a few exceptions. For example, vitamin A is more available in cooked carrots. Most protein foods need to be cooked. Undercooked foods, with due allowance for digestibility, are better than over-cooked foods. The stir-fry method used by the Chinese permits food to be cooked quickly and to retain many of the nutrients and flavor found in uncooked foods.

By partaking of the many digestible parts of the living whole, and by concentrating on natural foods, you will get all of the known nutrients in proper and natural proportions rather than in artificial concentrates. You will get all of the essential nutrients that have been discovered by science, and you should get those that have yet to be discovered; not only the vitamins and minerals of today, but the vitamins and minerals and other nutritional factors still undiscovered. This approach to nutrition is also more economical, and doesn't require a science course. It will protect you against ill health and at the same time supply you with a variety of choices to please everyone in your family.

## WHAT TO AVOID

**Chemical additives.** The fewer the additives the better! Civilization, although it has brought much progress, has also created some real problems in nutrition. In common use today in the food industry are a large number of chemicals that are added to enhance color or prolong shelf life. Much more study needs to be done to determine just how safe these chemicals are. In the meantime, since some of the chemicals have not been properly tested and their safety is uncertain, it seems wisest to avoid them. Read the labels on bottles, cans, and packages and choose those items that have the fewest chemicals or dyes. Better still, whenever possible, prepare your own food from the best products available.

*Getting little ones involved in food preparation helps them learn about good nutrition.*

**Sugar.** One of the chief offenders in confusing our appetites is sugar. Sugar is the principal seducer of the appetite. Used excessively it can dull the palate for the delicate flavors of fresh, natural food. Sugar can be easily misused and is especially bad for infants and young children, primarily because it satisfies hunger and displaces healthful, natural foods. Sugar is obvious in many desserts, candies, and soft drinks. But there is also an amazing amount of "hidden" sugar found in many other commonly used packaged and/or bottled foods. It is very important to your good health that you acquire the habit of reading the label on every packaged or bottled food item you buy.

Many of the best cooks in La Leche League have learned to cut out sugar entirely or greatly reduce it in as many recipes as they can. They have found that even in dessert recipes a sharp reduction in the amount of sugar called for works equally as well, and does not detract from the flavor. If your family is fond of gelatin desserts, for example, prepare your own using unflavored gelatin. Let ripe fruit be the only sweetener. If your little ones are served fresh fruit gelatin from the beginning, they'll love it. As you and your husband wean yourselves from too much sugar, your taste buds will begin to appreciate the flavor of natural sweetness.

**Salt.** Salt (sodium chloride) can be another offender in our diet. Like sugar, it is often misused in an attempt to enhance the flavor of our food. This may result in an excess intake of salt, which can be harmful. Excessive use of salt is linked to high blood pressure in some individuals. (Hypertension can lead to stroke—a leading cause of death in the United States.)

Salt was originally added to foods as a preservative and to cover up the unpleasant taste of foods that were spoiling because of lack of refrigeration. We are better off if we reduce the amount of salt we use. Many excellent cooks have found other ways to enhance flavor; they use lemon and/or a variety of herbs, spices, and other seasonings.

**Highly processed cereals and grains.** These products provide another source of confusion to our appetites. Many cereals and grains are converted, in processing, from natural to unnatural foods. This processing robs the cereals and grains of important minerals and vitamins. To correct this problem, an enrichment process was developed. From the public-health point of view, this was the most efficient way to correct the nutritional deficiencies that were occurring because of the preference people were developing for refined foods—(white instead of yellow or brown, fine instead of coarse, etc.). But *this enrichment is only an enrichment of an inferior product;* it does not make it into a superior product. It bears little resemblance to the original.

Cereals, with which we often start the day, have also been depleted of many nutrients, which have been sparsely restored by so-called enrichment. Pre-sweetened cereals are especially bad since they contain a bare minimum of food value and large amounts of tooth-decaying, appetite-seducing sugar. Whole-grain breakfast cereals, both hot and cold, are delicious, and there's a wide variety to choose from.

# How to Eat Well

By following the basic approach we have outlined so far, and adding the art of making foods tasty and attractive, you'll bring the joy of eating to the family table and you and your family will benefit nutritionally. Here are some practical tips to help you and your family eat well.

## READ THE LABELS

Acquiring the habit of reading the list of ingredients on food packages, cans, and bottles is most important. This will help you select foods that provide the most wholesome ingredients and avoid those that contain too much sugar, salt, chemical additives, or ingredients to which you or other family members may be allergic.

Another reason it is important to read the list of ingredients is because labels can often be misleading. A can labeled "fruit juice drink," for example, is just an artificial fruit-flavored drink. It is *not* pure fruit juice. By calling it a "drink" the company has stayed within acceptable labeling standards. Another confusing item is "milk drink." Sometimes the company lists the vitamins they've added, but these "fortified drinks" offer much less food value than real milk.

Be aware also that there's a difference between cheese food, processed cheese, and unprocessed, natural cheese. Only the latter has nothing added and nothing subtracted from the original product. Most grocery stores carry natural cheese; again be sure to read the label.

If an ingredient is listed on the label as "wheat flour," it refers to white flour. It must say "100% whole wheat" to mean that. You should also know that ingredients are listed in descending order of amounts found in the product. For example, if flour is the first ingredient listed, it means there's more flour in the product than anything else. If the second item is sugar, dextrose, or corn syrup, that means that next to flour there is more sweetener than anything else, and so on down the line. The chemicals are usually listed last, but some highly processed items may have more chemicals than food: for example, coffee-cream substitutes, some pudding desserts, and some ice creams contain more chemicals than anything else.

## CHANGING FOOD HABITS

Food habits don't change overnight. Introducing new foods requires tact, patience, and imagination. In the beginning you'll want to choose alternatives that resemble familiar foods. When you are shopping and reading labels, don't even bring home the foods you don't want your family to eat. If the adults in the family continue to snack on cookies and chips, the children will want to follow their example.

Creative approaches can make new foods more appealing. Melted cheese on whole-grain bread may look better to a toddler if it's in the shape of a triangle or a butterfly. A melon slice on salad greens can be a sailboat salad. Tickle your toddler's imagination by calling the crunchy inside slice of an apple an apple "cookie." Colorful sliced vegetables with dip have eye appeal. Even unusual containers can pique children's interest. Serve snacks on toy dishes, in special cups, or in a toddler's very own lunch box. Try a blender drink of bananas, milk, some ice, and a little vanilla. If it's served in a shake glass with a straw, what child could resist?

## USING WHOLE GRAINS

Introducing whole grains to your family can be an enjoyable change because there are hundreds of ways to use them. If your family doesn't like oatmeal for breakfast, try cornmeal, either as a cereal, good old-fashioned fried cornmeal mush, or when you have time, nice hot corn bread. Some recipes use a combination of cornmeal and whole-wheat flour, others use cornmeal only. Kasha is an old standby from people whose origins are in the Middle East and Eastern Europe. It is both nutritious and easy to cook. It can be used hot or cold, much like rice. The smell of spicy raisin-bran muffins baking will draw people to the table. A hot bran muffin is hard to resist. What a pleasant way to get your family off to a good, energetic start for the day! Try using granola, too. Granola recipes abound and it's fun to make your own, since the commercial varieties are often heavy on sweeteners and fats.

Husbands and older children have been known to balk at the introduction of whole-wheat bread. One suggestion is to offer them "half and half" sandwiches for a while—using one slice of whole-wheat bread and one slice of white. Very young children whose tastes have not had time to become conditioned usually like the whole grain bread right away.

If you do a lot of baking, you can introduce whole-wheat flour gradually into your baked goods. Just substitute a small amount of whole-wheat flour for the white flour you usually use in the recipe. This is especially easy to do in homemade breads. Many mothers have found that baking their own bread is great fun and a lot easier than they expected. If you gradually increase the amount of whole-wheat flour to the white flour over a period of months, eventually you'll be making a one hundred percent whole-wheat bread that no longer tastes "strange" to your family. It may even become more desirable than the white bread they used to like, especially when it's hot from the oven!

If you do use white flour in your recipes, be sure to use un-bleached flour, so as to avoid the extra chemicals used for bleach-ing. For extra nutrition, place one tablespoon of soy flour in each cup of white flour. Soy is high in protein, so it will add to the food value of the baked goods and will not be noticed in the final prod-uct. Dried skim-milk powder is also a nutritious supplement if milk allergy is not a problem. A tablespoon or two can be added to vari-ous cake, bread, muffin, or pancake recipes without changing tex-ture or flavor.

## USE NUTS AND SEEDS IN RECIPES

Plain raw nuts and seeds are too full of goodness to overlook. Even when roasted they are still nutritious, though less so than when raw. You can increase the food value in your potato salad, or chicken or tuna salad, by adding a tablespoon or two of hulled, raw, un-roasted sesame seeds. They are so tiny and bland in flavor that even the pickiest member of your family won't notice them. A sprinkle of raw sunflower or hulled raw sesame seeds over breakfast cereal or yogurt also will increase food value and add both flavor and a bit of crunch. In just about any kind of batter you make, you can add sesame seeds or finely ground nuts, and no one will be the wiser. Nuts and seeds are delicious in waffles, pancakes, muffins, and breads.

Nuts and seeds packaged by the ounce and sold in the grocery store are relatively expensive, as well as often stale. Look for one of the new, "old-fashioned" stores where you can scoop nuts, seeds, and dried fruits from big bins and buy them by the pound. These usually offer considerable savings over the packaged variety, and they are likely to be fresher and better flavored. Store them in the freezer to keep them fresh longer.

A caution is needed about giving nuts to children under three or so. The young child may not chew them well and there is a dan-ger of small chunks being inhaled into the lungs instead of going down the throat.

## EAT LESS MEAT

If your family is accustomed to eating only beef and chicken, try this easy way to prepare fish. Start with fillets, about one-inch thick, completely boned, either fresh or frozen. Broiling is the easiest and quickest way to cook them, and the shorter the cooking time the more nutrition is retained. Spread a thin coating of melted butter or oil on the fillet and broil about five minutes on each side, longer if frozen or if fillet is more than an inch thick. Before serving, sprinkle with dill weed, paprika, curry powder, or whatever spice you prefer then squeeze on some fresh lemon juice or place lemon slices on the serving plate as a finishing touch.

## BETWEEN-MEAL SNACKS

Make between-meal snacks nutritious and not just something to fill up on. If you or the children are ravenous and supper isn't ready, try raw vegetables or fresh fruit. If the apple or orange you offer a hungry little one is sliced, peeled, and cut into small portions, even the most finicky little eater is less likely to refuse. Even if a light eater's appetite is somewhat lessened by the before-meal snack, it really doesn't matter as long as the snack is nutritious. Just consider it part of his meal. Many times a nutritious morsel is gobbled avidly when handed out beforehand when it might have been scorned had it appeared cooked on a dinner plate. This reminds us of a mother who routinely cooks only half of the vegetables for a meal, serving the remainder raw at the table so each child can take his choice. You'll have to be careful of raw carrots, though, for the child under three. They may not be chewed properly, and can be inhaled rather than swallowed. Young children can usually handle other raw vegetables and fruits quite well.

Frozen snacks have special appeal in hot weather. While toddlers are teething, frozen foods can also be soothing to sore gums. Some nutritious frozen snacks are: yogurt and fruit juice popsicles, frozen blueberries, strawberries, slices of peach or pear, and even frozen green peas. Frozen bananas on a stick are much better for your children than ice cream bars.

Dried fruits, including raisins, are nutritious, but should not be eaten as a daily snack. They are hard on the teeth because of the high natural sugar content. Because of their sticky texture they also tend to stick in the crevices of the teeth, evading the toothbrush and thereby contributing to tooth decay. In addition, many dried fruits have been sulphured, and dipped needlessly in honey or rolled in sugar, which you don't need. If you have access to sun-dried fruits, with no sugar or honey added, they make excellent sweeteners for cakes, cookies, or muffins made from whole-grain flour. Used in baking they are easier on the teeth.

## QUENCHING YOUR THIRST

Unsweetened fruit and vegetable juices provide food value as well as quenching your thirst. There are many varieties of canned or bottled apple, grape, tomato, grapefruit, and pineapple juices that are unsweetened, with no chemical additives. But you have to read the labels and avoid any that are called "fruit drinks." Frozen orange, apple, grape, and other juice concentrates are also available in unsweetened brands. Freshly squeezed orange or grapefruit juice is delicious when available. Try adding carbonated mineral water to fruit juice for a bubbly treat.

If you begin having these juices on hand, chilled and ready, your family will learn to enjoy their natural sweetness. Of course, you'll want to completely avoid buying colas and other soft drinks. If they aren't even in the house, the natural drinks will be more appealing.

**Don't forget water!** To really quench one's thirst there is nothing like it! Sometimes when it comes from the refrigerator it is more appealing to the younger set. Water will seem more attractive poured from a brightly colored container than if it were just "plain old water from the faucet." A slice of fresh lime in a glass of ice water on a hot summer day both looks and tastes refreshing. Because of the pressure to serve soft drinks, parents have to be patient and persistent in resisting, and imaginative in providing substitutes.

## GROW IT YOURSELF

One of the best suggestions we can offer is to plant your own vegetable garden. If you have space in your yard, so much the better. If not, see if your local park district offers small plots of land to would-be gardeners. Or see if a friend or neighbor would like to lend you space in return for a few fresh fruits and vegetables.

There is something very special about the smell of a garden growing—the pungent scent of tomatoes, the sweet-sharp smell of carrot tops, and the rich warm smell of good dirt.

An advantage of growing your own vegetables is that they will be free of the chemicals commercial growers use in the soil, as well as free of the pesticides that are sprayed on the plants during various stages of growth. Unfortunately, some of these chemicals remain on the skin of the fruit or vegetables and cannot be washed off. When you peel them to get rid of the chemicals, you also lose some valuable nutrients. With homegrown produce, it's a choice you don't have to make.

# Special Hints for Nursing Mothers

We stated earlier that if you have good eating habits, there is no reason for you to make any major changes when you are breast-feeding. You do have to remember to eat enough to keep yourself in good health. Eating well is part of being a good mother.

## A FEW REMINDERS

Nursing mothers just naturally feel the need for extra liquids and should drink enough to satisfy their thirst. You can drink water, fruit and vegetable juices, milk, soup, or other liquids. In the excitement and bustle of caring for a new baby, you may not always notice that you are dry and thirsty. Some mothers take a drink of water whenever they sit down to nurse the baby. If you are producing large amounts of pale yellow urine, you are probably drinking all you need.

Constipation (hard, dry stools) may be a secondary sign of inadequate fluid. If you get constipated, increase your liquid intake as well as your consumption of fresh fruits and raw vegetables. And be sure you're getting enough whole grains (breads and cereals). Avoid commercial remedies. In fact, it is better to try to prevent the problem by starting during pregnancy to eat the proper foods and to see that you are well stocked with the necessary items to use after baby is born. Many new mothers have found that raw pears are especially effective for keeping bowels loose. Prunes, raw or cooked, and prune juice are also helpful.

## MILK PRODUCTS AND OTHER SOURCES OF CALCIUM

You don't have to drink lots of milk in order to make milk for your baby. If you are allergic to milk, you don't have to drink it at all. Cow's milk is a good source of calcium but it is also a very common allergen. If there is a history of allergy in your family you might want to cut down on milk during your pregnancy as this is when some babies become sensitized to it. The reaction shows up after the baby is born.

Even if you are not sensitive to cow's milk, you may not care for it. It is good to realize there are other products that will provide the calcium you and your baby need. Yogurt, hard cheeses (such

*A breastfeeding mother needs to take good care of herself.*

as cheddar, Swiss, and parmesan), and cottage cheese are good sources of calcium. Many people with milk allergies can tolerate at least small amounts of these. Blackstrap molasses and tofu, a soybean product that is becoming more widely available, are also good sources of calcium, as are cooked cabbage, collards and kale. Sesame seeds are especially rich in calcium. They can be added to baked goods, muffin or pancake batter, or sprinkled on salads or cereal.

Generally, meat and nuts are not good calcium sources but three exceptions worth noting are liver, almonds, and Brazil nuts. In the fish family, very high calcium is found in canned sardines and canned sockeye red salmon, both of which are normally eaten with bones. These bones, unlike the thin sharp bones found in most fish, are usually round and soft enough to eat. They provide a nice crunch to the softer consistency of the fish.

## CAFFEINE AND SOFT DRINKS

If you are accustomed to drinking lots of coffee, tea, or cola, you may wonder how the caffeine will affect your baby.

Excessive caffeine intake by the nursing mother may cause a reaction in her baby. If you drink more than two or three cups of coffee or tea a day and drink cola besides or eat chocolate frequently, you're getting quite a bit of caffeine. If you suspect it may be causing fussiness or slow weight gain in your baby, cut down for a week and see if it helps. Since people do become addicted to caffeine, cutting it out abruptly may give you a headache for a day or so. In general, it's best to get most of your daily liquids in water, juice, or milk and limit your intake of coffee or tea.

Remember that in addition to caffeine, soft drinks contain lots of sugar and no value. Sugarless soft drinks are not good either. Sugar substitutes may be easier on the teeth but could be hazardous to your health. Remember—if you as a parent consume soft drinks daily, you can be sure your children will want to follow your example.

## SUPPLEMENTS

Many people today report good results in preventing or eliminating certain deficiencies by taking vitamin or mineral supplements. Of course they are only supplements—they do not substitute for good food.

Your doctor may advise supplementary vitamins and minerals for you during pregnancy, particularly iron, to replenish and build up the stores from which your baby is building up his own supply of iron to carry him through his first half year of life. During the time while you are breastfeeding, your doctor may suggest that you continue taking them.

Many mothers report good results from taking brewer's yeast, a natural vitamin B-complex concentrate. Some feel that it definitely helps increase their milk supply; others report that it is a help in combating fatigue, depression, and irritability. Of course, the best way to avoid these things is by improving your daily diet and getting enough rest. But if you feel you need extra help, brewer's yeast might be right for you. It contains not only the B-complex vitamins but also large amounts of iron and protein.

There are some mothers who report fussiness in their babies when they take brewer's yeast.

# A WORD ABOUT DIETING

Mothers often wonder if it's possible to lose weight while breastfeeding. The answer is yes. In fact, breastfeeding makes it easier to shed the extra pounds put on during pregnancy. Those pounds were put there, after all, to store energy for producing milk. New mothers who do not breastfeed have to depend on diet and exercise for weight loss. Breastfeeding women have a head start, because the caloric demands of milk production are already using up extra energy.

According to Dr. Judith Roepke, a nutritionist at Ball State University in Indiana, and a member of LLLI's Health Advisory Council, lactation may be an ideal time to lose weight. Lactation seems to mobilize even fat accumulated before the pregnancy. But it's important to go slowly. Dr. Roepke suggests that nursing mothers do nothing to consciously bring about weight loss during the first two months postpartum. Your body needs that time to recover from childbirth and to establish a good milk supply, and most breastfeeding mothers will lose a few pounds anyway while following a normal diet. If after two months you haven't lost any weight, you probably need to increase your activity level as well as decrease your caloric intake by cutting back on starches and sweets. Put the baby in a stroller or baby carrier and head out of doors for a two-mile walk five times a week. At the same time, eliminate just 100 calories from your daily diet and you can expect to lose two or three pounds in a month. Not a dramatic weight loss, but one that guarantees that you and your baby will both stay well nourished. And the exercise has benefits that go beyond pounds and inches.

Crash diets, fad diets, and quick weight loss present problems for nursing mothers. Environmental contaminants like PCBs and pesticides are stored in body fat. Losing weight quickly releases these contaminants into your blood and can increase the levels in your milk. Unfortunately contaminants are a fact of modern life, but where possible, it's wise to minimize your baby's exposure. Exceptionally high protein/low-carbohydrate diets are potentially harmful because of substances released into the milk by the mother's altered metabolism. Any kind of drastic weight loss carries the risk of a drop in milk supply.

Many mothers find that weight loss takes care of itself while breastfeeding. Steering clear of sweets and "junk foods" (high-calorie foods with little nutritious value) and concentrating on good nutrition is often all it takes. Good nutrition will also help you combat the fatigue and emotional ups and downs that are an inevitable part of new motherhood.

## SOME SPECIAL PRECAUTIONS

**Smoking.** You probably know some of the disturbing statistics on the effects of smoking. The potential hazards of smoking during pregnancy may have been incentive enough for you to quit or cut down. However, despite your best intentions you may find yourself still smoking when your baby is born, and you wonder how this will affect breastfeeding.

The fewer cigarettes smoked, the less chance there is that difficulties will arise. By keeping smoking to a minimum, a mother can decrease the risk. Some mothers smoke and breastfeed with no problem. In general, if a mother smokes less than a pack (twenty cigarettes) a day, the amount of nicotine in her milk is not usually enough to cause any problem for the baby. Nicotine is not readily absorbed by the baby's intestinal tract and is rather quickly metabolized.

When a nursing mother smokes heavily (more than twenty to thirty cigarettes a day), the risks increase. Heavy smoking can reduce a mother's milk supply and on rare occasions has caused symptoms in the nursing baby such as nausea, vomiting, abdominal cramps, and diarrhea.

One study found that smoking lowers prolactin levels in nursing mothers. In other studies, smoking has been shown to interfere with the let-down reflex. If a mother smokes, she should not do so while she is feeding the baby.

Second-hand, or "side-stream" smoke, is potentially harmful for babies and young children. One study featured in *Lancet,* a British medical journal, found a significant correlation between parents' smoking habits and the incidence of pneumonia, bronchitis, and SIDS during their babies' first year of life.

There are legitimate concerns about the effects of smoking on a breastfeeding mother and her baby. The ideal solution is to avoid smoking. For those who can't seem to quit, cutting down is another option that might seem more within reach. When there are children in the family it's best to limit smoking to a separate room, away from the children. Keep a window open or use an exhaust fan. Better yet, smoke only outdoors.

**Alcohol.** An anxious, overtired mother may sometimes find that an occasional glass of wine or beer helps her to feel relaxed. Of course, as mother becomes less tense so does her baby.

The effects of alcohol on the breastfeeding baby are directly related to the amount the mother ingests. When the breastfeeding mother drinks moderately (two drinks or less per day), the amount of alcohol her baby receives has not been shown to be harmful. It is generally recommended that alcohol be avoided entirely during pregnancy.

At times, the use of alcohol has been suggested as a way to encourage a mother's let-down reflex. In some cases, because of its varying effects on the central nervous system, large amounts of alcohol can inhibit milk ejection.

Breastfeeding itself is an excellent tranquilizer, and relaxing is the key. Many mothers who choose not to drink alcohol find that tension drains away with a cup of hot or iced tea, or another favorite beverage. Lying down can do wonders, and listening to music is soothing. Especially nice is having your husband's reassuring arms around you when you're nervous about your new responsibilities.

**Drugs and Medications.** You should make it a practice not to take any medication whatsoever unless it is definitely necessary and has been prescribed or approved by a physician.

In general, there are relatively few medications that must be totally avoided by a nursing mother. This topic is discussed more thoroughly in a later chapter.

As for so-called "recreational drugs," these are best avoided by a breastfeeding mother. Reseach into their effects on the nursing baby have not been conclusive but they can be detrimental to a mother's ability to care for her baby. The use of marijuana, for example, has been found to cause significantly lower levels of prolactin, the "mothering" hormone that is important not only to an adequate milk supply but to the whole mother-baby relationship. THC, the active chemical in marijuana, appears in breast milk in small amounts. Why take a chance of exposing your baby to potential harm?

Taking good care of yourself and taking good care of your baby go hand in hand. Learning about good nutrition can improve your family's health and add to your overall enjoyment of life. You'll find it's worth your while to feed your family well.

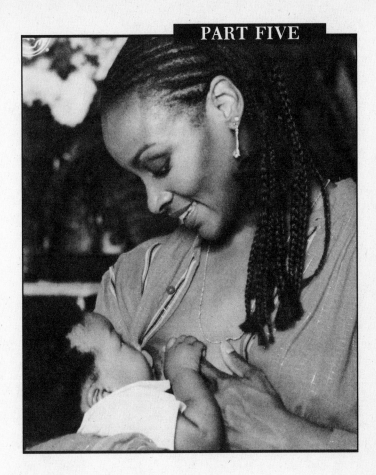

# PART FIVE

# As Your Baby Grows

# CHAPTER 13

# Ready for Solids

Hand in hand with bottle feeding of babies, a trend toward feeding solids earlier and earlier in infancy developed and took hold in the United States. A spirit of rivalry and competition arose among mothers (and sometimes doctors) to have the biggest baby who ate the most foods in the largest quantity at the earliest possible age. The baby food industry promoted and encouraged this trend. Mothers were led to believe that there was an advantage in giving solids early.

Today medical scientists have verified that breast milk gives the best assurance of proper nourishment because it is nature's complete food for the baby. Young babies do best without the early addition of solids to their diet. Breast milk is the perfect food for at least the first six months for the healthy, full-term infant, and there is usually no reason for adding any foods to the breastfed baby's diet before that time. In its 1980 recommendations, The American Academy of Pediatrics Committee on Nutrition advocates only breast milk until four to six months of age and does not routinely advise vitamin and mineral supplements for the full-term breastfed infant.

There are at least two good reasons for waiting. First, you want to maintain your milk supply, and the more solids the baby takes, the less milk he will want; the less he takes from the breast, the less milk there will be. It is the mother who starts solids early who will quite likely find that her milk supply is gone soon thereafter. She has substituted an inferior food for a superior food by adding solids to the baby's diet before he needs them.

The second reason for waiting is that the younger the baby, the more likely it is that any foods other than breast milk will cause food allergies. Cow's milk, used in most formulas, is the most common allergen there is. Most solid foods are poorly digested and may cause an unpleasant reaction in a two-month-old, but are readily assimilated by the same child if they are delayed until he is six months or older.

Until his immature digestive system develops to the point where it can utilize other foods without upsets, it is both kind and wise to give the baby the benefit of a few extra months of the food that nature has devoted millions of years to perfecting for him.

Some babies with a tendency to allergies will refuse solids even at six or eight months. This could be nature's way of protecting that baby from foods that will cause him problems. Such babies can continue to do well on breast milk alone until their systems are ready to tolerate other foods.

At some point around six or seven months, most babies start to teethe, and your baby's natural urge to chew and bite begins to develop. His mouth and tongue are ready for the new skills he will need, and his digestive system is probably ready to handle new foods.

Your baby will let you know when he is ready; watch him, not the calendar. If he suddenly increases his demand to be fed at some time around six months of age, and this increased demand continues for four or five days in spite of more frequent nursings, you can assume the time has come to start him on solids. If he is much younger than six months, however, don't get excited at these first signs and rush the start of solids, because his behavior might be due to other causes. A cold coming on might make him want the solace of nursing more often. If he is ill, this is not the time to begin new foods. Stepped-up activity on your part may be making you feel rushed and tense, and he is calling for needed attention. If he is fussy for some reason other than hunger, he will have enough to cope with. So play it safe and nurse more often for a few days before deciding it is really hunger that is responsible for his behavior change.

## VITAMIN SUPPLEMENTS

First, a word about vitamin supplements. If the nursing mother gets an adequate supply of vitamins from her diet, her milk will have an adequate supply of vitamins, in just the right proportions for her baby. Research continues to bear this out. Your physician may suggest that you continue taking prenatal vitamins while you are breastfeeding. Vitamin supplements for babies got their impetus as a supplement to formula, which is still not the perfect food for your baby. As long as your baby is thriving on your milk alone, he has no need for additional vitamins, iron, fluoride, or other supplements in the early months.

## BABY'S FIRST FOODS

By the time babies are ready for solids, they are also ready and able to sit up alone in a high chair and they just naturally want to put everything in their mouths. The simplest way to begin solids is to sit baby in his chair or, if he prefers, on your lap, and let him experiment with a tiny taste or so of his first food.

These first feedings of solid food usually go more smoothly if you nurse your baby first, to take the edge off his appetite. Otherwise he will be in no mood to try something new. With practice and patience on your part, he will catch on soon enough. These first few attempts are merely to introduce the idea of solids to him, not to fill him up. At first, use a small spoon and place just a small amount of food on it, about one-fourth of a teaspoonful. If you have an independent baby who balks at spoon feeding, provide him with finger food, small bites of food he can pick up and put into his mouth by himself. Learning to grasp small finger foods like cooked peas or beans will help him gain finger control and coordination. By the time he is a year old, he will probably be feeding himself, with very little help from you.

A word of warning is in order here. Most babies have an excellent gag reflex and manage to get up anything that goes down the wrong way. But while your little one is learning to handle food all by himself, you don't want to leave him alone and walk away. Also, be sure your baby is not given any foods to teethe on while he is lying down, as these could go too far back into his throat and cause him to choke.

## NEATNESS DOESN'T COUNT

Now is not the time to worry about neatness. A hungry baby is easily frustrated when instead of another tasty bite of food he is suddenly attacked by a wet washcloth. Squelch your tidy impulses for the time being. Your baby is just learning the basics of eating and isn't ready for lessons in manners yet. Put a big bib on him and move his chair off the rug or put a sheet of plastic under it. (A hungry dog is handy for cleaning up under the high chair!)

You will avoid some messes, though, and make the learning process easier for him, if you have only one thing at a time on his tray—one piece of the finger food, later one unbreakable dish with a not-too-large serving of one food, and (not at the same time) a small unbreakable cup, half full. Keep servings small.

New foods should be introduced one at a time. This means a single food, not a mixed food like stew or soup, or even a mixed-grain cereal. The reason for this precaution is that although the baby at six or seven months is not nearly so likely to have an allergic reaction as a younger child, it is still possible. If you introduce foods one at a time and he develops a rash or a sore bottom, potential indications of allergy, you will know what the most likely cause is and can eliminate the food temporarily. Wait until baby is at least a year old before introducing foods that cause allergic reactions in other family members.

It is a good plan to allow a week between each new food introduced. There is no advantage to be gained by striving for the widest variety of foods in the shortest time possible. Rather it is good for the baby to be given the opportunity to experience each new food thoroughly before going on to another. Start with about a quarter-teaspoon of a new food once the first day. Increase the amount little by little until by the end of a week he is getting as much as he wants two or three times a day. He will probably let you know when he has had enough by turning his head, clamping his mouth shut, spitting the food back out, or some other unmistakable gesture. Take his word for it. Don't start feeding problems by coaxing, pushing, or forcing. Give him only as much as he wants, not what you think he should have.

Babies have likes and dislikes about foods, as we all do. So if your baby turns away from any particular food, don't panic. Just skip it and try something else. Even if he has happily consumed three

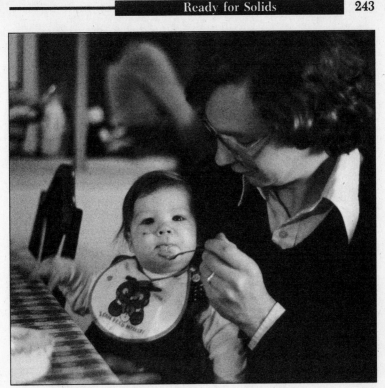

*Dad can help out when it's time for baby to start on solid foods.*

bananas a day for a week, and suddenly he won't look at one, go along with him. He's not sick—just sick of bananas.

Once a food has been started, try to keep at least a bit of it on his menu once a week or so thereafter, to avoid the possibility of an allergic reaction on its reintroduction after a lapse of time. This precaution should be kept up during the baby's first year.

# What Foods to Choose

Most of us find it unnecessary to use commercial baby foods at all. They are relatively expensive, and some varieties contain undesirable fillers and preservatives. If you do use commercial foods, read the labels to determine exactly what is in them. Though improvements have been made in recent years, for most babies, starting with table foods is easiest and best. If you understand good nutrition, and your family's eating habits are pretty good, then the food from your table will be fine for your baby, too. This also makes the transition to family meals easier. (See Chapter 12, "Nutritional Know-How.")

A blender or food processor can be used to make some table foods easier for baby to manage. However, a fork works nicely for most things you'll be giving him. If baby is six months or older when he's starting solids, he does not need foods pureed or liquified.

Here is a suggested guide for introducing solids to your baby.

**Raw, Mashed Banana.** This is a good food to start with, since it is fresh and wholesome and contains more food value than cereals. Babies usually love the smooth consistency of a ripe banana. After you've given your baby a small taste the first time and gradually increased the amount, you can offer the baby a whole piece of banana to handle himself, thus quickly eliminating one mashed food as well as pleasing the baby who likes to feed himself, and mash it himself, too...between his fingers!

If your baby doesn't care for banana, sweet potato (or yam) is a good alternative. It is preferable to bake it whole to better preserve all the nutrients. Sweet potato has a fine flavor and maximum food value. Most babies love it.

**Meat.** Meat is introduced early among solid foods because of its high iron and protein content. It is not difficult to reduce table meats to a consistency right for baby. Chopped beef, stew meats, or tender pieces of chicken can easily be cut up into small pieces or mashed with a fork. Better yet, scrape across a piece of raw meat with a knife. Tough connecting fibers will remain behind while the tender portions can be gently cooked for baby to eat.

When baby has had a week on one meat, try handing him a good-sized bone with no splinters or sharp corners, but with a few fragments of meat still on it. A chicken drumstick is good, and just about the right size for his grasp. (Be sure to first remove the needle thin splint bone.) Chances are he will chomp away on the bone with great relish, especially if he has the urge to chew and bite. He'll be developing muscle coordination in the process, too.

To make sure you have on hand the kind of meat your baby can handle, keep individual portions of cooked, chopped, or scraped beef or chicken, wrapped and frozen. When you have meat at the table that might be too difficult for the baby, put the frozen meat into a saucepan over low heat, tightly covered or still in its aluminum foil wrapper. The moisture from the frozen meat will steam it nicely in a few minutes.

**Fish** is another excellent protein food. It is entirely suitable for baby and rich in valuable nutrients, so if your family menu includes fish frequently, you can introduce baby to it, too. Watch out for bones. Check each piece between your fingers before giving it to baby. And wait until baby is older to introduce smoked and pickled fish or shellfish.

**Whole-Grain Breads and Cereals.** Finger-sized pieces of dried or toasted whole-wheat bread are good chewing foods for your baby and handy to offer him, perhaps between meals or while you are preparing dinner. Whole-wheat bread is the type most commonly available, but other whole-grain breads are also good. If you regularly serve a cooked whole-grain cereal you might want to introduce this; but be sure there is no sugar or other sweetener added, and cook it with water, not milk. Avoid mixed-grain cereals until baby has been introduced to each one. Baby cereals do not have quite as much food value as your own freshly cooked whole-grain cereals because they are more highly processed. They are an additional expense as well.

Another nice thing about whole-wheat toast (or a day-old heel of the loaf) is that it's good for spreading things on. A very thin layer of smooth peanut butter, for instance, is a popular spread, and it's very nutritious. Be sure to buy the natural variety, without added sweeteners and preservatives. Babies love it. Later on, cheese and homemade nutritious spreads can be added to the menu.

**Fresh Fruits.** Raw, peeled apple or pear can be grated, or scraped with the edge of a spoon, and put in a little mound on baby's high-chair tray. It won't be long before you can hand him a piece of peeled apple, ripe pear, or peach to munch on. Apricots, plums, and melons are good, too. If baby is eight months or older, other fresh fruits in season may be offered, but with caution. Some berries have seeds that babies are not old enough to handle well.

Frozen blueberries make wonderful finger food; baby will love the cold, crunchy taste, especially if he's teething. Citrus fruits can cause allergy, so wait with those until baby is about a year. Tangerine segments are good to start with, but be sure to take the seeds out.

Avoid canned fruits that contain sugar. They have less food value than fresh fruits, but unsweetened canned fruits are better than no fruit at all. Dried fruits such as raisins, dates, or figs should not be given at all in the first year, and later only on a limited basis. Although they are nutritious, they are very sweet and tend to stick between the teeth which can cause cavities.

**Vegetables.** Sweet potato, as we suggested before, and white potato are both good choices for baby. Don't add butter or margarine to baby's portion until after dairy products have been introduced.

Finely grated raw carrot can be mixed with grated apple or some of the other foods baby is getting. Cooked carrots are good, too. Other cooked vegetables may be offered from your table one at a time, just as you do with any new food. Some little ones enjoy frozen vegetables right from the package—especially frozen peas they can pick up and pop into their mouths one at a time.

Don't be concerned if, in the beginning, you find little bits of vegetable, virtually unchanged, in the diaper. Even cooked vegetables are harder to digest than many other foods.

Raw vegetables have more food value than cooked vegetables, but most of them are too hard for a little one to chew and digest. Some raw vegetables—particularly carrots and celery—can be dangerous as small chunks can be inhaled rather than swallowed.

**Eggs.** Since eggs, especially the whites, seem to be one of the more common causes of allergies, it might be best to wait until the baby is about a year old before introducing them. At first the egg should be hard-boiled. Place the egg in water and bring to a boil. Remove from heat, cover, and let stand twenty minutes. Peel under cool water. Feed baby only the yolk at first, mashed and moistened to suit his preferences. Start with no more than a quarter-teaspoon and increase gradually, a quarter-teaspoon at a time. After baby has been eating eggs well for a month or so you can give him scrambled eggs. Babies usually love to eat them as a finger food. Or cook an egg in with his cereal for extra nutrition.

**Cow's Milk and Other Dairy Products.** If there is a history of allergy in the family, or baby has already shown signs of it, avoid cow's milk entirely. The only milk your baby needs is yours. In some parts of the world, adults do not drink milk at all, but eat well otherwise, and the people are healthy and well-nourished.

Cottage cheese, yogurt, and natural cheeses can be introduced when baby is nine or ten months old. These dairy products provide calcium and other nutrients but they are much less likely to cause allergies than cow's milk. You can also add butter or margarine about this time, but do so sparingly.

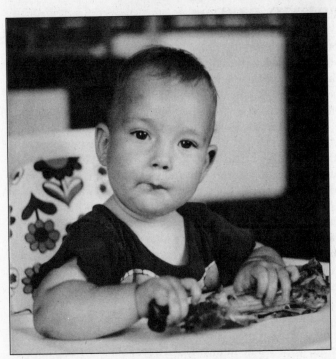

*It won't be long before your little guy is eating all by himself.*

## INTRODUCING THE CUP

At about ten months to a year you can start offering your baby water or juice from a cup once a day at mealtime or in between, whichever suits you best. There's no need to rush. For some time most of it will go down his chin. A tip on getting the baby started with a cup comes from Betty Wagner: let him drink through a short straw. (The bendable kind works well.) The sucking comes easily to him, and it's neater too—no drips or dribbles. Or, try the kind of plastic cup that comes with a tight-fitting lid and a spout, and doesn't tip over.

Baby's beverages should consist mainly of your milk, water, homemade soups (canned soups may contain a lot of salt and preservatives), and unsweetened fruit or vegetable juice. (Remember to check the label on the juice can.) No soft drinks please—these are heavy on sugar or sugar substitutes and sometimes caffeine, and are lacking in anything worthwhile. There is still no substitute for a good drink of water.

## WHAT TO AVOID

You will notice that from the beginning we are suggesting you feed your baby wholesome, nutritious foods. We would strongly urge you to avoid processed foods that are so often full of sugar, salt, preservatives, and chemicals.

Once you have given your baby the best start by breastfeeding him, we are sure you'll want to continue along those lines when he starts to eat other foods. Your baby will do just fine without cookies, pretzels, teething biscuits, puddings, cakes, and ice cream. Let him first develop a taste for the natural sweetness of fresh fruits and the natural goodness of whole grains. Now is the best time to start developing habits of good nutrition that will last a lifetime.

The whole process of starting your baby on solid foods may take from three to six months. Once he's eating a variety of foods without any signs of allergy or distress, you can be less concerned about mixing foods or introducing something new. As long as what you offer him is good, nourishing food, you can let his appetite be your guide as to what he wants to eat and when he wants to eat it.

As you are getting your little one well launched in the eating department, you'll want to learn as much as you can about good nutrition for your whole family. LLLI's cookbooks—MOTHER'S IN THE KITCHEN and WHOLE FOODS FOR THE WHOLE FAMILY—will give you good suggestions for keeping baby, and everyone else in the family, deliciously well-fed. For details, see the Appendix.

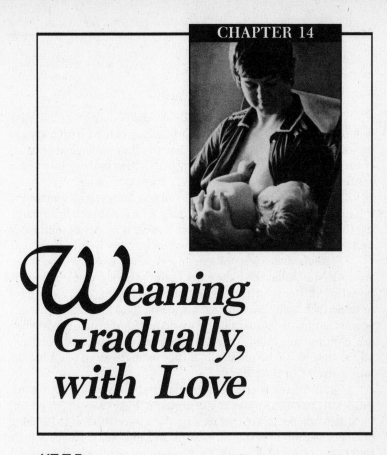

# CHAPTER 14

# Weaning Gradually, with Love

"When shall I wean my baby? How shall I go about it? How long will it take?" Some mothers begin to worry about weaning when their infant is only a few weeks old.

Why do mothers begin worrying about ending breastfeeding almost as soon as they've started? No doubt there are many reasons, but we suspect that not the least among them is the fact that society often expects babies to be weaned early. Mothers are uneasy about the thought that their babies might still be nursing after society expects them to be weaned from the breast.

We don't agree with society's attitudes about early weaning. We believe that ideally the breastfeeding relationship should continue until the baby outgrows the need.

One mother who had weaned because of criticism from others, had this to say about her decision: "I let pressure from people prematurely end one of the most meaningful experiences I have had with my son....I wish I had it to do all over again now that I am more sure of myself."

249

# More Than Milk

Your milk continues to provide special benefits for your baby as long as you nurse him. It doesn't lose its goodness with the passing of time. Research has shown that the immunological benefits of breast milk that protect your baby from illness in the early months continue to offer protection as your baby gets older.

If we consider breastfeeding only as a means of nourishing the infant, then we can see why it might be feasible to bring nursing to an end as soon as the baby can handle a variety of solid foods and milk from a cup—perhaps even before his first birthday.

It is when we view the nursing experience as a whole, when we understand that the baby has emotional needs which can easily be satisfied through the closeness of breastfeeding, that it is hard to understand why we must set a specific time for ending this important, intimate relationship. If we do not satisfy these needs when our children are small, they may be as undernourished emotionally as they would be physically if they were deprived of an important nutrient in their diet.

Dr. William Sears, pediatrician and author of THE GROWING FAMILY SERIES, makes this comment: "Early weaning is an unfortunate practice in western society. We are accustomed to thinking of breastfeeding in terms of months and not years. I have a little sign in my office which says 'Early weaning not recommended for babies.'"

## EMOTIONAL NEEDS

The breastfeeding mother and her baby build up a relationship based on their mutual needs, and the relationship changes gradually as the needs change. One of the most urgent needs of the tiny baby is food, and during this period of infancy the mother's physical need is to be relieved of the milk that fills her breasts for the sake of the baby. However, the mother and baby depend upon each other for many other things. The baby needs affection, and the mother enjoys responding to his need to be loved. The mother has a strong desire to be truly needed by this tiny one. But at some point, usually gradually, the baby's dependence on mother lessens. He begins to broaden his horizons, to try his wings. But nursing is still important, for it is a secure haven in a sometimes difficult world.

When the baby does not wean by a year or so, a mother may wonder if this means he is too dependent on her. She may fear that letting him continue to nurse will prevent him from growing toward independence. But weaning is a step toward growing up and, like walking or talking, a child takes these steps according to his own timetable. All children stop nursing sooner or later. Some have the need to continue the nursing relationship longer than others—but they do grow out of it eventually. And still they do not become overly dependent. We have been reassured on this point many times over because we have observed first-hand hundreds of babies who were considered "late weaners." Independence, not dependence, is one outstanding trait they seem to have in common as they grow up.

Dr. Sears confirms this with his observation: "Some of the most physically and emotionally healthy children in my practice are those who have been breastfed in terms of years."

Remember, too, that at a year or so your baby will not be nursing as often as he was at two weeks or six months. By the time he's nine months old or so he has probably cut down considerably, and the toddler who is "still nursing" may be only enjoying a bedtime snack or a "pick-me-up" when he bumps his head or has caught a cold. Nursing is so comforting to him when he's ill. It makes his recovery much smoother if he can nurse away his troubles.

## STILL NURSING?

It helps to keep in mind that all children wean eventually. Young children have a tremendous desire to move on to the next stage in their development. They want so much to be like the older members of the family that you can be sure they will stop nursing when they are able to do so. You are certainly not out to set a record for prolonged nursing. Late nursing is not something you strive for, but it is a very special relationship between mother and child.

One mother, Susan Redge from Michigan, tells how she and her son grew into and out of this special relationship:

*When my son was a newborn and he and I were at our first LLL meeting, the mother sitting next to me was nursing her two-year-old. I assumed that she came to get help with weaning. I was surprised to hear that instead she was there to learn more about toddler nursing. I was sure I would never need to learn about toddler nursing!*

When my baby was about eight months old, my mother-in-law couldn't understand why he didn't eat solid foods. Although I had offered him solids, he didn't seem too interested and I knew he was thriving on "mother's best." I was savoring our nursing time because I knew it couldn't last forever.

By the time he was a year old, my husband said "Don't you think he ought to quit? After all, it's been a year." I was ready for that and told him all about baby-led weaning and its benefits to both mother and baby. "Why some even nurse until three years old!" I said. "But, of course, our child will certainly wean before then!"

By the time he was two, I couldn't imagine not nursing him. I didn't think he would ever go to sleep without it. I was pleased that out of our chaotic life I could take time to relax and nurse knowing that I could close my eyes and the plants would be safe, he wouldn't be cracking eggs on my living room rug, or having a tantrum, or doing any of the other things two-year-olds might do. I felt real sympathy for mothers of two-year-olds who did not nurse.

By that time, no one asked me about nursing anymore. Most people assumed that he was weaned. I never dreamed I'd be nursing this long! He nurses at night to go to sleep, maybe once more in the wee hours, and usually once during the day.

The most important thing I have learned from La Leche League is to meet my child's needs. As a baby, he needed to be held close and nursed often. As he has grown, his needs have changed. He needs to know I am there for him and there are still times when nothing else but nursing can calm him. I've had the thought countless times that it is nursing that soothes the savage beast. It has many times turned a kicking, screaming, out-of-control toddler into a calm, smiling, confident and contented young man, bravely ready to face the world.

Now he's been telling me that only babies nurse, and he is a big boy. Sometimes he even falls asleep without being nursed. I probably will not have a nursing toddler much longer. I just hope I can continue to satisfy his needs as easily and with as much joy when breastfeeding is no longer a part of our lives.

*Your milk continues to provide special benefits to your baby for as long as you nurse him.*

## NATURAL WEANING

"But when will he wean?" you ask, as your two-year-old holds up his arms to be picked up and nursed again. Actually, he's been weaning himself ever since his first bite of solid food. To wean, says the *Concise Oxford Dictionary,* is "to teach the sucking child to feed otherwise than from the breast." While most people see weaning as the end of something—a taking away or deprivation—it's really a positive thing, a beginning, a wider experience. It's a broadening of the child's horizons, an expansion of his universe. It's moving slowly ahead one careful step at a time. It's full of exciting but sometimes frightening new experiences. It's another step in growing up.

In her warm and insightful book, MOTHERING YOUR NURS-ING TODDLER, Norma Jane Bumgarner talks about the "unpredictable course of natural weaning." She says there will come a time "at some age" when "your child will not find nursing so absolutely essential to her well-being. She may stop asking so often. Or she may be distracted sometimes from nursing....You will very naturally and with hardly a thought respond a little less quickly to her requests to nurse....In time—how much time no one can say—your child will abandon all but a very few favorite nursing times."

Norma Jane goes on to describe how some children will continue to enjoy one or more of these special nursing times for a while, dropping them ever so slowly until eventually they are weaned. She concludes: "Every natural weaning is unique so that it is impossible to guarantee anything about it except that it will happen."

## WHAT IF I WANT TO WEAN MY BABY?

Each of us must make decisions about breastfeeding and weaning in keeping with our family situations and personal circumstances. Perhaps you do not agree with the concept of natural weaning or you don't think it will work out for you. Before you decide that circumstances will make it necessary for you to wean your baby, think over all possible alternatives. Perhaps there are some compromises that could be made in order to allow the baby to nurse at least once or twice a day. Stop and think about whether weaning your baby will really improve matters. Norma Jane Bumgarner says, "Nursing makes the job of mothering easier, not harder." Remember that illness, medications, surgery, or returning to work do not necessarily mean you must wean before you and the baby are ready.

If at all possible, you'll want to take your time with weaning and proceed slowly. We talk about weaning as something to be done "gradually and with love." You'll need to step up the loving attention you give your baby in other ways during the time that you cut back on nursing him.

Dr. William Sears encourages the same thing when a baby is being weaned. He points out: "A wise baby who enjoys a happy nursing relationship is not likely to give it up willingly unless some other form of emotional nourishment is provided which is equally attractive or at least interestingly different."

Basically, weaning is accomplished by substituting other kinds of loving care for nursing. You'll want to cut out one nursing at a time, distracting your little one with a cup of juice, a story, or a walk around the block at the time he would usually nurse. Wait a few days to allow him to get used to this change and to avoid feeling uncomfortable yourself from overfull breasts, and then tackle another nursing time. This may take up to two weeks or so depending on how many times a day your baby has been nursing. It is not a good idea to rush things. Weaning is a big change for both of you and it takes time to adjust.

You may need to be flexible, too. If your little one reacts strongly to the idea of not nursing at naptime or bedtime or when-

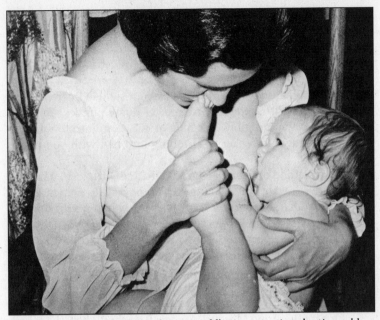

*Nursing provides a secure haven for your toddler in a sometimes hectic world.*

ever, you may decide to let him continue with that one nursing for a while. Weaning doesn't have to be an "all or nothing" situation.

If you decide to wean when your baby is under a year old and perhaps not drinking well from a cup, you'll probably want to talk to your doctor about giving him a bottle and ask the doctor what to put in it. If you are weaning from breast to bottle, you'll be substituting a bottle for some of the times you used to nurse the baby. Remember that your baby was nursing for comfort some of the time and will probably not need as many bottles per day as the number of times he was nursing per day. You'll need to double up on cuddling, rocking, hugs, and kisses throughout the day to make up for this. Instead of holding your little one in the familiar nursing position, bring his face close to yours and hold him cheek to cheek as you rock or comfort him.

With an older baby or toddler who is eating well and drinking from a cup, your basic weaning method involves lots of substitution and distractions. Keep tasty things to nibble on within easy reach. By frequently offering him drinks of water or, occasionally unsweetened juice, during the day, his thirst will also be quenched, often before he even realizes he's thirsty and asks to nurse. Chunks of fresh fruit are good, too—oranges, melons, or peaches.

Go out of your way to make the time at which you are omitting the nursing warm and happy in other ways. Your husband can be a tremendous help at this time, by taking the baby out for a stroll or putting him to bed at night, and perhaps by getting up with him if he wakes during the night.

Your toddler may be enthralled by your sudden interest in going for walks, visiting the playground, or doing puzzles. You may need to avoid the situations in which he is accustomed to nursing, such as in a favorite rocker or climbing into bed with you in the morning.

This method of weaning "gradually and with love" can be a lot of work. But abrupt weaning can be physically and emotionally traumatic and is never a good idea for you or your baby. By substituting lots of "other-mothering" you can help your little one come through the weaning process with his confidence and trust in you still intact. He may have a hard time understanding why he can no longer nurse, but at least he'll be reassured that his mother has not deserted him, she's still there with lots of love and understanding.

One mother from Missouri, Maggie Bryan, tells how the course of weaning took place with her son:

*While attending League meetings with my constant companion, Sean, I learned with great surprise about baby-led weaning and witnessed the wonderful closeness of mothers and nursing toddlers. The months slipped by; I was confident that he would eventually decide to stop nursing at his own pace, in his own time.*

*Imagine my dismay when I found myself becoming increasingly impatient with his continued nursing. I yearned to have a night free of bedtime nursing, to enjoy my bodily privacy once again, and a small thing, to read a few pages of the morning newspaper uninterrupted. It seemed to me that sometimes Sean was using nursing to trap my attention.*

*Whether or not my perceptions were accurate, my feelings were definitely a reality and had to be dealt with. So, with some trepidation, I decided to try to reduce the number of Sean's nursings and see if my impatience would lessen.*

*I began to ask him to wait a minute until I was finished with the morning paper, and, to my surprise, I found that he could cooperate for about five minutes. I found that delay also worked well in public situations. I found life with a nursing toddler becoming easier to manage. Sean nursed mainly at naptime, bedtime, and occasionally once at night.*

*As time passed, Sean began to give up naps and then stopped asking to nurse at night. On the rare occasions when he awakened, his Daddy held him close for a snuggle while he went back to sleep. Then to my astonishment Sean began to prefer to get up and have a bowl of cereal rather than stay in bed and nurse in the morning!*

*All of a sudden, it seemed, Sean was weaned! But actually the process had taken about six months. Sometimes I led, and sometimes Sean led. But his father and I only encouraged new behavior that he was ready and willing to learn. In this gentle way, I feel weaning was a maturing experience for both Sean and me.*

*Although our experience was not exactly the way I had imagined weaning would be, it did happen gradually and with love.*

# Toddler Nursing

Our culture today has geared us to thinking that all babies should be off the breast at an early age. But this is far from the custom that prevailed in centuries past. In biblical days weaning at age three was often mentioned, and still today in many parts of the world children wean themselves at ages up to three, four, or even older. Niles Newton, PhD, points out that in most periods of history and in most parts of the world babies have been breastfed for two to four years. She also observes that the changes in breastfeeding customs do not seem to have come alone, but in conjunction with a whole body of related customs. "La Leche League's repeated emphasis that breastfeeding is part of a whole philosophy of mothering is borne out by historical trends," she says.

Fulfilling your child's individual needs is the key. From the moment he is born, a mother strives to respond to the needs of her child. As the child grows, if he continues to express a need to nurse, it is a natural response for a mother to continue to meet this need.

If your toddler continues to enjoy nursing, you may find there are many advantages that continue to go along with toddler nursing. It is so easy to help an overtired or fussy child calm down and often fall asleep through nursing. If he hurts himself there is no better way to soothe him. Because nursing eases frustration, many families find that it helps turn the "terrible twos" into the "terrific twos," minimizing the usual competitive behavior of the two-year-old. Sometimes behavior that is normal for a toddler is blamed on breastfeeding if the child is still nursing. Behavior such as clinging and demanding normally occur at this age, whether the child has weaned or not.

Traveling with a child is much easier when he is still nursing. Even though you are away from home, your little one can be kept happy with the familiar comfort of your breast.

Your breast milk continues to provide immunities, vitamins, and enzymes for as long as your child continues to nurse. In one study, mothers reported fewer instances of illness requiring medical care in toddlers sixteen to thirty months of age who were still breastfeeding. If your child does become ill, nursing will be a comfort to him. If he has an upset stomach, he may be unable to keep anything down but breast milk.

You will probably find it convenient to encourage your child to use a special word for nursing. Choose carefully so that the word can contribute to discreet toddler nursing. One family uses "num num"; another calls nursing "mama." When the child shouts out, "I want mama!" in a restaurant, no one even turns around.

There will be occasions when it would be very inconvenient to nurse a toddler. If your two-month-old infant had begun to scream in a long check-out line at the supermarket, you might have pushed the basket to one side and gone out to the car for a few minutes to feed him. When he is older and demonstrated the ability to wait and understand the concept of time, you may offer him a nutritious snack and ask him to wait until you get to the car to nurse. If you are about to visit someone you know would be extremely upset to see your child nurse, you might encourage him to nurse before you go, in the hope that he would then not need to nurse during the visit.

## NURSING TOO MUCH?

Many little nursing persons nurse only occasionally, such as to fall asleep or for comfort when they hurt themselves. Sometimes however, a small child nurses much more avidly. If you feel your little one wants to nurse "too much" for his age, take a close look at what is happening in his—or your—life right now. Make sure he has lots and lots of other kinds of attention from you, and provide him with a nutritious snack or story before he asks to nurse. You can talk with him, sing, read, play games, or explore the outdoors together. Let him be a part of the jobs you do. He can wash pan lids while you do the dishes; he can carry socks to the clothes washer and push the vacuum cleaner around.

Is he away from you more than is comfortable for him? Are you home with him but busy with other projects? Are you spending lots of time on the phone? Are you going through a time of emotional upset? Moving? Is he making great strides in some other area of growth? Does he have an ear infection, allergies, or other illness. You can probably add your own ideas of things which might cause a child to want the extra reassurance of increased nursing.

When your child asks to nurse, if you are unsure that he really needs to nurse, you may choose to offer an apple and a story instead of nursing. If the child is happy with this, fine, but if he asks repeatedly or cries to nurse, this would indicate that he feels a real need. You can respect the laws of inner growth and individuality, nursing him with the confidence that he will grow away from this kind of closeness at his own pace.

Some little ones continue to want to nurse several times a night as well as during the day. When your little one wakes up during the night, pick him up, cuddle him, take him into bed with you, and nurse him if he wants it. Then, if he's willing, put him back into his own bed. However, he may sleep better and wake less often if you keep him in bed with you. There are a number of reasons why toddlers want to nurse often at night. He could be teething, which is a common cause for little ones to fret. Perhaps he's hungry or thirsty during the night and needs a nutritious bedtime snack. Or it could be that he's been so busy all day he hasn't had his share of hugging and cuddling and just needs time to be close to you.

## WHAT DO YOU DO WHEN THERE'S NOTHING TO DO?

Sometimes a mother needs to evaluate the nursing relationship she has with her toddler and consider whether things are really going well. In some situations, nursing can become the easy way out, substituting for other kinds of attention the toddler really needs.

An older baby or toddler may want to nurse simply because he has nothing more interesting to do, or because it is the only way to get mother's attention. As your little one is growing out of the infant stage, his need for mother does not really lessen. It changes, certainly, and mothering a toddler requires a great deal of ingenuity and even physical dexterity. His whole being is growing. His mind as well as his body needs stimulation. He needs conversation, and a companion to explore and experience all the new and exciting things his broadening horizons have brought into focus.

No one can better share these things with him than you, his very own teacher, guide, protector, and special person. No one knows his "language" as well as you do, nor understands so well his interests and needs. You know best when he's hungry and needs a snack to tide him over until dinnertime. You know when he's over-tired and needs to wind down in your arms.

One mother tells this story about how she realized her daughter needed more kinds of loving attention besides just nursing. Freda Main from Arizona writes:

*A month ago Celeste was a two-and-a-half-year-old nursing child who had become increasingly demanding of me. She seemed discontented and often angry at everything and everyone including herself and me. This is not unusual, I know, for a child whose sister had come into the family five months ago. I had always assumed Celeste would eventually stop nursing when she was ready, with no part played by me.*

*One day the light dawned. I had been thinking, "This child does nothing but nurse!" Then I realized this was precisely the case. I had not stopped thinking that nursing met all of Celeste's needs—as indeed it had for a long time. I had not observed until then that I was not giving Celeste the attention she deserved at times when she was not nursing.*

*For me nursing had become so easy and effortless that I had fallen into the trap of not growing in my relationship with my daughter. What had always worked so well before was not meeting her needs now.*

*I began to change my complacent ways. I began faithfully spending time with Celeste each day and giving her my undivided attention. We did many things together: making playdough, collecting popsicle sticks and gluing them together, and reading many stories. I would sit and hold her and hug her and kiss her even without "nursies." We talked. When my five-month-old slept, I spend the*

*time with Celeste instead of crossing off items from my
list of things to be done. We started having regular meal-
times, reading bedtime stories, and following daily routines. I started to be conscientious about eye contact and
really made an effort to do less talking and more
listening.*

*To my amazement, in a matter of days the little girl
whose nursing I had once seen no end to, was hardly
nursing at all. I was becoming more attuned to what she
really needed and was giving more of myself to meet her
needs.*

*It was hard for me to change. In weaning myself,
Celeste weaned also. Now I no longer think of baby-led
weaning as "mother doing nothing." As in everything else,
experience is the best teacher.*

## PREGNANT AND NURSING?

If you find that you are pregnant, there is no sudden need to
wean. Your child may wean himself early in the pregnancy when
a few little ones notice a taste change in the milk, or he may stop
nursing around the fourth month when some women notice a reduction in the milk supply. He may even wean toward the end of pregnancy when the milk changes to colostrum, or after the birth
because of the separation if you are in the hospital for several days.
If he seems to have a strong desire to nurse in spite of the changes
which occur during pregnancy, feel free to continue if you wish.

You may have some concerns about continuing to nurse while
you are pregnant. If you are eating a well-balanced diet including
a variety of nutritious foods there should be no cause to worry about
either baby being harmed. Some mothers may worry that nursing
through pregnancy will cause a miscarriage. There is no evidence
that breastfeeding will cause a miscarriage and some mothers who
have previously miscarried have not done so while nursing a toddler. The hormones that cause uterine contractions during the early
days of breastfeeding, and which are so helpful in preventing hemor-
rhaging after birth, have much less effect during pregnancy.

During your pregnancy, you may find that you are just not
happy about continuing to nurse your toddler. In this case, we suggest you consider following the recommendations that are given for
weaning "gradually and with love." It is up to you to make the decisions that will work best in your own family.

In a study of 503 La Leche League members who became pregnant while still nursing, researchers found that 69% of their babies weaned at some time during the pregnancy. Of course, there was no way to know how many of these little ones would have weaned if their mothers had not been pregnant.

## TANDEM NURSING

If you nurse through your pregnancy, you will probably find yourself in a situation called "nursing siblings who are not twins" or more simply, "tandem nursing." If nursing is still an important part of your older baby's life, it would not be fair (or wise) to cut him off abruptly when the new baby is born. Mothers find there are advantages as well as disadvantages to this somewhat unique situation.

It can be reassuring to the older child to continue nursing and sharing these special times with his new sibling can help to avoid feelings of jealousy. You may worry, however, that your new baby will be somewhat deprived of milk or of the intimate one-to-one relationship with just you. You may want to restrict your toddler's nursing to only certain times of the day, or establish a rule that he only nurses after the new baby is finished. Most mothers, however, find these things work out and the new baby gets plenty of milk without any problem.

One mother, Brenda May from California, tells how nursing two worked out in her family:

*When I became pregnant with our fourth child, my son Jon was a very active toddler who still enjoyed his frequent nursings. I soon realized he was not ready to wean himself, and I did not feel it was necessary to encourage him.*

*By the sixth month of my pregnancy, my lap seemed to completely disappear. This made our nursings somewhat awkward, but with the help of a pillow under his head, Jon continued. As my birthing time grew nearer, my milk supply decreased, and I thought Jon might decide to wean. However, he still continued, seemingly content with whatever he received at the breast.*

*On the morning of what was to be our fourth child's birthday, Jon and I lay in bed together nursing. It helped me to relax, as my labor had already begun. Six hours later, Jacob Allen was born at home with his family all*

*As your little one grows out of infancy, his needs change—but he still requires lots of love.*

*sharing in the experience. That day we began tandem nursing. Jon was twenty-one months old.*

*For the next three weeks, we spent most of our days nursing. Jon had increased his nursings, and Jake was nursing every hour or so. Soon after, my toddler went back to his regular routine but clearly enjoyed the abundant supply of milk now available.*

*I didn't know anyone who had tandem nursed; no one in our LLL Group had done it. So I felt unsure at times, but I just trusted my mothering instincts that told me what I was doing was right for myself and my children.*

Occasionally, after apparently completely weaning himself, a toddler might suddenly ask to nurse again. (This sometimes happens when the new baby arrives.) Don't be afraid to let him try it. Most likely, instead of nursing he will giggle and slide off your lap, reassured by your willingness to go along with his request. A mother from Ohio, Mary Beard, recalls:

*After Julian was born, Elliott asked once if he could nurse. I said, "Yes," and he said, "Oh," and walked away. Apparently he only wanted to make sure he could. Once he was reassured, we never heard anything more about it.*

If, on the other hand, your toddler reacts with enthusiasm and delight at the discovery of this bounty, relax and let him nurse. The more ambivalent your feelings about it, the less sure he is that you still love him, or even want him around. Many little ones still need lots of this kind of reassurance. Jan Wilcke of Kansas writes about her experience:

*When Ardith was twenty-eight months old, Carrie was born and I weaned Ardith. The weaning would have been too abrupt by itself without the added burden of a new sister contending for mommy's affection. Ardith seemed more tense, and I was unhappy about the situation. So, after two months, Ardith began nursing again.*

*For about six months after that, Ardith nursed twice a day. She now nurses once every few weeks. I believe this occasional nursing is important to her in a way different than it is for Carrie. Her need to nurse occurs quite often when she's had a bad morning and we're both "nearing the end of our rope." It's as if she's asking, "Do you love me as much as Carrie? Do you love me enough to let me nurse?" I think tandem nursing, while difficult at times, is a wonderful way to reassure a toddler when a new sibling arrives. And a warm lap with some mommy's milk is a safe retreat for the child when the demands of his enlarging world are too much for him.*

All aspects of nursing a toddler past a year or so are discussed in Norma Jane Bumgarner's book, MOTHERING YOUR NURSING TODDLER. Norma Jane, a long-time LLL Leader, shares the experiences of other mothers as well as advice from experts. It is an excellent resource for mothers who are nursing toddlers, considering weaning, nursing while pregnant, or tandem nursing. You can order a copy from La Leche League International or your local LLL Group. For details, see the Appendix.

# CHAPTER 15

# *Discipline Is Loving Guidance*

A s parents, our goal is to have the wisdom to guide our child's growth so that he can become an independent, mature, loving person, with his talents and abilities developed to their fullest.

Our first job is to meet his physical and emotional needs as fully as we can, so that a secure foundation is laid for his advance to maturity. Through breastfeeding we are getting him off to the right start. The breastfeeding relationship itself makes us more sensitive to his needs, so we are quicker and surer in devising ways of meeting them. As our child grows, his needs change. We must progressively let go of him as he assumes the direction of his own life. This process will not be complete until he is fully grown, but it starts in babyhood. This book, therefore, would be incomplete if we did not look into the beginnings of independence.

Before your baby enters the toddler years, it is important for you and your husband to share your feelings and ideas about discipline with each other as you develop your own style of parenting.

# Setting the Stage

Discipline is an integral part of everything we do for and with our children. Having developed a philosophy of mothering our babies and toddlers through breastfeeding and weaning, we are now ready to go on to develop other aspects of mothering our young child. "If you have been doing a good job of mothering, you are already doing a good job of disciplining," says Dr. Hugh Riordan, psychiatrist and LLL father.

In his book, BECOMING A FATHER, Dr. William Sears tells how parents begin the process of disciplining their child.

*By being available and responsive to your baby during the first year you learn to read your baby's cries. You learn to anticipate the behavior that will follow certain cues. You learn to interpret what your baby is feeling by watching how he is acting. Learning to read the feelings behind a baby's actions sets the stage for a very important part of discipline in the older child: determining the feelings behind a child's actions.*

## A NEED FOR GUIDANCE

As the baby-child grows, he will need guidance, instruction, and sometimes correction to learn the ways of our world. If the foundation of secure love was laid when he was a baby, and if he sees his parents as kind, polite, and considerate people, he will try to imitate them, because he wants to act in ways that will please them (most of the time). We still have to respect his growth patterns and not ask of him more than he is capable of giving at his stage of development, but we can and should give some direction to his inexperience. How to do this is where the difficulty often lies. Before we can successfully begin to discipline our little ones we must have a clear idea of *why* we are doing what we are doing and *how* we should go about doing it. There should be no sharp break in our ways of guiding our child's development. From infancy on, children need loving guidance which reflects acceptance of their capabilities and sensitivity to their feelings.

Elizabeth Hormann, an experienced mother and League Leader, wrote this about toddlers' needs:

*We would like to think that children learn the civilizing virtues—caring, compassion, consideration—simply by our good example, but most children need a little more than that. A clear definition of acceptable behavior, our expectation that they can meet that standard, and periodic guidance when they stray—all of these are necessary. Sometimes we have to thwart our wee ones....We have to be alert so that they don't hurt other people or their possessions; we need to know the difference between the normal behavior of toddlers and small children and behavior that becomes disruptive and out of hand. It is not easy to guide a small child when she clearly wants to go in another direction, but she needs us to do that for her.*

*It is not really so very different from what we did when they were babies. We looked to their needs, met them, and tuned out the critics who said we were spoiling them or babying them or ignoring our own needs too much. We were confident we knew our babies and ourselves best—and for the most part, we did. That hasn't changed. We still know our children better than anyone else. Because we know them and love them so dearly, we are better equipped than anyone else to guide them through the complex steps of growing up, of learning the rules, of developing character.*

*Guiding our children—lovingly—is an important part of caring for them and helping them be loving and lovable to people within our families and beyond. Next to breastfeeding, it is the best gift we can give a small child; and like breastfeeding, the benefits last a lifetime.*

# Discipline and Punishment

Discipline is a much maligned word, often associated with punishment and deprivation. Yet discipline actually refers to the guidance which we as parents lovingly give our children to help them do the right things for the right reasons—to help them grow into secure, happy, and loving persons able to step out into the world with confidence in their own ability to succeed in whatever they set out to do.

In *How to Really Love Your Child,* Dr. Ross Campbell explains how a child's emotional needs are a vital part of discipline:

*M*eeting a child's emotional needs and applying loving discipline will permit a healthy, strong, positive love-bond between parents and their child. When any problem with a child occurs, parents must re-examine the child's needs and fill them before doing anything else.

And how does punishment fit into this definition of discipline? Dr. Campbell goes on:

*D*iscipline is training the child in the way he should go. Punishment is only one part of this....The better disciplined a child is, the less punishment will be required. How well a child responds to discipline depends primarily on how much the child feels loved and accepted. So our biggest task is to make him feel loved and accepted.

Other experts speak out against punishment being confused with true discipline. In *Creative Parenting,* Dr. William Sears has this to say:

*P*unishment stops actions, but may ignore the feelings which prompted these actions....A child whose behavior is motivated by punishment is often easily, but deceptively, controlled. His behavior is submissive and compliant but may lack spontaneity and self-confidence. He may be the picture of a docile child but inwardly he is anxious. The child sooner or later rebels.

*There are always new challenges for parents as their children grow.*

## WHAT ABOUT SPANKING?

Outwitting a determined toddler is a challenge. His pranks and explorations are to him just innocent fun but they may be dangerous or destructive. It's our job to teach him and set limits for him. But we have found that in the long run, spanking a defiant toddler only leads to tears, resentment, and an uncontrollable (and understandable) urge to hit a baby brother or sister. Our children learn by the examples they see, and parents are the ones they most desire to imitate. So we must ask ourselves what kind of example we want to set for them. Punishing young children by spanking and slapping frequently reflects the impatience and frustration of the parent. It is not the kind of behavior we would want our children to imitate. Spanking does not help a child learn self-discipline.

As psychologist and popular columnist Eda LeShan writes in her book *When Your Child Drives You Crazy:*

*Is spanking a helpful, constructive form of discipline? No, it is not. Unequivocally! It may relieve our anger and clear the air when the atmosphere has gotten pretty tense and wound up, but it does not teach any constructive lessons about human relations, and after all, that's what discipline is all about: the way in which we try to teach our children to live in a civilized fashion with themselves and others....*

*Even when we think we are being rational about spanking, we're still not teaching any terribly valuable lessons. We say, for example, "I have to give you a spanking in order to make you remember how dangerous it is to run across the road." The lesson there is: "Here I am, a grown-up—a college graduate, even—and the only resource I have at my disposal to teach you the dangers of traffic is physical violence!" What a discouraging picture of human potential!*

Of course, there are other things parents do that can be harmful to a child. Physical punishment is only one aspect. Parents can undermine a child's self-esteem in other ways, too. Sidney D. Craig, clinical psychologist and author of the book, *Raising Your Child, Not By Force But By Love,* explains:

*Whenever a parent expresses disapproval, lectures, scolds, reprimands, criticizes, or punishes a child, the child suffers some loss of self-respect.*

# Normal Toddler Traits

Parents sometimes find it difficult to make the changeover from the total giving that a baby needs to the more active role of meeting the needs of a toddler. Over the years many of us had to unlearn some of the attitudes about discipline we had been raised with. We learned to relax a little, laugh a lot, and be incredibly quick on our feet.

A large part of mothering a toddler is helping him through the transition from babyhood, when his every wish was a real need, to later on, when he becomes an outward-looking youngster just starting to become aware of the needs of others. In the process he needs help in learning that not all his wishes are needs, and in fact, some of them, if granted, would most surely not be good for him at all.

While most people tend to respect the growth pattern of the infant, the eighteen-month-old or two-year-old is another story. When little fingers reach for electrical outlets, pennies go into mouths, and lamps are toppled over, parents face a new challenge. Of course, we can't permit utter chaos in our home, or unrestricted freedom. But we need to recognize that another stage of growth is taking place. The toddler is discovering the world around him, so he wants to touch, feel, and take apart everything he sees. He is an inquisitive two-year-old private eye, investigating everything. This is normal behavior for his age; punishing him is entirely out of place and will only frustrate him. That doesn't mean that you should do nothing at all. What's needed here is distraction and firm but gentle steering in another direction.

Not all children are alike; with some it is only necessary to caution them a few times about a forbidden object. If a child can learn to respect a few taboos without being nagged or scolded and without frustration on his part, then this method is fine. Usually it is wiser to remove dangerous or breakable objects from sight.

If your explorer discovers a "forbidden" object, one good way to satisfy his curiosity is to sit down with him and let him touch, feel, and even hold it himself. Show him how the electric hair dryer works, and explain in simple language, with lots of gestures, that we must be careful because it can be dangerous, break, or come apart. Give him plenty of time to explore it with your guidance. Then change the subject, distract him, and put the forbidden article away—out of sight or reach or, better yet, both. (Remember that toddlers are great climbers.)

## AN OUNCE OF PREVENTION

The time-honored adage, "An ounce of prevention is worth a pound of cure" can be most important in avoiding upsets with your busy little toddler. "It makes good practical sense," says Nancy Stanton of Florida, "to baby-proof your house as much as possible, because otherwise you'll spend your entire day battling with your child. It's hard enough to protect your child against the things you have no direct control over (such as cars on the street), so, especially if you have several preschoolers, keep your home environment as simple as possible. One mother even suspended her kitchen garbage can from the ceiling."

Nancy continues: "With very active toddlers, extreme measures are sometimes necessary to preserve your sanity. Someday you can put the knobs back on your kitchen cabinets. Most likely you have already given up at least one lower cupboard to your toddler anyway. Be sure to fill it with real utensils—an old coffee pot or spatulas."

## DANGEROUS SITUATIONS

In the case of a really dangerous situation such as chewing on an electric cord or running out in the street, mother should allow herself the full emotional expression of her fears; the child will gradually adopt these justifiable fears of real dangers and avoid them. A sudden shriek of alarm, accompanied by some fast footwork gets the message across pretty well when your little one reaches for the electric plug or runs toward the street.

In any case, always keep an eye on your toddler, for his own safety. Pediatric experts who have carefully studied accident patterns in the very young child state that it is only when a child has reached the age of approximately three that you can *begin* to teach him how to protect himself. Until that age he can only be protected by the watchful eyes of his caretakers, and it's up to you to make sure the eyes are there.

## LOOK TO THE CAUSE

When your little one is crabby and uncooperative, there may be a variety of reasons. Is he tired? Bored? Hungry? Over-stimulated? Sometimes figuring out the cause of misbehavior is a good way to avoid future problems.

Little children (like grown-ups) are often at their worst if they are over-tired or hungry. Nancy Stanton observes: "Toddlers usually need some extra sleep in the daytime, but they don't want to miss anything. If your child is really tired, stop everything—close the drapes, turn off the TV, don't do anything yourself—put a pillow on the floor and both of you lie down. At least one of you will drift off to sleep."

Or maybe his behavior is a signal to mother, telling her it's time to stop talking on the phone or visiting with the neighbors, or whatever it is she is doing that takes her away from her little one, mentally if not physically. It's time to get back down on his level and notice him.

*Really getting to know your child well is the key to effective discipline.*

## SAY WHAT YOU MEAN

"Come in the house right now, Kate," you call for the fifth time. Kate, still ignoring your summons, goes right on playing. Do you really want her to come in "right now" or don't you care? If you don't care, then don't call her until you do. Then, call her once. Wait a couple of minutes and call again. If she doesn't respond, go out, scoop her up, and carry her cheerfully and speedily into the house. She will soon learn that you mean what you say.

"To a two-year-old child, a call to stop playing and come in for lunch may on certain days be too much," says Edwina Froehlich, one of LLL's founders. "Try going out there ten minutes in advance with a nutritious snack you know he'll like, and when that's finished start the getting-in process."

## LIMIT TELEVISION TIME

Television programs can be a tremendous influence on young children's behavior. You need to monitor the kinds of programs your children watch as well as how much time they spend watching TV. A young child needs to learn from a variety of activities and interactions. Television does not offer the opportunity for these types of learning. What children do learn from TV may not be in keeping with your family's values. Preschoolers often cannot distinguish fantasy from reality and programs depicting violence can be particularly upsetting and frightening for them.

But often, it's not so much what's happening on the television screen that causes the biggest problem—it's what's *not* happening that matters most. Too much televison interferes with active communication among family members.

There are, of course, educational programs directed toward young children which you may find of value. As a parent, you have the responsibility to make informed judgments. Even so, you need to be aware of the hazards of commercials. A child can be enticed into wanting expensive toys and non-nutritious food products simply because he is bombarded with advertising campaigns.

## TEMPER TANTRUMS

On the subject of toddlers and tantrums, Edwina Froehlich recalls her own experiences:

*Temper tantrums can be devastating to both mother and child. Having had to cope with two children who had tantrums, I did learn a little. I followed the usual suggestions with the first boy—a spank on the bottom made him scream harder, of course; trying to firmly take him to his room was hard on my shins; a stern reprimand couldn't be heard over his screaming. Ignoring him was the best of the lot, since at least it didn't add to the child's hysteria. Still, this neither solved anything, nor prevented future tantrums. As I became better informed about our nutritional needs, I became aware that the timing of the tantrums often coincided with periods of hunger. They seldom occurred immediately after a meal. Once in progress, you can't stop a full-blown tantrum by offering*

*food, but understanding the cause at least enables you to
cope better. Better still, it can perhaps show you the way
to help prevent or at least lessen future tantrums.*

*When our youngest was about two and a half, a
friend had come for lunch, and Peter was for the most
part amusing himself. But late in the afternoon, when I
told him to stop something he was doing, his tolerance
level burst and he had his first tantrum! I went over and
sat on the floor beside him and reached over to pat him
gently. At first he rejected my hand and literally threw it
back at me. So I just sat by him and waited, whispering,
"I love you Petey." He quieted very quickly and rolled
himself over to me, burying his face in my lap, and finished sobbing in comfort. When the storm was over he
had forgotten what started it and we trotted immediately
to the kitchen. While I was happy and relieved to know
that I had been able to calm him, I girded myself for repeat performances. To my surprise, he had only two or
three more tantrums, and they were mild and quickly
over.*

If your child has tantrums often, try to determine if there is
a pattern. Do the tantrums occur at the same time each day? Only
with certain people? What seems to be the source of the frustration? Can you possibly remove the source? Do what you can to avoid
the frustrating situations that cause him to explode.

If your child does have a tantrum, he'll calm down sooner if
you remain calm and nonthreatening, As soon as the child will permit it, touch him gently and try to help him recover. When the sobbing has stopped you can offer him a nutritious snack if you suspect
he is hungry, but be sure it is not a sweet, or he may react with
another tantrum soon afterward.

The tantrum a child throws in public is no harder on *him* than
if he were at home, but it is agonizing for the parent. Onlookers
are quick to show their disapproval of your "naughty" child. Em-
barrassing though it is, the basic approach to handling the tantrum
is the same—the parent cannot react in anger, but must remain calm
and speak in quiet, soothing tones. Both mother and child are in
a state of distress in this situation, but the child is the more helpless
of the two. He cannot just turn off his rage on command. If it is
at all possible, pick the child up and move to a more secluded spot
where he will bother fewer people. But you may have a baby in

your arms, or the enraged child may be too heavy or kicking too wildly to permit removal. Any attempt to reason with him in this highly emotional state will be wasted. The only thing you can do is stand by quietly and wait it out.

## THE BITING CHILD

What about the child who bites or hits? This seems to be a rather common problem, and a difficult one, especially when other children are around. Norma Jane Bumgarner, author of MOTHER-ING YOUR NURSING TODDLER, tells this story:

---

*About* two years ago (at an LLL meeting), my beautiful, superbly mothered, absolutely perfect toddler was bitten by somebody's rotten, neglected, little monster—or so it appeared to me at the time. As I comforted my baby I shot reproachful glances in the direction of the little culprit's mother, making no attempt to hide the feelings we all have when somebody hurts our child.

As proof that there is justice in the world, our next child turned out to be not only a biter, but the most determined, dangerous biter I have ever seen. This is one of the most difficult things I have ever dealt with in my life, and it was made even harder for me by those few mothers who reacted the way I did two years ago.

---

Naturally, when we realize this is going to be a problem with our youngster, it behooves us to be ever watchful and intervene by removing him from the scene with great dispatch and firmness. Speed is of the essence. Yelling, spanking, or biting the child back doesn't solve the problem. Diane Kramer of New Mexico writes, "Young children are usually very oral in reaction. They use their mouths to feel, to love, to test, and to argue, and it takes time and maturity for them to realize that not all these reactions are accept-able. Meanwhile, love them, cuddle them, help them through their frustrations, and recognize that this too shall pass."

If your child seems to resort to biting when confronted with groups of children, you may need to avoid these situations for a while. Help him learn to get along with just one other child at a time, with careful vigilance as he does so.

## THE SANDMAN COMETH NOT

In some families, bedtime is a source of frustration, with everyone ending up exhausted and exasperated before finally getting to sleep. Planning a course of action ahead of time may help to avoid disaster! While it may not matter whether or not your preschooler goes to bed at a predetermined time every night since he doesn't have to get up early the next morning, some bedtome regularity is a good idea.

Don't set bedtime too early though, or he just won't be sleepy. Children can only sleep a certain number of hours, and if your child goes to bed at seven, he may be up bright-eyed at five in the morning. You can't have it both ways.

When bedtime comes, make it a cozy, quiet time, with no rush or hurry. A warm bath with time to play in the tub, a nutritious snack such as an apple, and a quiet story while you snuggle together under the covers, all lead to a relaxed little person, ready and willing to go to sleep. He may want you to stay with him for a while, and of course, you should. It's scary all by himself.

# A Look Ahead

As your children get older, discipline becomes even more of a challenge. Children will keep pressuring you, testing the limits, on into their teens. If they know that you are and always have been firm and consistent and loving, and that you trust them, it will be easier.

As you set limits for your older child you may find that at times he may be really angry with you, but he'll get over it soon as long as he knows that you really love him. Show him you love him by your actions, even when you have to say "no." As Dr. Ross Campbell reminds us: "The first fact we must understand in order to have a well-disciplined child is that making a child feel loved is the most important part of good discipline."

Whatever happens, remember that each child is an individual, and you can't lay down hard and fast rules that will be appropriate for all children. In this matter of discipline, if you have the intimate understanding of your little one that the breastfeeding relationship fosters, and if you are clear in your mind about the real nature of discipline, you can safely follow your own instincts as parents. "It's not our job as parents simply to take care of our children, but to help them learn how to take care of themselves," says Norma Jane Bumgarner. Jalelah Fraley, a mother from California, once remarked: "Out of all this will come sons and daughters well on the road to meeting the needs of our grandchildren in a wholesome, happy way—we shall see an era of 'gently nurtured' loving human beings."

When your child is born, you devote yourself to meeting all of his needs; you nurse him when he is hungry and hold him close as long as he needs and likes it. As he grows, he wants less snuggling and more sociability; you prop him up in the midst of the family from time to time. As the days and weeks and months go by, he becomes more independent in other ways; he starts eating solid foods and does not nurse so long or so often. Soon he picks up bits of food to bring them to his mouth himself. And one day, he is feeding himself, handling a spoon with dignity and aplomb, albeit with occasional spectacular messes. Now he is drinking from a cup, and as the months speed by, taking no more than a friendly nightcap from the breast. You are still there when he needs you. There is never an abrupt withdrawal of your love as expressed first through the warmth and closeness of breastfeeding and later in other ways. Secure in knowing that he can retreat for a bit into babyhood if he wants to, he ventures further and further into childhood, and finally (all too soon, it seems in retrospect), he isn't a baby anymore. Before you know it, he will be on his way to school, with a cheerful wave good-bye as off he goes.

The years go by, and though parenting does get somewhat easier, it is always challenging and interesting. Our children will never stop needing us in one way or another, thank goodness! But we have to learn when to stand back and when to offer our help. And someday, your little boy will be standing over his own wife as she happily nurses their baby, or your daughter, looking so like her mother at that age, will be proudly nursing hers. All the work and worry, the time and the endless patience, will have paid off. It was all very much worthwhile.

With your understanding guidance, your child will grow from dependence to independence gradually, and always with the love that is his birthright, and the great need of our world.

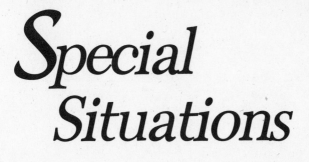

# PART SIX

*Special
Situations*

# $\mathcal{P}$roblems at the Beginning

$\mathrm{B}$reastfeeding in special situations often requires patience and commitment, but mothers have continued breastfeeding in almost every situation imaginable. They have discovered that when the circumstances surrounding breastfeeding are less than ideal, the special benefits of breastfeeding become even more important.

New babies and mothers struggling with special problems after birth appreciate the emotional closeness and reassurance of their unique breastfeeding relationship. Breastfeeding helps them get to know one another despite the complications. In addition, breast milk's nutritional and immunological benefits are especially important for the baby at risk.

The circumstances that might temporarily prevent you from nursing your baby are extremely rare. If you or your baby become ill, make it clear to your physician that you want to breastfeed your baby in spite of the special circumstances, and ask for his or her cooperation in bringing this about. Your positive attitude toward breastfeeding is a most important factor and one your doctor will take into consideration. Be confident that your milk is best for your baby if he can have any liquid or food by mouth (or even by nasogastric tube inserted through the baby's nose and into his stomach). Not only is breastfeeding safe for the sick baby, it is one of the best medicines for him. Doctors have often commented on how quickly a breastfed baby seems to recover. Your insistence on continuing to breastfeed whenever possible during a period of medical treatment can make a difference in the type of treatment the doctor may advise.

In the case of an unusual breastfeeding situation, your doctor may wish to contact La Leche League; encourage him or her to do so. Many doctors and nurses take advantage of the League's information and experience with mothers breastfeeding in unusual situations.

If your doctor is not familiar with La Leche League and its Professional Advisory Board, you can tell him or her about the League's resources. You'll also appreciate the support of your local La Leche League Leader. She may be able to put you in touch with another mother who has breastfed in a situation similar to yours. If your doctor is unwilling or unable to take positive steps to keep your baby nursing, you have a right to seek other medical advice and assistance. Your baby's welfare comes first.

# Breastfeeding after a Cesarean Birth

Of course you can breastfeed your baby despite a cesarean birth. You will probably get off to a somewhat slower start, however, as a cesarean section is major abdominal surgery, and it will take time to recover. If you are going to have a planned cesarean, you'll want to find out in advance as much as possible about cesarean births. Many mothers who have previously had cesarean deliveries have been able to have vaginal deliveries for subsequent births. Often the reasons for the first cesarean do not apply to subsequent births. But if it is necessary for you to deliver your baby by cesarean, or if you are reading this after you've had a cesarean birth, you can be confident that a cesarean birth need not be a deterrent to a happy breastfeeding experience.

Babies born by cesarean may be sleepier and more lethargic than those born without the aftereffects of anesthetics. It may take

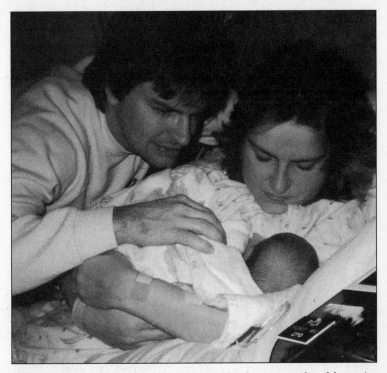

*Breastfeeding immediately after a cesarean birth creates a bond between mother, father, and newborn.*

a few days for this sleepiness to wear off, and your baby may temporarily have a weak sucking reflex. Try to discuss the choice of anesthetics with your doctor ahead of time. While a general anesthetic may be the easiest to administer, it will make you unconscious for the birth and drowsy for some time afterwards. This may postpone your first contact with the baby you have waited so long to hold and nurse. Ask if you can be given a regional anesthetic so that you can be conscious for the birth and hold and nurse your baby soon after he is born.

It is important to breastfeed your baby as soon as possible not only because of the importance of early contact and bonding, but also because breastfeeding helps the uterus to contract and return to its normal size more quickly. This also aids healing.

Breastfeeding can begin on the delivery table in the operating room, although you will need help in positioning and holding the baby. Because the IV will still be in one arm, and the arm may be strapped down while the doctors finish stitching the incision, it will be difficult for you to maneuver the baby. Your husband can help you place the baby flat on your chest to nurse, moving him gently toward your nipple. If your husband has never done this before he may feel awkward. If so, you can ask the nurse for help.

If you are breastfeeding for the first time in the recovery room, prop the baby with pillows or blankets to allow him to reach your nipple easily. You will probably be flat on your back due to the anesthesia, so make sure he is close enough to you to easily latch on. You should be fairly comfortable, since the anesthesia is still in effect. Again, feel free to ask for assistance in positioning the baby.

Some hospitals still require a twenty-four hour waiting period before allowing mother and baby to be together following a cesarean birth. This rule can be waived if your doctor understands how important it is to you to spend time with your baby right after birth, assuming there aren't any problems. Also ask your doctor to write orders for you to have your baby on demand, instead of only on the usual three- or four-hour feeding schedule.

## THE EARLY DAYS

Rooming-in is a wonderful way to get to know your baby and get nursing off to a good start. Some hospitals do not allow rooming-in for cesarean mothers for the first day or two, but most mothers find it comforting to have their babies with them all the time.

For the first few days after giving birth your abdomen will be sore and tender. Most medications that are given for pain will not affect your baby through your milk.

Get up and move around as soon as you can. Physical activity hastens the healing process. Drink plenty of fluids and get lots of rest.

## POSITIONING WHILE LYING DOWN

It may be easiest to nurse while lying down for the first day or so. You and your baby can nap together, enabling you to spend more time with him without becoming fatigued.

With the bed in a flat position, place the side rails of your bed in the "up" position and use extra pillows behind your back for additional support. Carefully roll to one side while grasping the side rail and relaxing your abdominal muscles. Move slowly to avoid any strain. Cover your abdomen with a towel or rolled-up blanket to protect you from baby's kicking. Flex your legs and place a pillow between them for more support and less strain on your stomach muscles. Lean back into the pillows behind your back.

Ask your husband or a nurse to place the baby on his side facing you so you are positioned chest to chest. His head should be resting on your arm or a rolled-up blanket. His mouth should be at the level of your breast. In this position, the baby should be able to latch on well.

It is important to nurse on both breasts at each feeding, which means you will have to roll over. The first day or so you may have to ask for assistance until you get the knack of turning over. Have a nurse place the baby on the other side while you turn.

Turn your hips a little at a time with your feet positioned flat on the bed. Move slowly, being careful not to pull suddenly on your incision. Again, use the side rails to help. Reposition the pillows and have a nurse help you ease the baby onto the other breast.

Once your incision is less tender, you can roll over in bed by yourself while holding the baby on your chest. Use the technique described above while securely grasping the baby.

## POSITIONING WHILE SITTING UP

It is wise to use several different nursing positions in the early days in order to speed your recovery. Some women, despite a tender incision, prefer to nurse while sitting up. Again, place the side rails of your bed in the "up" position. This will make it easier to find a comfortable sitting position.

Place the head of your bed upright while elevating your legs slightly. Flex your legs from time to time to help circulation. Prop a pillow (or rolled-up blanket) under one arm while placing baby on a pillow over your incision. This not only raises him to your breast, but also protects your sore abdomen. Hold baby very close to your breast, chest to chest, resting his head on your arm for support. This allows your free hand to support your breast if necessary.

## FOOTBALL HOLD POSITION

This is a good way to avoid direct pressure on your incision as baby is lying beside you, not on your lap. While sitting in an upright position, tuck a pillow under one arm. Place baby's head close to your breast, facing up, with his body tucked under your arm. His body should be bent at the hips, with his bottom against the back of the chair or bed you are leaning against. Support the back of his neck with your hand. Be sure he is up at the level of your breast so you are not straining to reach him.

## WHEN YOU GET HOME

Because you have had major abdominal surgery, as well as having given birth, you will need plenty of rest when you go home. Put the baby in a cradle right next to your bed so you don't have to get up and down. With plenty of diapers, a pitcher of juice or water, and a snack, you'll be set for several hours. Or else tuck baby right into bed with you. That way you both get lots of rest while getting to know one another.

Avoid cooking and other household tasks. If at all possible, find someone to come and help out with these chores while you rest in bed. Ask friends to bring meals, entertain toddlers, or do laundry.

Finally, while most families will have little trouble adjusting to a cesarean birth, some women may feel emotional pain along with the physical pain. Major surgery, especially when unexpected, can be upsetting when other plans had been made for the birth experience.

In many parts of the United States, mothers who have had cesarean births have organized support groups to share their common problems and experiences. For further information, see the Appendix. La Leche League can also help you through your local Leader, who can provide suggestions, support, and more information about breastfeeding and mothering after a cesarean birth.

Ann Hague, a mother from Georgia, writes:

*Although a cesarean mother and baby may have to be more patient and persistent, the rewards are well worth it. My surgery healed nicely, and my baby and I are experiencing a beautiful relationship through breastfeeding. A cesarean birth can be an apprehensive time, but it should not rob you of the remarkably loving experience of breastfeeding.*

# What If Your Baby Is Jaundiced?

Your baby may be only hours old, but more likely he is two or three days old. You notice that the whites of his eyes as well as his skin have a yellow cast. The doctor informs you that the baby is jaundiced and may refer to the bilirubin level in the baby's blood.

Jaundice is common in babies during the first weeks after birth, whether they are bottle fed or breastfed. In almost all cases, no treatment is necessary. The jaundice disappears, and the baby is none the worse for the experience. Even when treatment is called for, there are a number of ways to avoid any separation between mother and baby. You can continue to nurse your baby, and both of you can be assured of receiving breastfeeding's ongoing benefits. In fact, nursing your baby soon after he is born and frequently thereafter is an excellent way to keep jaundice from becoming a problem. Explaining the various types of jaundice may help you understand what's happening.

## NORMAL OR PHYSIOLOGIC JAUNDICE

Physiologic jaundice in the newborn is a common and usually harmless condition. Nearly half of all newborns appear jaundiced in the days after birth to a mild or moderate degree with no ill effects. In most cases the jaundice will disappear by itself in seven to ten days.

Normal or physiologic newborn jaundice refers to an excess of bilirubin which is temporarily stored in the baby's blood and tissues. The bilirubin is an orange-yellow pigment which gives the baby's skin a yellowish cast that is characteristic of jaundice.

In the normal course of events, new blood cells are continually being produced and old ones broken down. Newborns have an excess of red blood cells because the oxygen supply in utero is limited and the baby needs the extra red blood cells to carry oxygen. After birth, the baby's lungs supply plenty of oxygen and the extra cells are no longer needed. The breakdown of these old cells frees iron and bilirubin. The iron is stored in the liver and other tissues to be used later in the manufacture of new blood cells.

Current scientific knowledge indicates that bilirubin is simply a residual product of this process, which must be disposed of by the liver. When a newborn's immature liver cannot eliminate the bilirubin as fast as it is produced, the result is jaundice.

Physiologic jaundice usually appears on the second to fourth day in normal, full-term babies. In most cases, it gradually disappears by itself in about a week or so. Normal jaundice is not a disease; it is a harmless condition that has no aftereffects. There is no reason for breastfeeding to be interrupted because of normal or physiologic jaundice.

# PATHOLOGIC OR ABNORMAL JAUNDICE

Pathologic jaundice in a newborn is caused by an abnormal breakdown of red blood cells or any other cause of increased bilirubin production or reduced excretion by the liver. This situation is most commonly caused by Rh or ABO blood incompatibilities. While Rh incompatibility is becoming relatively rare, ABO incompatibility, a much milder condition, is still quite common. Your doctor will know whether he needs to watch for either of these conditions by checking your blood type before your baby is born.

In contrast to physiologic or normal jaundice, abnormal jaundice is often visible at birth or within the first 24 hours and the bilirubin level may rise quite rapidly. Medical treatment may be necessary in cases of pathologic jaundice, but breastfeeding can continue during treatment and can often help to reduce the jaundice.

# THE DANGER OF KERNICTERUS

High levels of bilirubin are of serious concern because of the possibility of brain damage. (A level of 20mg/dl or above is considered to be high in cases of Rh incompatiblity; 25 mg/dl or above is considered a high level in other cases. Problems can occur at lower levels in small premies.) Kernicterus, the technical term for the brain damage that can be caused by excessively high concentrations of bilirubin, is a staining by the bilirubin of certain brain cell nuclei. It is associated with a risk of brain damage. Kernicterus is quite rare, and is of greatest concern in the premature or sick baby with pathologic (abnormal) jaundice.

# LIGHT THERAPY AS TREATMENT

To determine if treatment is needed, the bilirubin level is measured with a blood test. If the baby has an abnormally high level of bilirubin, these blood tests may be repeated several times in the first week in order to monitor the changes in the bilirubin level.

If your doctor feels that your baby's jaundice requires treatment, he will probably prescribe light therapy. "Bili-lights" are similar to daylight fluorescent tubes and they are used to speed up the elimination of bilirubin. This treatment is designed to keep the bilirubin from approaching critical levels when, in extreme cases, an exchange transfusion may be necessary.

Generally speaking, the earlier and more rapid the rise in the bilirubin level, the sooner light therapy will be started. It might be started at 15 mg in a full-term baby. Sick or premature infants who are jaundiced present special problems, and medical treatment is often necessary at lower bilirubin levels.

If your baby needs to spend time under the bili-lights, he can still be breastfed. Since frequent nursing is important in helping the baby get rid of excess bilirubin, you'll want to be sure he nurses approximately every two hours, or ten to twelve times per day.

Light therapy does not have to be continuous to be effective. When you nurse your baby, remove his eye patches, cuddle him close, and look into his eyes. Holding and stroking him even when he is under the lights will be reassuring for both of you.

In some cases, you may be able to have the baby and the bili-lights moved into your room. You'll feel better with the baby close by, and keeping up frequent nursings will be that much easier. Some hospitals position the bili-lights over both mother and baby to minimize mother-baby separation even further and to promote uninterrupted nursing.

## THE BENEFITS OF BREASTFEEDING

Breastfeeding will benefit the baby with any type of jaundice. Frequent nursing right from birth will help control or prevent physiologic jaundice. Early and very frequent feedings usually result in minimal rises and prompt declines in bilirubin levels. The colostrum or "pre-milk" is especially important because of its laxative effect. Bilirubin in the blood is picked up by the liver and passed into the bile, which goes into the intestine. The meconium, the baby's first black, tarry bowel movements, contain large amounts of bilirubin. If it is not moved out it can be reabsorbed into the system. Because the colostrum helps the baby to pass the meconium, it helps prevent this reabsorption.

## "FLUSHING OUT" JAUNDICE

At one time, it was thought to be advisable to give the baby bottles of water, to "flush out" the jaundice. But research has shown that water supplements given to newborns in the first few days do not help to reduce jaundice. In fact, one study showed that the more water the baby received the higher the level of bilirubin reported.

Bottles of water have the detrimental effect of reducing the amount of nursing the baby does. Anything that makes the baby less interested in the breast or interferes with nursing at least ten to twelve times per day can increase jaundice in the breastfed baby. Frequent nursing is one of the best ways to help the baby get rid of the excess bilirubin.

## LATE-ONSET JAUNDICE

An unusual form of jaundice which usually does not appear for five to seven days after birth has been found to be caused in certain babies by a variation in the composition of their mothers' milk. This type of jaundice, also known as "breast milk jaundice," may last up to ten weeks. There have been times when babies showed signs of physiologic jaundice but their mothers were erroneously led to believe that their milk was contributing to their baby's jaundice and babies were weaned unnecessarily.

The specific variation in the milk of mothers whose babies have late-onset jaundice is unknown, but it seems to cause an increase in intestinal absorption of bilirubin. These babies are healthy and continue to thrive. Breastfeeding can usually continue without interruption. In rare cases when the serum bilirubin level reaches extremely high levels, your physician may recommend a change to another milk supply for a brief period (one to three days).

In more than twenty years, since this type of jaundice was identified, no case of harm to a nursing infant due to breast milk jaundice has ever been reported. But no systematic studies of the neurologic performance of these infants has been undertaken.

## GOING HOME FROM THE HOSPITAL

If your baby is otherwise healthy but is still being treated for jaundice when it's time for you to be discharged, talk to your doctor about continuing treatment at home. Frequent nursing is important and you can provide daylight (not direct sunlight) at home. In some parts of the country you can rent bili-light units for use at home. Of course, you will probably need to return to the hospital for the necessary blood tests to monitor the baby's bilirubin level.

Parents are understandably concerned if they are told their newborn shows signs of being jaundiced since this can have a wide range of causes. However, in the majority of cases, the situation is not serious.

# If Your Baby Is Premature

Premature babies come in many sizes. Some may weigh two pounds or less; other premies may be fully developed and weigh close to five pounds. Some will be able to nurse soon after birth, while others will have to be kept warm and protected in an isolette and will not have the strength to suck. If your baby is very small, he may have to stay in the hospital for several weeks or more. But knowing you can give him your milk will help you overcome the worry and fear you feel about his condition. Providing *your* milk for *your* baby is something only *you* can do. If your baby is very tiny or sick, nurses at the hospital will feed your expressed milk to your baby through a tube inserted through his nose to his stomach, or they may use a bottle with a special premie nipple. Often, when the baby is ready to take milk from a bottle, he is able to start nursing. Kathie Patten of South Dakota writes:

*It was a good feeling knowing that I was able to do something for my baby. Giving birth prematurely had left me with subtle feelings of guilt. Even though I could not give our baby the warm, loving feelings of motherly touch and sounds, I knew I was the only one who could provide him with superior nourishment.*

Later on, breastfeeding helps make up for the separation you and your baby have experienced. Rebecca Strasser from Tennessee was happy that she persevered in her efforts to breastfeed her son Jonathan who was born twelve weeks early weighing just under three pounds. She explains, "Nursing Jonathan has soothed the pain of our early separation....I am forever grateful to all who encouraged me to persevere so that I could know the precious joy of nursing."

## BREAST MILK IS BEST

Your baby benefits in many ways when he receives your milk. Research shows that milk from mothers who deliver prematurely adjusts to meet the special needs of their premature babies. The immunities in your milk protect your baby from illnesses to which premature infants are especially vulnerable. Human milk is easy for your baby to digest; it doesn't place any additional strain on his body as he struggles to adjust to life outside your womb. When you provide your own milk for your baby you are making a critical contribution to his care. Medical technology cannot duplicate mother's milk, the perfect food for your baby.

If your premie is unable to nurse directly from the breast, you'll want to start pumping or expressing your milk as soon as possible. Colostrum is especially important for him. Remember too, that as soon as he is able to take anything by mouth (or nasogastric tube), your milk is best for him. Very frequent, small feedings (about every hour or two) are best.

It will take time to learn how to pump or hand-express your milk. Thinking about your baby, looking at his picture, and calling the hospital for a report on his progress will help bring in more milk. Don't despair if the supply decreases somewhat as time goes by. Your body doesn't respond to a pump the way it would to a cuddly baby. Your supply will go up again when you begin to nurse your baby directly. (More information on pumping and storing your milk can be found in Chapter 7.)

Start out by pumping or hand-expressing from both breasts every two or three hours, about as often as your baby would be nursing. You do need to get extra sleep, though, so it's all right to go for a longer stretch of five or six hours at night without pumping.

Ideally, your milk should be stored in a refrigerator and fed to your baby within hours of collection without any kind of processing. Heating the milk destroys many of its protective qualities. If your milk cannot be fed immediately to your baby, it should be frozen. This will keep bacteria in the milk from multiplying and will do minimal damage to the milk's other components.

The hospital may provide you with containers for collecting your milk. If not, any sterilized container may be used. Use plastic containers, because some important immunological components of breast milk may adhere to a glass receptacle and these are especially important to a premature baby. Be sure your hands are scrupulously clean when you pump your milk. However, your daily shower is enough to keep your nipples clean, and it is not necessary (or even desirable) to clean them with soap, since nature has provided its own antiseptic secretions.

The appearance of your milk may surprise you. It is generally thin and bluish-looking; yet, if you let it stand awhile, you will find that cream rises to the top. From one pumping session to the next, the amount of cream will differ—and this is as it should be.

Remember, *your* milk is the right milk for your baby, and its over-all composition suits him perfectly.

A very tiny premie, born more than two months before his due date, may require a vitamin and mineral supplement in addition to mother's milk. If your doctor finds your baby needs this type of supplement, don't think that something is wrong with your milk. It's just that such very tiny premature babies may need more of certain nutrients to grow and develop properly. Your milk still provides the basis of the special nutrition your premature baby needs.

## A NEED FOR SUPPORT

Hospitals vary in the amount of support and cooperation they extend to mothers of premature infants. It is a real asset when the doctors and nurses caring for your infant encourage and support you in your efforts to provide breast milk and realize that you alone are able to provide the perfect nourishment for him. They can help build your confidence in your ability to nurse your baby.

If, however, others are less supportive than you'd hoped, you can still be successful. If you find you are having problems with the hospital staff, try to discover why. Sometimes a nurse who cares for prematures isn't fully aware of how to help with breastfeeding, and it's difficult for her to assist you. Knowing that many other mothers have nursed premature babies is bound to increase your self-confidence. A supportive La Leche League Leader can help at times like these.

Be persistent about keeping in touch with the hospital and doctor about the baby's progress. Most professionals are very understanding about the need for parents to know what is happening to their baby. They will also encourage you to come in and give your baby as much personal care and attention as possible. Even when the baby is in an isolette, he needs human contact, and you need to be with him, too. Linda O'Brien of Arkansas tells of traveling forty-five miles to be with her son in an intensive care nursery.

*No one seemed to understand the need I had for Jeff or the need I knew he had for me. On every hand I had people ordering me to rest—"Go home," they said, "Sleep! We can take care of your son." At times I felt maybe they were right and I tried. However, once home I could only weep. So I returned to the hospital prepared to stay. Jeff was crying when I arrived but responded to my voice and stroking. It was very evident he knew his mother even though he was only two days old.*

Although the benefits of mother's milk for premature babies are becoming more widely recognized, there may be some reason why your milk cannot be given to your baby for a while. If this is the case keep up your supply by pumping regularly. You can freeze the milk for later use; you may need it during those first days of breastfeeding when your supply hasn't quite adjusted to your baby's demands.

## THE FIRST TIME BABY NURSES

Depending on his size and gestational age it may be days or weeks before your baby is finally ready to suck. A pacifier or a "premie" nipple may be used initially to stimulate his interest in sucking, but, whenever possible, mother's breast is always best. If a premie nipple or pacifier is used, it should be used only briefly and efforts should be made to put the baby to the breast as soon as possible.

Getting a premature baby to nurse for the first time is often a difficult task. Both the new mother and the nurse, who may not have had a great deal of experience with helping premature infants breastfeed, may easily become frustrated at the slow progress the baby seems to make.

Keep in mind that he isn't really very strong and will need much cuddling, coaxing, and patience. He may not be able to suck well for more than a few seconds at a time. You need to be as relaxed and comfortable as possible, which sometimes isn't easy. Try to arrange for a quiet spot with a rocking chair. Use pillows under your arm and in your lap, and settle your baby and yourself in a comfortable position. To avoid tiring your baby, express a little milk until you have a let-down, and then put the baby to your breast. Be calm, gentle, and patient. Initially, he may or may not show interest in the milk-giving breast. Since he has received other types of feedings, he may become confused. Reassure him with calm, gentle handling.

He may latch right on and start nursing, or he may just play around and do some half-hearted sucking, or even merely lick the nipple. This will be a learning experience for both of you. Remember that a baby may not nurse very well during the first several at-

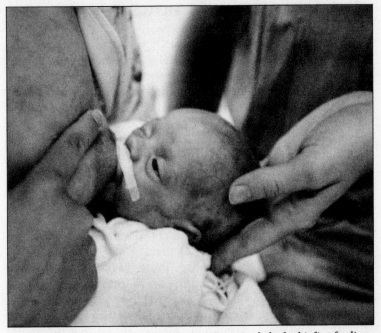

*You may need some help in positioning your premature baby for his first feedings.*

tempts. Often these first nursings are made up of more loving and cuddling than actual nursing. Both of you are benefiting from the close contact. Gently try to place your nipple in his mouth, but if he doesn't suck or seem interested this time, he will probably do better the next time—or the next. Remember your first attempts at feeding will take time. Allow fifteen minutes or so between each attempt to nurse him.

In her book, *A Practical Guide to Breastfeeding,* Jan Riordan, RN, MN, describes in detail the techniques needed to get a tiny premie started at the breast. She says, "The usual positions for feeding a large, healthy infant require adaptation for the small premature infant." She suggests holding the baby in the arm opposite the breast that will be used. The mother's arm extends along the length of the baby's body and her hand grasps his head to stabilize his position in relation to the breast. The mother's other hand is used to position her breast for the baby to grasp. The author, who is also a La Leche League Leader, goes on to explain, "This position allows the mother unrestricted visibility of the infant in addition to giving her complete control over his movements while at the breast. Mothers have found it universally effective."

## TAKING YOUR BABY HOME

The long-awaited day will finally come when you can take your tiny baby home from the hospital at last. You'll probably find yourself feeling somewhat unsure of your ability to care for your baby, since up until now his life has been so dependent on technical knowledge and complex medical equipment.

Be assured that your loving arms and warm milk are what he needs most at this point. Prematures have a lot of loving and nursing to catch up on, and they need all the time and closeness you can offer. Sleep with him, carry him in your arms or in a baby carrier, keep him feeling the nearness of you in every way. Give him lots of skin contact, with only his diaper between you and him. Keep your breast readily available to him.

If he has been on supplements, ask your doctor for guidelines on how quickly you can withdraw them. Make it clear that your eventual goal is total breastfeeding. You will know that your baby is getting enough by counting the number of wet and soiled diapers. As usual, six to eight good wet diapers and three to five bowel movements per day are good indications that he's getting plenty of milk.

If it is necessary to continue supplementing your premature baby, try using a nursing supplementer. Continue putting him to your breast often and check the information in Chapter 7 for tips on increasing your milk supply.

With lots of closeness and loving care your premature baby will grow and thrive. Is it worth the trouble to keep up your milk supply in order to breastfeed your premie? Jo-Anne Montgomery of Manitoba, Canada thinks so. Her daughter Shannon was born nine weeks early. She says, "Nursing my baby daughter has been and still is one of the greatest pleasures of my life. I encourage any mother who wants to nurse her premature baby not to give up."

# A Baby with Special Needs

The baby born with a handicap or medical problem needs breastfeeding even more than a healthy baby does. The baby with special needs benefits particularly from the love, attention, and reassurance that go with nursing at the breast. If your baby has a problem, contact your local La Leche League Leader or LLLI for information and help with breastfeeding.

A mother and daughter who are both La Leche League Leaders have written a book for parents of handicapped children. A SPECIAL KIND OF PARENTING, by Julia Good and Joyce Good Reis, offers practical help and reassurance on topics that range from the early days of acceptance to caring for your child when he needs to be hospitalized. They write:

*When a handicapped child is born, there is an immediate and serious impact on the parents and the whole family unit. . . . Whenever the news comes that the baby has a birth defect or a medical problem of some kind, it is a great shock to the parents. . . . The emotional impact is greatly influenced by the manner in which they are allowed to interact with their baby. . . . Breastfeeding can be a normal experience in emotionally trying situations where little else seems normal.*

Their book is available from La Leche League Groups or La Leche League International. See the Appendix. If your baby has a health problem that complicates nursing, remember that breastfeeding is nearly always possible and should be encouraged.

## THE BABY WITH DOWN SYNDROME

For the baby with Down Syndrome, a loving home environment, with maximum interaction between baby and the rest of the family, will help to develop his capabilities to the fullest.

Breastfeeding, with its enhanced interpersonal relationship, demonstrates to your baby your love and affection in a very special way. Breastfeeding is especially important for Down Syndrome babies because they have a greater susceptibility to infections than do normal infants, so the immunity factors found in colostrum and breast milk are especially valuable. And mother will find joy and delight in breastfeeding her baby and meeting his needs.

The baby with Down Syndrome responds readily to love and returns it enthusiastically to those around him. He is often a delight to the whole family. Lucille Clancy says this about her son, "My heart said 'I love him,' my head said 'I wish it didn't have to be this way,' but soon Chad's big, happy smile thanked me a million times for the extra love I had given him."

Many mothers have said how important the emotional support they received from their husbands was in helping them adjust to having a handicapped baby. As Louise Wills puts it, "I cannot underestimate my husband's help with Erika. Because of him, I have been more able to think of Erika *first* as a child, and *second* as a child with a disability." Remember that by drawing on each other for support and understanding, you and your husband will both grow stronger in the process.

A baby with Down Syndrome is often sleepy and may have a poor sucking reflex, so extra help and patience with breastfeeding are in order. Be calm and patient as he learns to suck and swallow. The rewards of nursing your baby are well worth the extra effort, so don't be discouraged if you encounter problems. With your loving help your baby will catch on.

Above all, remember that this special baby who has been placed in your care will give as much as he receives. As Lucille Clancy explains, "Loving Chad is a continually growing experience which teaches us love, acceptance, patience, and humor. There is a sadness in knowing that something is missing, like a piece of a puzzle, but there is joy, too. The added dimension that Chad has given our family will continue to enrich us as we live and grow together."

## A BABY WITH A CLEFT LIP OR PALATE

These two conditions often occur together, although a cleft palate is somewhat more common. The baby with a cleft lip can usually nurse at the breast even before surgery to close the cleft. With a cleft palate, an opening in the baby's palate (top of his mouth) makes it difficult for him to maintain the suction that helps him nurse. But unless the cleft is extremely severe, you and your baby can probably discover a way for him to breastfeed.

This does not mean breastfeeding will always be easy. It may in some cases be very difficult, and in a few, impossible. But even if your baby is unable to nurse at the breast, your milk is still very important to him. By holding him close to your breast as you feed him, you will be able to give him even more of the warm closeness of the breastfeeding relationship.

One mother used an electric pump for eight months to express milk for her eighth child, giving it to her baby in a special bottle.

As a result, the baby was in the best of health before undergoing the necessary surgery, and recovery was quick.

Edith Grady, a La Leche League Leader from Indiana, found that if she held her breast in baby Andrea's mouth, Andrea, who had a cleft of the soft palate, could "milk" the breast with her gums and tongue. It is mainly the baby's jaws, tongue, cheeks, and gums that work to draw the milk from the breast. Edith managed to keep her breast in Andrea's mouth by holding it with one hand and keeping the baby's head very close to the breast throughout the feeding.

At first she also pumped her milk and gave it to Andrea in a bottle after nursing her. By four months, Andrea was strong enough to get all of her milk at her mother's breast.

This technique and other information about breastfeeding a cleft-palate baby are explained in La Leche League's Information Sheet titled, "Breastfeeding My Baby with a Cleft of the Soft Palate." This is available from your local League Group or LLLI.

If the baby is bothered by milk running into his nose during nursing you may have to stop from time to time for a breathing spell. These babies often nurse better sitting up, or lying on a particular side. Experiment in your first weeks of nursing with different positions. Be patient with this special baby of yours, as it will probably take him longer to learn to nurse.

Cleft palate repair usually comes between one and two years of age. Your nursing toddler may not want to suck immediately after the operation because the roof of his mouth will be sore. He may want to lie at your breast or simply hold your nipple in his mouth without actually nursing. But as he recovers—in a week or so—he'll return to nursing, maybe with more enthusiasm than ever since the repair surgery makes it so much easier to breastfeed.

If your baby has a cleft lip, he will probably be able to breastfeed with few problems. Your doctor may want to perform some type of repair surgery while he is still nursing. Lip-repair surgery is usually performed while the baby is still quite young and receiving only breast milk. Tammy Shaw from Illinois persuaded her doctor to allow her son Peter to nurse immediately after his lip-repair surgery. She writes:

*My husband and I showed Dr. Johnson the information about nursing. He enthusiastically agreed to allow me to breastfeed soon after surgery. He believes in the mother-child bond, and therefore understood my wish to nurse Peter right away. He assured me that if any stitches pulled out after nursing, it would not harm Peter in any way to have him quickly replace a stitch. He agreed it was important that Peter be comforted. After the surgery when Dr. Johnson appeared and saw that Peter was nursing happily, he commented that it was nice to see him calm and not crying so soon after surgery.*

Another mother, Valerie Hawkes-Howat from Massachusetts, learned that it was not easy to find a doctor who was willing to allow her son to nurse immediately after lip-repair surgery. The story of her extraordinary efforts to find the right doctor appeared in a newsletter published by Children in Hospitals and later reprinted in La Leche League's publication, NEW BEGINNINGS (January-February 1986). Children in Hospitals is an organization that supports parents in their efforts to meet their children's needs despite hospitalization. For details, see the Appendix.

In the end, Valerie was able to nurse her son Willie immediately after his lip-repair surgery. The repair healed beautifully and the scar is barely noticeable. Valerie writes about Willie's first nursing after his surgery:

*When Willie was brought down from surgery, his bright eyes looked up at me and his little mouth opened into a wide, sleepy smile. I could have wept with relief. The only bandage on his face was a trio of narrow "steri-strips" across the upper lip. The nurse helped me take him into my arms and get him settled in my lap without disturbing the IV in his foot. I snuggled him and he began to root at my breast, so I immediately began to nurse him. He showed only profound pleasure to be back at my breast again—no signs of discomfort whatsoever. I noted the way his upper lip lay over the top of my areola, completely free of stress. There was no swelling or bruising around the sutures.*

*So Willie finished his first postoperative nursing by falling peacefully asleep in my arms, completely and blissfully ignorant of how hard both his parents had worked to make this possible.*

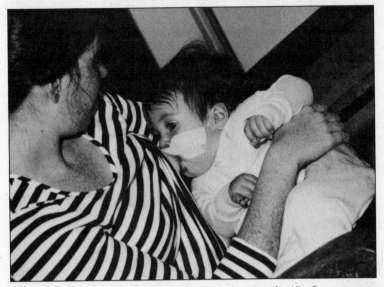

*Tammy Shaw was able to breastfeed her son, Peter, immediately after surgery to repair his cleft lip.*

## CYSTIC FIBROSIS AND OTHER MALABSORPTION DISEASES

Babies with cystic fibrosis, celiac disease, or other malabsorption problems do very well on mother's milk. In fact, such malabsorption diseases are often delayed if baby is breastfed. Later, when baby is older and the disease does begin to manifest itself, it is far easier to treat and manage. Whatever the baby's problem, it would be rare indeed if he were unable to nurse.

Kathleen Winterer's son, Ben, gained weight steadily on breast milk despite cystic fibrosis; Ben was much healthier because he was breastfed:

*At the time of Ben's hospitalization we were told we could expect one or two bouts with pneumonia his first year, and I am very happy to say Ben just turned two last month and hasn't had any yet. Of course, I like to think that colostrum's benefits in the beginning helped him through that first crucial year.*

# Losing a Baby

The death of a baby, whether through miscarriage, stillbirth, shortly after birth, or later through illness or accident is an experience most of us never consider. Sadly, the lives of many families are touched by such tragedies. Parents who suffer this terrible loss are usually shocked and grieved to find themselves coping with the fact that the mother's body doesn't immediately realize what has happened; milk will begin, or continue, to be made.

Mothers suffering the loss of a newborn, a stillbirth, or miscarrying after twenty weeks gestation, are often discharged early from the hospital. So the process of the milk coming in will take place at home. It helps to be prepared for what will happen, but often mothers experience engorgement—hard, painful swollen breasts—as a complete shock.

Sometimes dry-up medication is offered after the birth, but this seems to have little, if any, effect on the appearance of milk, and may produce unpleasant side effects such as nausea. Mothers losing a baby when the milk supply is well established will also experience engorgement, and will need to seek relief.

Women are often afraid to relieve their discomfort by expressing milk for fear of encouraging their breasts to make more milk. However, expressing some milk is probably the most useful thing to do. Even a few drops may be enough to help you feel more comfortable. A hot shower or a hot bath is a good preliminary to expressing some milk. Not only will the warmth enable you to handle your painful breasts, but the warm water often helps the milk to be released. At first, you may need to express a small amount of milk several times a day, and at night too, if you wake in discomfort. The point of expressing a little milk is first to alleviate discomfort, and secondly to prevent undue accumulation of milk sitting in the ducts, which could lead to a breast infection.

When the milk supply is already fully established, some mothers report that expressing and donating some milk to a local milk bank helps because they feel they are doing something positive to help another baby. If you choose to do this, you will be able to cut back gradually and decrease your milk supply more comfortably. You may also find it helpful to wear a firm bra for support and comfort. One size larger than usual may be necessary.

Many mothers are taken aback by the way the let-down reflex can be triggered just by thinking about the baby. This often seems to happen during the baby's funeral. Comforting hugs from friends may also make the milk let down. Wearing bra pads, loose and patterned clothing, even taking a change of clothing with you on outings all help.

## HOW CAN FRIENDS HELP?

Support from friends, family, and involved health professionals is vital. Celia Waterhouse, from Great Britain, whose baby Leo died at three months, offers this suggestion to friends. "Say simply how sad you are to hear about it. Your saying so will not make the mother any sadder for being reminded of her baby—as if she could ever forget! Even if nothing further is said between you, your acknowledgement of her sorrow will have helped."

Certainly practical help will be welcome—help with meals, laundry, or the older children—but having friends willing to talk, cry, and listen is wonderful in itself.

Whatever your feelings are, accept them as normal. Grief can continue for a very long time indeed. Remembering the baby's birthday and the anniversary of the funeral, sharing photographs, naming the baby even if he was stillborn, all can help. Couples need to support each other and understand that grief may affect husband and wife in different ways, at different times. Often there is a lot of help provided initially, but after some months people may expect parents to "get over it." This is a vulnerable time for bereaved parents, who may find grief welling up repeatedly. Dr. Penny Stanway, a British physician whose third baby was stillborn, says: "Most women find that they want to go over the circumstances of their baby's death time and time again with whoever will listen. A mother will have to have time to incorporate her loss, and the best way of doing this is by repetition of the event in her mind or by talking, as if 'to learn,' to stamp on her mind, what has happened."

There are several support groups for parents who have lost a child. They offer a chance to share feelings and experiences with other bereaved parents. See the Appendix.

# CHAPTER 17

# *When Extra Care Is Needed*

In certain circumstances, additional information or specialized techniques may be needed in order for breastfeeding to proceed smoothly. After reading this chapter, you may still have questions or concerns. Remember that your La Leche League Leader is available to provide information and encouragement. Don't hesitate to call on her for help.

## Multiple Births— Multiple Blessings

Can a mother breastfeed twins? Of course, she can. In fact, mothers who breastfeed their twins find that the benefits of breastfeeding are multiplied when they have two babies to love. Because twins sometimes come in smaller packages, they need the protection of mother's milk even more than single babies.

In her book, MOTHERING MULTIPLES, Karen Gromada, a La Leche League Leader and mother of twins herself, writes about the benefits of breastfeeding twins:

*The advantage of breastfeeding one baby are even more important and intense for multiples. How nice to save twice the money and twice the preparation time. And it is twice as nice to curl up at night for feedings in bed, rather than awaken to crying babies who must wait for you to warm their meals.... One advantage is particularly important.... Breastfeeding ensures maximum skin contact with each baby.*

## PLENTY OF MILK

All of the doubly blessed mothers agree that having enough milk is no problem. The tried and true maxim for breastfeeding holds for multiples as well as for one baby—the more you nurse, the more your milk supply builds up. A mother who lived in Illinois, Lee Mueller, had twins who each weighed eight pounds at birth, yet she found no need to resort to supplementary bottles or to start solids earlier than usual. A Wisconsin mother of twins, Judy Latka, commented, "I've taken breastfeeding a baby so much for granted that it surprises me when people are amazed that the twins are nursing. That part is easy—it's the extra set of loving arms that I need." Judy was aware of the importance of nursing the babies soon and often, and she adds, "I had discussed my desires many times with my doctors, and it was well worth the effort. My hospital stay was brief. I went home when the babies were twenty-eight hours old."

In planning for two or more (and we hope you have prior notice so you *can* plan), take the hints for easy housekeeping and mothering and multiply them to fit your needs. Cut your housework to a minimum. Your babies need the same relaxed loving attention that every baby deserves, and a tired mother is hard pressed to give this. If you possibly can, get help with the house for the first few months. Your spare minutes should be spent resting and relaxing not catching up on laundry.

*This mother nurses both twins at once with one in the usual cradle hold position and the other in the football or clutch hold.*

One mother who breastfed twins after her efforts to breastfeed with her previous six children had been short-lived, says, "Can You imagine my finding the answer to relaxed mothering with my twins, when I never seemed able to nurse the other six?"

With two babies on the way, a Massachusetts couple, Marge and Jon Saphier, outlined a plan of action. Marge explains:

*We decided to try to relieve me as much as possible from the housework so I could dedicate my time to the twins and our four-year-old daughter. Fortunately, we were able to have a graduate student live with us. She was given room and board for making two meals a day, cleaning up the kitchen, and cleaning up the general clutter of the house. We also decided to buy food in bulk; our cellar now looks like a supermarket. I only had to buy fresh produce weekly. This not only cut down on my time in the supermarket but also reduced our food bill.*

Marge offers the following five hints for functioning effectively as a nursing mother of twins: "(1)Get as much rest as possible. (2)Drink plenty of liquids. (3)Eat good, nutritious meals and snacks. (4)Have help with meals and household tasks. (5)Last, but certainly not least, contact LLL. Although I am a League Leader, I cannot tell you how much I needed and appreciated the support everyone in the League gave me."

A question that was uppermost in Paula Johnson's mind as a new mother of twins was how to feed both babies when they decided to nurse at the same time. This Missouri mother tells of her experience:

*The first try was hilarious! If you're holding a baby in each arm, what do you do when a newborn loses the nipple? Wish for a third hand, that's what! I soon discovered pillows, and we've got the system down pat now. For a couple of frantic weeks, they refused to nurse at the same time. But with practice and the aid of pillows we finally discovered a lying-down position that is comfortable for all three of us. The nicest part is that now I can doze off while nursing, whereas before I sat upright until both were finished. That made for short nights!*

*Looking back now, I realize I did little else but nurse the babies in those first couple of months. But now, here we are at four and a half months, the girls are both completely breastfed, and believe it or not, things are going pretty smoothly for us (well, most of the time). I have a fantastic husband who helps by preparing breakfast and by accepting my relaxed housekeeping. You can't be too hung up on those little details when there are twins to nurse. Our son, Aaron, who is two and a half, gets in on the act by finding a vacant place and just snuggling in. He sometimes gets out his babies to nurse while I'm nursing mine. He's sure babies only come in twos!*

From Texas, Patti Lemberg reflects on the trying times and also the rewards she found in breastfeeding two:

*They nursed about every two hours for twenty minutes at a time and slept one four- or five-hour stretch a day. The*

*Using lots of pillows helps keep both babies in position to nurse well.*

*hardest time for me was the six-week growth spurt when each of them nursed every forty-five minutes. It was a bit much, but I just took the same attitude I had taken during the last weeks of pregnancy: "Next year at this time they'll be toddling around, so cute—I won't even remember this day."*

*The most important advantage I have gleaned from the whole nursing experience is confidence. I know my way of mothering is good, and that makes me happy. This in turn relaxes me into a patient frame of mind.*

In discussing how to position the twins for simultaneous nursings, Patti goes on to say:

*When they were tiny, each rested in the crook of an arm, bottom at my hand, legs extended along my thigh. If one wiggled out of place I caught the back of the diaper and pulled him back. In fact, I still use this position if they both want to rock and nurse at the same time. Another good position is sitting on the couch with heads in lap and bodies extended under my arms onto the couch. This one is great because both hands are free to hold a book and sip a beverage. When they are still tiny it's best to put a pillow under each for height and comfort. These days, we prefer to nurse lying down on their bed (a mattress on the floor), with David on the left in the standard nursing position for lying down and Alan on the right across my chest. That may sound awkward, but any position that is comfortable to all is fine. You need to work with the furniture and pillows until you find what's best for you.*

*The most valuable piece of furniture I owned during the first six months was a big overstuffed rocking chair my dad bought at a garage sale.*

A New York mother, Patricia Berg, considers her twins "Happy baby times two!" Pat and her husband, Ted, worked as a team in keeping their lively production going.

*T ed took time off work when I returned home from the hospital. We spent a wonderfully peaceful vacation with our children. We didn't hire someone to come in after Ted returned to work. In retrospect I think it would have been helpful to have a high school girl come for a few hours a day to help. Those first weeks were tiring, but a patient husband who was willing to rock and soothe a fussy baby made it much easier.*

*I got to know baby Megan very quickly since she slept little and needed a great deal of nursing and contact. My relationship with Joelle was a little slower in forming as she was quieter and it seemed we had less time together in the beginning. I realize now that I often hesitated to nurse the girls simultaneously during those early weeks. However, when I did nurse them together (their feet toward my back, heads on a pillow) I found that the rush of good feelings so familiar to the nursing mother came even more easily. There's just something about four little eyes looking up at you so absorbingly! I also found that nursing the babies together would bring on a very strong let-down whenever I felt my supply a little low, usually in the late afternoon.*

Whether to nurse the babies together or separately is one of those things that mothers work out quickly to suit themselves and their babies. Another League Leader and twin mother, Carolyn Johnson of Illinois, described her method of satisfying two hungry babies:

*When time was a factor, I nursed the twins together, sitting in a rocker, with Jill on Judy's lap. Otherwise, I found it much easier to nurse the babies separately. I would awaken one about half an hour before the other was "due" to get up so as to avoid nursing them together. Of course, I alternated so that one twin wouldn't always have "first pickings."*

*If one was still hungry after nursing on one side, I would offer the other breast. Then the next one would begin on the breast last nursed by the other. Usually, the last to be nursed would be the first to wake up hungry. There were times when they would want to nurse again after only one and a half to two hours, and this served to increase my milk supply to meet their demands. Usually it would take two days of very frequent nursing and they would again be satisfied with a less demanding schedule.*

*I always made sure the twins were nursed at least every three hours and would awaken them if necessary. At night I didn't watch the clock, but kept them alongside our bed in a bassinet and buggy, and all I had to do was scoop the hungry one into bed, doze and nurse until the other one awakened, and then switch. This was a marvelous system for me because it gave me the sleep I needed. I also didn't change them at night unless they had soaked through everything. They never got diaper rash and didn't seem to mind not being changed at night.*

Almost all mothers who nurse more than one baby comment on their hearty appetite and increased thirst. Some make a practice of eating an extra meal before going to bed. Carolyn Johnson says:

*I noticed my appetite and thirst increased quite a bit during the first few weeks (I think I ate about six times a*

*day), which is probably nature's way of providing the
extra fluid and food for nursing two. I lost twenty pounds
when they were born and an additional seven pounds in
the next two weeks, which put me a little underweight.
However, these pounds gradually came back so that by
the time the twins were six weeks old we were all in fine
shape.*

Regarding the work of managing more than one baby, one
mother of twins commented, "The rewards are great, but during
the first three months you won't have time to think about them."

With more than one baby, your attention is focused on the
babies in a special way. Just watching them—noticing their differences, their uneven growth patterns, their inherent temperamental
leanings—is an ever-interesting, ever-changing spectacular. It can
give you insight and knowledge that add greatly to your compe-
tence as a mother, as well as to your enjoyment of your babies. As
one twin mother puts it, "I'm afraid having one baby will be rather
dull after watching two bloom and grow!"

If you are expecting twins (or have them already), you'll find
additional information on breastfeeding and caring for twins in
MOTHERING MULTIPLES, a book that's available from La Leche
League Groups or La Leche League International. See the Appendix for details.

# Relactation and Induced Lactation

In the usual course of events, a mother's body is prepared for
lactation during pregnancy, and the birth of the baby signals the
mother's breasts to begin producing milk. With the baby's eager
sucking, the milk continues to be produced. If the baby is not put
to the breast after birth, or if breastfeeding ceases soon afterward,
the milk "dries up." Relactation is the process by which a mother
is able to re-establish her milk supply several weeks or months after
lactation has stopped. It is a difficult and time-consuming process,
but it can be done. This is possible because the sucking of the baby
stimulates milk production. In fact, some mothers have been able

to establish a milk supply for an adopted baby without the impetus of pregnancy and birth. This is called induced lactation.

Often mothers who have attempted relactation have been those whose babies could not tolerate any artificial formula and needed breast milk to survive. Beth Robertson from Tennessee tells of her experience with relactation:

*I started breastfeeding my son Zachary in the hospital. My pediatrician was not supportive of breastfeeding and told me I should give it up. I followed his advice and quit breastfeeding after only seven days. I felt miserable about it but thought that the doctor must know what was best.*

*When Zachary was seven weeks old, he developed severe diarrhea and diaper rash. After almost four weeks of trying different formulas and medicines, his new doctor said we had gone as far as we could go with different formulas and breast milk was probably the only solution. He suggested that I find out about relactation.*

*I contacted Marty Wilson of La Leche League, and she assured me it could be done, but would require time and patience. She also arranged for donors to give us milk until mine came in. I used a nursing supplementer to give Zac the donated milk.*

*The first day I gave Zac the donor milk the diarrhea stopped entirely. It was a miracle! During the second week I began to express a few drops of milk and was delighted. I continued giving the donated breast milk at every feeding until Carol Blanton, another Leader, suggested I try cutting off the donor milk entirely for a day or two, with permission from the baby's doctor, and just nurse Zac more often to see if my milk increased. The doctor agreed. The next few days were rough going, to say the least, but things began to improve. By the next week Zac had gained seven ounces, and at the end of another week the doctor had me stop all supplements. I was finally on my own!*

*Relactation was a difficult process, harder than I had anticipated. I got discouraged many times, but I did make it at last. Zac is now thriving and gaining weight and is quite a happy and contented baby. We are both very grateful to La Leche League and everyone involved in helping us.*

Another mother, Kimberly Fradejas from Florida, was understandably concerned when her daughter Brandy didn't seem able to tolerate any of the formulas they had tried. When the baby was three weeks old, they took her to see a nurse practitioner at the clinic. Kimberly tells what happened next:

*I asked if it was too late for me to breastfeed. I had taken the dry-up pills for ten days after Brandy was born. The nurse said it might not be too late. She showed me how to guide the baby to the breast, and Brandy took right to it. She nursed for the first time right there in the office. I never will forget the look on her cute little face. It was as if that was what she had wanted and needed all along. The nurse then advised me to let Brandy nurse first whenever she was hungry, then to supplement her afterward with a small amount of formula. Every day I decreased the amount of formula Brandy was taking until she no longer needed a supplement.*

*The nurse arranged for me to talk with a La Leche League Leader, who gave me information on increasing my milk supply and books on breastfeeding. Since I knew nothing about nursing a baby, she invited me to come to La Leche League meetings where I could meet other nursing mothers.*

*Brandy is four-and-a-half months old now and weighs nearly twenty pounds. She is a very healthy and happy baby. I am proud to be doing the best I can for her. My only regret is that I didn't begin nursing her the minute she was born.*

## NURSING ADOPTED BABIES

After hearing stories of mothers who had successfully re-established their milk supplies for their allergic babies, mothers who were planning to adopt babies began to wonder if they could also provide breast milk for their babies. The first few adoptive mothers who were in touch with LLL were nursing their toddlers when they adopted their new babies. By putting the young baby to their breast often, they were able to increase their milk supply to fully meet the infant's needs.

Carol Marino from Connecticut tells us about her experience when she adopted a baby girl from Korea:

*When Carol Ann Ree Ja, just four months old, arrived to join her homemade sister, Judea Vera, she was tired and hungry. I put her to my breast and she nursed beautifully. It was surprising to me that she took to nursing so readily, since she had been bottle fed from the time she was born until she came home to us.*

*Judea was seventeen months old when Carol Ann Ree Ja arrived. She had been gradually weaning herself and was only nursing occasionally—maybe once every week or so. I realized that I'd have to build up my milk supply, and I started pumping a month ahead of time—five minutes on each breast four times a day the first week, eight times a day the second week, and from then on each hour during the day, until the last three days, when I pumped five minutes on each breast every two hours around the clock. This pumping brought in plenty of milk so I had a good supply when Carol Ann Ree Ja arrived.*

*Judea stepped up her nursing when the baby came home, and during the first month I often nursed two children at the same time, one on each breast. Finally one day Judea pointed authoritatively to my breast and announced, "Baby's!" She never nursed again.*

Encouraged by these success stories, other mothers planning to adopt babies became interested in nursing them. Even mothers who had never been pregnant were able to establish at least a partial milk supply so that their babies were receiving some breast milk even though they also received formula or other supplements.

Jo Young, from England who had never been pregnant, was able to bring in her milk for her adopted son, Peter. She began when he was three weeks old and explains it this way:

*With great effort and sacrifice from a small handful of people I succeeded in my effort to induce lactation, and incredibly, Peter was completely nourished and sustained at my breast by the time he was three and a half months old. He remained solely breastfed from then until he began to experiment with solids at about six months. During the early months when he was basically dependent on formula, Peter looked rather fragile and unwell, suffering from constant colds. I am convinced that the breast milk he has had is responsible for the marvelous changes in his looks. His skin has cleared and he is now a large, bouncy, blooming, typical breastfed baby.*

*I can never hope to convey totally the depth of my gratitude to the friends who helped us. I think they realize the wealth of the gift they have given Peter and me.*

---

The practice of nursing adopted babies has become so well accepted that some adoption agencies hold meetings for the mothers who plan to breastfeed. Mothers report that the extra effort required in building a milk supply for their adopted babies is well worth it. The closeness and intimacy of the breastfeeding relationship is extremely important to these adoptive mothers. From Arizona, Anne Sanger writes:

---

*It seems like such a short time since we took Lisa from the adoption agency into our family. She was four days old then and seemed so small. Now she is a happy, beautiful one-year-old.*

*I was able to nurse Lisa with the help of a nursing supplementer. I did a lot of preparation prior to her arrival. When Lisa was ten months old, we were able to discontinue using the supplementer. We are still a happy nursing couple.*

*It is difficult for me to explain what it means to me to be able to nurse Lisa. I wanted to give her the gift of love and the wonderful way of communicating that the nursing relationship opens to mothers.*

*I know that breastfeeding my adopted child was not the easiest thing I ever did in my life, but it has been one of the most rewarding. We feel very fortunate to be the parents of such a happy child.*

The basic technique for relactation or induced lactation is to encourage the baby to nurse as often as possible. This is how you stimulate the breasts to produce milk. Adoptive mothers can often begin establishing a milk supply before they have their babies. It helps, of course, to know when you'll get your baby. Use a pump or hand-express for three to five minutes on each breast several times a day, gradually increasing the number of times per day. If this is kept up faithfully, the breasts will begin to produce milk—usually in two to six weeks. It may only be a few drops at first, but this will increase once your baby starts to nurse.

One of the most difficult aspects of relactation is getting the baby interested in sucking at the breast if he has been used to bottles for several weeks or months. This requires a great deal of patience and determination. The mother who is attempting to relactate needs a generous amount of support and encouragement. It's a good idea to be in touch with a La Leche League Leader who can provide further information.

You will need to continue giving the baby some formula or donated breast milk. You should nurse the baby first, for as long as he is willing, before you offer the supplement. Many mothers avoid bottles completely and use a spoon, cup, small flexible bowl, or feeding syringe. A nursing supplementer can be used that allows the baby to receive his supplement as he nurses at the breast. (See the Appendix.)

If you are putting the baby to the breast as often as possible and giving the supplement only during or after a feeding, you may be able to gradually cut back on the total amount of supplement you give the baby as your milk supply increases. If you write down the amount of supplement he takes each day, and you see the total decreasing slowly, you'll know your milk supply is increasing. You'll need to watch the baby's wet diapers and bowel movements to be sure he is still getting plenty to eat.

While you are establishing a milk supply, it is very important to keep in touch with the baby's doctor and check the baby's weight on a weekly basis to be sure he continues to gain weight.

Many adoptive mothers continue using a nursing supplementer to give their babies formula at every feeding until the baby starts taking large amounts of solid foods. Even though they continue using a supplement, they find that feeding their babies at the breast provides a closeness that is beneficial to their relationship.

The mother who is relactating finds that for a time she is working almost around the clock feeding her baby as often as she can.

Of course, the more often the baby nurses, the more he benefits from his mother's milk, and the more milk there will be waiting for him the next time.

Information from mothers who have nursed adopted babies has been compiled into a booklet by League Leader Kathryn Anderson. *Nursing Your Adopted Baby* includes details of establishing a milk supply and the importance of keeping your perspective about the situation. Copies are available from your local La Leche League Group or LLLI. See the Appendix for details.

# What If Mother Is Ill?

"How can I take care of my baby if I get sick?" This is a common question of anxious mothers. Of course, caring for an active, healthy baby is a demanding job at any time, but when mother is ill it can be of real concern. It is reassuring to know that nursing your baby makes caring for him so much easier. For minor illnesses, such as a cold or the flu, you needn't even consider interrupting breastfeeding. The germs are not transmitted through your milk, and the baby has no doubt been exposed to the illness for at least as long as you have, and certainly was exposed to it before you knew you had it.

Breast milk can protect the baby from getting sick. A nursing mother produces antibodies to the specific germs her baby has been exposed to. These antibodies are transmitted to the baby through her milk. Continuing to breastfeed also helps you get the extra rest you need when you aren't feeling well. Sudden weaning would not be good for either you or your baby.

If your illness is more serious—for example, if you have pneumonia, hepatitis, or even tuberculosis—doctors on our Professional Advisory Board still advise continued breastfeeding. Breastfeeding requires a minimum of effort for you, giving you the most rest. In addition, your milk provides special protection for your baby against the virus or bacteria causing your illness.

If you become seriously ill and your doctor suggests weaning the baby, explain how important breastfeeding is to both of you. If your doctor still insists that weaning is necessary, remember that you are always free to consult another doctor before making a decision as serious as weaning your baby. It would be a good idea to discuss your situation with your local La Leche League Leader as she may be able to recommend another doctor who will be more supportive of breastfeeding.

## HOSPITALIZATION

If you can remain at home during your illness, so much the better. Get help with the necessary housework, laundry, and meals, and caring for the older children. Tuck your little one in bed with you, where he will be close by all the time and able to nurse whenever he wants.

If a serious illness or an accident requries hospitalization, you will want to make some special arrangements to have your baby kept with you, or at least brought to you. Nursing mothers have found all kinds of ingenious ways to avoid being separated from their babies during hospital stays. Discuss your needs and those of your baby with your husband and your doctor. Your condition, the hospital's facilities, and your baby's age and usual nursing pattern will all influence the situation.

More and more surgery is being performed nowadays on an outpatient basis under local anesthesia. You can then return home to rest and nurse your baby without any prolonged separation. Procedures such as dental work can nearly always be carried out without interruption of breastfeeding. When the potential surgery is elective, your doctor may be willing to postpone it until the baby is older.

If you must stay in the hospital overnight or for several days, your husband or a friend or relative can bring the baby in to visit you and nurse. Some hospitals may be willing to admit the baby and allow him to room-in with you, though they may require that someone stay in the room with you to help care for the baby.

Be flexible and polite as you talk over your requests with the doctors and hospital. If you are willing to cooperate with hospital personnel, they will usually be cooperative, too. Let them see how much it means to you to keep your baby with you.

## MAJOR SURGERY

Even when a mother is required to have major surgery, arrangements can often be made to allow her to continue breastfeeding. If some feedings must be missed, you can plan on using a breast pump so your breasts will not become engorged.

In some cases where a few days of separation are unavoidable, your little one will more than likely be willing and eager to return to nursing once you are back together. Marilyn Mastro of Florida needed to have a hysterectomy when her daughter Frances was a year old and still nursing. She tells her story:

*The surgery was successful. There were no postoperative complications, and my husband was allowed to bring the girls in to see me four days later. Frances was allowed to nurse (with a pillow under her to protect my stitches) for the first time in four and a half days. I had used a breast pump to relieve the engorgement and to keep up my milk supply. Pete said that after that short period of nursing, Franny slept better than she had during any of the other nights while I was away.*

*My doctor discharged me the next day and I came home and resumed breastfeeding and mothering my family. I had presumed that "complete hysterectomy" would mean the end of the joys of nursing, and this thought was very depressing and frightening. As my daughter suckled my milk supply back to her satisfaction I realized how important motherhood and nursing had become to me. I'm glad my doctor hadn't convinced me to wean Franny completely because I need her closeness now almost as much as she needs me.*

## MEDICATIONS FOR THE NURSING MOTHER

Be sure to check with your doctor before taking any medication while you are breastfeeding, even drugs that are available without a prescription. Usually the amount of the drug found in mother's milk is so small that it won't affect the baby at all, but you still want to avoid unnecessary drugs for your own sake while you are nursing your baby.

If any doctor is prescribing medication for you, be sure he or she is aware that you are breastfeeding your baby and knows how important it is for you to continue. There are three questions when a breastfeeding mother needs medication: Will the drug harm the nursing baby? Will weaning harm the baby or the mother? What are the options?

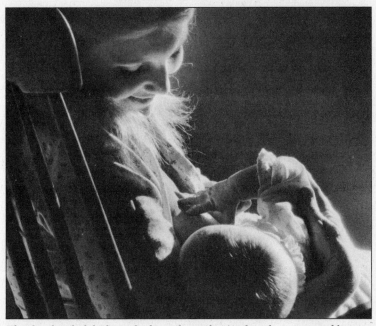

*The close bond of the breastfeeding relationship need not be interrupted because mother or baby is ill.*

When prescribing a medication for a nursing mother, some physicians routinely insist on weaning as a precaution. In reality, few drugs have been proven to be harmful to the nursing infant. Abrupt weaning is traumatic for mother and baby. Mother may develop painfully engorged breasts, risking a breast infection and compounding the problems for which she was advised to take the medication in the first place. Also, the mother/baby relationship is affected. Caring for the baby and keeping him content becomes difficult or impossible; the baby is often utterly inconsolable.

There are other contraindications for even temporary weaning. A baby with a family history of allergy may be placed in jeopardy of asthma or eczema when exposed to cow's milk or formula. In addition, he no longer enjoys the benefits of the many immune factors known to be in human milk, including antibodies to a number of infections to which infants are particularly susceptible—antibodies which, in many cases, may protect him from his mother's illness as well.

Most doctors have found that options are available that will permit breastfeeding to continue in almost all circumstances. If a particular drug poses a potential risk for the baby, usually it is possible to substitute another drug with lesser or no risk. The same is true when little is known about a drug's effect on a nursing baby.

Another drug about which there is more information can often be used instead. It may also be possible to alter or postpone treatment until the baby is older.

We are encouraged by the increasing number of studies being done on the subject of medications and their effects on breastfeeding. If there is any question about the safety of a drug for a nursing mother and her baby, it's a good idea to check with someone who is knowledgeable about medications as well as supportive of breastfeeding. Several reference books listed in the Appendix include information about the effects of medications on breastfeeding. A La Leche League Leader may be able to help, or guide you to someone who can give you accurate information.

If your doctor insists on prescribing a certain medication and advises you to wean the baby, remember that you have a right to seek a second opinion.

## DRUGS THAT SHOULD BE AVOIDED WHILE NURSING

There are a small number of drugs that are contraindicated while you are breastfeeding. The American Academy of Pediatrics publishes a listing of drugs that are are safe to take while breastfeeding and also those that are contraindicated.

Radioactive compounds used in diagnosis or treatment are contraindicated while breastfeeding. If these are needed, it will be necessary to discontinue nursing temporarily as these materials can be excreted in your milk and are dangerous to your baby. Your doctor or the radiologist supervising the treatment can advise you as to when it is safe to resume nursing. In the meantime, you will have to pump your milk and discard it.

Many authorities believe that combined oral contraceptives that include estrogen should be avoided while a mother is breastfeeding because they have been found to affect the quality and quantity of a mother's milk. There is concern, too, about possible long-term effects on the baby of hormones that are found in the mother's milk.

Illegal drugs, such as heroin, cocaine, and marijuana should also be avoided while you are breastfeeding. Their potentially harmful effects on your nursing baby include not only their presence in breast milk but also their interference with your ability to care for your baby. The use of marijuana has been found to cause a decrease in levels of prolactin, the "mothering" hormone that is especially important in assuring an adequate milk supply.

There are some other drugs that physicians agree should not be taken by a nursing mother. Be sure that anyone prescribing medication for you knows that you are breastfeeding.

## IMMUNIZATIONS

If your blood is Rh-negative and your baby's is Rh-positive, you will probably receive an injection of Rh antibodies (RhoGAM) very soon after you deliver. RhoGAM is used widely to prevent Rh complications, and it is not harmful to your nursing infant.

Along with RhoGAM, many other vaccines do not affect the breastfed baby through his mother's milk. According to the Center for Disease Control of the United States Public Health Service: "Most vaccines can be given safely to the mother of the nursing infant." Acceptable vaccines include: smallpox, typhus, typhoid, yellow fever, oral polio, tetanus, diphtheria, pertussis, rabies, measles, rubella, cholera, and influenza.

With regard to immunizations for your baby, the same schedule is followed for the breastfed baby as for bottle-fed infants. There is no need to refrain from nursing the baby before or after administration of any vaccine, including the oral polio vaccine.

# Mothers with Special Problems

A mother who is handicapped in any way will find it much more convenient to breastfeed her baby. This is true of blind mothers, deaf mothers, mothers who are confined to wheelchairs, and mothers who are recovering from illness or injuries. Breastfeeding requires less effort than bottle-feeding plus the satisfaction of nourishing her baby with her own milk provides comfort and reassurance to a mother with a disability. Many LLL publications are available on cassette tape or in Braillon for use by blind or handicapped parents. See the Appendix for details.

Mothers with chronic illnesses also benefit from the ease and satisfaction of breastfeeding their babies. Illnesses such as diabetes, lupus, arthritis, epilepsy, or multiple sclerosis need not interfere with a mother's decision to breastfeed her baby. Breastfeeding makes life easier. One mother with diabetes says:

*When a mother breastfeeds, she doesn't waste her time sterilizing bottles and preparing formula. The mother only has to bring the baby to bed, relax, and enjoy. Probably the biggest advantage is that the baby is healthier. Breastfeeding saves many trips to the doctor's office with ear infections, digestive problems, and allergies.*

Breastfed babies also tend to be less fussy because breast milk is more easily digested than formula. If a breastfed baby is fussy, often just putting him to the breast is enough to calm him.

One physical advantage of breastfeeding is especially noteworthy. Many women with chronic illnesses find that the normal hormonal changes of pregnancy result in a temporary remission of their symptoms. When a woman breastfeeds, her hormonal levels do not revert back to their pre-pregnancy state right away; this happens gradually. If weaning occurs at a natural pace, her symptoms often return much later than if she were bottle feeding, giving her better health when her tiny baby needs her most. Temporary remission during pregnancy and breastfeeding has been reported by mothers with rheumatoid arthritis, multiple sclerosis, lupus, and diabetes. Some diabetic mothers need only half as much insulin while nursing than they needed before they became pregnant. This makes the first months after birth easier on a mother who already has other problems.

For the woman whose illness is debilitating, nursing can contribute to her self-esteem and her self-confidence as a mother. These kinds of positive feelings may also have a favorable effect on the course of her illness. One mother with epilepsy says:

*Breastfeeding has been a salvation for me, especially on days when I knew there was very little I could do for my child. At least I was giving the very best of myself in extremely important areas—food, warmth, affection, touching, and caring. I could never have gathered the strength or had the energy to give bottles.*

There may be some things a mother can do, depending on her illness, to make nursing easier. For the mother with rheumatoid arthritis, it might help to set up a comfortable place to nurse with good support and extra pillows. An epileptic mother needs to have a safe place to lay the baby in the event of a seizure and to nurse in a chair that is well-padded or in a bed with guard rails or extra pillows.

Another benefit of breastfeeding for the chronically ill mother is the emotional closeness it adds to her relationship with her baby and the sense of normalcy that it brings to her situation.

Gail Stutler, who was recovering from brain surgery when her second child was born, recalls that she "couldn't even name a diaper." But she continues, "I could scoop up a tiny bundle, put her to my breast, and nurse her close to my heart. I could satisfy at least one of the desperate needs I had when deprived of all my capabilities."

**Diabetes.** In recent years medical science has made pregnancy and childbirth safer for diabetic women, and more and more of them are deciding to nurse their new babies. Many diabetic mothers find that nursing improves their condition. The easier transition from pregnancy to nursing makes for less of an adjustment, because your body continues to support both your baby and yourself.

A diabetic mother will have to make adjustments in her diet depending on how often her baby nurses from day to day. If she takes insulin, she will have to regulate the dosage as carefully as she did while she was pregnant, in order to keep her diabetes under control while nursing. The insulin itself will not hurt the baby. La Leche League's information sheet, "The Diabetic Mother and Breastfeeding," provides further information. See the Appendix for details.

**Epilepsy.** Mothers with epilepsy benefit from the nursing hormones and the relaxation engendered by natural mothering. If the mother must take medication to control her epilepsy, she should check with her doctor about the drugs' effects on breastfeeding. Most drugs prescribed for epilepsy won't harm the nursing baby. If your doctor is uncertain about the effects of a particular drug, perhaps one that is so new little is known about it, he or she may be able to prescribe another drug instead.

If you are a mother with a handicap, disability, or chronic illness, it would be helpful for you to be in touch with your local LLL Leader. She will be able to offer you additional information and encouragement and may be able to put you in touch with another mother who has nursed her baby in circumstances similar to yours. Contacting someone who has "been there" can help give you the confidence you need to feel that you can do it, too.

# If Your Baby Gets Sick

Most of the time your breastfed baby will be happy and healthy. You will be pleased and proud to know that your milk is contributing to his good health. But what's best for your baby if he does develop an illness, such as vomiting or diarrhea?

First of all, remember that not all loose stools constitute diarrhea. If your baby is otherwise well and thriving, it really doesn't matter how loose his bowel movements are. In the breastfed infant it is quite normal for baby to have very loose, runny bowel movements. Many breastfed babies, especially in the early weeks, have as many as six or eight stools a day; later on, as they get older, they may have only one a week or even fewer. All this is well within the realm of normalcy. Even the occasional green, watery stool in an otherwise healthy baby is nothing to worry about.

When a baby is not running a fever, it is wise to consider other possibilities before assuming that illness is the cause of diarrhea or vomiting. If vitamin, iron, or fluoride supplements have recently been started, they could be the cause. (These are not necessary for most breastfed babies.) Sometimes vitamin or iron supplements taken by a nursing mother can cause digestive problems in her baby. An occasional bottle of formula could result in diarrhea or vomiting in a sensitive baby. Diarrhea is also a common side-effect of certain medications, such as antibiotics, taken by the mother or the baby. Another possibility is that baby is sensitive to a new food that has been introduced. In some cases, a food eaten by the nursing mother may affect her baby.

Because of the immunological protection received through mother's milk, a breastfed baby is less likely to become ill when colds and flu are going around. When a nursing mother is sick, it is best for her baby to keep on breastfeeding. The baby has already been exposed to the germs causing the illness, and breast milk will help protect the baby. In fact, the nursing mother can produce antibodies on demand to the specific germs that challenge her baby. For example, the baby picks up a germ and passes it to the mother. Her more experienced immune system begins to manufacture the necessary antibodies; she gives these back to the baby through her milk.

Even so, breastfed babies do sometimes get sick with diarrhea. If a baby is having twelve to sixteen stools a day, or if the stools have an offensive odor or contain flecks of blood, the baby most likely has diarrhea. Usually symptoms will improve in three to five days, but diarrhea occasionally causes more serious problems in babies and young children. The lining of the intestine is inflamed and irritated, and it tends to leak fluids and pass nutrients through the body too rapidly. The loss of water and salt can lead to dehydration and eventually to shock. Signs of dehydration include listlessness, lethargy, dry mouth, less than the usual amount of tears, minimal urine output, and fever. You should call your doctor if you suspect your sick baby is becoming dehydrated. You can help prevent dehydration by making sure that your baby gets plenty of fluids. The best way to do this in a breastfed baby is to offer small, frequent nursings.

Some doctors routinely advise that the baby or toddler who is vomiting or has diarrhea be taken off everything by mouth—including breast milk. When confronted with this advice, a nursing mother may well question it. Mothers with breastfeeding babies or toddlers know that abrupt—even if temporary—weaning can make life miserable. When the familiar source of solace is taken away, a sick baby becomes even more frustrated and upset. Meanwhile mother's breasts become fuller and more uncomfortable.

There are several options open to the nursing mother when her doctor's medical advice goes against her instincts and her other sources of information. Some mothers might seek out another, more like-minded doctor, one who is more knowledgeable about breastfeeding. Other mothers might be tempted to do things their own way without telling their doctor. The best answer is to work with your doctor to arrive at a solution acceptable to everyone—physician, mother, and baby.

Recent studies support the idea that a baby with diarrhea should continue breastfeeding. Much of the work on this subject comes from developing countries where diarrhea can be a serious, even life-threatening problem in infants and small children. Even breastfed babies may experience frequent bouts of diarrhea in areas where sanitation and hygiene are poor. Taking babies off the breast for a few days with each episode of diarrhea risks malnutrition and premature weaning, and hence, more severe attacks of diarrhea. A 1985 study conducted in Burma concluded that keeping babies breastfeeding was the best treatment.

For the breastfeeding baby with a mild case of vomiting or diarrhea, special measures are usually not necessary. In her book, *A Practical Guide to Breastfeeding*, Jan Riordan, RN, MN, writes:

*If a breastfeeding infant develops flu symptoms, he may have a low fever, irritability, vomiting, and diarrhea for a few days. If he is willing to take anything by mouth, it should be breast milk. Although many health professionals advise that even breastfed infants avoid milk products in the case of vomiting and diarrhea, this is a grievous error. . . . Because breast milk is digested so rapidly, even the infant who is vomiting regularly will absorb some of the nutrients and fluid of the milk before it is regurgitated. . . . Only in moderate to severe diarrhea is supplementing breast milk with an electrolyte oral solution such as Pedialyte necessary, but this is rarely a problem in the breastfeeding child.*

So the rule of thumb for the breastfeeding baby is: If a baby can take anything by mouth, it should be breast milk. As long as he is having at least two or three wet diapers per day during his illness, he is not in danger of dehydration.

For the baby who's vomiting, it will be best to take him off solid foods for the duration. If his stomach is very upset, it might help to hand-express most of your milk and let him nurse for comfort on a fairly empty breast. By keeping down the amount of breast milk he gets at each nursing (but nursing fairly often), the baby may be less likely to lose it all again. After a few hours of tolerating these smaller feedings, the baby can begin to take more milk at each nursing. If even the smaller feedings quickly come back up, you should call your doctor and watch for signs of dehydration.

For the baby who is six months or older, or the toddler who is begging for something because he is thirsty, perhaps a few ice chips or water from a teaspoon will satisfy him for a while. The advantage of ice is that it goes down slowly and is an interesting distraction to boot. If you can hold him off with something like that, fine. If not, let him nurse on the emptied breast but don't give him anything else. In any case, weaning is not necessary or advisable.

**Breast milk is the best food there is for the sick baby, and as long as he can take anything by mouth it should be your milk.** When a nursing baby is sick, the comfort he receives at the breast may be the most important benefit of all.

## LACTOSE INTOLERANCE

Occasionally, when a baby has very frequent, loose stools it may be suggested that he has something called lactose intolerance, and you may be told to take the baby off the breast. There is no need to do that. True lactose intolerance is virtually unknown in babies and young children under weaning age. As children grow beyond weaning age, the enzyme lactase, with which they were all born and which is necessary to digest milk sugar (lactose), begins to disappear from their systems. This occurs because after weaning, milk is no longer a necessary part of the human diet.

Lactose intolerance is not a problem for the totally breastfed baby. On the other hand, cow's milk allergy (sensitivity to the protein in cow's milk), is frequently confused with lactose intolerance, and should be ruled out as a possible cause of baby's diarrhea. Sensitive babies may react to cow's milk products in their mother's diet.

If baby is ill or has been given certain medications, such as antibiotics, he may develop something called "secondary lactose intolerance," which shows up as diarrhea. The best thing to do in such situations is to take baby off everything by mouth **except your milk.** For the toddler who has been on lots of solids and other liquids, you may need to give water by cup also, as your milk supply may not be enough for him. As the effects of the illness or the medication wear off, his stools will return to normal. In the meantime, because of the special closeness and comfort he derives from the breastfeeding relationship, as well as the physical benefits of your milk, he will recover much faster.

Regardless of the age of your nursling, whether he is a little newborn or a sturdy toddler, remember that if he develops diarrhea, don't panic. And whatever else you do, keep nursing.

# Slow Weight Gain

Slow weight gain in an otherwise healthy breastfed baby is a warning signal. It calls for a close look at baby, mother, and the nursing routine. If you find yourself in this situation, don't rush to replace breast milk, the most complete food for babies, with an artificial substitute. Adjustments can be made, and breastfeeding, with its long-term benefits, can continue.

Why do some babies gain weight slowly? There may be one simple explanation or a combination of reasons. Could a minor illness be causing the problem? Often, a baby who is not feeling well does not nurse well. Of course, the baby's doctor will check him over thoroughly to be assured that illness is not the cause of the problem. And if the baby *is* sick, nursing is of even more value. An all-out effort to maintain breastfeeding, along with appropriate treatment for the illness, will speed recovery.

In all cases of slow weight gain, the baby should be under the care of a doctor. In the majority of these cases, the baby is doing well and most breastfeeding difficulties can be readily resolved. Look over the section in Chapter 7 called "Is Baby Getting Enough?" It explains many of the breastfeeding management techniques that help to increase a mother's milk supply and help baby gain weight.

Remember that most babies lose some weight after birth. Baby's weight gain should be figured from the lowest point, not from his birth weight.

What is a good average weight gain? About a pound a month, or four ounces a week, is an acceptable weight gain for a breastfed baby. Some put on twice that much in the early weeks, while others fall a bit below that average for a time. If the baby has 6-8 wet diapers and 3-5 bowel movements a day, and is alert and active and doing well in other respects, a gain of slightly less than a pound a month may be his normal growth pattern. Increases in length, head, and chest circumference are also signs of growth. Good skin tone also indicates that baby is getting enough to eat.

## TIME AT THE BREAST

If a baby is not gaining well, the first question is how often is the baby being nursed? Not nursing often enough is probably the most common cause of low weight gain. Breast milk is quickly digested, and frequent nursings are easier for the baby and provide him with a steady supply of nutrients. If slow weight gain is a problem, it's important that you nurse on both breasts at least every two hours, with perhaps one longer stretch of three to four hours at night if baby is asleep. If a feeding begins at eight o'clock, put the baby to the breast again at ten, regardless of how long the eight o'clock nursing lasted. Plan to nurse the baby ten to twelve times in each twenty-four-hour period.

## "SWITCH NURSING"

If your baby is not gaining well, always nurse on both breasts at each feeding, and change breasts several times during the course of a feeding. This means that you'll nurse on one side for as long as baby is actively sucking and swallowing. Then as he slows down and begins to lose interest, switch to the other breast. For some babies, this can be as long as ten minutes on each breast; for others it will be only two or three minutes before you switch. Be sure to let the baby nurse from both breasts at least twice at each feeding. If baby tends to fall asleep, changing his diaper before switching sides can wake him up.

"Switch nursing" keeps a sleepy baby more interested in nursing and helps a baby get more milk because he sucks more actively. It also encourages more let-downs for the mother, along with giving her breasts more stimulation so she will produce more milk. A few days of "switch nursing" can sometimes bring about a dramatic improvement in baby's weight gain.

## NIPPLE CONFUSION

Using a pacifier, nipple shields, or supplemental bottles of water, formula, or juice can cause nipple confusion and interfere with baby's ability to suck effectively at the breast. Just one bottle is enough to confuse some babies, especially in the early weeks. A baby uses totally different techniques to remove milk from your breast than he uses to drink from a bottle. You'll want to be wary of bottles or pacifiers if your baby is gaining slowly as nipple confusion can add to rather than solve the problem.

## THE EXTRA-PLACID BABY

The slow gainer may be a placid baby, a quiet infant who regularly sleeps for four or five hours at a time. This little sleeper isn't gaining well because he just isn't nursing as much as he should be. If your baby is one who sleeps a lot, you may be thinking, "Such a good baby." But don't be lulled by such placidness. Keep a careful check on the number of wet and soiled diapers. After the first week, you should be getting at least six to eight really wet diapers a day. A new baby, under six weeks, will usually have three to five bowel movements per day. As he gets older, the number may decrease and he may only have a bowel movement every three or four days, but in these cases, the amount will be substantial.

With a sleeper, mother takes the initiative and actively encourages her baby to nurse more often. You have to become a clock-watcher. For a time, you are the gentle prod encouraging your baby to nurse. Handling baby and nursing him often helps to rouse him. He needs this stimulation as much as he needs your good breast milk. It all works together to get him going.

## ENCOURAGING THE SLEEPY BABY

To wake a sleepy baby who needs to eat more often, strip him down to a diaper and hold him, skin-to-skin, next to you. (If you are chilly, throw a blanket loosely around the two of you.) Rub his back or feet. Talk or sing to him. One mother of a sleeper said that every time her baby opened his eyes during a nursing, she'd say loudly, "Yes! Good! You can do it!" Each time he responded to her words by nursing well for another minute or so. Whether it was mother's pep talks or her all-around attentive mothering we can't say, but baby's thinness was soon replaced by dimpled elbows and chunky legs.

If baby is still too drowsy to nurse, try sitting him in your lap with his chin in your hand and bend him forward at the hips. Or gently bring him from a horizontal to a vertical position with one hand supporting his head. Or try walking your fingers up and down his spine.


## TINY AND FUSSY

Occasionally, a baby is wakeful—fussy even—and spends a considerable amount of time at the breast, but still lags in the weight department. The question then is—how well is the baby sucking? Is he taking the nipple well? He should be getting at least one inch of the areola, the dark area surrounding the nipple, into his mouth. The baby who sucks in a fluttery manner on the end of the nipple will get the milk that has already collected in the breast, but he will not take in the additional milk that comes when he draws the nipple further into his mouth and sucks vigorously. He isn't getting as much milk as he should, nor is it the richest milk, with the highest fat content.

If you suspect that your baby has such a sucking habit, look carefully at how he is nursing. When there is concern about the baby's weight gain, his position at the breast is very important.

Check over the section in Chapter 4 called "Breastfeeding in Slow Motion." Be sure baby is positioned so his whole body is facing you and he does not have to turn his head in order to take your breast and nipple in his mouth.

You may want to try using the football-hold position in order to have a better view of baby's position and sucking techniques. Be sure his body is bent at the hips and he does not arch his back.

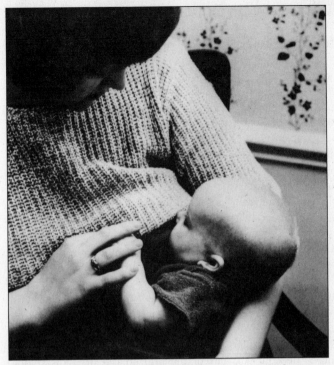

*Babies are meant to grow and thrive but sometimes breastfeeding techniques need improvement so this can occur.*

## AN OVERABUNDANT SUPPLY

Occasionally a mother who seems to have an overabundant milk supply has a slow gaining baby who nurses often but is fussy, very gassy, and has loose greenish stools. He seems to be getting too much milk and may even spit up after feelings. A mother whose baby shows these symptoms may need to let the baby nurse his fill on the first breast letting him pull away himself when he is satisfied before offering him the other side. It may help to offer only one breast per feeding for a while to see if baby shows signs of improvement. It may be that the baby is getting too much of the thinner foremilk and not enough of the rich hindmilk that comes later in a feeding.

# CHECKLIST FOR MOTHERS

If your baby is slow to put on weight, you'll want to take good care of yourself so you can build up your milk supply to meet baby's needs. Are you doing too much and not getting enough rest? One pediatrician's prescription for slow gainers is to put mother and baby to bed together for a few days. Try to reduce outside stress in your life. Make your baby your main concern for the time being.

Are you eating well? Think now—what did you have for breadfast today? Was lunch "on the run?" Are you drinking enough water or juice? Your liquid intake can include some coffee and tea, but keep in mind that excessive amounts of beverages containing caffeine have been known to adversely affect the weight gain of some babies. The same is true of smoking, especially if the mother is a heavy smoker.

Are you taking oral contraceptives that contain estrogen? These have been found to affect the quantity and quality of a mother's milk. Could it be that you are anemic or have an underactive thyroid? Both of these conditions can affect a mother's milk supply if they are left untreated. Check with your doctor about these possibilities.

When a baby is not gaining as well as he should be, there is bound to be concern. But taking him off the breast is seldom, if ever, the answer to the problem. There is always the possibility that this will introduce a whole new set of problems.

# TAKE SPECIAL NOTE

When babies do not gain well on breast milk alone, everyone becomes concerned. The mother may feel frightened and inadequate. The doctor stresses that something needs to be done, but lack of knowledge about breastfeeding can lead to inappropriate interventions. The following points can be reason for concern and indications that some changes, perhaps even supplemental feedings, may be needed for a time. Determining the cause of the low weight gain and taking appropriate action can relieve everyone's concern and boost the baby's weight.

• If baby's weight gain is below the recommended range of four to seven ounces a week or at least a pound a month.

• If baby has not regained his birth weight by two to three weeks of age.

- If there are too few wet diapers or scanty bowel movements.
- If the baby is not waking to nurse at night.
- If the baby is nursing fewer than ten to twelve times a day.
- If the baby has gotten into a habit of taking only the end of the mother's nipple or will only stay at the breast for a very short time, or refuses the breast.
- If the baby nurses "all the time" but is mostly sleeping or "mouthing" the nipple, not actively sucking and swallowing.
- If mother has persistent sore nipples in spite of treatment and correct positioning of baby.

These situations may indicate the baby is not sucking effectively. A baby who is not sucking well cannot build up his mother's milk supply to meet his needs. This mother and baby require the help of someone familiar with sucking problems.

In such cases, breastfeeding can and should continue but the baby may need to receive supplementary feedings for a while.

Using a specially designed nursing supplementer, you can give the supplement while baby nurses. This avoids any nipple confusion from artificial nipples and continues to provide the sucking stimulation that your breasts need in order to produce more milk.

First choice for supplementing the breastfed baby is the mother's own milk which she hand-expresses or pumps. This continues to provide your baby with all the benefits of breast milk and also stimulates your breasts to continue producing lots of milk. When baby is able to suck more effectively, there will be plenty of milk there to reward his efforts.

Do not give your baby formula or any other food without the advice of your doctor.

## THE DOCTOR'S ADVICE

The doctor should be seeing the baby regularly to assess his weight gain and overall condition. If weight gain is very slow, and the doctor suggests a supplement, discuss the possibility of waiting for a week or two while working to improve the breastfeeding routine, or perhaps you can pump or hand-express between feedings and supplement with your own milk.

If the doctor insists on a supplement, you may want to seek a second opinion especially if the baby is healthy and gaining at least four ounces per week; improved weight gain may be possible with better breastfeeding techniques.

If the doctor finds that the baby's weight gain is seriously low and does not want to delay while you attempt to build up your milk supply, it is important to give the supplement as recommended while taking steps to improve the breastfeeding situation. Avoid using bottles and artificial nipples.

In all cases of slow weight gain, keep in touch with your doctor, watch the baby's progress carefully, be aware of the baby's wet and soiled diapers, and continue efforts to improve breastfeeding techniques.

## FURTHER HELP

A mother whose baby is gaining weight slowly needs additional information along with lots of encouragement. Your La Leche League Leader can provide the support you need if your baby is not gaining well. She may be able to offer specific suggestions that can help you, or she may refer you to a more experienced Leader or a lactation consultant for extra help. Your baby may need special guidance in learning to suck effectively and there are experts available who can show you how this can be done.

Babies are meant to grow and thrive and everyone is happy when they do. If your baby is not gaining well, there may be reason for concern, but be assured that your milk is still the perfect food for him. He just needs to get more of it! Once he does, his glowing health and fat cheeks will be a source of pride and satisfaction for you in the months and years ahead.

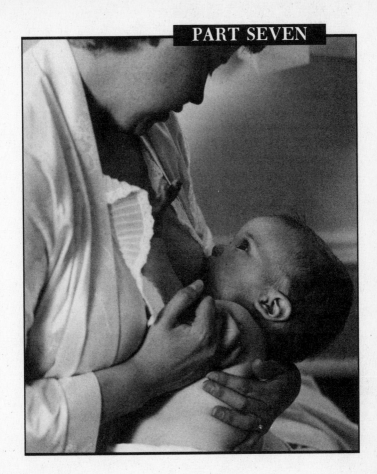

# PART SEVEN

# Why Breast Is Best

# CHAPTER 18

# The Superior Infant Food

Breast milk has long been recognized as the superior food for the infant. It contains all the nutrients your baby needs to grow and develop.

The comment, "My, how that baby has grown," is music to a mother's ears. Your baby's rate of growth during the early months is far greater than at any other period of his life. The human brain is one-third its adult size at birth and reaches the two-thirds mark by age one. Your baby's head grows about four and one-half inches during his first year to allow for the tremendous growth of his brain.

Good muscle development and an increase in length are significant signs of progress, along with baby's weight gain. Getting bigger is serious business for a baby, and milk is the means by which he grows.

Since milk is intended as the sole food for the baby for a critical period of time, the first requirement is that it be a complete food—one that supplies all that is necessary in ideal proportions. No formula can make that claim.

Secondly, if an infant food is to do no harm, it should also agree with his still developing digestive system. Artificial infant feeding again falls short. Human milk, custom-made for the human baby's digestive system, is more readily assimilated than cow's milk. The addition of other foods to the diet of the young baby only interferes with the finely tuned balance between breast and baby. Your milk is truly compatible to your baby's nutritional makeup. Breast milk will sustain, strengthen, protect, fill out, and put a recognizable bloom on your baby's skin. It is all he will need until he is ready for solid foods at about the age of six months, if he is full-term and healthy when born. A highly respected researcher, the late Dr. Paul György, said: "Human milk should be considered superior to cow's milk as the initial physiologic food for the human infant.... Breastfeeding reduces both morbidity and mortality rates, especially the latter.... Human milk is for the human infant, cow's milk is for the calf."

# Designed for the Human Baby

Milk differs from species to species just as the other cells in a mother's body are unlike those of other species. Human milk and cow's milk, like the milk of all mammals, consists mainly of water, protein, fat, lactose (a sugar), and a generous dash of vitamins, minerals, and salts, as well as traces of hormones. While both of these milks weigh in with the same caloric value—an average of twenty calories to an ounce—the proportions of the different components are different. In the preparation of infant formula, cow's milk is diluted with about an equal amount of water, and sugar must be added to recoup the lost calories. Both milks are the expected white color, although mother's milk may sometimes look thin and blue compared to artificial homogenized formulas. What you cannot see is how perfectly your milk adapts to your baby's digestive system and nutritional needs. As J. Ross Snyder wrote in *The Journal of the American Medical Association* as long ago as 1908: "The deft manipulation of cow's milk to duplicate breast milk is not unlike the claim that by clipping its tail and ears one can so modify the calf that it can be substituted for a baby."

When comparing breast milk to cow's milk or any other artificial formula as a food for the baby, the similarities fade and the differences are pronounced. After all, human breast milk is the only food uniquely designed by nature for the human baby.

## PROTEINS ARE THE KEY TO GROWTH

Of all the substances that make up living things, proteins are the most distinctive, the most characteristic of the species. Certain key proteins in your milk are as different from those in cow's milk as you are from a cow. In their most notable function, proteins break down into amino acids, the building blocks of body tissue. Your milk contains all of the essential amino acids in the proper proportions that your baby needs. The large amount of casein protein in cow's milk forms large, tough, rubbery curds, that are difficult for the human baby to digest. This explains why a formula-fed baby remains "full" longer than the breastfed baby. Whey protein, which is more plentiful in mother's milk, is perfectly suited to the human baby's digestive system and easy for him to digest. It is also higher in nutritive value than casein protein.

Specific proteins in milk are capable of destroying harmful bacteria or protecting the young against infections that may enter the bloodstream. Those in cow's milk furnish protection against diseases in the cow. Your milk protects your baby against threats to him from his environment. When proteins are heated, as is true in the preparation of formula, these special properties are easily destroyed.

Cow's milk has more than three times as much protein as human milk. This disparity makes sense when the goals of bovine and human growth are examined. The calf is on his feet within hours of birth, and his prime bodily needs are muscle and bone growth. In less than two months, the calf is expected to double his weight, adding an average of 65 pounds. In contrast to the calf, the human infant does not add such bulk and generally doesn't double his weight until five or six months of age. He won't walk until close to a year.

Of crucial importance to the human infant during the early months is having the right nutrients for the continued development of his brain and the rest of his nervous system. As Jelliffe and Jelliffe state in *Human Milk in the Modern World,* "In the case of the human neonate, rapid brain growth is *the* characteristic of the species."

According to an analysis reported in 1989 by M. F. Goldfarb:

*Human milk matches protein content to protein needs and provides a vast array of support molecules which can never be provided in formula. Human milk contains a complex mixture of several hundred proteins.*

*Human milk is uniquely designed for the human baby.*

## AMINO ACIDS AND TAURINE

One distinctly significant aspect of human milk is the appropriate ratio of amino acids. Amino acids must be present in certain amounts and proportions if they are to work well individually and collectively. When there is an excess of some amino acids and a depletion of others, the baby must work to get rid of the excess. Harmony prevails when the baby is breastfed. All the amino acids in breast milk are used by the baby.

Taurine is one example of an important amino acid found in high concentrations in human milk that is virtually absent in cow's milk. Evidence is accumulating that taurine has an important biologic role in the development of brain tissue as well as the stability of the retina. The human infant is unable to synthesize taurine, so he is completely dependent on his food to supply this amino acid. Because of its potential importance to brain development, it is currently being added to some prepared infant formulas. Taurine has always been available to the infant who receives his mother's milk.

## FATS PROVIDE ENERGY

The fat content in milk readily illustrates the tailoring of milk to the species. It varies in amount in different mammals by almost thirty-fold. For example, the young of sea mammals must quickly acquire a layer of blubber to protect them against icy waters; this need is reflected in the high percentage of fat in the milk of the seal.

For your baby, the fat in your milk means high energy in the form of calories for growth and a reserve store of fuel. The resulting layer of fat tissue blankets a baby against heat loss. Along with his soft skin, it makes him especially nice to cuddle. A breastfed baby has firmer flesh and feels more solid than a formula-fed baby.

On an average, human milk has close to four percent fat, which accounts for over forty percent of the total calories in breast milk. Mothers who are severely undernourished and have no fat reserves of their own to draw on, tend to produce milk that is somewhat lower in fat than that of well-nourished mothers, though the protein and lactose content of their milk is still within the acceptable norm.

Unlike the predetermined fat content in a bottle of formula, the amount of fat in a mother's milk varies from feeding to feeding and from week to week, but over a period of time it meets all the needs of the infant. The fat content of the milk changes even during a feeding, so the practice of having a mother express a sample of milk, in order to examine it for the level of fat, is useless for determining if the milk is "too rich" or "not rich enough."

The kind of body fat an infant develops depends on the kind of fat in his diet. The infant on cow's milk or formula has fat deposits of a different composition than those of the infant on mother's milk.

Certain fat products are optimum in the development of the brain and nervous system, and it is of concern that some fats in formula are biologically inappropriate and less than optimum for the infant.

According to a 1989 article in the *American Journal of Clinical Nutrition*:

*It is virtually impossible to supplement the diet of formula-fed infants to match the long-chain polyunsaturated fatty acid intake of breastfed infants with currently available whole foods.*

If fat cannot be absorbed, it is useless to the baby. Fat that is not absorbed may even act as a bandit, robbing the baby of calcium, since fat and calcium can form an insoluble "soap" which passes right through the baby's digestive system.

The fat of human milk is absorbed and utilized by the baby with remarkable efficiency. Such a harmonious state comes about because a fat-digesting enzyme, lipase, is in mother's milk. This maternal lipase complements and augments the infant's lipase. It is activated in the baby's intestine and aids in the digestion of the infant-tailored fats or lipids in the milk.

In order to increase fat absorption in formula feeding, the butterfat in cow's milk is replaced with linoleic acid, a vegetable oil. The changeover to vegetable oils in formula gives the baby a greater amount of unsaturated fats and a decreased supply of cholesterol. Attention has focused in recent years on reducing the amount of cholesterol in adults' diets—but a baby in the first two years of life needs cholesterol. It is utilized in the covering—or myelination—of nerves which, in turn, permits muscular coordination. Your baby will sit, crawl, and then walk as the process of myelination is completed.

Research on animals has suggested that exposure to cholesterol in human milk may be advantageous in later life, enabling a person to better handle dietary cholesterol as an adult. Giving babies a physiologically sound start in life still seems to be the best insurance against future disease.

## LACTOSE IS ESSENTIAL

Sharing top nutritional billing with protein and fat is the sugar lactose. It is found only in milk and is frequently referred to as milk sugar. Among sugars, lactose has remarkable properties that benefit the newborn. In the familiar role of carbohydrate, it is a source of quick energy, but that is only one of its functions. Lactose may contribute to the optimal development of your baby's brain and central nervous system. In general, the bigger the brain the higher the percentage of lactose in the milk of the species.

Lactose also enhances the absorption of certain minerals, calcium in particular, that are necessary for good bone and tooth development. It also determines to a great extent the environment of your newborn's heretofore sterile gut, or intestinal tract.

Mother's milk contains one and a half times as much lactose as is found in cow's milk—a fact that is readily verified by the sweet taste of breast milk to the adult palate. The sugar content of cow's milk must be increased for use in infant feeding, and in many instances table sugar, sucrose, is used. Sucrose and other substitute sugars are not the equal of lactose. Lactose breaks down and releases its energy at a slow, steady pace, thus avoiding the highs and lows in blood sugar that are characteristic when sucrose is used.

This high level of lactose in mother's milk is related to a correspondingly low level of minerals and salts in the milk, an arrangement that is ideal for the human infant. In cow's milk, this ratio is reversed.

The lactose in your milk is ideal for your baby because of its special effect on the microinhabitants of the intestines. Milk sugar promotes the growth of a select group of bacteria, mainly *Lactobacillus bifidus,* which thwarts the development of the undesirable bacteria that are responsible for severe diarrhea in the young. Aiding the growth of these good bacteria is a substance called the bifidus factor. Mother's milk contains much more bifidus factor than does cow's milk or formula. Evidence of its effectiveness may be recognized by anyone who changes a breastfed baby's diaper. The bowel movements of the totally breastfed baby have a distinct, not unpleasant, buttermilk-like smell. This is proof that the small world within is populated by a preponderance of beneficial bacteria. The formula-fed baby's stools have a strong odor—very unbecoming to the baby.

Until your infant's own immune defenses are more fully developed, your milk not only provides superior nourishment, it is also a major safeguard against infantile diarrhea.

## VITAMINS AND MINERALS IN PERFECT BALANCE

Vitamins and minerals are essential to growth and health. Supplies must be replenished daily, and breast milk is the best and most balanced source for infants. Dropping a supplemental dose of vitamins or minerals into your baby's mouth "just in case" is not a good way to avoid problems. The need for iron is a case in point.

When iron supplements are given, the baby's delicately balanced use of iron may be put in jeopardy. Two specialized proteins in mother's milk, lactoferrin and transferrin, pick up and bind iron from the infant's intestinal tract. In scooping up this iron, they stop harmful bacteria in their tracks. The bacteria, including the potentially dangerous *E. coli,* which may cause diarrhea, are deprived of the iron they need for growth. When iron supplements are given to the breastfed baby, the iron-binding abilities of lactoferrin and transferrin are overwhelmed, and bacteria thrive.

The iron in mother's milk, while low in quantity, is just enough, since the baby can absorb it extremely well. Up to fifty percent of the iron in breast milk is absorbed, as compared to four percent iron absorption when fortified infant formula is given. As he grows older, the iron that your full-term, breastfed baby receives from your milk is meant to be naturally supplemented by the iron reserves he acquired at birth.

The store of iron comes about mainly as a result of the blood flowing to the baby from the umbilical cord following birth. Your baby receives his full quota of blood if the cord is not clamped or cut until it changes from being thick and blue to being a thinner, white cord, about five to ten minutes after the baby is born. With this procedure, your newborn receives several ounces of additional blood, about a thirty percent increase in blood volume. The extra blood carries additional oxygen to your baby's newly operating systems. When the blood cells are broken down, the leftover iron is stored for future use. In this way, the full-term baby's supply of iron will be adequate well into the second half of his first year.

**Calcium, Phosphorus, and Vitamin D.** Calcium and phosphorus are two major minerals found in milk and are generally thought of in tandem. Calcium, in particular, is well-known for its role in the formation of strong bones and teeth. Cow's milk has high levels of calcium and phosphorus—much higher than those in human milk. This is necessary in cow's milk because the calf starts walking from birth. Despite this large supply of calcium in cow's milk, rickets, a disease of young children caused by lack of calcium, was rampant in the United States in the early 1900s as populations shifted to the cities and artificial infant feeding replaced breastfeeding. The sight of older children with abnormally bowed legs was all too common until it was learned that a high concentration of calcium in the blood means nothing if there isn't sufficient vitamin D to activate it. Better late than never, the essential vitamin D was added to the cow's milk sold for human consumption.

Some experts have expressed concern about the low levels of vitamin D found in human milk. Over the years, however, rickets has rarely been found in fully breastfed infants. This is true even in northern climates where there is less exposure to sunlight, which activates the formation of vitamin D.

A 1989 study in the *Journal of Pediatrics* reported that "unsupplemented human milk-fed infants had no evidence of vitamin D deficiency during the first six months." Of course, you will want to take your baby outdoors, weather permitting, so that he benefits from the natural sunlight. A few minutes a day of sun on your baby's cheeks is all that is needed.

The story of calcium also revolves around its neighbors, phosphorus and fat. If the concentrations of calcium and phosphorus are not in the right proportions, the usefulness of these minerals to the infant is impaired. Again scientists had to tinker with the amounts of these two minerals in cow's milk to bring them in line with mother's milk. As mentioned before, unused fat reacts with calcium in the baby's system. In the breastfed infant, fat is well absorbed, and calcium and phosphorus are in balance. The comparatively low levels of calcium in your milk notwithstanding, the retention of this mineral in your breastfed infant is still generally higher than that found in infants on formula, and the supply is adequate for your baby's needs.

**Zinc.** Your breast milk contains less zinc than cow's milk, but what is present is better absorbed by your baby. In fact, breast milk is a specific treatment for a rare, inherited metabolic disease called acrodermatitis enteropathica (AE). Infants with this condition suffer a zinc deficiency brought about by a reduced ability to absorb zinc. Whereas babies prone to AE develop the disease on cow's milk, which has more zinc, babies with AE who are switched from cow's milk to breast milk, with less zinc, are cured. This special property of zinc in breast milk was only discovered in 1978. It is now understandable why AE is a disease that increased in incidence as breastfeeding declined.

Other minerals, such as copper and manganese, have been found to have a significantly better biological availability in human milk than in cow's milk formula.

**Vitamin B$_6$ and B$_{12}$.** A pioneer in breastfeeding research, the late Dr. Paul György is renowned as the discoverer of riboflavin and vitamin B$_6$. Prior to his work, no one knew that babies needed vitamin B$_6$. This lack of information was reflected in the preparation of infant formula at the time. Some infants on a well-known formula inexplicably developed convulsions. The problem cleared with the addition of vitamin B$_6$, a substance that was already an integral component of mother's milk.

Scientists now also know that a certain protein in mother's milk has the capacity to bind vitamin $B_{12}$. The protein is, in a sense, a strong security agent, keeping the vitamin $B_{12}$ under lock and key for the baby's use and making it unavailable to any threatening pathogens. This binding action, as with that of lactoferrin, deprives the problem bacteria in the baby's gut of the resources to grow. Thus a potential problem is averted.

**Vitamin C.** The milk of an adequately nourished mother contains all the vitamin C her baby needs. Scurvy, a disease caused by lack of vitamin C, is virtually never seen in the breastfed infant.

Keep in mind that this important vitamin is not stored in the body and therefore must be replenished each day, more or less, by the breastfeeding mother. This is seldom a problem since a wide variety of fruits and vegetables contain vitamin C. Giving vitamin C supplements directly to the baby is inadvisable. If there is a questions of vitamin C adequacy, a supplemental dose can be taken by the mother. She not only benefits herself, but dispenses the vitamin in the proper form and amount to her baby through her milk.

**Fluoride.** Fluoride is currently receiving a great deal of attention, linked as it is to sound teeth and decreased dental caries. Mother's milk contains some fluoride, and while the amount is small, it seems to be perfectly suited to the baby's need. Even so, there's often pressure on parents to give their babies fluoride drops. Some mothers have found that fluoride supplements cause their babies to be fussy.

# Breast Milk—An Arsenal against Illness

Mothers who breastfeed their babies have often noticed that when the rest of the family comes down with a cold or flu, the baby remains free of it or has only a mild case. But until recently, a mother's conviction that breastfeeding protects her baby in a special way could be substantiated only by comparative studies of breastfed and bottle-fed babies. The studies, which go back to the turn of the century, show that breastfeeding definitely prolongs the period of natural immunity to many viral diseases, including respiratory infections. They also show that breastfeeding protects against

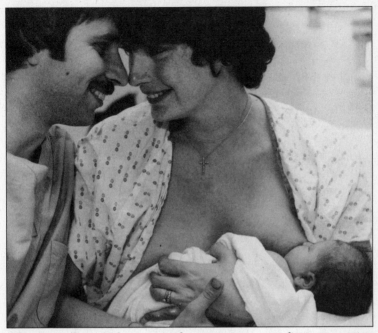

*Baby's first feedings of colostrum provide an important source of protection against disease.*

a number of bacterial diseases. And it has long been known that breastfed babies have fewer problems with diarrhea than artificially fed infants.

With the advent of the 1970s, scientists developed more sophisticated techniques for examining the immunologic factors in milk, and new information came to light. Thus researchers now know some of the scientific reasons for what the early studies indicated and what many breastfeeding mothers believed all along. The story that is unfolding is more amazing than had ever been imagined. Dr. John W. Gerrard, a Canadian researcher, wrote in *Pediatrics* in 1974, "We presumed that the function of breast milk was little more than the provision of nourishment. We now know that breast milk also provides effective protection, more effective than antibiotics, against certain common enteric pathogens, and that it can also be expected to provide relative freedom in infancy from allergic disease, a growing problem of modern feeding habits."

Dr. Herbert Ratner coined a phrase that aptly describes breast milk's unique qualities—"nature's vaccine for the newborn." This unique protection starts with your baby's first feeding of your colostrum.

## "NATURE'S VACCINE"—STARTING WITH COLOSTRUM

The first milk from your breast, which is called colostrum, is low in fat and carbohydrates, and high in protein. It is exceptionally easy to digest and is a superb "pick-me-up" for the newborn. In the days that follow, the thick, creamy-looking colostrum begins to change into thinner, mature milk.

During the 1970s, researchers found that colostrum, which had previously been virtually ignored, contains living cells that defend the newborn against a number of potentially harmful agents. It is now recognized that mother's breast takes over in protecting the baby where the placenta leaves off.

Your infant arrives in the world with a supply of antibodies—protective proteins that come to him from your blood via the placenta. The antibodies, which are also known as immunoglobulins, have been manufactured by your immune system in response to infections that you have been exposed to. These include some of the common contagious diseases of childhood. While the immunity you have to these diseases is lifelong, the immunity which is passed on to your unborn baby give him only temporary protection until his own immune system begins to develop.

In addition, protective antibodies to germs that you have come into contact with in the course of daily living in your home environment also cross over to your baby while he is in the womb. These immunoglobulins permit your newborn baby to enjoy the same immunity as you have when he enters the familiar environment of home. Until recently, scientists believed that the full extent of a mother's gift of antibodies to her baby came by way of the placenta. They were misled by information derived from studies on cows, which are highly researched because of their importance as food.

Research had shown that the calf, unlike the baby, receives no antibodies before birth. A calf's full, and only, allotment of protective cells comes in the first feed from the mother cow within hours after birth. As every dairyman knows, the calf that is deprived of colostrum is soon a dead calf. Research also revealed that the predominant antibody in this lifesaving colostrum is the immunoglobulin G (IgG). When the scientists turned their attention to the human baby, it was found that IgG is the primary antibody present in his system when he is born.

The conclusions drawn from these early studies, while not unreasonable, were not exactly correct either. It was assumed that the transfer of antibodies from mother to baby occurred before birth. Because the important IgG is already present when the baby is born, it was thought that human colostrum was of little importance in the fight against infection.

With advanced technology, scientists found that colostrum abounds in immunities. Scientists found them in concentrated forms and in new modes that even surpass those acquired by the baby through the placenta.

Scientists made the surprising discovery that colostrum has an abundance of an antibody that is new to the baby, secretory immunoglobulin A (IgA). They found that colostrum (and the later milk as well) is alive with protective white cells—leukocytes. These white cells, which are also found in blood, are the body's chief defense against infections. They have the ability to destroy or thwart the bacteria and viruses that can cause serious disease.

The presence of live white cells in milk means that milk is a living tissue, very much like blood. Even before scientists knew about these live white cells, breast milk was referred to by some doctors as "white blood," precisely because it has life-giving properties associated with blood.

A stir of excitement occurred among scientists with the discovery that there are about as many leukocytes in breast milk as in blood. White cells come in a variety of forms, each with unique properties. Some of those in breast milk produce the important secretory IgA.

## THE PROTECTIVE SHIELD— HOW IT WORKS

Secretory IgA acts as a first line of defense in the body. Whereas IgG, the main antibody coming to the baby through the placenta, is a blood-circulating or humoral antibody, IgA exerts its protective effect directly at those points where germs are most likely to arrive on the scene, at the portals of entry to the body, such as the throat, lungs, and intestines. These areas are covered by mucous membranes, which act as barriers against pathogens, and it is here that IgA is secreted in the battle against infection. The leukocytes migrate to the baby's intestinal tract, for instance, and continue to manufacture IgA. This antibody's somewhat different construction from its relative in the blood allows it to resist the processes of digestion. The immunoglobulins stand as sentries along the frontier that is the lining of the gastrointestinal tract. They prevent penetration of germs or foreign proteins that are capable of causing allergies.

A leading specialist in the protective roster is the macrophage, or "big mac." A type of leukocyte, the "macs" are capable of engulfing troublesome organisms. They swallow the germs, and with the help of a protein enzyme, lysozyme, destroy them. (Lysozyme, it was found, is also in good supply in mother's milk.) Once the offender is destroyed, the macrophages move on to the next challenge.

The concentration of these antibodies in your colostrum is at its highest in the first hours after the birth of your baby, which provides yet another reason for putting baby to your breast as soon as possible. And no other fluid—glucose, water, tea, formula—comes close to being as good for your baby as colostrum.

As the weeks of breastfeeding go by, and colostrum gives way to mature milk, the concentration of antibodies in your milk decreases. While fewer of these immunities are found in each ounce, the amount of milk your baby takes is increasing. In this way, he continues to receive ongoing protection against many organisms, both viral and bacterial.

Researchers have found that the presence of IgA in breast milk stimulates the infant's own immunologic development, so that the baby is protected not only by the IgA in the milk but by the immunoglobulins produced in his own gastrointestinal tract. The early stimulation of the immune system may have far-reaching effects in protecting infants from disease in later life.

Studies continue to confirm the importance of the IgA in breast milk and its effect on the infant's gastrointestinal tract. One study reported in the *American Journal of Public Health* in 1985 found that "the risk of acute gastrointestinal illness in infants receiving formula was six times greater than in infants receiving breast milk and 2.5 times greater than in infants receiving cow's milk."

Another study reported in a Scandinavian medical journal in 1988 showed that IgA antibodies protect babies against toxin-induced infantile diarrhea. In 1989, the *British Medical Journal* reported that breastfeeding protects infants from respiratory tract illnesses even when other risk factors are present. And in 1986, the *Journal of Pediatrics* reported that breastfeeding protected infants from *Haemophilus influenzae* type b (Hib) disease for up to six months. This is the bacteria that is associated with meningitis, a very serious illness in young children.

## SPECIALIZED PROGRAMMING
## AGAINST ILLNESS

In Hong Kong researchers discovered that certain leukocytes in mother's milk react to the presence of a virus by producing interferon, a protein that warns the surrounding cells of impending danger. The interferon manufactured by breast milk leukocytes closely resembles that produced by blood leukocytes and is added protection for the infant against a variety of viral diseases.

Another fascinating finding was the discovery that the breast can deliver a particular antibody in response to a new threat to the baby even when the needed immunoglobulin was not previously present in the mother's blood. A chain of events begins when the fully breastfed baby is beset with a new germ. As he continues to nurse, perhaps even more often than usual because he is not feeling well, the offending organism is passed from baby to mother. In ways not yet fully understood, the breast produces a matching immunoglobulin on site, locally, and sends the protective element along to the baby in the milk. This is a system of "specialized programming," with the nursing mother making antibodies on demand to germs that challenge her baby. The baby places the order, and mother programs the cells and delivers the appropriate antibody.

The discovery of breastfeeding's direct dynamic role in preventing illness helps to explain how babies, as long as they are breastfed, can survive in a highly infected environment. It is an advantage that, unfortunately, is most apparent in its absence, a fact that came home to the world in modern times following the introduction of bottle-feeding in underdeveloped countries.

# Breastfed Babies Are
# Proven Healthier

Breastfeeding is important to infant health. Even in parts of the world where overall infant mortality is low, breastfed infants are likely to be sick less often and less severely than their bottle-fed counterparts. In developing countries, breastfeeding can be critical to infant survival.

A World Health Organization study in rural Chile in 1970 showed an alarmingly high number of deaths among infants. On examining the data, researchers found a strong correlation between the method of feeding a baby and the baby's well-being. Those infants who received formula or cow's milk before the age of three months were at a three times greater risk of dying than babies on breast milk alone. Young babies who were partially formula-fed fared little better than those who were completely on artificial feedings. Mothers in higher income groups were more apt to give bottles and so, unknowingly, increase the amount of risk to their babies. Breast milk, it was concluded, provides a remarkable safeguard against infection for the young child.

## MORE RECENT STUDIES

More recent studies continue to confirm the beneficial effects of breastfeeding for babies living in poverty. In a 1982 study of infants in the Philippines, deaths from infection and diarrhea were many times higher in babies who were fully bottle-fed than in those who were even partially breastfed. Changes in hospital policies that produced an increase in breastfeeding from 40 percent to 87 percent were accompanied by a 95 percent decline in deaths from serious infection. A study of infant deaths in metropolitan areas of Brazil found that the risk of death from diarrhea was 14.2 times higher in infants who were weaned from the breast than in fully breastfed babies; the risk of death from respiratory infection was 3.6 times greater. Infants who were partially breastfed were at greater risk than those who were fully breastfed, but were better off than those who were fully bottle-fed. In Bangladesh, breastfeeding was associated with a 70 percent reduction in the risk of contracting severe cholera; breastfed children up to 30 months of age were less likely to become severely ill, despite cholera epidemics.

These are only a few examples of the dramatic effect breastfeeding has on infant health in parts of the world where poor sanitation, unsafe water supplies, poverty, and lack of medical care contribute to enormous public health problems. Mother's milk is the first line of defense for the community's smallest, most vulnerable members. Data from all over the world show that breastfeeding rates are declining as the infant-feeding patterns common in the United States, where formula-feeding is thought to be "safe," are exported to the developing world, with often-tragic results. But even in affluent areas of the United States, Canada, and Western Europe, breastfeeding improves infant health. This was true sixty years ago, and it is true today.

*A breastfed baby's good health is a source of joy to parents.*

## STATISTICS TELL THE STORY

The well-known Grulee study followed over 20,000 babies in Chicago in the 1920s and 30s. Mothers regularly brought their babies to the Chicago Infant Welfare Society for checkups, and the youngsters in the study were followed for at least nine months. Grulee and his associates divided the babies into three groups based on how they were fed: breastfed, almost half of the babies, 9,747; those who were partially breastfed, 8,605 babies; and totally artificially fed, 1,707 babies. A record was kept of deaths from all causes and illnesses due to infections.

In all of the babies, respiratory infections were by far the most common cause of illness. A noticeable difference in the three groups was found in the ages at which the babies came down with respiratory illness. Once past five months, only a small number of breastfed babies developed respiratory infections, while such illness among the artificially fed group remained high. An even more telling difference among the three groups was the number of deaths from respiratory infections—four of the more than 9,700 breastfed babies, 44 of the 8,600 partially breastfed babies, and 82 of the 1,700 babies of the artificially fed group died of respiratory illness. Deaths from respiratory infections in bottle-fed infants were 120 times greater than among breastfed babies.

The second biggest problem for these babies was gastrointestinal infections such as diarrheal diseases. The breastfeeding babies had far fewer intestinal infections compared with both partially breastfed and artificially fed babies, fewer even than respiratory problems. When figures were compiled on the total number of deaths from infections of all kinds, it was found that in all, 129 of the artificially fed babies and 75 of the partially breastfed group died of infections. If the rate of deaths among the totally artificially fed infants were applied to the completely breastfed group in the study, it could be expected that there would be over 730 deaths in this large number of infants. But the records show that only 13 of the over 9,700 breastfed babies died from infection. Even in the light of today's modern medical advances, the low mortality rate in breastfed infants as recorded by Grulee from the Infant Welfare Society reports stands out as an enviable record.

An updated comparison of illness among breastfed and bottle-fed infants was made in 1977 in the United States. The babies in the study were from middle-class families who enjoyed a high level of medical care, education, and housing. Dr. Allan S. Cunningham found that episodes of significant illness in the 164 breastfed babies were uncommon, and when there was an illness, it occurred at a later age than in the artificially fed babies.

## FEWER DOCTOR VISITS

A recent study cited in the *American Family Physician* reviewed illness in babies as measured by visits to the doctor. Records were compared on 66 bottle-fed and 40 breastfed babies. Only 25 percent of the breastfed babies had to be seen by the doctor even once in their first six months because of illness. For the bottle-fed babies, this figure was 97 percent. By the age of a year, the breastfed babies who did become ill required from one to five visits to the doctor, while the bottle-fed babies who were sick made up to sixteen visits to the doctor. A study from 1980 reports that formula-fed infants were hospitalized three times more frequently during the first three months of life than were breastfed babies.

Over the years, research in industrialized nations has found that many specific kinds of infectious diseases are less likely to occur in breastfed babies; these include respiratory infections, diarrhea and gastroenteritis, ear infections, pneumonia, and meningitis.

Studies also show that breastfeeding has a protective effect against chronic health problems, such as allergy. Breastfeeding has been associated with lower rates of juvenile diabetes, celiac disease, childhood cancer, and severe liver disease.

The resistance to disease that human milk affords a baby cannot be duplicated in any other way. Your milk is indispensable to your baby. As Dr. James Baggott, a biochemist who is well-versed in the study of human milk, has observed, "The preventive powers of breast milk should be used to their maximum." Even when babies have every other possible advantage, breastfeeding gives them an extra boost on the way to good health. Human milk is the very best infant food available. And when mothers in the trend-setting developed world choose to give their babies human milk, rather than a costly industrial product like infant formula, they send an important message to women everywhere: your own milk is important to your baby. Breastfeeding is best for babies, no matter where they live.

# How The Breast Gives Milk

A mother's breast is a superior food source. The way in which it supplies milk for the baby is as remarkable as the milk itself. In a bottle-feeding culture, a person may unconsciously think of the breast in terms of a bottle and transfer some characteristics of the bottle to the breast. Mothers are told to wait until the breast feels full before offering it to the baby, just as a bottle is filled before giving it to the baby. Mothers may sometimes be advised that "the breast must fill before the milk will flow."

Not so. Your breast may feel empty, but as your baby nurses, milk will be there. While a nursing bottle is a container and nothing more, a nursing mother's breast is the manufacturing site. It is never totally empty and is always capable of producing more milk.

Your baby's eager sucking is the key to milk production. While the making of milk is usually associated with the birth of a baby, there have been instances throughout history of women bringing in a milk supply for a baby other than their own simply by encouraging the baby to suck frequently at the breast. A member of the League tells of having been breastfed by her grandmother following the death of her own mother. Her grandmother had nursed all of her children and felt that this was the least she could do for her motherless granddaughter.

A picture of the inner structure of the breast could remind one of branches of a tree. The top branches are deep in the breast, coming together at the trunk, leading to the nipple. Small buds represent the milk-producing cells, known as the alveoli, which select the nutrients and protective agents needed to make the milk. Droplets of milk pass through the small ducts and are stored in reservoirs just behind the nipple.

There is a continuous build-up of milk that collects in these reservoirs between feedings. Over a period of time, this supply can make the breast feel quite full, but it is only a fraction of the milk the baby receives. The milk that collects between feedings, known as the "foremilk," usually accounts for about one-third of a baby's intake at a feeding. The remainder and greater portion of milk comes directly "off the production line" as your baby nurses. This process begins as his strong sucking action makes contact with the nerves in your nipple. Impulses from these nerves travel to the pituitary, the master gland in the brain, by way of the hypothalamus, which is near the pleasure center of the brain. Nature intends for mothers to enjoy breastfeeding their babies.

Two powerful hormones, prolactin and oxytocin, are then released in sequence. Milk is secreted under the influence of prolactin, while oxytocin moves it from the ducts. With your baby's vigorous sucking, band-like cells around the alveoli constrict and squeeze out larger, more concentrated fatty globules and proteins than are found in the foremilk. Baby is then getting the "hindmilk." It is a tasty reward for his continued nursing and for your patience in keeping him at the breast. It's also the milk that puts weight on your baby, which is the reason babies need to suck well in order to gain well. Since babies need to nurse long enough to receive the hindmilk, it is not a good idea to set a time limit on how many minutes a baby should nurse.

The length of a breastfeeding session should be determined by the baby's interest and response. He will usually suck eagerly, swallowing often, for the first ten minutes or so. Then the flow of milk may decrease and he begins to doze or lose interest. That's the time to switch him over to the other breast. As long as he is sucking correctly, you can let him nurse as long as he wants on the second side.

## BREASTFEEDING HORMONES

Niles Newton, PhD, professor of behavioral sciences at Northwestern University, has investigated oxytocin and prolactin, the hormones related to lactation. She calls oxytocin "the hormone of love" and says the presence of oxytocin is one reason a breastfeeding mother is physically different from a mother who does not nurse her baby. Oxytocin triggers nurturing behavior, which is "an essential ingredient in the success of reproduction," according to Dr. Newton.

Current research indicates that the secretion of oxytocin is a conditioned response. A mother's body can produce oxytocin in response to familiar sights, sounds, and activities, not just from the direct stimulation of breastfeeding. In 30% of the mothers studied, oxytocin levels increased when their babies became restless and in 20% an increase was found as they were preparing to nurse. Prolactin levels were found to increase only when the baby actually sucked at the breast.

## THE MILK-EJECTION REFLEX

Oxytocin is responsible for triggering the let-down or milk-ejection reflex. Manufactured and released by the pituitary gland, oxytocin causes the milk to be released into the milk ducts where it becomes available to the baby. When this occurs, a mother may feel a tingling, cramping, or pins-and-needles sensation in her breasts. A few women may find this feeling intense enough to make them catch their breath. It is an obvious sign that the milk is flowing into the ducts, but it is not something to wait for anxiously and worry over. A let-down occurs several times during a feeding.

Whether you feel the milk ejection or let-down reflex is not important. One way to recognize that it is occurring is to watch and listen for changes in the rhythm of your baby's sucking and swallowing.

For some babies, the first rush of milk may come too quickly and catch them unaware, which results in some choking and sputtering. If this happens, take baby off the breast to let him catch his breath and have a spare diaper or other cloth handy to absorb the excess milk. This is usually a temporary problem as baby gradually learns to keep up with the milk. But if it happens often, it may help to hand-express some milk before baby nurses until the initial spray subsides. It can also help to hold baby in a more upright position while he is nursing.

If the milk-ejection reflex is a little slow in the early days of breastfeeding, it may be because you are somewhat nervous and your body is still adjusting to this new experience. It won't be long before mother, milk, and baby are in tune with each other. You may then find that your milk lets down at the first sound of a baby crying—your own baby or any other baby!

Fright, or sudden shock, may temporarily inhibit the let-down of your milk, especially in the early days of nursing. This may give a mother the impression that she has "lost" her milk. Milk is still there, and more will come, once mother and baby relax. Scientists believe that this interesting phenomenon in milk letting down developed in the early periods of the human race. When a wild creature or some danger threatened a mother and her baby it was time for mother and baby to flee, not sit and nurse.

There are no longer wild animals at our doors, so even when you feel anxious there's no reason to flee. Just snuggle down with your baby and imagine your milk pouring out to him in all of the profusion of a glorious Milky Way. A sixteenth century artist, Tintoretto, portrayed what has been identified as the milk let-down in a painting, appropriately titled, "The Origin of the Milky Way." It shows Hercules nursing at Juno's breast as her milk ejects in a spray of stars.

## Mother's Milk Cannot Be Duplicated

Mother's milk is a unique and unmatched commodity. In their definitive book on breast milk, *Human Milk in the Modern World,* Jelliffe and Jelliffe state, "There is no possibility of cow's milk being humanized biologically. The two products are much too complex and dissimilar."

There are components of breast milk that still have not been identified. A researcher in the field, Dr. W. Allan Walker of Massachusetts General Hospital, has stated: "What we now know about human milk is just the tip of the iceberg. . . . We'll discover a lot more factors in milk that enhance its protective and nutritive value."

Your milk is not an inert combination of ingredients that can be identified, measured, and fairly well-duplicated. Even if it were possible to incorporate all the unique proteins of human milk into a formula, many would subsequently be inactivated in the processing needed to make formula safe. The president of a well-known formula manufacturing company summed up the contribution of industry to infant nutrition by saying, "We're second best to the breast." And we would add, a distant second.

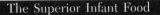

*This baby seems to know his mother is giving him nothing but the best.*

In a 1989 article titled "Science and Politics of Breastfeeding," T. B. Mepham states:

*Not only are attempts to mimic breast milk by modifying cow's milk increasingly revealed as inadequate, but the non-nutritive advantages of breastfeeding, such as in disease prevention and through its contraceptive properties, are assuming greater human and economic significance.*

Mother's milk cannot be duplicated because, in reality, no two mothers produce identical milk. Even the milk of an individual mother varies from day to day and during different times of the day—just as other fluids and systems in our bodies fluctuate. The colostrum your baby receives on the first day of his life is quite different from the colostrum on day two or three. Even the taste of the milk changes with the diet of the mother. You could say that your milk is programming your baby's taste buds for coming fare on the dinner table. During one feeding, your milk varies from skim to creamy, permitting your breastfed baby to enjoy a change of tastes that could be compared to a multi-course meal.

Breast milk is recognized as the superior food for the infant, but there seems to be no end to the promotions aimed at a mother to persuade her that her breastfed baby needs something in addition to her milk. The "something," it seems, is always for a price. Glossy advertisements will congratulate you on nursing your baby and then smoothly slip in a statement to the effect that some vitamin or other popular and important-sounding item is "borderline" in mother's milk. The ready solution, we are to believe, is to give the baby the commercial product. But what is "borderline" is the scientific background for such ads.

In a paper presented at La Leche League International's Breastfeeding Seminar for Physicians in California in 1976, Dr. W. G. Whittlestone of New Zealand, international authority on lactation, stated, "Milk is, in effect, a source of biological information which carries on those processes started in the placenta and completed with weaning and the total independence of the growing young."

We can say with confidence that the baby ingesting his natural food, his mother's milk, is on the right track, nutritionally speaking. There is a certain predictability that no longer holds true when the script has been changed. The newborn receiving a foreign food is on an uncharted course.

To quote Dr. Herbert Ratner: "The script of nature gives rise to the prescription, and what wise nature inscribes is the perfect prescription. Art, however, is only imitative of nature, and like any imitation, only approximates but never matches nature's product. That is why the best of formulas, artificial as they are, will always fall short of nature's formulation—human milk, perfected as it was through time."

# CHAPTER 19

# *Advantages of* Breastfeeding

Throughout this book we've explained the advantages and benefits of breastfeeding for you and your baby. In this chapter we explain just a few of these points in greater detail.

## Avoiding Allergies

Protection against allergy is one of the many advantages a baby receives from his mother's milk. Your baby will not be allergic to your milk; you can count on this with certainty. It is a law of nature that infants never become sensitized to their natural food.

Proteins make the critical difference. The protein in your milk is totally compatible with your baby. The proteins in cow's milk and in formulas based on cow's milk are potential troublemakers for the human infant. Some babies, when exposed to these foreign proteins, become sensitized. When again fed cow's milk or cow's milk formula, they react with a variety of symptoms, depending on the part of the body that is sensitized. An allergic reaction can mimic a respiratory or intestinal infection by producing the same kinds of severe symptoms.

Not only will a baby never be allergic to his mother's milk, but breastfeeding can be a factor in protecting the baby from future allergies. In October 1974, John W. Gerrard, MD, a pediatric allergist from Canada who is a member of La Leche League's Professional Advisory Board, wrote this in *Pediatric Annals:*

---

*T*he evidence that breastfeeding prevents allergic disease is based on five factors. First, allergists such as Glaser, who practiced when breastfeeding was common, noted a greater prevalence of allergies in infants brought up on formula than in those brought up on the breast. Second, breastfed babies, after developing allergies when given supplemental foods, recover from their allergies when these foods are avoided. Third, babies on the breast alone may develop allergies that subside as soon as the food to which the baby is sensitive is eliminated from the mother's diet. Fourth, some babies—approximately 20 percent in our experience—grow out of their cow's milk allergy by the age of twelve months. (Such babies, if brought up on breast milk and not given cow's milk until the age of twelve months, would not be expected to develop cow's milk allergy.) Finally, it has been our experience....that babies with gastroenteritis due to cow's milk allergy often develop normal gastrointestinal function when given breast milk alone.

---

Dr. E. Robbins Kimball, a pediatrician and also a member of La Leche League's Professional Advisory Board, found in a study of 1378 children that the incidence of allergies is closely related to the length of time a baby is breastfed. Babies who were bottle fed from birth, or breastfed four days or less, developed the highest percentage of allergies. Nursing a baby for six months or longer provided the greatest protection from allergies. Of the 528 babies in the study who were breastfed, or as Dr. Kimball says, "had only mother" for six months, none developed an allergy when there was no family history of allergies.

In a 1988 study reported in *Annals of Allergy*, allergies were less likely to occur among breastfed infants. In fact, the research showed that breastfeeding, even for a short period, was clearly associated with a lower incidence of wheeze, prolonged colds, diarrhea, and vomiting.

For some parents, preventing allergies is a major reason they choose to breastfeed their babies. One mother, Brenda Bane, writes:

*We have three lovely children; Stephen is seven, Brian is six, and Sara is now thirteen months. Both of my sons were bottle-fed. I would like to share the advantages I have experienced firsthand of the breastfed first year as compared to the bottle-fed first year.*

*During their first year, both boys went to the doctor at least once a month, mostly with bronchitis and tonsillitis. Sara has been there only twice in her life. Both boys were allergic to formula, while Sara thrived on my milk. Both boys are still allergic; Stephen's allergies are quite severe. To date, Sara has no known allergies.*

*As babies, the boys had colic very badly; Sara had none. The boys averaged only five hours of sleep per night at age one, while Sara enjoys about eleven hours. She is such a happy baby; the boys cried all the time, making me nervous and naturally tired and grumpy quite often.*

*Last but not least, let us not forget the cost of hypoallergenic formula, cereal, baby food, bottles, sterilizers, and vitamins as compared to only mother's milk for most of the first year and then finger foods from the table. As for me, I eat better, am much healthier, and have really enjoyed relaxing along with my daughter.*

## A DESPERATE PLEA

For some infants, breastfeeding serves as both a preventive measure and a cure for allergic disease. One of the most dramatic cases of an extremely ill baby getting well on breast milk came early in La Leche League's history. Lorraine and Emil Bormet's two-and-one-half-month-old David, bottle-fed since birth, had been suffering from almost continuous diarrhea, breathing difficulties, and eczema. Different formulas were tried, including soybean and meat-based varieties, with no improvement in David's condition. Almost as a last resort, the doctor suggested that breast milk was probably the only thing that David could tolerate.

Lorraine located a nursing mother several miles from their Illinois farm home, and the mother agreed to help. Following David's first feeding of breast milk late one evening, his astonished mother reported that, "he fell asleep and slept through the night for the first time in his life."

Convinced of the value of breast milk, the Bormets dared to hope that Lorraine could bring in her own milk, even though it had been almost three months since the baby's birth. She contacted La Leche League for advice. Milk production, we could assure her, is stimulated by the baby's sucking, and so she began the painstaking work of encouraging David to take the breast. Lorraine stayed in close touch with Marian Tompson, one of La Leche League's founders, and David continued to receive breast milk from generous donor mothers. Eight days after she began her efforts to breastfeed, drops of milk appeared. Some weeks later, Lorraine Bormet was completely nursing her baby, who by then was symptom-free, healthy, and content.

In the years since the Bormet story unfolded, other mothers with similarly allergic babies have contacted the League, and many have found that, despite a late start, they could provide their own milk for their babies.

## WORTH A TRY

Other enthusiastic accounts come from parents who had problems with cow's milk allergies with an older child and decided to go with mother's milk when expecting a new baby. They comprise a large group and are probably among the strongest advocates of breastfeeding. Kathy Driskell of Illinois tells the story of Michael, the Driskell's second child:

*We had experienced a series of problems with our first child, Jennifer, who was bottle-fed. She vomited after almost every feeding until she was nearly six months old. This was followed by chronic diarrhea until she was past two. Her pediatrician changed the formula numerous times, but to no avail. He finally concluded that it was an inherited allergy.*

*Needless to say, I was eager to avoid this nightmare with Michael. Some of my friends had tried to encourage*

*Good health continues into the toddler years when baby starts out at mother's breast.*

me to breastfeed, but frankly, it scared me to death. Coming from a large, close-knit, strictly bottle-feeding family, I had visions of my relatives shaking their heads in pity at my poor starving baby. Finally, after much debate, my husband, Ed, and I decided the best thing for Michael would be to give breastfeeding a try for a week or two. Now, fourteen months later, I have to look back and laugh, for Michael turned out to be the chubbiest, healthiest child I could have imagined. Needless to say digestive problems were nonexistent (he rarely even spit up). Nursing my son has been an experience I wouldn't have missed for anything.

## BABY CAN STILL BE ALLERGIC

A baby may react to foods other than cow's milk, of course—early solids, for instance, or even vitamin or fluoride drops—so you'll do your baby a favor if you're careful to limit what goes into his tummy to what is compatible to his young system. Your milk alone is your best bet for about six months. While your baby remains on breast milk, his intestinal tract is protected and is given time to mature. Potentially allergenic foods, which he may eat later on, such as egg white, citrus fruits, corn, and wheat, will be less likely to cause problems. If your baby shows signs of a reaction to a new food or if there is a history of allergy in your family, you may want to postpone giving solids longer. Be sure to read Chapter 13 on starting solids before introducing your baby to other foods.

Jani Howd of South Dakota did not think allergies would be a problem in her family, but she later found out her daughter was highly allergic:

*Avoiding allergies was not one of my primary reasons in deciding to breastfeed our first child. Now, two years later, I definitely know that it is an advantage that should not be taken lightly.*

*During her first year, Angie was a perfect example of a contented, healthy breastfed baby. Her only problem seemed to be a supersensitive skin. When I began introducing table food to her at about five and a half months, she ate willingly with a good appetite. At twelve months any attempt to feed Angie cow's milk or eggs resulted in a reaction. By eighteen months, eggs were no longer a problem, and at twenty-one months she seemed to tolerate milk.*

*Shortly after this, Angie developed eczema. We immediately took cow's milk away, but the eczema did not disappear completely until I put Angie on a strict elimination diet to determine exactly which foods she was allergic to. Then the fading eczema wasn't the only change noticeable in Angie. Starting about the age of eighteen months, temper tantrums and sleepless nights had become a matter of course, along with a loss of appetite. John and I attributed it to her growing independence and tried to handle her with love and patience.*

*Now that she is eating foods that agree with her, it is a rare sight for her to have a temper tantrum. She is our happy, contented, breastfed toddler. Her appetite has returned and the change in her disposition is almost unbelievable. Breastfeeding does not entirely prevent allergies, especially with a very allergic individual like Angie, but it was reassuring to hear her dermatologist tell me that had she not been breastfed, her allergies would be more severe, in greater number, and that she would have had food-related skin problems sooner, and have kept them longer.*

If there is a history of allergies in your family it is generally a good idea to avoid eating an excessive amount of any food during pregnancy. There is evidence that a baby can become sensitized before birth to a food that his mother eats.

## CAN BABY REACT TO SOMETHING MOTHER EATS?

In some instances, a food that a breastfeeding mother eats will cause a reaction in her baby. The protein from cow's milk, eggs, or some other food in the mother's diet may penetrate her gastrointestinal tract. These "stray" proteins in her blood can find their way into her milk. If her baby reacts to these "strays," it's an indication of a pronounced sensitivity to that food, and very likely the baby has a strong tendency toward developing allergies. In such a case, the answer is to exclude from the mother's diet the food containing the specific protein. Mother's milk itself is fine; the stray protein riding along is all that needs to be eliminated. Switching the baby to an artificial infant food would overwhelm him with a large dose of a potential allergen and more than likely make the problem worse.

When looking for reasons why a baby is unusually fussy, has a rash or diarrhea, or develops other allergic-like symptoms, it's important to remember that the cause could be something quite simple, so consider the most common possibilities first. Is the baby receiving any supplemental bottles of formula or juice? Vitamin or fluoride drops? He may be crying because he's coming down with an illness. A baby who is nursing very frequently may be going through a growth spurt. Consider your own situation. If you're continually tired or rushed, make life easier for yourself and your baby by slowing down. Are you taking any medication? This could be the problem. Something that the baby comes in contact with could be causing a rash. A few common possibilities include detergents, soaps, fabric softeners, dyes (colored sheets), wool, feathers, lotions, spray deodorants, and hair sprays (place a towel around your shoulders when you spray your hair).

If the rash, fussiness, or whatever persists, your totally breastfed baby may be reacting to something you are eating. Fortunately, there is a relatively simple and cost-free method of finding out if your diet is involved. Start by eliminating a particular food for a week or so and see if there's a difference in the baby. Since cow's milk is one of the most troublesome foods in this regard, you might want to try eliminating milk first. Be sure you also exclude other dairy products and all foods that are made with milk or dried milk solids. You'll have to read the labels of any prepared foods to be sure you are avoiding milk products completely. It may take five to seven days to clear your system, so don't expect your baby's reaction to clear up immediately.

If there's no change in your baby when you avoid dairy products, you might want to try eliminating other foods one at a time (or several at once) for a week or so to see if baby's symptoms disappear. Other common allergens are eggs, wheat, citrus fruits, corn, chocolate, and nuts. If baby seems to improve when you eliminate a group of foods, try reintroducing them one at a time in order to identify the source of the problem.

Occasionally, a mother can eat a small portion of a food as part of a meal with no reaction on the baby's part, but a large amount taken alone at one time will spell trouble. If you have a highly allergic child, a little detective work may be necessary on your part, but you're already ahead of the situation by breastfeeding.

If you have a baby who is sensitive to the foods you eat, you'll want to be especially careful to delay the introduction of solid foods and cautious about the foods you give him.

## WHAT ABOUT CHEMICAL CONTAMINANTS?

Man-made chemicals such as DDT, PCBs, dioxin, and heptachlor were once used widely in industry and agriculture. They have since gained the reputation of being contaminants—waste products littering our environment. Traces of such contaminants are found in milk, both human milk and cow's milk. The situation can become intensely personal for a breastfeeding mother when large amounts of a contaminant are discovered in the area in which she lives. What are the implications for her and her baby?

Our advice is to use common sense. Put the matter of contaminants in perspective. First of all, there is no evidence to date of any harm coming to a breastfed baby because of the presence of these substances in his mother's milk. They are found only in minimal amounts. Even when mothers were suddenly exposed to

*Your baby's growth and development will continue to amaze you.*

high levels of pollution, such as resulted from the accidental contamination of livestock feed with PBBs in Michigan in 1973, breastfed babies didn't show signs of toxicity. When the United States Senate Subcommittee on Health and Scientific Research held a hearing on environmental toxins and breastfeeding in 1977, one of the participants, Dr. Mark Thoman, editor of *Veterinary and Human Toxicology* and a member of LLLI's Health Advisory Council, testified: "On the basis of the research to date, no risks to the human infant from contaminants in human milk have been demonstrated, and no official group that has studied this matter has recommended the blanket discontinuance of breastfeeding."

In a policy statement, the American Academy of Pediatrics affirmed: "There are no known effects in children at levels found in people in the United States." As chairman of the Academy's Environmental Hazards Committee, Dr. Robert Miller said, "For the health of their babies, we strongly encourage mothers to breastfeed their babies." Dr. R. J. Roberts, chairman of the American Academy of Pediatrics Committee on Drugs (1988-89) points out, "Our ability to indentify contaminants exceeds our knowledge of their effect on the breastfeeding infant."

Contaminants are not to be taken lightly, of course. They pose a risk to all of us, and research must continue to determine the overall extent of this risk. But when media attention focuses on the amounts of contaminants in breast milk, there's a tendency to lose sight of what is happening at other periods in the baby's life, before birth for instance. As Dr. Thoman points out, "The chemical insult from any toxin is more crucial in the first six to eight weeks of pregnancy than it is during the months of lactation."

By giving serious thought to what you eat and the products you use in your home, you can lower the amount of contamination you, your baby, and the rest of your family receive.

We suggest that you discontinue the use of pesticides and other sprays in your own home or on your lawn. According to Dr. Thoman, "Certain chemicals are considered safe, but when introduced near young babies, they are not. I have found so-called nontoxic sprays can be hazardous." You can also avoid laundry products containing chemicals. Clothing treated to resist weather, moths, or wrinkling may also be suspect. Permanently moth-proofed garments may contain dieldrin, which is absorbed through the skin.

As much as possible, try to avoid eating foods with pesticide residues. Fruits and vegetables should be peeled or thoroughly washed under running water. When you are pregnant and nursing, freshwater fish from waters that are known to be contaminated should be avoided. Fat can be cut from meat and poultry, since most of the noxious substances are concentrated in the fat. Contaminants are stored in body fat, which explains why it is unwise for a nursing or pregnant mother to go on a crash diet to lose weight. A sudden weight loss releases some of these accumulated chemicals and increased amounts may cross the placenta or enter the milk supply.

Periodically, it is suggested that breastfeeding mothers have their milk tested for contaminants. When mother's milk is analyzed, it is not unusual to find levels of one or more of the contaminants that exceed the currently established limit for commercial foods. It does little to clarify the situation. Dr. Edward Kendrick of the University of Wisconsin spoke to the issue in *Pediatrics*, 1980: "It should be clear to all that risk/benefit analysis leads to different conclusions for commercial milk as compared to human milk. The analysis leads to different conclusions because the alternatives in the two cases are so markedly different. The application of particular contaminant limits to commercial cow's milk does not lead to the use of a substitute food but rather to the use of cow's milk with a lower contaminant level. However, the application of these limits to human milk leads to the use of a substitute and possibly inadequate food for the infant, namely infant formulas."

In addition, a baby being fed a formula is exposed to other contaminants peculiar to artificial feeding, such as lead and contaminants in the water used to prepare the formula. Furthermore, analysis of human milk shows variability on a day-to-day and even a morning-to-evening basis, so testing a single milk sample would be inconclusive. A study in Norway on insecticides in human milk showed a dramatic variance in the same mother's milk at different times. In most cases, the repeated testing and careful analysis required to give meaningful results is time-consuming and expensive.

Dr. Kendrick speaks for many other authorities when he explains: "To ask mothers to have their milk sampled voluntarily when neither the experts nor local physicians can decipher the results not only wastes health-care dollars but generates maternal anxiety with no useful outcome. We must await the clear demonstration of risks associated with breastfeeding before making such suggestions. At present, it is a balance of potential risks against known benefits, and the known benefits must take precedence."

# Jaw, Teeth, and Speech Development

The body-building enthusiast working out in a gym and the little one at your breast—his fists tightly closed, drops of perspiration on his brow, and his jaws working vigorously—are both engaged in body shaping routines. The gymnast's exercise may result in developing big muscles; your baby's exercise in eating will affect the shape of his face, his smile, and his ability to speak clearly.

Of course heredity lays the foundation for facial structure. A square jaw or a narrow chin, for example, may be a family trait. But whatever your child's potential, it is enhanced by the simple, repeated motion of sucking at mother's breast. Breastfeeding encourages proper facial development and may indeed spare your child dental or speech problems in future years.

A baby sucks differently on an artificial nipple than he does at his mother's breast. The sucking techniques used in bottle-feeding may lead to underdeveloped facial structure and may also encourage baby's tongue to thrust forward, causing the baby to develop an incorrect way of swallowing. If this habit persists beyond bottle-feeding days, there's the possibility that the alignment of permanent teeth will be affected. A rubber nipple, a pacifier, or baby's thumb may also press against the roof of his mouth, narrowing the upper dental arch and limiting the amount of room for teeth. Researchers from Johns Hopkins School of Public Health reported on a study of nearly 10,000 children in which they found that the longer the duration of breastfeeding, the lower the incidence of malocclusion. Children who were breastfed for a year or more required 40% less orthodontia than those who were bottle-fed.

## DENTAL CARIES

Bottle-feeding mothers are often cautioned not to allow a toddler to fall asleep with a bottle of formula or sweetened liquids because this practice has been found to contribute to rampant tooth decay. It has sometimes been suggested that breastfeeding can also contribute to dental caries, especially if a toddler nurses frequently at night. There are reasons to believe that this is not the case. Breast milk does not usually flow from the breast unless the baby is actively sucking, which triggers him to swallow. A bottle nipple held loosely in a toddler's mouth can still drip liquids which pool around his teeth and cause decay.

If breastfed toddlers do develop tooth decay, improvement can often be seen with better dental hygiene and careful monitoring of sweets and snacks. It is not usually necessary to limit nighttime nursing.

Dr. Otto Schaefer, Director of the Northern Medical Research Unit of the Canadian Department of Health and Welfare, reports that his personal experience with several thousand Eskimo children who were breastfed traditionally for two to three-and-a-half years shows no evidence of rampant tooth decay.

## FACIAL DEVELOPMENT

When your baby nurses at your breast, your nipple responds by shaping itself to his mouth in a way that no artificial nipple can. A mother's nipple is soft and flexible. Your baby moves your nipple back into his mouth and up against the hard palate with his tongue, elongating the nipple and bringing his gums and lips around some or all of the areola (dark area). His cheek muscles are extremely active, enhancing facial development.

Through honest labor, baby earns his dinner and prepares his tongue and mouth to make the complex adjustments needed to form the sounds used to speak clearly. This extra "speech training" through breastfeeding is especially important to our sons, for boys are gener-

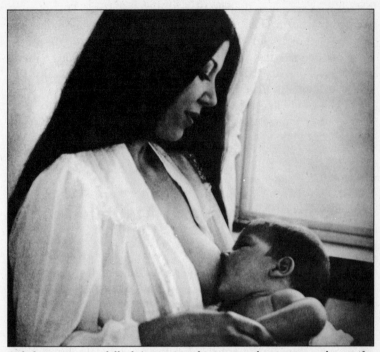

*As baby nurses peacefully, he's exercising his jaw muscles to prepare the way for clear speech.*

ally less mature at birth than their sisters and seem to need speech therapy twice as often as girls do when they reach school age.

Two speech surveys in New Zealand, one in 1971 and the other in 1973, tested whether "factors influencing the development of the sucking response could have an effect on improving the muscles required for speech." Frances E. Broad, who conducted the survey, looked for "any differences in speech between breastfed and bottle-fed children." She also examined "influences likely to affect early reading ability," because, she explained, "it has always been thought amongst speech teachers that if a child could speak clearly he had a very good chance of being able to read well." Her study covered 319 children, ages five and six. Dr. Broad writes, "The Putaruru and West Coast surveys show that improved speech and reading ability coincide with breastfeeding and that the improvement is dramatically seen in the case of the male child."

Clear speech also depends on good hearing. Repeated ear infections early in life can make it difficult for a young child to hear the fine differences in sounds. Breastfeeding's protection against infection is an added bonus. Ear infections can occur in bottle-fed babies who are given their bottles while lying down. The pressure created by sucking on a bottle can force milk into the middle ear, causing irritation and sometimes infection. Nursing at the breast does not require this kind of suction, so a breastfeeding mother can nurse her baby lying down and not worry that this practice will cause an ear infection.

The good effect breastfeeding has on a baby's ability to speak is, of course, enhanced when his mother and father talk to him and respond to the first attempts at speech from their budding linguist.

# Social, Motor, and Mental Development

All parents take pride in their baby's development and carefully watch his progress as he learns to roll over, sit, crawl, stand, and walk. You watch his social development, too, as he responds with smiles and coos and learns to play peek-a-boo and patty-cake. Every baby is an individual and develops these skills at his own pace. Such things are hard to measure and tabulate, but a study was done in 1984 indicating that your breastfed baby does have a significant advantage over his bottle-fed peers in psychomotor and social development in the first twelve months. Breastfeeding has also been associated with optimal physiological organization and increased responsiveness. A 1987 study suggests that the tendency of breastfed babies to cry more often for feedings during periods of wakefulness serves to stimulate an increase in mother-infant interaction which has positive results in terms of the infant's development.

A study that was done in 1988 showed a small but significant relationship between the duration of breastfeeding and scores on the Mental Development Index of the Bayley Scales at one and two years of age. A study done on low birthweight infants found the ones who were breastfed had an 8 point advantage in mean Bayley Mental Developmental Index over infants who had not been breastfed.

But no matter what the experts say, you can be sure that your baby's growth and development will never cease to amaze you. You won't believe how quickly your helpless newborn changes into a toddling, babbling one-year-old. And your baby will no doubt grow to become the cutest, sweetest, brightest, and most cherished child in all the world.

# Breastfeeding and Your Reproductive Cycle

As breastfeeding begins, your reproductive cycle moves into a rest period. If your baby nurses often, day and night, you probably won't have menstrual periods for several months after delivery. The time when you can again conceive is postponed. While you may be able to become pregnant while still nursing, it will not be as soon as it would be if you were not a breastfeeding mother.

Almost all mothers who are totally breastfeeding their babies are free of menstrual periods for the first three to six months or longer. This is called lactation amenorrhea. Total breastfeeding means the baby relies completely on mother for nourishment and for all of his sucking needs.

A study done in Mexico in 1988 showed that "In the absence of bleeding or supplementation, 100% of breastfeeding mothers remained anovular for three months postpartum, 96% for four months, 96% for five months, and 96% for six months."

Many mothers find that their periods do not return until the baby is a year old or older. By this time, he is nursing less often and eating a variety of foods. Dr. Herbert Ratner notes: "It is the baby's sucking that controls the mother's ovulation. The more the baby has a need to suck, the less ready he is to be displaced by another. The less the baby has a need to suck, the more ready and able he is to cope with a new sister or brother."

This rest period in your reproductive cycle comes about because your baby's frequent nursing inhibits the release of hormones that cause your body to begin the monthly preparations for a new pregnancy. Ovulation, the release of an egg, usually does not take place, and you do not have menstrual periods. A state of natural and healthy amenorrhea is produced while the mother is totally breastfeeding her baby.

A 1990 report in *Lancet* showed that the risk of ovulation is reduced by a higher frequency of feedings, longer duration of each feed, and less supplementary feeding. The chance of ovulation occurring during the first 6 months postpartum was 1-5% among amenorrheic women who were exclusively breastfeeding.

## HOW IT WORKS

Studies show that it is the frequency of nursings that inhibits ovulation. In a study of the !Kung mothers of Africa, it was found that births were spaced on an average of forty-four months apart due to breastfeeding. These mothers put the baby to the breast for a brief period several times an hour. They keep their babies with them most of the time, at night as well as during the day. Mother's milk is the baby's only source of sustenance for the first half year or so, and breastfeeding continues well into the second year.

A marked increase in short intervals between births—a baby every year—is regularly seen in cultures that give up total breastfeeding for artificial infant feeding. This is not the way nature programmed a woman's body. Breastfeeding is recognized as an important controlling factor in the growth of a population. John Knodel of the Population Studies Center at the University of Michigan, wrote in 1977 in *Science*, "Recent estimates suggest that the total woman-years of protection against pregnancy provided by breastfeeding in the Third World is quite substantial and may well be larger than the total amount of contraceptive protection achieved through family planning programs...."

Numerous studies over many years have confirmed the effect of breastfeeding on fertility. We learned this, too, from personal experience, our own and the experience of the thousands of breastfeeding mothers who have been associated with La Leche League. John and Sheila Kippley, founders of the Couple to Couple League, gathered data on American women who practiced total breastfeeding and found there was an average of 14.6 months without periods following childbirth. LLL Leader Sheila Kippley writes in her book, *Breastfeeding and Natural Child Spacing*, "This is only an average. Some, an exceptional few, will experience a return before 6.0 months postpartum. Others will go as long as 2.5 years without menses while nursing."

In a 1986 study, women who nursed more frequently than eight times per day, and continued to nurse at night, found their periods were delayed much longer than mothers who supplemented early or whose babies did not nurse at night.

While there are many factors still to be identified in the relationship between breastfeeding and ovulation, breastfeeding does lengthen the time before menstrual periods resume and naturally postpones the possibility of another pregnancy.

When your reproductive cycle is in this resting state, you are less likely to have problems with anemia and the fatigue that goes with it, since there is no monthly loss of blood. Also, you will not have the tension or other mood swings that often precede menstruation. One husband listed this as an added advantage of breastfeeding because he found the "living was easy" during the months his wife was breastfeeding.

*Nature did not intend a woman to have babies too close together in age.*

## WHEN YOUR PERIODS DO RETURN

While some nursing mothers go for two years or longer without menstrual periods, other women who are totally breastfeeding have early menstrual periods following childbirth.

Total breastfeeding will always delay ovulation for a time, but the resumption of regular periods is usually an indication that ovulation is occurring. For some women, especially those who are still exclusively breastfeeding, the first one or two menstrual periods occur without previous ovulation. But a mother who has regular periods should consider herself able to conceive again. When menstruation does return, there is no reason to stop nursing the baby. Breastfeeding can and should continue.

When baby gets older, is nursing less, and eating a variety of other foods, a mother who has not been having periods may resume ovulation without a prior menstrual period and conception can take place before menstruation resumes. This can also happen if a mother returns to work and is separated from her baby for several hours each day, of if a baby who was nursing often suddenly starts to sleep all night.

Any time the amount of baby's sucking at the breast is reduced, the mother should realize that her hormone level could be affected and her menstrual cycle may resume. More importantly, if this change in nursing patterns has happened suddenly, ovulation could be more likely to occur before the first menstrual period.

Early periods may also be more irregular than they were before you became pregnant, since it takes a while for your cycle to settle into a more predictable schedule after childbirth, whether a mother is breastfeeding or not. You can find a more detailed and thorough explanation of the physical changes in your reproductive cycle while breastfeeding, and how you can become more aware of them, in Sheila Kippley's book, *Breastfeeding and Natural Child Spacing*. See the Appendix for details.

## CONTRACEPTION AND BREASTFEEDING

Although breastfeeding has been shown to significantly delay the return of fertility, you may plan to use other forms of contraception while you are still nursing. Use of the oral contraceptive pill is not recommended as the method of choice for breastfeeding mothers.

However, there are differences in the results of studies done on the use of combined oral contraceptives, those that contain estrogen, and the progestin-only minipill. Combined oral contraceptives have been found to affect the quantity and quality of a mother's milk.

There is also concern that the synthetic hormones found in the milk may have long-term effects on the baby. In a series, *Population Reports*, Robert Buchanan wrote, "Nearly all studies report that combined oral contraceptives appeared to decrease the volume of milk produced or to shorten the duration of lactation in some women. . . . Some women using orals have produced milk containing decreased protein, fat, lactose, calcium, and phosphorus. Many questions remain to be answered."

Research on the effects of the progestin-only minipill has not shown the same result in terms of the quantity or composition of the milk in well-nourished mothers. However, long-term effects of the hormones that are passed on to the baby through the mother's milk are of concern to some experts.

The chemically treated IUD may contain some of the same hormones as the birth control pill, and is not recommended for breastfeeding mothers. Some studies show that there is a greater risk of uterine perforation from the use of the IUD in lactating women.

# Breastfeeding and Breast Cancer

Are women who breastfeed their babies less likely to develop breast cancer than those who do not? The answer to this question is still being sought, and the search is complicated by the fact that other factors also influence the rate of breast cancer in a population. Yet researchers keep coming back to breastfeeding as an important consideration in the prevention of breast cancer. Dan H. Moore, PhD, American Cancer Society Research Professor at Hahnemann Medical College and Hospital in Pennsylvania, noted at a symposium on breastfeeding at the University of Pittsburgh in 1979: "In populations throughout the world where breastfeeding is practiced most, the incidence of breast cancer is relatively low."

Among the Eskimos in Canada, only one case of breast cancer was found in the fifteen year period from 1954 to 1969, even though the population had grown from 9,000 to 13,000. As the traditional Eskimos were assimilated into Western culture and the length of time that a mother nursed her baby decreased (or the bottle replaced the breast altogether), the incidence of breast cancer increased. Dr. Otto Schaefer, from Canada, comments, "We have noted remarkable changes in regional breast cancer epidemiology in Eskimos and other people, which appear to be directly related to the local duration of lactation. In both Alaska and Greenland, breast cancer has been found only recently among native people. It was not seen in earlier times."

A predominantly bottle-feeding society, the United States has had a mortality rate from breast cancer of 23 per 100,000 women for the past forty-five years. "In contrast to the relatively high mortality rate in the United States," Vorherr and Messer wrote in the *American Journal of Obstetrics and Gynecology* in 1978, "The breast cancer mortality rates in Thailand, El Salvador, Egypt, and Japan are only 0.9, 1.4, 3.0, and 4.4 per 100,000 respectively." In these countries, breastfeeding is still a common way to feed babies.

A possible explanation of breastfeeding's protective role has to do with the hormonal state found in the woman who is totally breastfeeding, which differs from that of a woman who nurses little or not at all. In support of this thinking is the fact that women who have no children have one of the highest incidences of breast cancer.

One factor that seems to be closely related to the low incidence of breast cancer in nursing mothers is the total number of anovulatory months during the reproductive years. Among the Canadian Eskimos studied by Dr. Schaefer, the mothers commonly breastfed their babies for three years or longer. Another pregnancy followed, with more years of nursing. Pregnancy and nursing continued over a prolonged number of years.

A study in New York in 1964 by M. Levin and Associates points to the length of nursing time as an important factor in the protection against breast cancer. There was a decreased risk of breast cancer among women with a history of seventeen or more cumulative months of breastfeeding. A total of thirty-six months or longer of breastfeeding was associated with a "marked decline" in the incidence of this cancer.

More recent studies have confirmed that breastfeeding offers mothers protection against breast cancer. A 1985 study found that women who had breastfed for twelve or more months had one quarter the risk of developing premenopausal breast cancer compared to women who had never lactated. In 1986, one of the largest studies ever done on breast cancer confirmed that women who had breastfed were at less risk of developing premenopausal breast cancer and that the risk decreased as the duration of breastfeeding increased. This study, reported by W. Douglas Thompson of the Yale School of Medicine, also suggested that breastfeeding may affect rates of breast cancer after menopause as well.

Another 1986 study reported in the *American Journal of Epidemiology* showed that the risk of breast cancer decreased among both premenopausal and postmenopausal women, with increasing duration of lifetime breastfeeding experience, although the effect was consistently stronger for premenopausal women. In 1989, the *Journal of Clinical Epidemiology* reported a study which included 4599 women, 20-55 years of age, identified as having an initial diagnosis of breast cancer. The same number of women of similar ages were selected at random from the same geographic areas to be a control group. After age at first full term pregnancy had been factored out, number of pregnancies and duration of breastfeeding were shown to have a strong influence on the risk of breast cancer. Compared with women who had given birth but had never breastfed, women who had breastfed for 25 months or more were one-third less likely to develop breast cancer.

Breast cancer and breastfeeding were also in the news some time ago with the widespread reporting of research linking a cancer virus in the milk of a mother mouse with breast cancer in her female offspring. Subsequent research disproved the theory that such a cancer virus, transmitted in the milk, plays a role in human breast cancer.

# Economy, Convenience, and Enjoyment

"As a mother who has done both, I can tell you that nothing is more convenient than breastfeeding," states Katie Hartsell from Kansas. "When the baby begins to cry, the mother has a readily available supply of milk at the right temperature. There is no waiting for the bottle to be warmed. There is quite a savings to the family budget and no waste."

The cost advantage of breastfeeding is considerable, especially compared to premixed formulas and disposable bottles. One young couple, trying to budget for their new baby and their first apartment, were shocked by the "substantial jump" in their weekly food bill with the regular purchase of formula.

Viola Lennon, one of La Leche League's founders, suggests that the money you save by breastfeeding might be used to purchase a major appliance. A father from New Zealand, Harry Parke of Cambridge, told a group of fathers, "My wife and I figured that by nursing our first son, Christopher, we saved considerably in the first year by not using formulas, sterilizers, early solids, electricity, birth control means, etc. Raewyn immediately decided that the money saved was to be a deposit on a freezer, and it now stands in the hall!"

In the United States, formula costs have increased at such a rapid pace that the entire industry is being investigated by the Federal Trade Commission. The price of infant formula has increased six times faster than the price of cow's milk. The current price of premixed formula on supermarket shelves ranges from $20-$25 per week.

Low income mothers in the United States can receive food supplements for themselves, their babies, and their young children through the WIC (Women, Infants, and Children) program developed by the federal government. Formula prices have escalated the cost of this program. In 1986, only 38% of WIC mothers were breastfeeding their babies at hospital discharge. In a 1987 Summary Report from the US Department of Agriculture, it was estimated that 29 million dollars could be saved annually if WIC mothers breastfed their babies for just one month.

## WORLDWIDE IMPLICATIONS

In Third World or developing countries, the impact on the economy would be devastating if mothers chose to abandon breastfeeding. Gabrielle Palmer, a nutritionist and breastfeeding counselor from Great Britain, writes in *The Politics of Breastfeeding:*

*Human milk is a commodity which is ignored in national inventories and disregarded in food consumption surveys, yet it does actually save a country millions of dollars in imports and health costs. The Mozambiquan Ministry of Health calculated in 1982 that if there were a mere twenty percent rise in bottle feeding, in just two years this would cost the country [the equivalent of] 10 million US dollars, and this did not include fuel, distribution, or health costs. They also calculated the fuel required for boiling the water would use the entire resources from one of the major forestry projects. Inventors of fuel-saving cars are rewarded, why not energy-sparing women? For every three million bottle-fed babies, 450 million tins of formula are used. The resulting 70,000 tons of metal in the form of discarded tins is not recycled in the developed countries.*

Once you become an experienced nursing mother, you will probably spend two or three hours a day relaxing in your favorite chair, casually offering your baby the emotional, nutritional, and immunological benefits of breastfeeding. You will take this for granted as part of your daily routine. You may pause for a moment to reflect on the fact that you're giving your little one the very best start in life—but you may never stop to realize the global implications of what you are doing. You may not be aware that a mother's decision to breastfeed has economic, ecological, and political significance.

Worldwide trends toward artificial feeding have drastic consequences in terms of maternal and infant health. We can be proud of the involvement of La Leche League in efforts to reverse this trend. Thirty-five years ago, the seven founders wanted to help their friends and neighbors experience the benefits of breastfeeding their babies. Now the organization's outreach extends to mothers in every part of the world who need that same kind of mother-to-mother support and encouragement.

Women who choose to breastfeed their babies are making a difference in the world. Becoming a member of La Leche League and contributing to the organization are positive ways to convey a

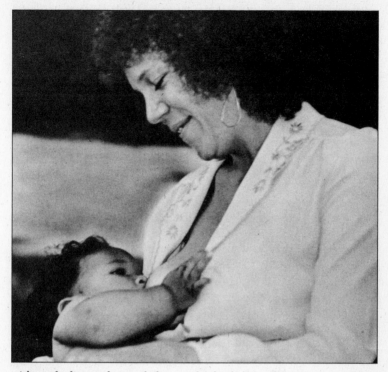

*A breastfeeding mother can feel secure that her baby's milk supply is always readily available.*

message of support to mothers all over the world who want to give their babies the best start in life.

## YOUR MILK IS ALWAYS AVAILABLE

As a nursing mother, you can take off on short notice for a family excursion, a long trip, or that full-day picnic when formula can spoil. You can make your plans and pack your bags without worrying about having an adequate supply of formula for the baby—a formula that may not be available everywhere. You won't even have to be concerned that a strange water supply will make your baby ill, since a breastfed baby does not need extra water.

Wherever you and baby are, so is your milk. It's a most reassuring thought, particularly in the rare, but always stressful time when the usual, normal supplies of food are cut off. This doesn't happen too often, but we do hear from mothers who have had such

experiences and are most grateful that their little ones were spared
the brunt of this disturbing situation.

In the Midwest, an unexpected and severe snowstorm stranded
a family in their car. While the husband went for help, his wife snuggled the baby under her coat, keeping them both warm, and the
baby nursed and slept. This young mother found the feeling of normalcy associated with feeding the baby helped to keep her own
fears in check until a rescue crew came for them.

## EMERGENCY SITUATIONS

Another family unexpectedly spent a night in the mountains.
The four Walkers of Ohio—mom, dad, five-year-old Scott, and one-
year-old Adam, in a backpack atop his father's shoulders—set out
for an afternoon's hike and didn't make it back to their camper for
twenty-one hours. "We had hiked these trails so often we thought
we knew them all thoroughly," Judy Walker wrote. But when the
Walkers started down the trail they thought led back to their car,
they inadvertently went down another trail, which they learned later,
"went right off the map." The night spent in the isolated area was
cold, rainy, and so dark "we couldn't see each other." Judy concludes
her story: "My husband kept scooping leaves over us trying to keep
us dry, and all night, at least once an hour, Adam woke, hungry,
wet, screaming. Each time I nursed him, as it was the only thing
that calmed him. I thank God that throughout that cold, wet night
I had warm milk to fill my baby's tummy and to comfort him."

Kay Troisi from Alabama tells of her family's experience:

*A hurricane came roaring through our community with
little advance warning of its nearness or intensity. A lot of
damage resulted, including many fallen wires, and snapped
pine trees perilously perched on power lines. Consequently,
we were without electricity for two and a half days.
During this time, I realized even more what an advantage
breastfeeding is. Our daughter, Tamara, was only three
weeks old and not having to worry about how to feed her
was an immense relief. There was no concern over
preparing formula, not to mention sterilizing, storing, or
heating it without electricity. Not only did I have ready
nutrition and reassurance for Tamara, but baby and
mother were also consoled by our nursing session during*

*the worst of the storm. We could be in our own little world while nursing, oblivious to the external ragings. After the storm, continuous closeness ensured a peaceful baby, contented mother, and overall a happier family, during a time when other families might have been in chaos.*

## A PLEASURABLE EXPERIENCE

Breastfeeding is intended to be a pleasurable experience for a mother. A woman who breastfeeds with pride and satisfaction is aware that breastfeeding is a sensual experience. She also knows that this is a perfectly healthy and normal aspect of her sexuality. Dorothy V. Whipple, MD, wrote in the *Journal of the American Medical Women's Association:*

*Suckling a baby, for the woman who accepts and enjoys her femininity, is a particularly moving experience. The physical sensation is pleasant, the guzzling eager mouth against the sensitive erectile tissue of the nipple is enjoyable in itself. It also brings peace, contentment, fulfillment to the whole body and personality. The sensation is not orgasmic; it is more like the peaceful afterglow of orgasm. It brings to the woman a deep and personal understanding of her role as a woman. It brings to her also a bond with women in distant times and cultures. The mature woman who carries out the totality of her feminine functions knows she has a niche in the ultimate scheme of things.*

And Selma Fraiberg, in describing how a baby learns to love, tells about the mutual satisfaction of breastfeeding:

*In breastfeeding, the infant is cradled in the mother's arms. Pleasure in sucking, the satisfaction of hunger, intimacy with the mother's body, are united with his recognition of her face. The baby learns to associate this face, his mother's face, with an enjoyable and comforting experience. As we watch the nursing baby we see how gradually the skin surface of the body is suffused with pinkness—a sensual glow of pleasure and well-being.*

*When the baby is held at his mother's breast the entire ventral surface of his body is in contact with her body. And this sensual pleasure heightens his awareness of his own body. Nursing mothers also experience sensual pleasure through the baby's sucking. This should lead to no embarrassment. It is simply one of the rewards, one of the ways in which* **mutual** *sensual pleasure binds the mother to her baby and the baby to her.*

To the list of breastfeeding's unique characteristics, we add yet one more—its universality. The baby at the breast represents the common language of mothering. Babies have basic needs that do not change, regardless of when or where they are born. And the beautifully natural act of nursing your little one has this same timeless quality. It is a link to other mothers and a sign, even, of womanly power. The ability of a mother's body to nurture her child is a source of strength to her. And through breastfeeding's gentling effect, an island of peace is secured. It is a small miracle, belonging rightfully to mothers, babies, and families the world over.

# PART EIGHT

*Mothers Helping Mothers*

# CHAPTER 20

# About La Leche League

La Leche League began with a wish—a dream, really—that all mothers who want to breastfeed their babies would be able to do so. The seven of us who founded La Leche League had overcome a variety of difficulties before we were able to breastfeed with ease and confidence, and we knew of too many mothers who were unable to breastfeed at all simply because they had no one to turn to for information and advice.

## How It All Began

It was at a church picnic that Mary White and Marian Tompson decided there had to be a way to help their friends who wanted to breastfeed their babies but found only frustration and failure when they tried. With their own nursing babies cradled in their arms on that summer afternoon in 1956, Mary and Marian talked about finding a way to help those women experience the joy and deep fulfillment of breastfeeding.

In the weeks that followed, Mary talked to Mary Ann Kerwin, her sister-in-law, and Mary Ann Cahill, who casually mentioned the idea to Betty Wagner. Marian contacted Edwina Froehlich, who got on the phone to call her good friend Viola Lennon. Each had nursed one or more babies. We had no grandiose plans about how to go about helping our friends, but we were willing to try. Two local physicians, Drs. Herbert Ratner and Gregory White, advised us on those aspects of breastfeeding and mothering that were commonly associated with the medical community.

Confident of our information, and enthusiastic about breastfeeding, we invited our pregnant friends to a meeting at Mary White's house one October evening in 1956. What we offered to interested neighborhood mothers then — and what the 28,000 La Leche League Leaders who have followed us continue to provide — was information, encouragement, and support. Personal mother-to-mother warmth and caring have been a cornerstone of our organization since its inception. Although La Leche League has grown into a worldwide organization with over 3,000 groups in forty-eight countries (located in communities throughout the United States, Canada, New Zealand, Europe, Africa, Asia, and South America), our focus still remains on the personal one-to-one sharing of information and encouragement that provides a new mother with the confidence she needs to breastfeed her baby.

Today La Leche League stands as the internationally recognized authority on breastfeeding. La Leche League has been contacted by mothers, fathers, doctors, nurses, and other professionals throughout the world for our expertise on breastfeeding. La Leche League International serves on the Board of Non-Governmental Organization Consultants to UNICEF, an agency of the United Nations, a registered Private Voluntary Organization for the Agency of International Development, and is an accredited member of the US Healthy Mothers, Healthy Babies National Coalition.

La Leche League's Annual Seminars for Physicians, held in North America, attract doctors from all over the world. They are accredited by the American Medical Association — Category 1 of the Physician's Recognition Award, the American College of Obstetricians and Gynecologists, the American Academy of Family Physicians, the American Osteopathic Association, and the American Academy of Pediatrics.

Workshops for Lactation Specialists are scheduled each year in the spring and fall to meet the needs of the emerging health professional who specializes in caring for the breastfeeding dyad. Continuing education credits are available to board certified lactation consultants and to registered nurses.

# How LLL Can Help You

Over the years it has been La Leche League's privilege to help hundreds of thousands of mothers breastfeed their babies. La Leche League, to us, is simply a mother with a baby in her arms and a smile on her face, proud of herself and eager to share all that she has learned and experienced. Mothers, like you, who find fulfillment and delight in nurturing an infant are the heart and soul of La Leche League.

La Leche League Leaders everywhere rejoice in the knowledge that by helping mothers to breastfeed their babies, they are playing a part in strengthening and deepening the love ties formed in infancy that will last a lifetime.

## OUR ORGANIZATION

Our name, La Leche, is Spanish and is pronounced la lay-chay. Simply translated, it means "the milk." The name for our organization was inspired by a shrine in St. Augustine, Florida, dedicated to the Mother of Christ under the title "Nuestra Senora de la Leche y Buen Parto," which translates freely, "Our Lady of Happy Delivery and Plentiful Milk."

Our international headquarters, located in Franklin Park, Illinois, USA, is staffed by 40 employees. Every year they respond to thousands of pieces of mail and answer countless phone calls from the many people throughout the world seeking breastfeeding help or information. There are LLLI Affiliate organizations in Canada, Great Britain, Switzerland, Germany, and New Zealand. La Leche League is a nonprofit organization and is entirely supported by donations, memberships, and sales of materials.

## PROFESSIONAL SUPPORT

La Leche League has a Health Advisory Council comprised of doctors and health professionals from all over the world. This council is consulted about medical situations and evaluation of new research. Members of the Health Advisory Council review La Leche League publications that include medical information. Complementing the Health Advisory Council are doctors throughout the world serving as Medical Associates of La Leche League.

A Legal Advisory Council and a Management Advisory Council complete the LLLI Professional Advisory Board.

## PUBLICATIONS

La Leche League's basic manual, THE WOMANLY ART OF BREASTFEEDING, has sold more than two million copies and is available in nine languages, on audiotape, and in Braillon. Other LLLI publications are available in more than 30 languages.

La Leche League is the world's largest resource for breastfeeding information. Currently, we publish 20 books and distribute more than 3 million publications annually. A selection of nearly 200 books, information sheets, and pamphlets are listed in the *LLLI Catalogue*.

## CONFERENCES

International and Area Conferences are held periodically for parents and professionals. Speakers include experts in breastfeeding, parenting, childbirth, nutrition, childcare, and related topics. Doctors, educators, researchers, authors, and parents represent a wide range of experiences and opinions.

## MEMBERSHIP

Members of La Leche League International care about giving their babies the best. This caring starts with breastfeeding and nursing mothers often have questions which can be answered by other nursing mothers. LLLI has developed into a worldwide network of mothers with breastfeeding experience who share information, support, and encouragement.

Membership in La Leche League offers you these benefits:

• *one-year subscription (six bimonthly issues) to NEW BEGINNINGS, a magazine filled with inspiration, practical hints, photos, book reviews, and breastfeeding information.*

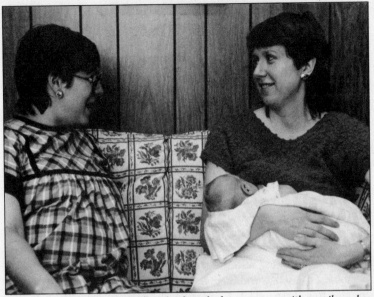

*Perhaps La Leche League can best be described as a woman with a smile on her face and a baby in her arms eager to help other mothers learn about breastfeeding.*

- *a 10% member's discount on most purchases from the **LLLI Catalogue** which features a wide variety of outstanding publications on breastfeeding, childbirth, nutrition, and parenting.*

- *the opportunity to share the companionship of other mothers of babies and young children at monthly meetings of your local LLL Group and learn even more from the carefully selected books in the Group's library.*

- *participation in LLL special events, including local and international conferences, with a special member's discount on registration fees.*

When you become a La Leche League member you support the efforts of your local Group Leaders who are volunteers, and you join an international mother-to-mother helping network with over a quarter of a century's history of practical mothering wisdom.

## LA LECHE LEAGUE MEETINGS

LLL meetings are informal discussion groups usually held in the homes of members. Information is presented following a planned schedule of topics that cover the practical, physical, and psychological aspects of breastfeeding.

La Leche League meetings offer a wonderful source of information and encouragement, and a ready source of new friendships among mothers who have many things in common.

At these La Leche League meetings, the LLL Group Leader shares her knowledge about breastfeeding and related topics and encourages mothers to ask questions and share their own experiences. For every question or difficulty that might be brought up, there are usually several mothers at the meeting who are able to offer various solutions or suggestions. It is both exciting and reassuring to watch other babies in the group thrive and grow. It is fun to see how unique each baby is, and the wonderful, warm way in which each mother and baby relate to each other. Babies are always welcome at LLL meetings.

In addition to providing breastfeeding information, LLL meetings are a wonderful place to learn more about the world of mothering an infant from other women who have "been there" and are delighted to pass along their insights.

Our Leaders are primarily mothers who have breastfed their own babies and are willing to share their knowledge and enthusiasm about breastfeeding with mothers who look to them for help. The personal experience and special training of each Leader prepare her for this role. Every LLL Leader has completed a specific application process before she is considered qualified to act as an official representative of La Leche League.

## HOW TO FIND LA LECHE LEAGUE

With over 3,500 La Leche League groups meeting every month all around the world, the chances are excellent that there are one or more groups in your community. Group Leaders make every effort to publicize their meetings so that mothers will be able to find the local LLL group quickly and easily.

Nearly all groups place meeting notices in the local newspapers. Watch your paper, or simply call the newspaper office and ask if they know how to get in touch with the La Leche League groups in the area.

In some of the larger cities, you will find La Leche League listed in the white pages of the telephone directory. If there is no listing, try calling the maternity wards of the larger hospitals or some of the obstetricians and pediatricians in your area. Childbirth instructors or your local library may have information about La Leche League groups in the community.

Be sure to ask around among your friends and neighbors who are pregnant or have young children. You will more than likely find one or more of them have been to League meetings and would be delighted to put you in touch with a local Leader.

In the USA, we currently have a toll free number you can call for immediate answers to breastfeeding questions, a free copy of our Catalogue, or the name of a La Leche League Leader near you. Just call 1-800-LA LECHE.

Or you can write us at La Leche League International, 9616 Minneapolis Avenue, PO Box 1209, Franklin Park, Illinois, 60131.8209 USA. Our regular telephone number is 708-455-7730. Business hours are from 9:00 AM to 3:00 PM, Central Time. At other times, a prerecorded message will refer you to another number for immediate breastfeeding help.

## WOULD YOU LIKE TO HELP?

Perhaps you are not able to locate a La Leche League Group in your community and this book has been your only source of guidance for your breastfeeding experience. As the months go by and your baby grows and thrives on your milk, you may notice other mothers asking you questions about breastfeeding. We know, because that's how we got started! If you find this is something you enjoy, why not write to us for information on starting a La Leche League Group?

La Leche League needs mothers just like you who have read this book, followed its recommendations, and happily breastfed their babies. If there is no League Group in your area and you think you'd be interested in becoming a La Leche League Leader, write to LLLI Headquarters, c/o Leader Accreditation Department, and request a copy of our free brochure, "Becoming a La Leche League Leader."

# About This Book and Its Authors

When the seven of us wrote the first edition of THE WOM-ANLY ART OF BREASTFEEDING in the 1950s, we were all mothers at home full-time. Writing was done in between other chores, while the baby napped or played nearby, perhaps with a preschool brother or sister. More often than not, the desk was the family dining table, and manuscript pages had to be hastily gathered up at mealtime.

We had mutually agreed that our families were our first priority. This understanding freed us to set aside League work when our families needed us. As our children grew and circumstances changed, some of us took on salaried jobs at La Leche League Headquarters. The interest that we shared thirty-five years ago has not abated. All of us continue as members of the Founders' Advisory Council and Betty Wagner and Mary Ann Kerwin still serve as active members of LLLI's Board of Directors. Betty Wagner, Viola Lennon, and Mary Ann Cahill are currently employed by La Leche League.

When we started the League, each of us knew one or more of the others, but some of us were getting acquainted for the first time. We were far from being carbon copies of each other. Some had bottle-fed older children; others had been fortunate enough to have breastfed their first babies. There is a span of sixteen years in our ages and great diversity among us. What solidly unites us is our belief in the importance of mothering and the value of breastfeeding.

Since our philosophy is based mainly on what we have found through experience to be most valuable, we include some information about us as individuals.

**MARY ANN CAHILL, McHenry, Illinois:** Mary Ann was well along in her first pregnancy when she found a copy of Grantly Dick-Read's book, *Childbirth without Fear,* on a sale table in Marshall Field's basement in Chicago. "I read passages aloud to Chuck over that summer before Elizabeth was born," she recalls. "I was convinced that our baby would be born naturally and, of course, I would breastfeed." Unfortunately, the dream of a natural delivery vanished with the routine administration of a spinal, and breastfeeding amounted to "a noble try." When the Cahills moved to Franklin Park in 1951, they learned of the "radical Dr. White." Under his care, the rest of the Cahill babies arrived without medication and thrived on mother's milk.

The family moved to Libertyville in 1960, and over the years, the red brick tri-level often echoed to the antics of ten growing youngsters, the nine Cahills—Bob, Elizabeth, Tim, Teresa, Mary, Joe, Margaret, Charlene (Charlie), Fran—and little friend Janet, who for a number of years was part of the family and as a young woman still joins in family get-togethers. These days, such occasions are often held to celebrate marriages and the arrival of grandbabies. Mary Ann has been working for LLLI, mainly as a writer, since Chuck's death in 1978. Currently, she is the Associate Director of LLLI's Funding Development Department.

In 1981, Mary Ann took great pride in the publication of the third edition of THE WOMANLY ART OF BREASTFEEDING as she had done the major work of writing and revising it. In 1983, LLLI published THE HEART HAS ITS OWN REASONS, authored by Mary Ann.

Mary Ann Cahill                  Edwina Froehlich

**EDWINA FROEHLICH, Franklin Park, Illinois:** Edwina was one of the few women in the 1950s who devoted considerable time to a career and married late. She was thirty-six years old when she and John began their family. There were dire warnings from all sides about the perils of having a baby at such an "advanced" age. And certainly, it was said, no woman over thirty could produce enough milk to satisfy a baby. Paul was born naturally at home, and those aged mammary glands produced an abundance of milk for him and the two brothers, David and Peter, who make up the Froehlich family. Early in her mothering, Edwina found it quite a struggle to give up the organized approach to life that had served her so well in the business world. It was only after she relaxed and accepted the unscheduled needs of her baby that she was able to truly enjoy motherhood.

The Froehlich family now includes three daughters-in-law, Marilyn, Sharon, and Paula, "who are outstanding young women and we dearly love them." Edwina has retired from her LLLI staff position but remains active as a member of the Founders' Advisory Council. She is also the Leader of a local LLL Group in Franklin Park, Illinois, where the League started 35 years ago. Edwina enjoys her role as Grandma to Leanne, Kristin, Steven, Katrina, Michael, and Laura, with another grandchild expected soon.

**MARY ANN KERWIN, Denver, Colorado:** When Mary Ann and Tom Kerwin became parents for the first time in 1955, Mary

Ann was eager to breastfeed even though not one of her friends was breastfeeding. The combination of her inexperience and a sleepy baby made it difficult to get started. Helpful advice and support were forthcoming from Greg and Mary White (Mary is Tom Kerwin's sister). Soon, Mary Ann and her first baby were a contented nursing couple. Mary Ann's major regret regarding her first breastfeeding experience is that she weaned at nine months. It was a painful and upsetting time for both mother and baby, but Mary Ann learned from this experience. All of the other babies were allowed to wean at their own pace. The Kerwins have eight children: Tom, Ed, Greg, Mary, Anne, Katie, John, and Mike. A ninth child, Joseph, born in 1959, died at six weeks of age — a victim of Sudden Infant Death Syndrome.

After serving as Chairman of LLLI's Board of Directors from 1980-83, Mary Ann returned to school and received her law degree in 1986. The education she received from her children gave her the necessary determination and self-discipline to achieve this goal. She continues as an active member of LLLI's Board of Directors and is currently practicing law in Colorado.

Mary Ann now has three grandsons. Her first two grandchildren were born prematurely to her daughter, Mary. Although Michael was two months premature and was a sick baby initially, Mary was able to breastfeed him completely within a few weeks. The hospital staff was very supportive and knowledgeable. Ben was born five weeks early but he began breastfeeding in a few days. Happily, her son, Ed, and his wife, Karen, had a full-term baby in February 1991, Lewis Joseph. All three grandsons are thriving, due in large part to successful breastfeeding.

Being a breastfeeding mother and a parent is never easy, but Mary Ann believes her children have a head start in that regard, thanks to the influence of La Leche League International. She says, "Whatever I might have done to help others has come back to me a thousandfold."

**VIOLA LENNON, Park Ridge, Illinois:** Vi's ten little Lennons came in all sizes, and just to prove that no challenge was too much for her, she even produced a set of twins in 1961. It was considered quite an accomplishment to nurse even one baby in those days, so Vi caused quite a stir in the neighborhood when she calmly proceeded to totally breastfeed both Catherine and Charlotte. Cathy was wakeful as an infant, nursing at least every two hours, while sleepy Charlotte nursed much less often, but gained more rapidly than her sister. She also weaned five months later than Cathy. The twins were sixth and seventh in the lineup, with Elizabeth, Mark,

*Mary Ann Kerwin*                 *Viola Lennon*

Mimi, Rebecca, and Matthew preceding them, and Martin, Maureen, and Gina following. Mimi was colicky as a baby, and Vi assumed that indicated a high-strung personality, but Mimi has grown into an easygoing, serene young lady.

Vi is currently the Funding Development Director for the League, helping secure outside funds to finance La Leche League's ever-expanding work. Viola was the last of the founders to become a grandmother, but currently she has four grandsons and two granddaughters, all under the age of four.

**MARIAN TOMPSON,** **Evanston, Illinois:** Even though she changed to a new doctor with each of her first three babies, Marian was unable to breastfeed for as long as she would have liked. Each doctor gave her the standard advice of the time—nurse no more than every four hours, offer supplementary bottles, and start solids at six weeks. It was with their fourth baby, in 1955, that Marian and her husband, Tom, found more supportive help from Dr. Gregory White and

*Marian Tompson*

his wife, Mary. Baby Laurel was nursed until she weaned herself, as was true for the succeeding babies. The seven Tompson children, Melanie, Deborah, Allison, Laurel, Sheila, Brian, and Philip, are grown up now and her five daughters are all married. Marian considers herself particularly blessed to have been present at the births of most of her twelve grandchildren.

Marian was La Leche League's first and only president. During the twenty-four years of her presidency, she spoke out clearly and with love in many parts of the world for breastfeeding mothers and babies. Currently, Marian manages a toy store near her home and dispenses breastfeeding information to new parents along with rattles and teddy bears. She continues as a member of LLLI's Founders' Advisory Council and also serves on a number of advisory boards for organizations concerned with nutrition, childbirth, and family life.

**BETTY WAGNER, Franklin Park, Illinois:** Betty has breastfed all of her children, beginning back in 1943, thanks in large part to her mother, who was able to give her the practical help she needed. It was baby number six who presented Betty with new challenges. Dorothea cried a good deal and wasn't happy anywhere but in her mother's arms. Betty found it necessary to curtail all outside activities and rearrange her life around this little one who needed her so intensely. Dorothea was past her third birthday before she would venture very far from her mother, but about the time she was three and a half, she blossomed into a very self-confident, outgoing little girl. The Wagners had seven children — Gail, Robert, Wayne, Mary, Peggy, Dorothea, and Helen. Betty's daughter, Mary, was the first of the founders' daughters to become a La Leche League Leader.

As the Executive Director of LLLI, Betty is responsible for the day-to-day operation of the League. She also serves on the Board of Directors and the Founders' Advisory Council. Betty has twenty-one grandchildren and one great-granddaughter; all have been happily breastfed.

**MARY WHITE, River Forest, Illinois:** Mary's first attempt at breastfeeding was just like that of most mothers in the 1940s — disastrous! In a short time, baby Joseph was a bottle-fed baby. When her second baby was born, her doctor husband, Greg, was home from the Army, and she had the support that a nursing mother needs. Bill, Peggy, Katie, Anne, Jeannie, Mike, Mary, Clare, Molly, and Liz were all happily breastfed with never a bottle in the house. Only

*Betty Wagner*                    *Mary White*

the first three were hospital births; the others were born at home, and arrived at intervals of two to five years due solely to the most natural family planning of all, breastfeeding. Now eight children are married and her 36th grandchild has just arrived. All of the grandchildren have been breastfed, and all but two were born at home. Liz, born when her mother was forty-seven, is now a junior in college and Mary has time to enjoy being a grandma while still remaining active in the League.

Mary's devotion to the special kind of mothering that is so much a part of breastfeeding has always been a guiding influence in La Leche League. If you were to ask Mary, she would tell you that she believes her most important job as a mother is to instill in her children a love and trust in God for all of their lives.

## THOSE WHO HELPED

A dedicated office staff and many professional consultants worked long hours to prepare the manuscript for the third edition of this book in 1981. Mary Ann Cahill did most of the writing with lots of help from the other founders. Since the book is intended for mothers, you won't find footnotes or references in the text, but you can be assured that we have sound authority behind the statements we make.

The fourth revised edition, published in 1987, was compiled and edited by Judy Torgus, long-time League Leader and Executive Editor of LLLI's Publications Department. Judy had worked on the 1981 edition, and she was able to pull together the needed information from a variety of sources in order to make the fourth edition as complete and up-to-date as possible. The founders carefully reviewed the final manuscript, along with Sally Murphy and Gwen Gotsch. Last minute typing needed to get the book out on time was done in the evenings and on weekends by Joyce Kasheimer.

This edition was published to commemorate La Leche League's Thirty-Fifth Anniversary. A chapter has been added that reflects on the organization's history and its future. This information was compiled by Marlene Sweeney. Other revisions have been made where newer recommendations replace the previous information. Ongoing research continues to disclose new benefits of human milk and substantiate the benefits already recognized. Revising and editing of this edition were handled again by Judy Torgus, Executive Editor of LLLI's Publications Department, assisted by Elayne Shpak and other members of LLLI's Headquarters Staff.

Most of the personal stories that are included came from the pages of NEW BEGINNINGS, our bimonthly members' publication. We want to thank the parents who shared their experiences with us, as well as those who posed for photographs. All of the photos used in the book were provided to us by the photographers at no charge.

We are deeply grateful to each of the above and to many others—too numerous to mention—who helped to make THE WOMANLY ART OF BREASTFEEDING a classic.

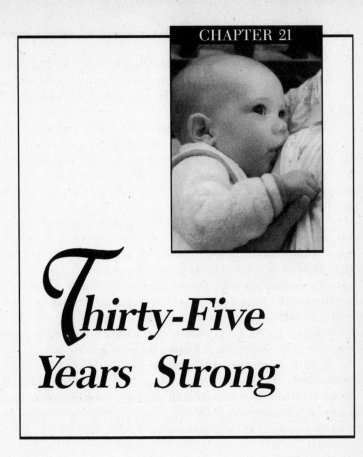

# CHAPTER 21

# *T*hirty-Five Years Strong

The year was 1956 and a confrontation was taking place in the Middle East. The new Egyptian President, Abdul Gamal Nasser, had seized control over the Suez Canal. Life was uncertain.

In the United States there was a sense of growing prosperity and increased consumerism. Women were beginning to seek careers outside their homes. The American dream was defined by "bigger and better."

The incidence of breastfeeding at one week was 18%. Mothers were encouraged to adhere to a strict doctor-imposed schedule while caring for their babies. Information about breastfeeding was almost non-existent.

In the year 1991, a confrontation is taking place in the Middle East. People all over the world are involved and concerned. Consumerism in the United States is rampant but family values are beginning to emerge and receive recognition.

And the incidence of breastfeeding is at 50.6%. Mothers are searching for ways to be with their babies without affecting their careers. Information about breastfeeding abounds—books, articles, tapes, videos.

Some things change and some things stay the same.

So, as we celebrate the 35th Anniversary of La Leche League, we reflect on our past, rejoice in our present, and reaffirm our future.

Many of the changes that have occurred in infant-care practices over the past thirty-five years have been attributed to La Leche League's influence.

In 1956 babies were routinely introduced to solids between one and three months. Based on valid medical research as well as their success in keeping up their milk supply by delaying solids, the founders of La Leche League recommended postponing the introduction of solids for four to six months. Today the American Academy of Pediatrics agrees with delaying the start of solid foods, and few mothers are told to give solid foods in the early months.

When La Leche League began, babies were routinely separated from their mothers following birth for as long as twenty-four hours. La Leche League spoke out—babies need their mothers, and mothers benefit, too, by early nursing and uninterrupted bonding. Today women expect to hold their newborn baby immediately after birth. What was unheard of thirty-five years ago is common practice now, and LLL helped mothers achieve this.

Dr. Ruth Lawrence, author of *Breastfeeding: A Guide for the Medical Profession,* collects historical data about breastfeeding. Quoting from magazines and advertisements dating from the 1940s and '50s, Dr. Lawrence points out that considerable doubt was posed in the mind of the average mother at that time. She was led to believe she should rear her child according to the advice of "experts."

The women of the fifties came to La Leche League with very basic questions. How do I know if I have enough milk? How do I know when the baby is hungry? When will my child sleep through the night? Today's women still come to LLL in search of answers, encouragement, and the mother-to-mother support that we have become known for. The most common reason still given by mothers who stop nursing in the early weeks is that they didn't think they had enough milk.

Lynn Werner, a historian and lecturer with the Women's Studies at Northwestern University, describes La Leche League as the precursor of the Feminist Movement. Seven women set out to give the baby back to the mother at a time when male experts dominated the child care field. She believes this empowerment of women

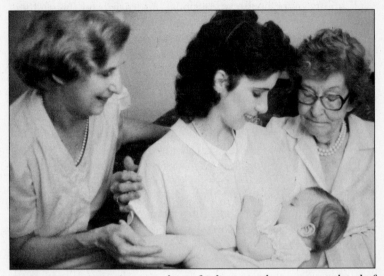

*From generation to generation, breastfeeding provides a common bond of love.*

was the beginning of self-help groups and women's control over health-care issues.

From its small beginning, La Leche League has grown into an international organization, recognized worldwide as an authority on breastfeeding. Today there are 3,000 LLL groups in 48 countries. La Leche League has matured into an experienced, well-seasoned, vital women's group making an impact on the world in which we live. La Leche League International is accredited by medical associations to present annual Seminars for Physicians. These are attended by doctors and other health care professionals from all over the world. A series of Lactation Specialist Workshops, accredited for lactation consultants and nurses, is presented each year.

A doctor who spoke at a recent LLLI Seminar for Physicians, Method A. Duchon, MD, a perinatologist from Ohio, pointed out that obstetricians and pediatricians are often unable to provide much education and support to nursing mothers because their education, background, and experience with breastfeeding has been so limited. In reviewing leading obstetrical and pediatric journals, current textbooks, and continuing medical education offerings, he found that breastfeeding was minimally represented, and the information he did find emphasized disease, problems, and suppression of lactation. "What I know of breastfeeding, I learned from my wife," he said, urging other health professionals to learn from the mothers they help.

Last fall, Betty Wagner, LLL founder and the Executive Director of LLLI, represented La Leche League at the United Nations when heads of government met at the World Summit for Children. La Leche League remains in the forefront of placing the needs of the nursing baby on the world agenda, acting as a non-governmental advisor to the United Nations by serving on the Board of Consultants to UNICEF, the United Nations agency concerned with the welfare of the world's children. La Leche League is directly involved in a variety of programs around the world to promote and support breastfeeding.

In the United States, a La Leche League program was developed to encourage breastfeeding among low-income minority mothers which has since spread to other countries. LLL's Breastfeeding Peer Counselor Program works in cooperation with local community health care agencies, including WIC clinics in the USA, to offer accurate breastfeeding information along with mother-to-mother support.

## WHAT THE FUTURE HOLDS

Recently, the founders of La Leche League and members of the Board of Directors were asked to share their views about La Leche League's future. Here's what they said:

*Today practically all reputable sources agree that breastfeeding is best for mothers and babies. Why is La Leche League still needed?* Betty Wagner responds: "Reputable sources may agree and the medical community may give lip service to the superiority of breastfeeding, but our current culture is definitely a bottle-feeding culture." Since health-care professionals often lack the practical know-how, our mother-to-mother support is unique and valuable in today's world.

Mary Ann Cahill, another of LLL's founders, suggests, "Breastfeeding is a long-term commitment. In order to succeed, a mother needs the encouragement and companionship of other mothers. La Leche League succeeded in the beginning and continues to work well because it meets this dual need for sound, practical information and loving support. Babies don't change and neither do mothers, though the circumstances in which they find themselves differ from one generation to the next."

Mary Ann Kerwin adds: "Breastfeeding is a gift from the past that was in the process of being abandoned when we started LLLI. The incidence of breastfeeding in the United States decreased from 60% in the 1940s to less than 20% in the 1960s, probably the lowest in the history of the world. No previous culture dared to discard such a valuable resource. Mothers have always needed support in breastfeeding their babies, but the support system had broken down. We began to revive the womanly art of breastfeeding simply by providing a mother-to-mother support system. In an increasingly fragmented society that too often separates mothers and babies, LLLI is not only still needed but more needed now than ever."

***Breastfeeding issues change with the times. What do you see as the breastfeeding issues of the '90s?***    Almost all of those surveyed agreed that encouraging breastfeeding among mothers employed outside of the home would continue to be a challenging issue.

Viola Lennon feels the international arena presents many new challenges concerning infant mortality and morbidity. Barbara Heiser, a member of the LLLI Board of Directors, believes, "Bottle-feeding needs to be seen as a high-risk behavior if we are going to make a difference in Third World countries."

***How is the breastfeeding mother of today different than her counterpart of 1956?***    Marian Tompson says, "Breastfeeding was simpler in some ways in the 1950s and 60s. Most mothers of small children stayed home to care for them." The mother of today has more demands on her time, more pressures to be "all things to all people." The nursing mother feels many outside forces pulling on her to place things and other people before her baby. Joan Crothers, a member of the LLLI Board of Directors, reminds us that LLL's approach can help mothers of the 90s set priorities and put "people before things."

According to Mary Ann Kerwin, "Breastfeeding mothers today are pulled in far more directions than their counterparts of 1956. Life is much more complex. The new opportunities for young women are also creating enormous pressures. The attitude of the 1950s included the belief that women, children, and babies inevitably would be taken care of whereas mothers no longer have that sense of security."

***How has the influence of La Leche League affected your family?***    There is no doubt that this question affirmed what every young mother wants to know—Yes, there are long-term benefits to your mothering style. All of La Leche League's founders are now grand-mothers, and each one of them attests to the influence La Leche League has had on the next generation. Edwina Froehlich explains: "There is no doubt that our three sons have somehow absorbed what I learned through La Leche League: the importance of the early mother-baby relationship, being aware of the emotional needs of infants and children, the importance of feelings in a one-to-one rela-tionship, as in marriage. I believe it is no coincidence that they chose women who join them in these beliefs to be their wives. All three of these young mothers seem to have started their motherhood way ahead of where I was when I started. They already have so much of the knowledge that I had to struggle to get. As a grandmother it delights me to observe my grandchildren being nurtured in such a loving way."

*In what direction do you see La Leche League heading as we approach the 21st century?* Our influence in the world is definitely being felt. Founders and Board Members alike envision La Leche League becoming a spokesperson for breastfeeding mothers worldwide. They could see LLL networking with, col-laborating with, and assisting world organizations in maternal and child health issues. "We will enhance the vision of breastfeeding as a process which encompasses a lot more than just providing the perfect food to the baby," Barbara Heiser predicts.

Mary Ann Kerwin says, "We are joining hands all over the world to focus on breastfeeding as a world health issue and to help mothers everywhere realize the joys of breastfeeding their babies."

Betty Wagner adds, "Our work is needed worldwide and mothers are answering that need and becoming volunteer accredited Leaders. In order for the rate of breastfeeding to increase, mothers need to know the benefits to their baby and themselves. A success-ful breastfeeding mother, more than anyone, understands the major benefits of breastfeeding. She is the one who is best able to spread the word to her sisters. La Leche League will continue to grow. League mothers know breastfeeding is so much more than giving milk to their baby."

Mary White summarized all of this by saying, "Our purpose is and always has been to foster good mothering through breast-feeding, and by so doing, to encourage good physical and emotional growth for the child and the development of closer and happier family relationships. That's the way we put it back in the beginning, and that's the way we see it today!"

# Mothers Express Their Appreciation

Perhaps the basic story of La Leche League's thirty-five years is best told by the mothers themselves who have found the support and encouragement they needed to breastfeed their babies—and sometimes to change their lives.

A mother from Colorado tells what happened in her life that led to an appreciation of La Leche League:

*I have been a member of La Leche League for almost nine years, and have often wanted to write and express my appreciation and thanks for the encouragement, support, and nurturing I've received.*

*I have three boys, ages eight, five, and two years. Nursing them has brought us all untold benefits—love, closeness, health, understanding, nurturing, and so much more.*

*I'm writing now because, for the past several months, I've been confronting pain from my own childhood. The realization that I grew up in a family where emotional needs were not met—creating a co-dependent situation. I'm having to face my childhood and learn that I can let go and learn healthier patterns for myself.*

*Most information on co-dependence and dysfunctional families says that you can't give what you didn't get. Well, I have given my children lots of love and nurturing and acceptance of them at each stage of development, and I have to give a lot of credit to La Leche League. From the birth of my first son, nursing has been the foundation of all I've done. Learning to answer their needs as infants has created a very nurturing way to parent. And we have three bright, happy, secure children.*

*Thank you, La Leche League, for helping me to give my children what they needed most! And in the process, I'm learning how to model healthy adult behavior, too. We're a healthy, happy, growing family and I'm very thankful for La Leche League.*

And another mother, Kristine Williford, who lives in Venezuela, agrees that finding La Leche League made a big difference in her life:

*I want to thank you for being there for so many of us. LLL has made a world of difference in our lives. I joined LLL when my son was two months old and going through a growth spurt. After trying my pediatrician's advice and making my son wait an hour and a half between feedings, I called the LLL number in the phone book. Talking with an LLL Leader solved my problems and lifted my self-confidence. I went to my first meeting two weeks later and was convinced of the wisdom in listening to our children. I'm blessed with a very supportive husband who has been enthusiastic about breastfeeding.*

*Since our son was born twenty months ago in California, we have lived in Texas, the Bahamas, and now Venezuela with month long stopovers in California in between. We're convinced that breastfeeding has provided stability and health in Sam's life. He's a great toddler and is comfortable meeting new people and seeing new places. At twenty months, he is beginning to wean during the day, but still loves nighttime snacks snuggled in between Mama and Papa.*

*I've never written letters to organizations before, but I wanted you to know that LLLI is important. Never doubt the effect you have on people's lives.*

Susan Doran of Tennessee relied on THE WOMANLY ART OF BREASTFEEDING to give her the help she needed while she was breastfeeding her sons:

*In 1978 my first son was born. We moved three times during his first year and had three pediatricians, each giving me conflicting advice. When I was told to start solids at two months of age, I resisted as a direct result of reading THE*

*THE WOMANLY ART provides a reliable source of breastfeeding help.*

*WOMANLY ART OF BREASTFEEDING. Another time, the day before we took to the road for a 700-mile interstate move, I was told to stop breastfeeding my five-month-old because he was vomiting. The next day, driving behind the moving van and listening to my baby cry, I finally pulled off the road, dug out my copy of THE WOMANLY ART OF BREASTFEEDING and read that it was certainly okay to breastfeed an ill baby. I immediately breastfed my son and the rest of the trip was a much more contented one. I am convinced that THE WOMANLY ART OF BREASTFEEDING made our nursing relationship a positive one.*

*I now have two more sons who were both breastfed. We have moved into nine different localities with the consequences of encountering a variety of different medical professionals. But all three revised editions of THE WOMANLY ART OF BREASTFEEDING were my continuing source of reliable breastfeeding information.*

April Meyer from South Dakota agrees. She writes, "Just wanted to drop you a note to thank you for all the support over the last thirteen months. Since we don't have a La Leche League group nearby that I could attend, your book THE WOMANLY ART OF BREASTFEEDING has been a lifesaver! I doubt I would have continued this long without it.

"Breastfeeding for me has truly been a wonderful experience. I had many doubts over the months, due mostly to the fact that I'm the first in our family in generations to nurse, but it's been the best way to nurture and feed our baby. I'm thankful for all the support from your organization."

Many health professionals turn to La Leche League's mother-to-mother support and find it invaluable when the time comes that they are breastfeeding their own baby. Dr. Eloise Skelton-Forrest, a prominent obstetrician/gynecologist from California and Director of the Alhambra Women's Medical Group, writes the following to congratulate La Leche League on its thirty-fifth anniversary:

*How* *special you are! It is exciting to know that you have been helping families for thirty-five years. I always smile when I think that my initial encounter with La Leche League was as a nursing mother with a hungry newborn. My training in obstetrics and gynecology prepared me for many things:, but it was La Leche League that gave me the practical skills I needed to make my relationship with my daughter most rewarding.*

*I encourage mothers to seek assistance from La Leche League on a regular basis. THE WOMANLY ART OF BREASTFEEDING and EL ARTE FEMININO DE AMAMANTAR are well used in the lending library we have for our patients. The world looks forward to many more years of your watchful and loving support.*

# Others Add Congratulations

*I am pleased to extend congratulations to La Leche League International in celebration of your thirty-five years as a supporter and promoter of breastfeeding.*

*As your Surgeon General, as a pediatrician, and as a woman, I wholeheartedly endorse breastfeeding. In today's modern world, breastfeeding is all too frequently circumvented when extraneous demands confront mothers. Yet, the many benefits of breastfeeding to infants and mothers are well documented.*

*First and foremost, breast milk provides excellent nutrition for proper infant growth and development. Properly initiated and sustained, it also provides infants protection from many common infections during the first year of their lives.*

*In this country, promotion and development of successful breastfeeding plays a key role in our Government's major initiative to achieve healthy children by the year 2000. Internationally, breastfeeding serves as a healthful means to the survival and well-being of mothers and their children, particularly in developing countries.*

*La Leche League's history of support to mothers is commendable and most valuable. Again, I offer congratulations on your past accomplishments and wish you success with your future endeavors.*

*Antonia C. Novello, MD, MPH*
*Surgeon General of the United States*

*La Leche League is one of the few nonprofit organizations where children really profit.*

*Don Aslett*
*Author of* Clutter's Last Stand

*Congratulations on your staying power. You were right to be outspoken, honest, scientific, and determined.*

*When I went to medical school a half-century ago, I believed everything I was told. The professors of pediatrics tried to be as scientific as possible. How can a doctor be scientific if the amount of ounces the baby is getting from the mother's breasts cannot be measured? One doctor said that breastfeeding would become acceptable to the medical profession if a flow-meter could be attached to the breasts. So we learned how to mix up formulas, and discouraged nursing. What a waste! We then created our own problems for ourselves as pediatricians.*

*Bottle-fed babies had more allergies, ear infections, anemia, rashes, gastro-intestinal infections, needed more house calls, and I discovered later, had more trouble with malocclusion when they grew up. I did not discover the wonders and benefits of breastfeeding until La Leche League International got through my prejudices.*

*Congratulations! You have helped turn me on to Mother Nature's way, the best way to rear babies. Once the breastfeeding mother and her newborn baby get locked into each other's needs and desires, the rest of the childrearing until the child is eighteen years old and out of the house comes easily and logically.*

*Congratulations! You have found out that what is best for the baby is breastfeeding and love. Our bodies were designed for this. Science cannot improve on what is the infant's birthright.*

*Lendon Smith, MD*
*Pediatrician and Author*

*O*n behalf of Kiwanis International, I am pleased to acknowledge the 35th Anniversary of La Leche League International.

La Leche League International has been an ongoing force emphasizing the many positive reasons for women to breastfeed their babies. They have continued to do this, in spite of what appeared to be trends to the contrary. It finally appears that the trends are returning to La Leche League International's point of view, where they belong.

The vision of this organization leads to the appropriate nutrition of the newborn. It lessens the likelihood of disease and increases the bonding so necessary between mother and baby.

Kiwanis International is pleased that La Leche League International is part of its Advisory Council, helping Kiwanis with its emphasis programs aimed at young children.

May you have more successful years to follow.

W. J. Blechman, MD
President
Kiwanis International

*W*hen I attended my first La Leche League meeting seventeen years ago, I didn't know much. I certainly had never seen a baby breastfed and I stared in veiled amazement. Yet, I wanted to do what was best for my baby. Breastfeeding was at its lowest point ever at that time and the first Series Meeting, "The Advantages of Breastfeeding" was a revelation. Now, thanks to La Leche League, breastfeeding is again on the rise and almost everyone knows that breast is best.

*But, La Leche League means even more to me
personally. Through La Leche League I learned how to
breastfeed, how to mother, and how to live in keeping with
my values. And, in addition, I learned how to speak in front
of people, how to lead a meeting, and how to interact with
people in an administrative position. When I first became
the owner of Mothering magazine in 1980, I modeled
everything I did after my experience in La Leche League.*

*For me, my life as a woman began with La Leche
League and I will always be grateful to those special women
at that first meeting, in that little house, on that quiet
street, who have enriched my life immeasurably.*

*Peggy O'Mara
Editor/Publisher*
**Mothering** *Magazine*

*When I opened my office to practice pediatrics in my
hometown of Jackson, Tennessee, in 1949, I was the first
full-time pediatrician in the central part of West Tennessee
(Population 250,000). And I was distressed to learn that
many (and perhaps most) mothers were being given
hormone shots to dry up their milk the day after delivery. I
would estimate that no more than 5% of mothers were
attempting to nurse their babies. And of those who started
breastfeeding, most stopped after a few days or weeks.*

*In spite of my efforts to educate obstetricians, parents,
and parents-to-be in my community, I had little success.
Then, some years later, a courageous and dedicated La
Leche League representative moved to Jackson from
Illinois.*

*She did many things, including holding LLL group
meetings in Jackson and appearing before the hospital
board of trustees promoting breastfeeding. She said in
effect, "You should make things easier for mothers to nurse
their babies."*

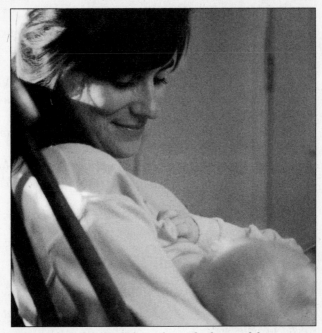

*What is best for the baby is breastfeeding and love.*

*Today, obstetricians and pediatricians routinely—even enthusiastically—urge mothers to nurse their babies. Few people in our community are unaware of the benefits of breastfeeding.*

*Some years ago, pediatrician Lee Forrest Hill of Des Moines, Iowa said in effect, "La Leche League has done more for the nutrition of infants than all of the learned pediatricians in the world." I agree!*

*William G. Crook, MD*
*Pediatrician and Author*

*T*wenty-two years have passed. Yet how well I remember that lonely, desperate night. I held Yvonne, my first born, six weeks old, as I sat in the rocking chair in the living room. It was 2 AM. In one hand I held a bottle; in the other hand a pacifier. On my lap lay Yvonne, refusing my breast. We were both crying.

During my childbirth classes someone had suggested that I contact La Leche League for breastfeeding information. But my stubborn Dutch pride rebelled. I don't need them! After all, I had come from Holland. I should know how to nurse a baby!

Then, on that awful night I suddenly realized how alone and bewildered I was. I made a resolute decision to call La Leche League the very next day. The rest is a successful history of breastfeeding and mothering.

Long before contacting La Leche League, I basically believed in everything it stands for. I could have done it all by myself; so why didn't I, or couldn't I? Why did I need La Leche League?

Because La Leche League gave me support. By being there for me, La Leche League took away the loneliness. By listening, they took away the desperation. By sharing their knowledge and wisdom, they allowed me to grow gently and firmly, in my own beliefs.

But most of all, La Leche League changed everything from a belief to a reality: a wonderful, supportive, loving reality.

Tine Thevenin
Author, speaker, and mother
Minnesota

*La Leche League has sown the seeds of a rich and ongoing legacy.*

*Over the past thirty-five years, La Leche League International has become a powerful force in saving the lives of babies and in providing emotional support, accurate information, and leadership to the young mothers and fathers across our nation and around the world. Through the vehicle of neighborhood-based meetings, local and international conferences, publications, and mother-to-mother support, La Leche League has sown the seeds of a rich and ongoing legacy ensuring that today's babies and millions of children in future generations can receive their rightful inheritance of sound human nutrition and loving, responsive care.*

*Breastfeeding offers not only profound physiological benefits to babies, it also offers deep emotional sustenance to both mother and child. The basic human level of physical intimacy afforded by breastfeeding teaches babies that the world is good, that it can be trusted, and that they are worthy of love. Such messages if not delivered at the intimate breast of a loving mother in the formative stages of consciousness may never be heard or received with such force again in the human lifespan. I clearly feel that the roots of the profound loneliness, the unrequited yearning and despair that have contributed to our nation's rising levels of adolescent substance abuse and suicide can be traced to the early severing of that primal physiological and emotional link between mother and baby.*

*I salute and embrace the founders of La Leche League, and the thousands of leaders who have given so unselfishly of themselves through all these years, who have touched the lives of so many families. And most of all, I salute the millions of babies who have smiled up at their mothers' faces as they nursed contentedly embraced in loving arms. Their security, their strength, and their vital health are the greatest tribute that La Leche League and its founders could ever have.*

*Sandy Jones*
*Author, speaker, and mother*
*Maryland*

# *Appendix*

A wide variety of books are available to help you learn more about breastfeeding, childbirth, parenting, and nutrition. We are proud of the books that are published by La Leche League International because they reflect the same philosophy you have found in the pages of this book. All of the books we publish can be ordered by mail and shipped directly to your home. Local La Leche League Groups also have these books available for purchase and/or loan, and some of them can be found in your local bookstore or public library.

We encourage you to read and learn as much as you can about your role as parents. Follow your instincts and natural inclinations in choosing the advice and information that seems right to you. The basic philosophy of La Leche League encourages you to learn about babies' and children's needs so you can understand and respond to those needs from earliest infancy and throughout the years as your child grows. And always remember, babies and children need lots and lots of love.

# Books That We Publish

**GROWING TOGETHER: A Parent's Guide to Baby's First Year** by William Sears, MD.

Over 150 black and white photographs and 16 pages of color photos illustrate the growth of motor, language, social, and cognitive skills from birth to one year. Dr. Sears, the author of LLLI's GROWING FAMILY SERIES, advocates attachment parenting, and tells how parents can enhance their baby's development by their responsiveness. GROWING TOGETHER answers parents' questions about "What will my baby do when?" and also tells how parents develop their own abilities right along with their baby. Includes tips on parenting, breastfeeding, and infant stimulation.
No. 273, $14.50

**BECOMING A FATHER: How to Nurture and Enjoy Your Family** by William Sears, MD.

Addresses the joys and problems of parenthood from the male perspective—everything from how to hold a tiny baby to sibling rivalry and organized sports. Dr. Sears, a pediatrician and father of six, writes from personal experience and promises that becoming a father will bring rich rewards, among them love, a better marriage, and maturity.
No. 266, $8.95

**NIGHTTIME PARENTING: How to Get Your Baby and Child to Sleep** by William Sears, MD.

Explains how babies sleep differently than adults, how sharing sleep can help the whole family sleep better, and how a particular style of nighttime parenting can lower the risk of Sudden Infant Death Syndrome. Helps to reassure parents that meeting nighttime needs is important to their baby's well-being.
No. 276, $7.95

**THE FUSSY BABY: How to Bring Out the Best in Your High-Need Child** by William Sears, MD.

Assures parents that meeting the needs of a fussy baby does not cause baby to be "spoiled." Suggestions include "back to the womb" security tips and a guide to interpreting a baby's cries. Chapters on coping with colic, feeding, fathering, soothing, and avoiding maternal burnout include plenty of support, reassurance, and day-to-day survival tips.
No. 269, $7.95

**MOTHERING MULTIPLES: Breastfeeding and Caring for Twins** by Karen Gromada.

> Full of practical tips from experienced mothers of twins. The author, herself a mother of twins, includes hints on streamlined housekeeping, baby equipment, family adjustments, and ways to comfort two fussy babies. Everything mothers need to know to cope with the challenge of more than one baby.
> No. 267, $7.95

**MOTHERING YOUR NURSING TODDLER** by Norma Jane Bumgarner.

> Warmth, wisdom, and wit illumine a lively discussion of breastfeeding past the age of one. Besides exploring the "why" of nursing a toddler, this book helps a mother cope with the challenges: getting enough rest, dealing with criticism from friends and family, nursing (or avoiding nursing) in public places, communicating with her husband, and finally, weaning.
> No. 268, $7.95

**A SPECIAL KIND OF PARENTING: Meeting the Needs of Handicapped Children** by Julia Darnell Good and Joyce Good Reis.

> Handicapped children challenge their parents' emotional and physical resources. This book can guide parents through the problems and help them discover their disabled child as an individual. The authors cover both facts and feelings about handicaps, parents' reactions to the initial diagnosis, the grieving process, and effects on the marriage and the rest of the family.
> No. 280, $8.95

**LEARNING A LOVING WAY OF LIFE** compiled and edited by Virginia Sutton Halonen and Nancy Mohrbacher.

> A collection of stories, photos, and poems that reflect La Leche League's philosophy told by parents themselves. Tells of the joys found in building strong family relationships. This book will help you understand and enjoy your own family more.
> No. 275, $7.95

**SAFE AND HEALTHY: A Parent's Guide to Children's Illnesses and Accidents** by William Sears.

> Dr. Sears guides parents through some of the most stressful episodes of parenting by answering the most frequently asked questions about childhood illnesses. Tells when you should call the doctor and how to handle situations that don't require a doctor's advice. Written by a pediatrician, this book is an essential guide to caring for your child.
> No. 281, $9.95

**OF CRADLES AND CAREERS: A Guide to Reshaping Your Job to Include a Baby in Your Life** by Kaye Lowman.

> Examines the family vs. career dilemma, with stories from mothers who have found ways to combine their working lives with mothering. The author's research adds a wealth of ideas for negotiating with employers, exploring self-employment, choosing substitute child care and achieving harmony at home. Tips on breastfeeding and working, job-sharing, and maternity leave round out a book that encourages women to explore a variety of options and helps them choose what works best for themselves and their families.
> No. 278, $9.95

**WHOLE FOODS FOR THE WHOLE FAMILY: La Leche League International Cookbook** edited by Roberta Johnson.

> Complete nutrition-conscious cookbook contains over 900 kitchen-tested recipes. Filled with time-saving make-ahead meals, ideas for using leftovers, special diet and allergy recipes, suggestions for baby's first foods, last-minute dinner menus, and a separate "Kids' Cookbook," this treasury of family-pleasing dishes uses only whole unprocessed foods and minimal amounts of salt and sweeteners. Complete with protein and calorie counts, recipes include meat and meatless main dishes, ethnic foods, wholegrain breads, desserts, snacks, and sandwiches—a wondrous variety of wholesome, delicious eating.
> No. 262, spiral-bound, $14.50

**MOTHER'S IN THE KITCHEN** edited by Roberta Johnson.

> Tasty and easy recipes submitted by LLL mothers. The classic LLL cookbook emphasizes low-cost nutritious recipes that families love.
> No. 260, $4.95

**PLAYFUL LEARNING: An Alternate Approach to Preschool** by Anne Engelhardt and Cheryl Sullivan.

> This book offers a workable and enjoyable alternative to traditional preschools: the at-home cooperative preschool. You and other parents can provide a learning environment while you share in your children's emotional, intellectual, and social development. Filled with quotes from parents and professionals that support its ideas, PLAYFUL LEARNING is designed to be a multi-purpose guide for adults who work with young children and includes a wide variety of craft projects, simple recipes, science experiments, plans for field trips, music activities, and much, much more.
> No. 279, spiral-bound, $14.95

THE WOMANLY ART OF BREASTFEEDING an Audio Guide
An exclusive audio-edition of LLLI's best-selling manual offers a basic guide to breastfeeding in two 90-minute tapes. Information is excerpted from the fourth edition of THE WOMANLY ART OF BREASTFEEDING. **No. 663, $15.95**

# Other Helpful Books

In addition to the books we publish, La Leche League International distributes a wide selection of books that offer helpful information to parents and professionals. Some of these are listed here. For a complete, up-to-date listing plus ordering information, send for a free copy of the LLLI Catalogue.

***Creative Parenting** by William Sears.*
Comprehensive child-care guide covers the basics and more. Dr. Sears' concept of continuum parenting describes a way of life in which family members respect and enjoy one another and parents feel confident about trusting their own instincts. **No. 331**

***The Working Woman's Guide to Breastfeeding** by Nancy Dana and Anne Price.*
This book offers practical advice for mothers who want to continue breastfeeding when they return to work. Includes personal stories from mothers. **No. 393**

***The Family Bed** by Tine Thevenin.*
Co-family sleeping is as old as the human race and yet has become controversial in the 20th century. This book explores the pros and cons and suggests that the family bed will help solve bedtime problems and create closer family bonds. **No. 345**

***The Natural Baby Food Cookbook** by Margaret Kenda and Phyllis Williams.*
Natural foods taste better and are healthier and more nutritious for your baby. Homemade baby foods also cost less. The recipes in this book will help you feed your growing baby easily. Chapters include information on allergies and vegetarianism and tips for enticing finicky eaters to the table. **No. 365**

**Your Child's Self-Esteem** *by Dorothy Corkille Briggs.*
Being able to understand a child's search for identify and self-worth creates confidence and patience in parents. These guidelines will help parents boost their child's self-image in the early years and lay the groundwork for self-esteem. **No 399**

**How to Really Love Your Child** *by Ross Campbell.*
Helping children feel and understand their parents' love is the key to emotional wholeness and family happiness. Dr. Campbell, a Christian psychiatrist, outlines techniques for communicating with and disciplining children at various stages of development, always guided by principles of unconditional love and acceptance. **No. 352**

**How to Talk So Kids Will Listen and Listen So Kids Will Talk** *by Adele Faber and Elaine Mazlish.*
The suggestions in this popular book, based on the work of the late child psychologist Haim Ginott, really work. The authors offer a method that stresses listening to your child, dealing with feelings, finding alternatives to punishment, and helping your child develop a positive self-image. With this kind of supportive, friendly communication between parents and children, everyone in the family can cooperate and live together harmoniously. **No. 353**

**Don't Shoot the Dog** *by Karen Pryor.*
In this entertaining and enlightening book, Karen Pryor, author of *Nursing Your Baby,* applies the principles of positive reinforcement to dogs, dolphins, and humans. The result is a constructive method of shaping behavior that works on everyone from whining children and lazy teenagers to sloppy spouses and cats who sit on the furniture. **No. 334**

**Methods of Childbirth** *by Constance Bean*
The third edition of this classic overview of childbirth options was published in 1990. Gives an up-to-date look at trends and attitudes among parents and professionals. **No. 363**

**The Cesarean Myth** *by Mortimer Rosen and Lillian Thomas*
A thought-provoking look at today's cesarean epidemic from the eyes of an obstetrician who believes in a natural approach to birth. **No. 324**

# PROFESSIONAL BOOKS

*The Lactation-Consultant's Topical Review of the Literature on Breastfeeding by Mary-Margaret Coates, MS, IBCLC*
> This guide to the published literature outlines a wide range of information needed by those who help mothers with breastfeeding. Subheadings, cross-referencing, and an index make it easy to locate citations in answer to specific questions. Published by La Leche League International. **No. 524, $25.95**

*An Overview of Solutions to Breastfeeding and Sucking Problems by Susan Meintz Maher, IBCLC*
> Outlines the steps needed to assess and solve the more challenging cases of nipple soreness, breast problems, and ineffective suck. Published by La Leche League International. **No. 67, $5.50**

*Lactation: Physiology, Nutrition, and Breast-Feeding edited by Margaret C. Neville, PhD and Marianne R. Neifert, MD.*
> Scientific book on the physiology of lactation, and the clinical management of breastfeeding. Includes chapters on nutritional and immunological aspects of breastfeeding, hormonal regulation of lactation, mechanisms of milk secretion, drugs and toxins in breast milk, and infant and maternal problems. **No. 358**

*Breastfeeding: A Guide for the Medical Profession by Ruth A. Lawrence, MD.*
> This authoritative reference on nearly every aspect of breastfeeding is a valuable resource for physicians, nurses, lactation consultants, and League Leaders. It applies recent research to practical situations and provides guidelines for the management of breastfeeding. **No. 319**

*Counseling the Nursing Mother by Judith Lauwers, Candace Woessner, and CEA of Greater Philadelphia.*
> Guides the breastfeeding counselor in helping mothers identify and resolve their concerns and problems. Chapters deal with family adjustments and infant development as well as breastfeeding problems and special situations. The three-ring notebook format, along with tables and study guides in each chapter, makes this a handy reference tool. **No. 330**

*Lactation Consultant Series Developed by the Lactation Consultant Department of La Leche League International. Series Editor, Kathleen G. Auerbach, PhD.*

> Counseling nursing mothers requires knowledge that goes beyond the basics of breastfeeding. LLLI's Lactation Consultant Series can provide that expertise with in-depth units on a wide variety of topics. Written in clear, non-technical language, the series emphasizes counseling strategies as well as breastfeeding techniques and background information. Each unit is 8 ½" x 11" and three-hole punched to fit a looseleaf binder, making it easy to add new units to your library. Send for listing of units that are currently available. **No. 288**

# BOOKLETS AND INFORMATION SHEETS

Various booklets, pamphlets, and information sheets on specialized topics are available from local La Leche League Groups and from La Leche League International. For an up-to-date listing plus complete ordering information, send for a copy of the *LLLI Catalogue.* Here is just a sampling of the items:

**Nursing My Baby with a Cleft of the Soft Palate**      No. 22

**The Diabetic Mother and Breastfeeding**      No. 17

**Breastfeeding a Baby with Down Syndrome**      No. 23

**Breastfeeding Your Premature Baby**      No. 13

**Legal Rights of Breastfeeding Mothers, USA Scene**      No. 59

**Allergies in Breastfed Babies**      No. 54

**Helping Love Grow: Parenting Adopted Children**      No. 56

**Nursing Your Adopted Baby**      No. 55

## Breastfeeding Rights Packet

> Resource material for mothers involved in divorce, custody, employment, or other legal controversies that threaten their continued breastfeeding. **No. 78**

# Breastfeeding-Aid Products

Most breastfeeding mothers and their babies get along just fine without specialized equipment or products. However, in cases where some assistance is necessary to ensure continued breastfeeding success, La Leche League has certain products available that can be of help. Some of these items are available through local LLL Groups, or you can order directly from La Leche League International.

### Medela Manualectric Breastpump/Feeding System

Engineered to operate with the same suck-release-relax cycle characteristic of a baby's nursing action, the Medela Manualectric Breastpump operates with a piston-type action. A special adapter fits inside the shield to adapt the pump to smaller breasts. Can also be used with the Medela Electric Breastpump. **No. 421**

### Gentle Expressions Breast Pump and Feeding System

Battery-operated pump operates with one hand. A suction release valve allows mother to provide intermittent suction with the touch of a finger. Lightweight and 7 inches small, the pump is easy to take along. Requires two AA batteries. **No. 417**

### Loyd-B Breast Pump

An efficient, durable pump used successfully by thousands of women over the last fourteen years, the Loyd-B features a squeezable handle which controls the pumping action and a release trigger which allows the mother to regulate the vacuum. It's small enough to take with you and easy to clean. **No. 420**

### Mag Mag Battery-Operated Breast Pump with AC Adapter

Unique stimulator assists in the let down of milk. This pump can be used with batteries or plugged into an electric outlet. All parts except motor are dishwasher-safe. **No. 408**

### Egnell Battery-Operated Breast Pump

Small and easy to carry, this pump is easy to use with one hand. Includes silicone areolar stimulator which helps increase milk flow. Dishwasher safe. Requires 2 AA batteries. **No. 413**

## Medela Supplemental Nutrition System

A thin tube taped to each breast carries supplement to the nursing baby from a plastic bottle hanging on a cord around the mother's neck. A valve in the bottle cap prevents the milk from flowing until the baby sucks; the two tubes make it easy to switch sides while breastfeeding. Helpful for mothers who are relactating or nursing a baby with a sucking problem. **No. 416**

## Medela Hand Expression Funnel

The Medela Hand Expression Funnel is a specially designed plastic funnel that fits onto an ordinary baby bottle and allows a mother to collect her hand-expressed breast milk without spills or splashes. **No. 423**

## Breast Shell Kit

Medela breast shells allow air to circulate around nipples to correct inverted nipples and protect sore nipples. **No. 422**

## Breast Shields

Two-piece breast shields recommended for use during pregnancy to correct inverted nipples. **No. 402**

# ADDITIONAL ITEMS OF INTEREST

## All New Breastfeeding Video
## Breastfeeding Your Baby: A Mother's Guide

One-hour video produced by Medela, Inc., in cooperation with La Leche League International. Families tell of the advantages of breastfeeding and experts give guidance on techniques. Celebrities like Linda Kelsey, Katharine Ross, and Cathy Rigby tell of their own breastfeeding experiences. **No. 601, VHS; No. 602, Beta**

## Nursing Reminder

Sewn on the lower band of a nursing bra, the plastic slide can be moved with the touch of a finger to remind mothers which breast to start with at the next feeding. **No. 403**

## Nursing Fashions Packet

Contains ideas on what to wear to breastfeed discreetly, sewing tips, and flyers advertising clothing and patterns for nursing mothers. Also includes information on homemade and commercial baby carriers. **No. 98**

**Baby Cuddler Baby Sling**
 A sling has been found to be the ideal way to carry a baby
 from birth to three years. Comfortable and adjustable, the Baby
 Cuddler Baby Sling distributes the child's weight over shoulders and hip to avoid back strain. **No. 401.**

**Lansinoh®** Lanolin for Nursing Mothers
 Nursing mothers have used lanolin for years to soothe sore
 nipples. Lansinoh's® patented process removes impurities and
 alcohols to create a pure medical-grade hypoallergenic anhydrous lanolin that is safe to use even for those allergic to wool.
 Order from LLLI's Catalogue. **No. 581**

# Organizations That Offer Support

Many of these organizations have local chapters. Check your
phone directory or contact their headquarters at these addresses:

*The American Academy of Husband-Coached Childbirth — The
Bradley Method*    *Box 5224 Department CB; Sherman Oaks CA
91413-5224.    800-423-2397*
 Founded by Robert Bradley, MD and Jay and Marjie Hatha-
 way for the purpose of making childbirth information available through films, classes, lectures, and workshops.

*American College of Home Obstetrics    47 Harrison; Oak Park
IL 60304.    708-383-1461*
 Can help parents find physicians who support home birth.

*American College of Nurse Midwives    1522 K Street NW;
Washington DC 20005.    202-289-0171*
 Can refer parents to health care providers who can offer a
 natural approach to birth.

*American Society for Psychoprophylaxis in Obstetrics, Inc. —
ASPO/Lamaze    1101 Connecticut Avenue NW, Suite 300;
Washington DC 20036.    800-368-4404 or 202-857-1128*
 Physicians, parents, and professionals offering training and cer-
 tification of prenatal class instructors in the psychoprophylac-
 tic method of childbirth preparation.

**Association for Breastfeeding Fashions**    *Post Office Box 4378;*
*Sunland CA 91041.*    *818-352-0697*
Offers information on companies that design fashionable clothing for breastfeeding women. Please call or send S.A.S.E. for
more information.

**Children in Hospitals, Inc.**    *31 Wilshire Park; Needham MA*
*02192.*    *617-482-2915*
Parents and health-care professionals concerned about the need
for ample contact between children and parents when either
is hospitalized.

**Cesareans/Support, Education, and Concern, Inc.—C/SEC**
*22 Forest Road; Framingham MA 01701.*    *508-877- 8266*
Provides information on many aspects of cesarean childbirth
in order to make couples more aware of their options.

**The Couple-to-Couple League**    *Post Office Box 111184; Cincin-*
*nati OH 45211.*    *513-661-7612*
An interfaith organization offering couples help with the practice of natural family planning. CCL teaches ecological breastfeeding and the full sympto-thermal method of predicting
ovulation.

**International Childbirth Education Association—ICEA**    *Post*
*Office Box 20048; Minneapolis MN 55420.*    *612-854-8660*
A volunteer organization which brings together persons
interested in family-centered matternity and infant care.

**International Lactation Consultant Association**    *Post Office Box*
*4031; University of Virginia Station; Charlottesville VA 22903.*
Can refer you to a lactation consultant who has been officially
certified as a health care provider.

**InterNational Association of Parents and Professionals for Safe Alter-**
**natives in Childbirth—NAPSAC**    *Route 1 Box 646; Marble Hill*
*MO 63764.*    *314-238-2010*
Parents, medical professionals, and childbirth educators who
promote education enabling parents to assume more responsibility for pregnancy and childbirth.

*Mothers at Home*      8310 A Old Courthouse Rd., Vienna VA
22182.    703-827-5903

An organization for the woman who has chosen to stay home
and devote her skills to the nurturing of her family. Also publishes a monthly newsletter, "Welcome Home"

*Parent Care, Inc.*      9041 Colgate Street; Indianapolis IN
46268.    317-872-9913.

Partnership of parents and professionals dedicated to improving the newborn intensive care experience and future for
babies, families, and caregivers.

*Parents of Prematures*      Post Office Box 3046; Kirkland WA
98083.

Support group for parents of prematures.

*Vaginal Birth after Cesarean — VBAC*      10 Great Plain Terrace;
Needham MA 02192.

Provides classes, lectures, and seminars for couples interested
in learning about vaginal delivery after a previous cesarean.

# Photo Credits

**PART ONE**

Pages 1, 17, 19, © Richard Ebbitt; pages 5, 35, 39, Dale Pfeiffer; page
9, Beryl S. Ward; page 13, William Sears; page 27, © Harriette
Hartigan; page 31, © Medela, Inc.; page 33, courtesy of the
Association for Breastfeeding Fashions.

**PART TWO**

Pages 45, 91, © Richard Ebbitt; pages 47, 103, 113, William Sears; page
49 © Harriette Hartigan; pages 51, 54, 121, 153, Dale Pfeiffer; page 69.
Terry Dusicsko; page 81, Shelley Langston; page 85, Edward R.
Cerutti; page 95, Beryl S. Ward; pages 97, 135, Darrell Rideout; page
119, Linda Ortiz; page 145, Eleanor Randall.

**PART THREE**

Page 159, Darrell Rideout; pages 161, 165, Therese Barry; page 177,
© Richard Ebbitt; page 183, Katie Costanzo.

**PART FOUR**

Pages 191, 216, 231, Darrell Rideout; page 193, Melody Reis; pages 197, 209, Dale Pfeiffer; page 200, William Sears; page 203, Gwen Gotsch; page 205, Cheryl Class Erickson; page 213, Maureen Cristall; page 219, © Richard Ebbitt; page 223, Robert McLeod.

**PART FIVE**

Page 237, Tom Jackson, courtesy of UNICEF; page 239, Linda Yackle; page 243, Pat Crosby; page 247, Susan Hammang; pages 251, 263, 265, 269, 273, © Richard Ebbitt; page 253, Joyce Bussell; page 255, Mary Sparks.

**PART SIX**

Page 279, courtesy of Nancy Dietrich; pages 281, 333, Dale Pfeiffer; page 283, Judy Torgus; page 295, Carol Rudzinski; page 301, courtesy of Tammy Shaw; page 305, Darrell Rideout; page 307 © Richard Ebbitt; page 309, Sandra Hansen; page 321, S. R. Kaeding.

**PART SEVEN**

Pages 337, 355, Darrell Rideout; page 339, Eleanor Randall; pages 342, 371, 379, Dale Pfeiffer; page 349, © Harriette Hartigan; page 361, Martha Schulte; page 363, Lisa Candelario; pages 367, 375, 385 © Richard Ebbitt.

**PART EIGHT**

Page 389, Pat Crosby; pages 395, 407, 413, 419, Dale Pfeiffer; pages 399, 401, 403, © Richard Ebbitt; page 421, Jane Schreiner.

# Index

Nipple
care, 28-34; 59
confusion, 62, 147, 331
preparation, 30-31
shields, 66, 124, 147
soreness, 52, 120-24, 127
Nixon, Janice, 151
Novello, Dr. Antonia, iv, 415
Nursing
corner, 85
fashions, 32-34, 434
pads, 78
reminder, 59
siblings, 262
special word for, 258
strike, 154-57
styles, 73-76
supplementer, 317-18
See also Breastfeeding
Nutrition
breastfeeding mother, 230, 333
for the family, 219-29
snacks, 209
Nuts, in recipes, 227; caution, 227

Obesity, in breastfed babies, 151-55
O'Brien, Linda, 293
Odent, Dr. Michel, xxvi
Ointment, for sore nipples, 124-25
Older children, 215-16
Olson, Sally, 41
O'Mara, Peggy, 418
Oral contraceptives, 148, 322, 334, 380
Oral polio vaccine, 323
Overtired baby, 100
Ovulation, delayed, 377-80
Oxytocin, 66, 358-59

Pacifier, 76, 149, 331
Paediatric Society of New Zealand, 11
Palmer, Gabrielle, 384
Parenting style, 217; as a team, 201
Parke, Harry, 383
Parker, Ann, 111
Paster, Barbara Ann, 142
Patten, Kathie, 291
Paul, Carolyn Keiler, 189
People before things, 19, 205
Pepe, Toni, 158
Phillips, Chris, 195
Phosphorus, 346
Physiologic jaundice, 287-89
Pillows

after a cesarean, 285
in nursing lying down, 53
in nursing twins, 308-10
Placid baby, 74, 147, 331-36
Plastic lining, avoid, 124
Planning for breastfeeding, 19-44
Playpens, 212
Pleasurable effects of breastfeeding, 8, 387-89
Plugged duct, 137-44
Pollock, Debbie, 24
Population growth, 378
Positioning baby at the breast, 28, 50-55
after a cesarean, 285
as it affects weight gain, 332-36
to avoid sore nipples, 120
twins, 308-12
Postpone going back to work, 165-66
Postpartum depression, 13, 88-89
Poverty, and benefits of breastfeeding, 11
Precautions for nursing mothers, 234-35
Pregnancy, 6-7, 261, 377-80
Premature baby, 291-96
Preparing your nipples, 28-34
Preschoolers, helping with house-work, 209-14
Pressure on nipples, to avoid leak-ing, 78, 169
Prevention of discipline problems, 271-78
Price, Karen, 121
Priorities, 171-72, 207, 216
Prolactin, 12, 358-59; affected by marijuana, 235
Proteins, 340-43
as cause of allergy, 369
in breast milk, 340-43, 363-64
Pryor, Karen, xv
Psychological benefits, 13
Psychomotor development, 376
Pumping your milk, 127-37
and storing milk 127-37
for a premie, 292
to stimulate milk supply, 317-18
when returning to work, 168-70
See also Hand-Expressing
Punishment, 267-70

"Quality time," 183

Radioactive compounds, 322
Rash, from mother's diet, 369

# Would You Like to Know More?

As you read through this book, you find that La Leche League is mentioned over and over again as a source of information, support, and encouragement. La Leche League Groups meet monthly in communities all over the world to share breastfeeding and mothering experiences.

Perhaps you'd like to be a part of this mother-to-mother network. It is easy to become an LLL Member. Just return the coupon below along with your annual membership fee. You'll receive six bimonthly issues of NEW BEGINNINGS, a magazine filled with personal stories, helpful hints, and up-to-date parenting information. Members automatically receive our LLLI Catalogues by mail and they are entitled to a 10% discount on most purchases. Term Life Insurance at special Group Rates is also available in some areas to LLL Members and their families. You don't need to attend Group meetings in order to join—though most members enjoy the interaction with other mothers that meetings provide.

Why should you join La Leche League? Because you care—about your own family and about mothers and babies all over the world!

---

Return this form to La Leche League International,
P.O. Box 1209, Franklin Park, IL 60131-8209 USA.
*In Canada, write to: LLLC National Office, 18-C Industrial Dr., Chesterville ON KOC 1HO*

_____ I'd like to join La Leche League International. Enclosed is my annual membership fee of $30.

_____ In addition, I am enclosing a tax-deductible donation of $ _____ to support the work of La Leche League.

_____ Please send me a copy of THE WOMANLY ART OF BREAST-FEEDING, softcover, $9.95 plus $3.50 for shipping and handling. *(In California and Illinois, please add sales tax.)*

_____ Please send me La Leche League's FREE Catalogue.

_____ Please send me a FREE copy of the Directory of local LLL representatives. *(Please enclose a self-addressed, stamped envelope.)*

---

*Name*

---

*Address*                                          *City*

---

*State/Province*              *Zip/Postal Code*              *Country*

6/91